To   Ray Usher

Auf Wiedersehn

PAT

Warmest wishes

from

Shirley Thompson

July 2012

Front cover: photograph of Pat in wrestling pose by permission of Norman Fletcher, Victoria Studio, Birmingham.

Auf Wiedersehen
PAT

The Joke's on me

Pat Roach &
Shirley Thompson

BREWIN BOOKS

First published by
Brewin Books Ltd, 56 Alcester Road,
Studley, Warwickshire B80 7LG in 2006
www.brewinbooks.com

ISBN 1 85858 292 X

A Cataloguing in Publication Record
for this title is available from the British Library.

Typeset in New Baskerville
Printed in Great Britain by
Cromwell Press Ltd.

CONTENTS

DEDICATIONS

This third biography in the Pat Roach Trilogy is dedicated to the memory of my very dear friend and writing partner Pat Roach. It chronicles his six-year battle with cancer and contains many heartfelt tributes from some of his family and close friends, including principal members of the 'Auf Wiedersehen Pet' cast and crew, and a wide range of celebrity wrestlers.

Writing this book was, ironically, an extremely sad, yet joyful experience: the sadness of working side by side with Pat on this book, over a number of years, in the sure knowledge that sooner or later, he was going to die. After the cancer had finally claimed him, in the early hours of a July morning, in 2004, there was the prolonged sadness of working alone on his tapes, and re-reading the notes we'd made together. Juxtaposed with this, however, is the tremendous joy of being able to share so many of Pat's remaining memories and thoughts (combined with those of his family and friends), with you, the Reader, in the pages that follow...

Shirley Thompson, September 2006

Driving down the winding country lane, on a hot summer's day. I park the Volvo over on the left, then enter through a side gate. Thought I saw his ancient red Mondeo parked a little way ahead… but that has to be my imagination – the sun must have got to me.

Finding the plot isn't particularly easy, but it's been just five days, so memory and instinct lead the way. Take one or two shots of my friend's final resting-place. He's lying peacefully, beneath a substantial quilt of wild flowers, with wreaths from loved ones, at either end. Flower heads nod knowingly, in the gentle breeze, sharing his secrets. The long rest that he spoke of is finally here – but his story continues…

ACKNOWLEDGEMENTS

The authors are indebted to the following people, companies and organisations, for their invaluable contributions, various favours and support, which have been of great assistance in the publication of this book:

Family:
Doreen Roach, Pat's wife; his mother, Dolly; Pete Meakin, his stepbrother; Shirley Meakin, Pete's wife; Pat's son and daughter-in-law, Mark and Diane Roach; their son, Patrick Roach Junior – Pat's grandson. His cousin, John Bevis, and second cousin, Joyce Taylor.

Close Friends:
Vic Armstrong; Ronnie Callow; Alfie and Harold Evans; Don, Eddie and Gordon Fewtrell; Tony Green; Bernard Guest; Georgie James; Robert Knight; Roy O'Neill; Kenny Schofield; Dave Talboys; Mick Walker.

Close Friends/Auf Wiedersehen Pet – Cast and Crew:
Noel Clarke; Chris Fairbank; Steve Gibson, Pat's chauffeur; Tim Healy and his wife, Denise Welch; Jimmy Nail and his wife, Miriam Jones; Timothy and Shane Spall; Julia Tobin; Kevin Whately and his wife, Madelaine Newton. Scriptwriters: Dick Clement and Ian La Frenais. Producers: Chrissy Skinns and Joy Spink. 'Gary', Chapter 9: Gary Holton's mother, Joan Pugh and his manager, John Harwood-Bee.

Companies and Associations:
Publishers: Alan and Alistair Brewin of *Brewin Books Ltd*.
We are most grateful for the continuing support of broadcasters, Professor Carl Chinn M.B.E, Ed Doolan, Julie and Tony Wadsworth, and, furthermore, to the BBC, for granting us permission to include extracts from their interviews with Pat on the *Carl Chinn Show*, *The Other Side of Pat Roach* and the *Late Show*, respectively. Also to the French series, hosted by Bernard Pivot, *Bouillon de Culture*: the original source of the ten questions, which Ed Doolan asked Pat, at the conclusion of *The Other Side of Pat Roach*.

Thanks are also due to the *Birmingham Evening Mail*, for permission to reproduce a copy of the article about Chris Fewtrell's funeral, which was kindly provided by Gordon Fewtrell, from his private collection.

Close Friends/Former Wrestlers/Boxers/Referees etc.:
Ron 'Ace' Allcard; Bobby Barnes; Brendan Breslin; Bill and Sarah Bridges; Spencer Churchill; John Crowhurst; Joe D'Orazio; Seamus and Mickey Dunleavy; Pete Evans; Ron and Steve Gray; 'Con' and Johnny Harris; Judo Pete Roberts; Killer Kowalski (John Hayles); Johnny King; Vince McMahon; Mick McManus; Jackie Pallo (now deceased); Jack Perkins; Frank Rimer; Ray Robinson; Tony St. Clair; Adrian Street and Miss Linda; Mel Stuart; Jack Taylor; Darren Walsh – (current World Heavyweight Champion); Tony 'Banger' Walsh; Billy Wooding. Also, to many others, who may be found in the book, via the Index.

Additional thanks to Pat's agent, Peter Charlesworth and his Associate, Sharry Clark. Also, *Medical Staff:* Pat's surgeon, Doctor Ian Geh; nursing sisters Christina Hughes, Jayne Illsley and Clare Horrobin. The *Cancer BACUP* Charity; in particular Michelle Rowley and Julia Nex; Doctor Kief and his daughter, Mia, at the Ludwigshafen Clinic in Germany.

Special thanks to world-renowned photographer, Rolf Konow, of Copenhagen, for permission to publish his photograph of André the Giant, with Doreen Roach. Also to Norman Fletcher of Victoria Studio, Birmingham, for the cover photograph of Pat, in wrestling mode.

Members of the Clergy and Associates:
The Reverend Tom Pyke, Vicar of St Paul's Church in Birmingham's Jewellery Quarter. Richard Grimmett, Master of the Bell-ringing Guild. The Reverend Nigel Marns, Vicar of St. John's and St. Andrews Churches, Bromsgrove. Nicola Currie, Communications Officer for the Diocese of Worcester.

Other friends/Associates:
Cynthia Berrington (now deceased); Poppy Brady of the *Birmingham Evening Mail*; Ken Collins; Jim Collins; Chrissie Doyle; Thomas Felkin; Lisa Flynn, owner of *Gems Wine and Dine Ltd*; Freddie Frost; Val, Brian and Karen Hastings; Rod Hearne; Chris Millward; Jean Newbould; Lynn Perkins; Dave Prowse – (Darth Vader); Josie Rudge; Ian Sandy; Paddy and Jill White; Mavis and Barry Wood.

FOREWORD

Pat Roach was a big man: big of stature, spirit and generosity. He embodied the old cliché of gentle giant. He filled the room with his presence and his smile.

When we first saw him in a rehearsal room for Auf Wiedersehen, Pet, it wasn't hard to guess which part he was playing. Pat was Bomber to a 'T'. It's impossible to imagine anyone else filling that role. It was the first time we had ever met a professional wrestler. We thought of asking him if it was all fixed, but thought better of it in case the smile vanished.

In the series, Pat is the voice of reason, the calming influence in the midst of disparate and sometimes desperate characters, as they deal with graft, fatigue, debt and depression, closeted together in a hut, or a villa, or a trailer on an Indian reservation.

In real life, the work can exert a toll on actors, when they're thrown together in strange places. And in the midst of it, there was Big Pat, with a permanent smile, a positive attitude and an appetite for life.

Outside the series, we worked with him one other time, when he played a very different role in the James Bond film, Never Say Never Again. We can't actually say he spoke our words, because there weren't any, but he did his level best to beat the living daylights out of Sean Connery.

Many of his film titles give a sense of the type of roles Pat was offered, with his size and his strength. Raiders of the Lost Ark, Clash of the Titans, Kull the Conqueror, Conan the Destroyer. How on earth did Portrait of a Lady sneak in there?

During recent years, only a handful of people knew that Pat had cancer. This was at his insistence. Those of us who did know watched him fight it with his customary courage and tenacity, refusing to let it get in the way of his life or his work. Being with the mates he loved, in the series he loved, was the best possible antidote and he was adamant about reporting for duty in AWP3, in Arizona, and AWP4 under the hot sun of the Caribbean. Tragically, he was not with us on our last venture, but everyone felt his spirit and presence.

In spite of all the success that Pat enjoyed, in sports, film and television, he always remained a modest, approachable and sweet-natured person. A bloke you could share a hut with.

Dick Clement & Ian La Frenais

They are very shallow people who take everything literal. A Man's life of any worth is a continual allegory – and very few eyes can see the Mystery of his life. Every biography, even the most material in its methods, is in fact a comment on the human spirit itself.

Robert Gittings: 'The Nature of Biography', Heinemann (1978)

Chapter One

SEVEN O'CLOCK THIS MORNING

(A conversation between the two co-authors, in July 1999, five years before Pat's demise).

If you can fill the unforgiving minute
With sixty seconds worth of distance run...

But where are we running away from – and what is the 'unforgiving minute'– in your particular life?

If each of us were asked to describe our own idea of true happiness and contentment, there would be as many versions as there are grains of sand in the sea. But perhaps they would have certain elements in common? Mine would be to walk along a deserted stretch of soft, white sand – miles from anywhere. We are holding hands, tightly. A gentle breeze caresses my skin. My companion is someone with whom I am in *total* harmony. He is making no demands on me – nor I on him – in a haven, away from all time and pressure.

I suppose, to some extent, happiness is being content with your lot, isn't it? So it means you can be happy with a million pounds, or you can be happy on the dole. We all have different standards of criteria.

Would you know if you were?

I'm happy enough to wake up in the morning, and I've always said that all my life – even when I was a young lad. Ted Edwards comes to mind, when I was a young lad of nineteen. Ted was a bit of a junkie. I believe he's dead now. He was a cockney and a former builder, and all of us kids used to look up to him: Alfie Evans, Harold Evans – all our mob. He lived in Handsworth, off Rookery Road. We became friends, although he was a foreman on a building site.

He was an old man. The reason I brought Ted up was that he used to say: "You can't buy seven o'clock this morning." That always stuck with me. I thought later on, how lucky you are to have experienced seven o'clock this morning. I've always thought about the people who wouldn't experience seven o'clock this morning.

Life is a very strange thing. Just when you think you know what to expect, you've planned everything to the nth degree, something happens. It hits you right between the eyes. Then... when the smoke clears... nothing is ever the same again.

For me, for my part, for my life, the most unforgiving minute was when the doctor told me I'd got cancer. At that moment, I didn't want to forgive anyone the minute – and there was no distance far enough to run. There was nothing to be quoted about length, or distances, or forgiving people... or anything. A numbness... and no forgiveness.

What goes through your mind? You're sitting there; you've already read it upside-down – that you have the cancer. The doctor sits there and tells you for the tenth time that day – delivering the message – perhaps it's a terminal message? He doesn't know. He cares – but only in a professional way, because unless he is professional about it, he can't help you.

You can't really forgive him for that: he doesn't really care. But he does care... but he doesn't care... but he does care; it's just that he's being professional: he has to tell you. And after all, you are the sort of person who wants to be told – 'straight from the elbow'. Well, you've got it – straight from the elbow. But you're not going to forgive him for saying it.

When you gaze out of the window, looking at a church spire in the distance, you're thinking: 'If I ran away and got to that church, would it divorce me from the situation? If I put a distance between here and there, would I then no longer have cancer?' But no... no, that couldn't happen. You'd still have a cancer. And you can't forgive anyone for anything at that moment. Because you're going to die.

When I first realised that something was wrong, I was internationally and competitively fit for wrestling – that means you're a bit special. But there it is – there's something wrong.

And you had no idea that you were going to be told that – when you went to see the doctor?

No idea at all.

What were you expecting?

A hiatus hernia. At the time you think: 'It's a thing I shouldn't put off. "Procrastination is the thief of time", and I don't want to be a party in letting my life be stolen away from beneath me. Let's do something about it.' I'd noticed something was wrong. I couldn't keep my food down. If I don't do something...

How long had you suspected that there was something wrong?

A few weeks, I suppose. Then I went to the doctor's. He referred me to Good Hope Hospital. I remember all the nurses making a fuss because they knew about me – a celebrity – I suppose. We were all giggling and chatting, and it was all very nice.

When I woke up, there was no one around – they'd all gone, except the doctor and myself who was a 'Sardagee': a Sikh – with a beard. 'Sardagee' means 'bearded one'. There were us two Sardagees!

I'd only just come round from the anaesthetic, and he looked at me and he said: "Yes Pat, you've got a tumour." I suppose I hadn't really thought about it at the time, as being cancer. I knew it wasn't very acceptable – having a tumour – but I still didn't think about cancer. Until I went to a later appointment at the East Birmingham Hospital. Then I read it upside-down – that I'd got it.

How do you mean – you read it upside-down?

Well I was in a room and my report was on the desk, and I read it upside-down. At about the time the doctor walked in, sat down and said: "Yes Pat, you've got a cancer."

So you knew before he told you?

Just seconds. And he said that there's only one way to get it out – that's surgery: cut it out. I said: "OK, yes." And we proceeded to, or tried to, talk about the operation, and... didn't get very far that day. I went away and I didn't tell anyone – kept it to myself. I didn't think that there was any need to upset anyone, and in fact, I didn't tell anyone until the night before I was going in for the operation. I told absolutely no-one.

But wasn't it terrible, keeping it to yourself?

No it wasn't. Because it would have been terrible to put everyone through the agony that I was going through.

But in a way it would have helped you, wouldn't it?

(Adamantly). No, not at all. What a cancer sufferer needs around him is strength: strong people.

And that's not *necessarily* the people closest to you?

You need the strength of people around you – not the weakness of people – sobbing and breaking down; every word they say to you, thinking of what they are going to say. So the best thing you can do is to be as normal as you can.

But you don't feel normal, do you?

Well, no. I had to tell my accountant, I had to tell my solicitor, and one or two other people, who I put on oath and told. I had to tell my agent, so he didn't book me into any long series – no more thirteen episodes of 'Auf Wiedersehen Pet'! Not even into a long movie, because who knows? Eventually, as I got closer towards the date, which was quite soon I have to add, from the time I was diagnosed with cancer, to the time I underwent the operation.

How long was that?

A couple of weeks, I think. I remember saying to one of the doctors: "Well, what exactly will happen? Because I'm not really quite sure." That surprised him. He said: "Come into this room and I'll tell you." We sat down and he discussed exactly what they'd do: how they'd cut me from where to where, possibly with a second cut, depending upon what was found when they opened me up. How they would then put all these tubes into me – and I'd be put in Intensive Care. He intimated that the danger area was not the operation, but getting germs while you were in hospital – funnily enough.

Of course, what he didn't say were things like: "When we open you up, we might find that the cancer's all over the place and we'll have to close you again"; that's what he didn't say. Luckily enough for me, when they opened me up – there it was – all by itself, and they chopped it out either side and stitched me up. As soon as I was moved from Intensive Care, into the Recovery Unit, I started doing exercises – calf raises – at the bottom of my bed, with seven tubes sticking out of me! And continued to do it.

How long ago was it, that you had the 'op'?

March 98 – wasn't it? I remember the nurses taking my 'Iron Lady' off me, my saline solution on wheels, because I was marching up and down and it was squeaking, driving everybody mad! They oiled it, then gave it back to me.

Brian, who came into the bed opposite me, had exactly the same thing: cancer of the oesophagus. While I was there, I went in under the name of Frank Roach and shaved off the beard, because I wanted to be anonymous. Didn't want my mother to know – and up until now, she doesn't.

In fact I checked into the hospital on a Friday – to get my bed – and once I'd got my bed I was OK for the operation on the Monday. I actually left hospital again on the Saturday, and visited my mother in hospital. I walked in and she didn't recognise me – quite. She looked at me and she said: "Oh, it's our Paddy!" Then she said: "There's something different about you, our Paddy – you ain't on drugs, are you?"

I went to see her again on the Sunday and told her that I was going to India – wrestling.

So you were only in hospital for six days?

Yes, about a week. By the time she saw me again, I think she was out of hospital too, and I wore a big coat I'd bought while I was doing my last wrestling tournament in Berlin, so that she couldn't see that I'd lost weight. The fact that I'd shaved my beard off made my face look thinner anyway. So it didn't show up – I got away with it. Months later she said to me: "Have you lost some weight?" She'd been seeing me on a regular basis, and some time had elapsed since I'd been in hospital. So she still doesn't know to this day. I'll tell her the day before this book is published, because I can't allow her to read about it in a book.

I was wondering about that – you'll have to have told her by then. What's the prognosis? What did the doctors say?

I have a seven per cent chance of lasting five years.

That was a year ago?

Yes, so I've now got a chance of lasting even less, because a year's gone by. I don't know whether those are national or international figures.

So how do you keep going, when you've had such a traumatic shock? When you're having to endure all of this, and you've been given that kind of prognosis?

The problem is that every day you're looking in the mirror... and what I'm doing now, is that I've got a little bit of weight now, as you can see. The reason I've got it is because the only way I'll know I've got cancer again, is when I lose weight, unless I get prostate cancer, and I have my blood test: that's the only cancer that shows up in a blood test. But while I've got this little bit of weight around my middle – I'm OK. If it disappears, I'll have a cancer again. That's why I'm content to have the extra weight now – I've never had it before. All my life I've been slim and trim.

If someone reading this book is in a similar situation, (obviously you wouldn't want to preach), but what would you say was the best mental approach for keeping yourself going?

What I've tried to do is tidy my life up. Anything that couldn't be tidied up by anyone other than myself, I've tried to tidy it up: tied loose ends up.

I've put a lot of thought into my own funeral. I now know how, if I hear anything, I can put my own funeral together. I'm starting to collect stickers now – you know – like when you go to Blackpool and Ilfracombe, and I'll stick them all over my coffin!

The places you've been?

Yes, but it's too late now to do it properly. I'll leave a big space at the end of my coffin, for where my feet will be, and I'll put a question mark there. I'll probably put 'Up or Down?' That's what I'll do. People can just come and have a laugh if they want to – I don't care! Depending on where I die from or where I get buried, I suppose. I think I'd probably want to go back to the ground, where I came from. I don't think that I want to be burnt.

I read somewhere, in one of Dolly's cuttings, that you would like to be buried in the Jewellery Quarter, somewhere around Saint Paul's. Do you still feel that way?

Well, I thought about going back to the Jewellery Quarter where I came from. What I might want to do is if any one of my family ever acquired a nice piece of land, I might want to be buried on that. At the time, it would depend on them.

Do you think that there's a chance that it might not happen – is there a chance of you surviving?

Yes of course there is, you never take any notice of figures, do you?

No, so what about that side of it? Do you think that maybe you'll just come through all of this?

Well I do come through it – I come through it every day, don't I? I have to say that at this time, my thoughts, daily, are with young Chrissie Fewtrell, who I have known for a great deal of my lifetime, who is obviously a member of the Fewtrell family – Eddie's brother. – Chrissie is faced with the fact that he's dying from cancer. He's so cheerful, so courageous, so brave. He's so thin and frail.

How old is he?

In his early 50s. He's so frail, so worn, so brave. He's even still buying old cars, doing them up and selling them. Daily, he's going to die – and he knows it. And you ring him up and he says: "I'm alright! I'm alright!" He's so brave... and he's an inspiration to me. I don't ring him all the time, because of the very idea that you ring him up every day because he's so very ill. But I do ring his brother, Gordon Fewtrell, almost every day, and ask Gordon how he is.

It's common knowledge that cancer is one of the biggest killers. If you look at recent statistics, at least one in three people will be affected by the disease in some way.

Every family can reach out and touch someone who has cancer. I'm in the organisation now – USANA, (a Greek word meaning 'health') which is to do with vitamins – and I tell you, – I've never been so impressed in my life. It's a very successful, multi-marketing company. I've already gained great physical benefit from it, through taking the vitamins.

So you don't feel as if you've got anything wrong with you?

No, no. I've been trying very hard to get back to my wrestling and training, but I haven't been able to, because of my illness – and I really want to try and get back to it.

Do you still go jogging every day?

No, I should do, but I don't.

You don't feel able to?

Well, I have big problems: I have to watch how I eat all the time now – because of my stomach situation – it's lack of capacity; so if I'm going to train, I need to eat regularly, but I can only eat such a little bit. I can't eat all the time because when I eat, I can't bend over, and things like that, because the food would just come back up again. I watch how I eat and when I eat, particularly when training. So there's a lot to think about. I have started training twice and I hurt my knee once. Now I'm under a new pressure, because I'm only able to do a few hours' work a week.

I have to do what the doctor says I can do, and have physiotherapy. If I didn't do any work, what I have around me would fold up, and I would go bankrupt. I don't want to go bankrupt for obvious reasons. Hopefully I would live to regret it. (Laughs). Hopefully! What I'm trying to do is keep it going while I sell the yard – I've got a lease round my neck.

The trouble is, you can have no idea of exactly how long you've got. So you're working in the dark, aren't you – playing it by ear?

I've just got to get rid of things and, basically, I suppose, accept the fact that I'm an invalid. The doctor seems to think I am and everybody else seems to think I am.

Do you feel like an invalid?

No, I don't.

You don't look like an invalid.

But if I really face facts, I'm really not able to do things that I used to be able to – without a great deal of consideration.

Chapter Two

VALENTINE'S DAY

Sadly, despite his fighting spirit, Chrissie Fewtrell died of cancer, in August 1999. Pat had known Chris since he was a schoolboy and was one of many who attended his funeral. He had worked for his elder brother Eddie in the nightclub business, changing in later years to the car trade. The following is a shortened extract from an account of events that happened, within the space of six months, recalled by Pat, in November of that year.

November 1999:

I kept in touch with Gordon Fewtrell, who told me that, day by day, Chrissie was getting worse. Every single day, his brother, Don, bless him, used to visit Chris. He was there every day, by his brother's side – right 'til the day he died. Good for you Don.

In an effort to prolong his younger brother's life, Eddie paid for the latest medicines. I visited Chris just a few days before he died, without realising that death was so close. We talked about all sorts of things: cars, and the old days when we used to play cards at the club. I tried to reassure him by telling him about my own cancer. I don't think he told anyone. We used to compare notes. He was still chasing people for money – even though he was in a terrible state.

Chris was quite compos mentis. If I'd been speaking to him on the telephone I'd never have known he was ill: absolutely 'on-the-ball'. Within a short time his condition worsened dramatically. I paid a second visit to his home where his wife, Lisa, was nursing him. I held his hand, because I was never going to hold it again. I wanted some contact with him – for a while. It was self-indulgence, but I wanted to do it. Then he focused on me, saw that I was holding his hand and pulled it away.

But eventually I couldn't last any longer. I suddenly stood up; I kissed him and went. Lisa said: "Would you like some tea?" I just walked away and shook my head. They didn't even see me downstairs. They just let me go. As soon as I got outside the house, I just broke down, because I knew I'd never see him again. He lasted another couple of days – then he'd gone. He was just a boy – I always remember him as a boy. Yes, young Chrissie Fewtrell will always stay with me all my life really – those last few days and hours; a very brave, very spirited young lad.

13 January 2000:

About fifteen months after my operation, I finally satisfied myself that I'd got fit enough, and even more important, hard enough, to wrestle again. So I actually accepted an invitation to Fairfield Hall, Croydon – probably five months from today. Then I accepted a date in Bristol, that followed about two weeks later, and another at Victoria Hall, Hanley, Stoke-on-Trent: a very famous hall. In each case they were Tag Matches, with a partner, which meant that I could keep out of the ring by some skulduggery or other.

Heavyweight Wrestling Champion Darren Walsh was Pat's partner for the Tag Match in Hanley. Darren recalls: "It was six years ago now, because I've got a character with a mask, called *Thunder*, which I do now; back then I was just myself. There were some big names at the Tag Match. There was me and Pat as partners, plus Tony St Clair and Chic Cullen. Brian Dixon was the promoter. The first team went into the ring. I was at the back of the stadium, waiting for the music to come on and they played the old Big Daddy music – "We're on our way to heaven, we shall not be moved" – so Pat was huffing and puffing!

"Because I was the young lad, (Pat would go mad if he knew I was saying this), I did all of the work – I took all of the knocks for him. But he never told me anything about being ill. When he was in the dressing room, he went into a corner and turned his back to everyone so that they couldn't see his operation scar, whilst he was changing into his leotard. That night he wore a black leotard. He'd normally wear maroon trunks, but this time, he definitely wore a leotard."

As he was likely to be thrown around the ring, Pat checked with his doctors beforehand. During his original cancer operation, as he so graphically puts it, "My insides had been removed, then put back again!" The doctor confirmed that it was safe for him to go back in the ring, and that nothing would become dislodged.

The last time I was at Fairfield Hall, in Croydon, I had kidney stone problems, would-you-believe? I walked into the hall that night but never wrestled. Finished up in hospital, just half a mile away. I managed to cover my tracks. I told people I'd been in hospital, afterwards, because kidney stones were no big deal. I did six matches in all; none of them televised, because British wrestling matches aren't these days.

I worked at a hall in Oldham and also for the promoter, John Freemantle. I worked at Gravesend and that's where I actually took the poster, with an enormous photograph, down from the board, having served its purpose. I sent it to the first of my two cancer surgeons, Professor Casson, in Newfoundland, Canada; he's moved there recently.

Bear in mind, just a few weeks before my operation, I'd been wrestling on the International Circuit. I was in Berlin on an international tournament. Again I didn't do very well, but I didn't know why. I had no idea! I haven't trained since Christmas: I've just had a terrible bout of 'flu, followed by a cold virus, that's lasted five weeks – as so many people have – almost an epidemic. I've just got rid of it.

Tuesday 13 March 2001:
I came in last Friday night, after I'd had a week of moving things around, sat down in front of my television set – one of the few things that I hadn't moved out of the room. I say that because, well – that particular night was different – I'd started to move all my 'goods and chattels'.

I'd had my... I don't know whether I want to use 'death sentence', because I don't want to sound sour – d'you know what I mean? I'd had my sentence – when an approximation of my last few months on earth was laid out before me, just a month ago – on Valentine's Day! Since then I've proceeded to get rid of all my bits and pieces.

This particular night, coming home to my club, I found myself sat on the floor, leaning against a pile of photographs and wrestling posters, which I would later move, and watching television. The telly was on the floor – and I was on the floor – and just about everything about me was on the floor, I suppose.

But day to day, I go about my business, getting rid of my bits and pieces. I make no excuse for repeating myself. It's just that that's what I'm doing – I'm repeating my actions too, on a daily basis – getting rid of my bits and pieces. What I didn't want to get rid of today, I have to convince myself that it really must go: I've got to find a new home for things. Things that hopefully, people will love, as I've loved having them around me over the years; I suppose for quite a different reason than anybody else will ever want, for my little things.

They might have some regard for them, because of what they've been involved in – a film, something to do with my past, wrestling. But everything I move has a meaning for me. I'm looking at a large framed photograph lying there, glass broken, it's one of Sean and myself, doing the fight scene in 'Never Say Never Again'. It's fallen on the floor and the glass has cracked – and it's all on its own in the corner.

There's a few chairs, tucked around corners, here and there. I asked my co-author Shirley the other day: "How much are they worth Shirl?" And she said: "Oh, I don't know, about 150 quid I suppose." So they'll go. I've still got my collages on the walls; they've followed me around various offices; quite heavy, men's stuff, I suppose. Got my boy, David, looking at me (glazed white statue) with his leaf around his private parts, flexing his left arm at me; showing me his 'six-pack': he's got to go.

Downstairs, in the club, there's lots of statues. My big Hercules – he weighs about seven to eight hundred weights. I bought him from 'Italia Classics' – from a friend of mine, Georgie Homer – and I've got various female statues, from mythology – five or six of those. We'll have to find a new home for those too.

As time goes on now, all I think about every evening is, 'I'm OK today, but how quickly will I go downhill? Once it starts, will I be mobile? And for how long – once I start to slide? How long will I be compos mentis – and how long will I fight the thing about not wanting to give in?' You mustn't give in. Then of course, there are my little chandeliers. The ones in this office are not so nice, but I've got my lovely crystal chandeliers downstairs; when those are pulled down, the place will look absolutely bare.

A few photographs: the big 'blow-up' of the 'Auf Wiedersehen' boys and myself – on the wall; I suppose I'll take that down soon. Then I'll have to decide about the Club's last moments – the club's demise; how it will run parallel with my demise (voice begins to break). When will I decide to close the door? I really don't know – it will all come.

I'm looking at some of my old cups now – and medals – things from Germany. A 'seiger' – German for winner. The Hanover tournaments – memories of Hanover: I used to call it my 'second home'. Friends I had there. I wonder how they'll find out? I suppose word will travel quite quickly, to some of the boys who're over there.

There must be quite a collection of wrestling posters – and I suppose they're worth some 'dough' – some money. I don't know whether I'll just put them in a suitcase and leave them to my grandson. If there was a very respectable Museum of Wrestling I'd donate them. But I wouldn't want them to vanish – it would be nice to keep them for the posterity of wrestling. Unfortunately it's vanishing day by day – all the old television stars that people remember. I was about to say: "They're all dying off." I think what I really meant is: "We're all dying off!" (deep chuckle). 'He laughs'!

Yeah, so at the moment I'm sat in what was my office, on part of an old three-piece suite. Shirley said she likes the pattern – I don't think she meant it! But it suffices, I suppose, for the last crossing the T's and dotting the I's of the book. The little things that Shirley wants to get right – Shirley's attempt at perfection – making sure that it's as I want it; as it possibly should be, or the best way that it can be, under the circumstances.

I don't want to be too guilty of rambling on – or the business of feeling sorry for myself, I'm not going to do that – because I don't feel sorry for myself. I feel well rewarded. I always think about my 'lifetimes' – never just 'my life'. (Whispers and repeats) "I think about my 'lifetimes'." You know, every time an Evergreen piece of music comes on – I mean a 'Golden Oldie', there's always something I can attach to the memory – something to remember.

In a very funny way, when the time comes that I will be immobilised, and I'll be sat around those last few days, I just hope that the morphine doesn't take over too much – and it leaves me that little room to think: to think back and back, and back.

And I hope that I don't get robbed of my memories for the last few days – 'cause they'll keep me happy – and I'll look forward to the rest. God... can you imagine? ... A rest!

It must surely be one of life's saddest ironies – that even when a man dedicates a large proportion of his life and career to physical fitness, there is still no guarantee that he will be protected from serious illness.

The title Pat chose for our first book – *If* – was a very appropriate one for someone with a thirst for life, who explores new situations with an *intense* appetite for adventure. But the time seems to be fast approaching when he may no longer be able to experience 'seven o'clock in the morning'. So maybe our story is heading towards an inevitable conclusion?

Pat, what do you think about this idea for Chapter Three?

SILENCE

Would you check this page with me?

SILENCE

I've put Ken Collins and his friends at the beginning....

Still no response...

So accustomed have I become to our conversations, and the easy rapport between us, that any second now I expect him to answer. But he can't... and I have no choice other than to speak on his behalf... and finish this final book of the trilogy – (he was always determined that we should). The new series of *Auf Wiedersehen Pet* was televised, in May 2002, and having enjoyed the unexpected happiness of an extra Christmas, Pat soldiered on to make a fourth series, in 2003. The inside stories of all four *Aufpet* series, and the *Christmas Special*, follow in later chapters.

By the end of 2003, Pat seemed to have conquered the demon disease, at least for the time being; a miracle, it seemed, had occurred. But the cancer was covertly biding its time. Pat continued to fight his illness, through both conventional means and a series of alternative treatments, (including two somewhat controversial remedies, from America and Germany). Sadly, despite his relentless efforts, this man, with a heart as big as his stature, finally passed away, in the early hours of Saturday 17 July 2004.

But let me take you back now, to a time when everything was new and exciting for Pat – when his whole life lay ahead of him, full of challenges – like an un-chartered map.

The cries of children echo across time – and the temperature has dipped to minus something. It's cold enough for snow...

Chapter Three

FROM SMALL BEGINNINGS

The muffled sounds of children, playing in the snow; their breath hangs in the icy air, like dragon smoke. In the dark, Ken Collins and his friends have night vision, their young eyes quickly adjusting to the 'Black-out'. The snow-covered ground is bathed in the pale light of a full moon, making everything seem much lighter... casting shadows. Ladywood children dash in and out of entries, playing 'Flash Gordon'. Torches flash on and off, like alien laser beams or ray guns. An occasional shriek echoes the length of Shakespeare Road, as an enemy torch picks out another child and he is 'zapped' against a wall, or collapses, vanquished, into a cushion of white.

Accompanying Pat through the fascinating Odyssey of his life promised to be rather daunting – like Homer's perilous epic journey. But halfway through writing our first book, *If – The Pat Roach Story*, I realised that Pat's encounters with characters such as Kubrick, Spielberg and Connery, or wrestling some fierce opponent, were far from the unnerving experiences of Odysseus, wrestling with Scylla and Charybdis. For the emotionally charged, often-traumatic experiences of his youth, had produced someone with an ideal disposition for negotiating the supposedly glamourous, but often precarious minefield of the entertainment world – not to mention life in general.

You can draw something from everything you do. I'm the sort of person who feels that if I wake up in the morning, I've swum the channel. It's great – all you've got to do is wake up! I believe that the only thing you're entitled to in life is a smack on the arse the day you're born. I think that's enough. If you're lucky enough to get a parent's love, or even more lucky to get two parents' love, and can go through life with both parents loving you and both grandparents loving you, then you're an extremely fortunate person. But if you don't have that situation, you have to make the best of what you've got.

At various places in our book, we've included, with Ed Doolan's kind permission, extracts from his insightful BBC WM 2003 broadcast, *The Other Side Of Pat Roach*, Pat's first record choice was Gracie Fields' classic recording, *Sally*, a favourite of Dolly's. When the record finished, Ed asked: "Happy childhood?"

Yes, I think so. Very disjointed – my father and mother split up, when I was very young. I went to live with my old grandmother, then various aunts and uncles. We lived in Balsall Heath for a while, on the Belgrave Road itself, went to Hope Street School, then I lived in Ladywood, with my old grandmother, Amelia. She was a bargee – a water gypsy. We lived in Shakespeare Road, Ladywood, which is no longer there. I went to Nelson Street School and Steward Street School. I was very happy, I suppose. We had our little pleasantries, which we did; in the early days, there was no television. We did all sorts of things.

Requesting a second record, Pat commented:

This one's for my old dad. He loved 'Danny Boy', and I love Joe Longthorne singing it – it's just wonderful – it really is.

According to Joyce Taylor, Pat's cousin: "I can remember mom and dad playing the piano, and they'd got a jazz band there as well." Her mother, Agnes, was Frank Roach's sister. " Frank brought his little boy to our house," she continues, "but he was very fair then – with curly hair. He was very small and he sat by the door. But that's the only meeting I had with Pat. He was about two years old."

The Doyle family lived at 90 Belgrave Road, Balsall Heath, Birmingham; Dolly, Pat and the Scotts lived next door, at number 92. Chrissie Doyle, a Care Worker, who lived at number 90, between the ages of five and eighteen, knew Dolly and 'Paddy', as she calls him, very well; she was just two years younger. Chrissie had three brothers and a sister. Her brother Jimmy Doyle was almost the same age as Paddy and used to go boxing with him. Her mother was Bridget ('Bridie') Doyle. Her father, William, had been in the army. "We didn't have a lot, but we were all good friends," Chrissie recalls, "we all looked out for each other."

Pat would have been about seven, when the Doyles moved in. According to Chrissie, "Dolly was a real 'diamond', because she would look out for everybody; whatever Dolly had, she'd share, and she was very protective of her children." A photo of Dolly, in a man's suit, cigarette in hand, portrays her as someone ready to take on the world! "Dolly's boys were good boys, but if they'd done something that they shouldn't, and you spoke sharply to them, Dolly would come out and say: 'Don't you speak to them like that. I'll chastise my children, but nobody else should!' She kept them in order herself, but she was very loving with them."

Harry Meakin eventually moved in with Dolly. They had two sons, Rickie and Pete Meakin. According to Chrissie, Harry drove around, mostly collecting old metal and 'tat'. "He was like many men at that time, if he got work, he'd work, but if not, he didn't. Harry was always getting summonses for his lorry, and so forth. One day he went out in the lorry and he came back with a horse!"

Another neighbour, 'Auntie Mary' was married to an Asian: her married name was Mary Mohammed. She's now known as Mary Evans, and was another good friend of Dolly's. "We were all close friends. Any problems, or anything that we ran short of, we either went next door to Dolly's or we went up to Auntie Mary," Chrissie remembers. "If they needed something, we shared it with them too – even to a bucket of coal. My mom would sometimes work from six in the morning until six at night." Dolly was employed at the 'Speedo Wilmot' as she used to call it – *Wilmot Breeden*; she'd also worked at *Bulpitt's,* in Ladywood. "They all worked hard – and they played hard – particularly on Saturday nights."

In *Pat Roach's Birmingham,* we describe how Dolly arranged outings for neighbours and friends in Balsall Heath. "To *The Old Dun Cow* and places like that," confirms Chrissie, – "they were hilarious at times! They all had to struggle, but they kept jovial with it; they weren't miserable people at all. Paddy was rather shy, but he wasn't standoffish in any way. He and my brother later went boxing together, so we began to have a few conversations, as he got to know us better."

Dolly held Jumble Sales in her back garden. "For the holidays she'd take the boys hop picking. I used to envy them, because I could never go. There was a Teenage Dance at *Moseley and Balsall Heath Institute*, on the Moseley Road. Paddy took me there, not as a girlfriend, but as a next-door-neighbour. Coming out, he'd met this girl, so I had to stand up on the open-backed part of the lorry, while she had the passenger seat at the front by Paddy. But I got my lift home!"

According to Chrissie, although Paddy was rather reserved, he was well mannered. "If we were walking down the street together he'd always walk on the outside. When you were crossing the road, he'd hold your elbow, to make sure you crossed safely." In a recent interview Julia Tobin observed that Pat was very considerate with female actresses. "He was something on his own, really, in that way," continues Chrissie. "As he got older, he stayed quite reserved, but he'd got a *lovely* sense of humour."

In the 1980s, Pat offered Chrissie a job, working in one of his cafés. "He'd be there to help you, when you needed it, but my brother said he's never want to cross him – because you'd know about it if you did! I never saw him angry, but my brother did once."

One of the four photos supplied by Chrissie was taken at *Digbeth Civic Hall*, after Paddy had just completed a wrestling match. "It shows a group of us having a drink, in the room below where the wrestling match had taken place, at the hall. His red, two-seater sports car was parked outside. Paddy won the match." At one particular dance, a man kept bumping into her. "Paddy took him by the arm and said: 'Come with me.' He took him round behind a board and the next thing – the man came up and apologised to me." That's very similar to an incident that referee Joe D'Orazio describes in Chapter 10, about when he and Pat were queuing in a London Post Office.

Pat's step-brother, Pete Meakin, was born in December 1948, when Pat was eleven years old. His brother Rickie had been born two years earlier. Pete recalls: "My first recollections of Pat are when he used to give mom five pound, so that she could take us to see him wrestling at various halls. I would be thirteen at the time, when I first really became aware of him, Pat would have been twenty-four. I had to go away to an Open Air School for some time, so that would be a gap out of my life with Pat too. Our neighbour, Mr. Robinson, had a car and he used to take the four of us, to watch Pat wrestling: mom, Rickie, my mate Geoff and myself. It was more like 'my brother the wrestler', rather than someone I'd grown up with – because of the age gap."

When Pete was four, fifteen-year-old Pat started working for his dad, and returned to live with Amelia, but would visit Belgrave Road from time to time. Pete's memories of their grandmother are rather sketchy, as he was only nine when she died: "My first recollections of my Gran would be when mom used to take us up to see her; sometimes we'd stop overnight. We'd just have a mattress on the floor. I really *loved* that, because we'd go up in the attic. There was absolutely nothing there, but it was just the novelty of going up there. It was a bit spooky, because the floorboards creaked! We'd explore it in the daytime, when we could see our way around. Nan lived quite close to the railway. It was *magic*, hearing the 'ch ch' noise of the steam trains, while we were sleeping.

"My Nan was deaf so we had to shout to her. She had dark hair, done back into a bit of a bun. She had arthritis, so her fingers were crooked, bunions the size of footballs, and a slim frame. Amelia used to love us, but there was always a musty smell, as it was an old house. Nan had a bit of a courtyard, with a mangle in. I remember playing with it. Rick put his fingers in and I mangled them; he didn't think much of that – but it was good fun! I can't ever remember having a hug from her, although I was probably too young to remember anything like that." By all accounts, Amelia was a kind-hearted person. She was nicknamed 'Feely', because, being small, she used to feel across the tops of mantle-pieces, for coins!

Pete confirms Chrissie's earlier comment: "Mom was very protective towards us. We lived in a very rough area. Any problems, fights or what-have-you, mom used to be straight round there, sorting it out. She could lift most people up with her one hand! She's the only woman I know with a cauliflower ear-hole!"

Jean Newbould has described Dolly as a brilliant storyteller. "Oh she was – yes. I think that's probably where Pat got his gift from – between his dad and his mom," observes Pete. "I think mom would have been a brilliant actress herself. She used to love being the centre of attention. One particular wedding we went to was at our friends, the Robinsons. One of the girls came over and said: 'Where's your mom Pete?' I said: 'Oh, she's just gone into the toilets, to tell some of the girls' fortunes,' so they all rushed in there, to get their fortune told! When we finished a cup of tea, mom would swill it round, get the leaves up the side of the cup, look into it, and the first thing she used to say was: 'Oh, there's a big tall man coming. Looks like the bloody Rent Man!' She could always read *something*. She'd show you, and explain what it meant. You'd look in the cup and think: 'Oh yes, I can see that.' But it was just imagination. The front door was locked, because of the Rent Man, but the back door was always open!

"There'd often be two or three people sitting on the wall at the bottom of the garden, which, I suppose, would be about seventy-five feet wide. With mom being protective towards us, we could do anything we liked in the garden; we could build underground dens, which were quite dangerous when you think about it. Me and my mates used to dig for hours and hours and go under the ground. There was never any work done on it. Nothing in our home was ever neat and tidy!"

Shortly after Pete was born, Pat met market traders Alfie and Harold Evans in the Bookies and café, in Little King Street. Alfie was thirteen and Harold was fourteen. "Pat used to come in to see his dad, and of course, you start talking and laughing and joking about," explains Alfie. "One day he asked if he could come to the dance with us, at Laura Dixon's: there was one in Navigation Street and one at the top of the High Street.

We said, 'You can come, if you put a decent T-shirt on,' continues Alfie. "Pat came back on Saturday night, with a shirt, but the collar was about three inches short around the neck. So we had to cut the back, to put a tie on him! Because Pat was useless – he could *not* dress. From that point onwards, we were very close friends. Until he met Doreen – and over a period of years, we just had a good laugh."

Alfie's brother, Harold, remembers: "Pat came in the Bookies, but he wasn't a big gambler. His dad used to have his half-a-crown and five-shilling bets. He thought he owned the place because he was a businessman, but he was really just a scrap dealer. Pat worked very hard for his dad, for £2.00 a day, using a pan shovel, loading as much rubbish on to the lorry as his dad could get, to dump at the Tip. At the time, Frank seemed a dominating figure. He had a driver called Billy Allen, who drove the big lorry, from the tip. He was a nice character, Jewish, bald-headed, with rimless eyeglasses. But Pat was a quiet, shy person, and very modest.

"As life went on, we took Pat to the Judo Club, in Blews Street, Aston, Birmingham. The instructor was Frank Ryder, who became European Champion; his brother Wilf was Assistant Instructor. Pat was very awkward in judo, and not many people could train him, because of his size: he was too powerful and knocked people about, so they didn't want to train him." If he was so awkward, how did he get his Black Belt within two years? "Well, what happens," explains Harold, "(and a lot of people don't understand this), it's the hours and the attendance that you put in. Some Belts, you get in with Attendance and also what you know about the sport. Pat could push people off the ground easily; he could pick you up and throw you where he wanted to. That's how he probably attained his status."

Harold is the last member of the Hart and Evans families to be trading in the Bull Ring market. "I could sell the stall tomorrow, but I want to keep the family name on. Once you lose it, your family history's gone. In the *Birmingham Museum and Art Gallery*, as you walk up the stairs, there's a portrait of a lady selling flowers. She's my Great Grandmother. She was presenting a posy to the lady Mayoress of Birmingham. The occasion is when they were given Flower Rights to sell, in the streets. Her name was Fanny Gosling (short for Frances). We've got Hart, Evans and Gosling, as family names. She's wearing an old-fashioned dress with a little hat. It's beautiful. When my dad's brothers got drunk they used to go and sit by the painting – and cry!

"We were still at school, when we met Pat," continues Harold, "but most of our family took their children out of school to work. We used to go out Saturday morning to help our mom, and we'd sell either cucumbers or lettuce, on the end of the stall. I was ten when I started doing that, in 1945, after the Evacuation. Pat used to pop in occasionally and say: 'How's it going 'H'?' When he was a lad he'd come and help our mom on the odd occasion, selling fruit.

"Our mom, Lily Evans, was a Barrow Girl – a real old character. Her maiden name was Lily Hart, (from the Bull Ring). But she was very well known by the police, through Fly Pitching and for her bad temper. She loved a drink and 'played up' terrible." Harold recalls that when Pat was only seventeen, "We were all betting him that he couldn't drink this whisky. Pat had a pint glass and we filled it up – nearly. Pat was game for a challenge. He sat there and drank it. His face was glowing – we thought he was going to explode! Pat was staying at our house that night, in Well Street, Hockley. We walked round to the Taxi Rank in Dale End. Pat was the only one of us who could drive. He learned to drive, early days, with his father. Pat got in the front passenger seat, but next thing we knew, he was dragging the taxi driver through the back of the taxi, saying: 'I'm driving this taxi!' So Vincie Turner, smart young lad – a good dresser – a modern type of person, kicked Pat straight in the face, so that he lay there unconscious, in the back of the seat – and that's the truth!

"We arrived home in Well Street. We had a big attic in our house, an old back-to-back house; lovely old times – you know? Anyhow, Pat was sick everywhere in the house. When our mom got up the next morning, she looked and said: 'I can see size thirteen, under the table!' Up came Pat, looking absolutely lifeless. He said, 'Oh Mrs. Evans, I'm sorry. They got me drunk.' Our mom said, 'Oh, you big so-and-so! Anyhow, come on, what do you want for your breakfast?' And that was our mom's attitude."

Eventually Pat and the Evans brothers drifted apart, as his career blossomed. Alfie recalls: "I was courting my Francis and Pat was seeing her sister, Pat, up in Manchester. One weekend we went up there, to the Races and we got 'skint' – as usual! So we had to hitchhike back from Manchester. We broke up and I was home within two hours. Roachie arrived six hours later. Nobody would give him a lift because of his size – they were frightened!"

Another of Pat's friends, Johnny Harris, explained that because Pat was so naïve, Harold and Alfie took him 'under their wing', helping him to become more streetwise. Harold confirms: "When we were ten or eleven, we'd already been working the market for a few years, so we were more educated in that respect, and we brought Pat out in the world. His dad was dominant and he made sure the lad worked." As Pat got older, that 'education' began to pay dividends. After a funfair, on Epsom Downs, they searched the poor lodging houses around London, and found a hostel, somewhere around Paddington. "There was a sliding door, and a man came to it, with a big hump on his back," continues Harold. "Paddy always called humps on people's backs 'Charlies'. So he said to me: 'Look at the Charlie on his back!'

"It was five shillings a night. We went up on the third floor; it was very late by then. We woke up the next morning, in bed. Pat, being as tall as he was, the sheets hardly touched him. We looked around us and there were Chinese Seamen, Jamaican's – all nationalities. Pat was wiser that me: he'd planted his money down his socks." Harold's money was stolen. "Later on when I used to meet him, Pat would say, 'Do you remember that bloke with the Charlie?' He never forgot it. It was like something out of Charles Dickens!

"We got on the train at Euston and I fell asleep. When we hadn't got a ticket, we'd jump the train. But when we arrived at Snow Hill Station, I was still fast asleep. The next thing I knew, Pat's carrying me under one arm, a suitcase under the other, and my legs are going like that. He's saying: 'Come on – let's go!' We used to run out of the back entrance to Snow Hill, where the railway carts were; the incidents you think of, with Pat!"

Alfie recalls an instance when his mother was Fly-pitching in the market, on a Saturday, but had no license: "Pat and I went down to see her. Dale, the copper, was coming up the market and we were shouting: 'Aye-aye Lily, here's Dale!' Pat got one end of the barrow, I got the other, and we were carrying it between us. The plums were falling off and rolling down the bloody Bull Ring! We finished up under the archway, in the Fish Market, where we used to hide – until the copper had gone. In all these instances, there was never any malice in it," explains Harold. Pat makes the same point in *Pat Roach's Birmingham*: despite the 'ducking and diving', there was never any intention of doing harm. "It was just a good laugh," continues Harold. "There were dares and challenges, and usually about ten of us running around together.

"Pat left his Gran's in Shakespeare Road and went to live back at his mom's, so then he broke away from us, when he met Doreen. Pat met Doreen at Laura Dixon's and you've heard the saying; 'He swept her off her feet'? Well that was the truth – because he picked Doreen up, they were dancing around the floor, and her feet were dangling; they weren't touching the ground. He was carrying her! She used to say, 'Oh Pat!'" Doreen and Pat eventually married in February 1957, when Pat was nineteen. "When he was courting Doreen, nobody knew for week and weeks. Then he'd go away and come back lots of times," explains Alfie.

"Dolly came to the market one day, to our stall," recalls Harold. "She said: 'Hey 'H', have you seen our Paddy?' I said: 'No Mrs. Roach.' I always called her Mrs. Roach, out of respect, and called my mom Mrs. Evans, you see? She said: 'Hey 'H', I've got to meet him here. He's going to get me a turkey.' Anyhow, she's waiting there. 'He'd better hurry up, because as soon as that pub's open, I'll be in there!' Then this big shadow came up, with a great big turkey on his shoulder: 'Hello Ma,' (giving her a kiss), 'I've got your turkey.' And all the gold was on her. That's the truth, honestly!" Dolly was always 'dressed up to the nines'.

Harold came to his youngest brother Ronnie's defence, giving the two lads responsible a good hiding. "The next thing, about six kids came up the street, firing pellet guns, and I was ducking. Down the yard came this giant figure, took his coat off, and stood in the middle of the road, with his arms like that, looking just like John L. Sullivan. Everybody took off on their bikes and rode for dear life! That happened in Burberry Street Park and they chased me to Well Street, just round the corner, in the Jewellery Quarter."

Alfie elaborates: "I was in the house with Pat, when we heard screams and shouts, and there was Harold – rowing. Roachie called him 'Brick-bottle Harold', because if there were bricks and bottles about, he'd throw them! He called me 'Candlestick Alf', because I used to hit Harold with a candlestick, in the house, because I couldn't fight. Anyway, the next thing we knew, Harold was throwing bricks and bottles at these lads. Then they got him on the ground. Roachie came out. A bloke had walked through the crowd, stripped to the waist, and said, 'Who am I going to have?' Roachie said: 'Me!' He took one look at Roachie and he ran – he flew! Pat's strength was phenomenal."

Pat was the only driver at one time, within their group. He had a V8 Pilot car, painted all colours of the rainbow. "We were all coming out of Laura Dixon's club the one night," recalls Alfie, "and we'd all bagged a bird, bar Roachie – although it was his car! There must have been about ten passengers. Pat had his right foot, shoved through the window. He's driving up through New Street, in Birmingham. The things we used to do - and we never got stopped by the police!"

They bought an old Buick for £18.00, which Pat drove. "We thought we were 'Jack-the-Lads', with big wall-rimmed tyres and a big bull-nosed Buick," recalls Harold. "We must have seen too many gangster films at the time! But those were the good old days." "He was a good lad, Pat was," observes Alfie.

Doreen recalls her first meeting with Pat: "He was about sixteen, I was nearly seventeen, (there's a ten-month difference in our ages), when we met at Laura Dixon's Dance School. The lads went there, just to play up, but I used to go with my sister and we took the ballroom dancing really seriously. They turned up just to watch – and 'take the Mickey'! Pick up the girls – yes."

According to Pat, he and his friends fancied Doreen and her sister. "Yes, my sister was beautiful," confirms Doreen. "She had long blonde hair, right down her back. I had short black hair. They never believed we were sisters – even when I had Markie. He was blond-haired, for a while. They used to think he was my sister's – not mine!" Dolly's father, Bill Bevis had reddish-blond hair, so that could account for it! Doreen also confirmed that Pat was always the scruffy one, whereas some of his friends were quite smart. One of Pat's wrestling friends, Pete Roberts, commented that Pat was quite eccentric in that way. He never seemed to place much importance on his appearance, although he *was* fastidious – as substantiated by Doreen's washing quota!

"Alf and Pat have fallen out several times," explains Harold. I think Alf is the only one who could go raving mad with him and he'd take it. Me and Pat have had friction too. When we were going to the park we'd nearly come to blows. As kids, five or six of us would jump on Pat and get him on the ground. The next thing, bodies would be shooting. He'd lose his temper and God help the one he caught! But when we went swimming, a big arm would come and you'd think you were drowning. You'd go: 'Pat – Pat!' He'd drag you up and down like a rag doll. He *did* frighten us, didn't he Alf – in the water?

"Frank had been on a murder charge in Canada," Harold continues. "That was Paddy's pride of his father, because all round our way, early days Hockley, people were always going to prison. Mr. Roach, or 'Stick of Troche' as we used to call him, was a bit of a 'blarney merchant' – that's my honest opinion." "He'd stutter, if he got excited," explains Alfie. "He used to get agitated with us, because he said we were leading Paddy astray. When Pat was working on the coal Shirley, he'd start work at six o'clock in the morning, then go to work for his dad for the rest of the day, after he'd finished!"

Despite losing contact with Pat after he met Doreen, the brothers were soon back in touch with him. Twelve months down the line, Alfie's wife was eight months pregnant with Bernadette, and Doreen was eight months pregnant with Mark. "Pat came to pick us up one Sunday at Mom's. Mark's around forty-nine now – the same age as Bernadette. We all went down to Stourport – Francis, Doreen, Roachie and me. We were sitting on the side of the bank and there was a pub across the road. Roachie says: 'Do you fancy a drink?' Now bear in mind that the two wives were eight months pregnant. So I said, 'Yes' – and we swam across the river, to the pub. But the ladies had to walk round. You can imagine what my missus said, can't you? I blamed Roachie – 'It was his idea!'"

In 2004, Adrian Goldberg interviewed Harold, for BBC Local Radio, as part of an outside broadcast about the history of the Birmingham Bull Ring Outdoor Market. Several other friends from Pat's youth would like to pay tribute to him, so we have included more of them in the next chapter.

Chapter Four

'TOWNIES'

One of the first coffee bars in Birmingham was called 'El Sombrero': that was in the Horsefair. A certain group of people would meet there on a regular basis. Pat was one of them; there were a few others, including myself. In those days, this group of people was known as the Townies. We used to frequent the same places, and you'd always see the same circle of people. If there was anything on, like races at Wolverhampton, or a good film at the cinema, everybody would be there. It was like a grapevine.

Tony Green

Mavis and Barry Wood were good friends of Pat, for the five years between 1954, when Mavis was sixteen, up until the end of 1959, when he became more involved with sports.

"When we knew Pat he was tall and slim, not yet muscular, and hadn't grown his beard."

During that period, according to Barry, Pat was a young working chap, who wasn't particularly into sports or showbusiness, but then progressed in that direction.

Mavis recalls: "I met Barry when I first came to live up here. We'd all meet, every week, at the *Turners Public House* in Turner Street, to decide where we were going. Pat used to say, 'Well, we're not going up to the *Sydenham*, or to the *Tower* again' – but we usually ended up at one of them. Pat was always keen to do something different; we were too, but there were lots of places that we couldn't go into – we'd been banned!"

Pat searched for variety and change throughout his life: Mavis' example being an early illustration of that trait. Johnny and Eddie Hart were group members too. "Ray Green, Barry and myself, Ronnie Masters and Pat also," adds Mavis.

"From the *Turners* we'd either go to the *Tower Ballroom* or the *Sydenham* in Golden Hillocks Road. Then Eddie started to court this girl in the Black Country, so we all 'courted' her – just so that he could see her! Sometimes we'd come out, at the end of an evening, and say: 'Oh, we're not going home yet. Anybody fancy Blackpool?' And off we'd go! There'd be Barry and myself, Ray Green, Pat and Johnny and Eddie Hart. We'd all pile in the back of this van, because in those days the drinking, driving and overloading regulations weren't so strict. You'd open the door sometimes and there'd be arms and legs everywhere – you didn't know who was who!"

Barry recalled that all the men in the group slept on the beach in Blackpool, being unable to afford lodgings. Mavis was the only woman amongst them: "I was courting Pat, Barry and *all* of them! I seem to remember being *really* cold, but that's probably because I slept in the van."

She describes an outing to Halesowen Town Hall, when Pat smashed a door down! Whilst visiting the Black Country, they'd attend dances. "Some were held at the Town Hall; we got banned from there, for fighting. Pat went in and tried to reason with them: 'Look, none of us are drunk. We've come all the way from Birmingham, to see Eddie's girlfriend Greta,' but they just wouldn't have it, so he punched a panel out of the door. Then he just stood there, nursing his hand and flexing it. Afterwards, we simply walked away. It was as if it was accepted – 'Oh – they're the lot from Birmingham!' It sounds terrible; although we weren't really that bad; but we used to fight and we'd all be singing. I don't ever remember anyone on drugs. Some of them used to smoke, although Pat never liked smoking, at all." A supreme irony indeed, as he was the one who eventually developed cancer of the oesophagus.

Pat was a natural group spokesman. "Being the biggest out of the lot of us, if there was a problem, he'd go in and sort it out," Mavis explains. "After the lads had been fighting, he'd go in and smooth it over, saying, 'They're not bad lads really. They start on us because we come from Birmingham.' He was very diplomatic; he would rather talk than get into a physical fight. But the lads in our group used to go crazy, probably because they knew that Pat would sort everything out. After they'd all had their fights and their noses were bleeding, and their eyes blacked, the new suits they'd just bought from John Collier's would be in a real state. If they had a suit from John Collier's, they thought they were 'the cat's whiskers'!"

Barry points out that, although Pat's height was very unusual then, it would be less so nowadays. "People used to tease him, saying things like: 'I bet it's cold up there, isn't it mate?' But on one occasion, in a Black Country coffee house, Pat 'turned the tables'. There were two old fellas in there, who were both a *head* taller than Pat. So *he* got the chance to say, 'I bet it's cold up there mates, isn't it!'"

"Sometimes they'd drop me off at the dance, then go into Halesowen for a cup of tea," explains Mavis. "They'd try and race there too – to see how fast they could go in the old van." With far less traffic, the trip was more of a novelty than it would be nowadays.

"Johnny Hart had an old Ford Eight van with a spare wheel on the side. We all went up to Cannock Chase, on a hot summer's day," Barry remembers. "Mavis was learning to drive." "I can see it now – the red and white gingham tablecloths were all laid out everywhere," remembers Mavis, "with people having picnics. I actually went over some of the tablecloths, because I couldn't steer properly! It was just like something out of a comedy film. It was so funny, and Johnny Hart was shouting: 'Put the brakes on!' We went straight into the river, which was a kind of reservoir. It was only shallow, but we couldn't get out without getting wet. Johnny waded to the bank. Pat saw me, waded out, opened the door and nodded his head from side to side, as if to say: 'Oh – not again!' Then he just picked me up. Everybody was laughing and they helped to pull the van out. Pat carried me back and put me down – as he always did; he was forever picking me up or doing something with me – throwing me up in the air!"

They'd sometimes take a taxi to the *Swan* at Yardley. "We were walking back," recalls Mavis, "and coming over Tyseley Bridge, right in the centre, Pat just picked me up and held me over the side; either he was telling me to sing, or trying to stop me from singing, I'm not sure which. But that was Pat. He wasn't doing it maliciously. I can't remember how long he held me there, but every time I pass that bridge now, I can still see it happening!"

Barry's father was Billy Wood. The family lived near the junction of Ladypool Road and Highgate Road, on the border of Sparkbrook and Balsall Heath. "Pat would come up the entry, and knock the back door. But there'd be nobody there when dad opened it, because Pat would still be in the entry part – he could lean over and just knock the door!

"We'd go to *Tony's Ballroom* in Hurst Street, and the *Crossed Guns* or *Crossed Keys Pub*. Pat would be in there: 'Get us a…' – all the bookies used to go in there, so Pat used the bookies signing code to tell me what sort of drink he wanted!"

There was a parking area outside the *Ballroom* where the coaches lined up; the soldiers used to meet up there. "Pat would put Mavis on the coaches and she'd be singing Shirley Bassey songs. He'd introduce her to the passengers!"

Mavis recalls Pat saying, on several occasions, that he was going to get somewhere in life – he wasn't just going to 'bum around'. By-the-same-token, four decades later, he told his co-writer that he never actually *planned* his career, but when an opportunity presented itself, he would make the most of it. Barry comments: "He also got on well because, being a head taller than anybody else, he stood out in a crowd."

Barry remembers meeting Doreen shortly after her first meeting with Pat, probably when he drove Pat to Doreen's home, in South Yardley. "Doreen seemed rather quiet at the time. I didn't recognise her at the Memorial Service, last November, because it's been years. I spoke to her, but she didn't recognise me either."

Barry recalls returning from Blackpool, in a van without tools. "We just went on 'spec' and on the way back, 'out in the sticks' we had a puncture. We stopped on this big drive – I think it may have been to a farmhouse. Pat went down and borrowed some tools and a 'jack'. We had hardly any money on these trips, and slept on the sands of the South Shore, because you could just drive the car on then. We'd simply have a 'whip round' for petrol and that would be it." "I was probably the only one working," adds Mavis. So *that's* why Pat was holding her over the bridge – to get the petrol money! According to Barry, "The lads told me that one of Pat's cars couldn't get up hills, so they reversed it up Mucklow's Hill – which used to be even steeper!"

In years to come, they would see Pat in various places around Birmingham, or when Barry was delivering cars. "That's when he started to grow his beard and to thicken up a bit. Of course, he was fighting by then." According to Barry, "...he was a genuine guy, he didn't look for trouble or get into trouble. We used to get on very well with him. He wasn't a shy person, but, by the same token, he wasn't aggressive at all."

"Pat could be quite old-fashioned in some ways," observes Mavis. "He didn't like women to swear and I don't think he swore much himself. He didn't like women to smoke, particularly Doreen. Nor to wear miniskirts or anything too revealing. He didn't like a lot of make-up either. But in other ways he was raring to go – 'let's do it' sort of thing."

"Before he met Doreen, we'd be going to Worcester," explains Barry. "There wasn't a motorway at that time, we'd be on the old road. There was a gent's toilet outside, with a wall around it. Pat would say: 'Here's two birds coming Baz!' Because he could see over the top of the wall! 'There's a big one – she's mine!'"

Rod Hearne and his family moved in three doors away from Dolly and Harry Meakin, at 98 Belgrave Road, Balsall Heath, after Pat had already moved out. He remembers Pat coming down, to visit Dolly and his two younger brothers, Rickie and Peter. "Rickie was a good mate of mine," recalls Rod. "We used to hang around together. We were almost the same age. I remember Pat bringing Mark down to Dolly's. At that time he didn't have any celebrity status. That was around 1960. I'd be about thirteen or fourteen.

"Rickie was a quiet lad, like Peter – never got into any trouble. Pat would come down the Varna Road entrance, which was the back way to all the gardens, then through a back gate into Dolly's garden. Dolly was alright, although she could be a bit 'loud' at times. They had a couple of Alsatian dogs; one of them was very vicious: it had distemper. When I came down the entry, the white Alsatian made a Beeline for me! Dolly would call it and it would come back to her. If I went to call for Rickie, I'd just shout from the bottom of the garden! I remember Dolly sitting in the back garden, on a summer's day, shelling peas. You could see across the gardens: there were just walls separating them; in Dolly's case, it was probably about four feet high." The sort of walls you could sit on? "You could have done," retorts Rod, "but you wouldn't sit on *her* wall, because of the Alsatian dog!"

Pat was quite new to wrestling, at that stage, having bouts at the *Waldorf*, on Waldorf Road, Sparkhill, and the stadium in Pershore Road. 'His mom watched him wrestle there," confirms Rod. "I heard that the reason he took up wrestling in the first place was that he needed money for an operation to take Mark to America – something to do with his ears; that's what we heard as lads. They needed about a thousand pounds for it."

Johnny Harris met Pat when they were both sixteen – only a couple of months apart, age-wise. "We worked on a building site together, in Buckingham Street, up Constitution Hill – towards the Jewellery Quarter," explains Johnny. "Pat was a big lad, but not as broad as he became. He was very strong nevertheless – and would pick people up on a big pan shovel, used for loading dirt onto the wagons. He picked me and my cousin up together, on the shovel – no problem! We were only about eight stone each, wringing wet, then."

Johnny first met Pat at Harold and Alfie Evans' house in Well Street – (the brothers featured in the previous chapter).

In *Pat Roach's Birmingham*, one of Pat's best friends, Brian Webb, explained that Pat deliberately held back, because of his size. In street fights, the local lads called him 'The Giant'. Sometimes they'd try to wind him up, because he was big; but he'd just fix them with a stare – which usually did the trick!

"It probably did," agrees Johnny, "but I think he was held back in his boxing career, because he hadn't got a vicious streak." Former boxer Johnny King made the same comment – that Pat wasn't aggressive enough. "He was too nice a man to make a successful boxer," adds Johnny Harris. Pat was past the boxing training stage, when the two of them met. "He was on the weights in the Weight Room, with the wrestling. Let's face it, wrestling is more about showmanship. We all loved it, but boxing is much more of a physical sport."

Like several members of Pat's circle, Johnny remembers Laura Dixon's Dance School, above Chetwynd's, in Navigation Street. "We went there practically every Saturday night; being a dance hall, they only sold beverages like pop, or coffee or tea. So half the time we used to nip outside and go to the *Swan* pub, in Navigation Street, for a couple of drinks, although I must say, Pat didn't drink a lot." He confirmed that the lads used to 'take the Mickey'. "Yes – *Come Dancing*! We were only there for the 'birds' weren't we? At half time, when we had a break, we'd nip out, but we'd have a dance, especially if we saw someone we fancied! It was a Dance School too – you could have private lessons in the daytime."

Johnny doesn't remember Doreen from the School, although he'd seen her elsewhere. Vince Turner was a couple of years younger than Pat and himself. Johnny's cousin, Albert Jordan, was one of their group, for a while, but he died young. "Pat drove us around town, although I never went much further afield with him than that." With regard to Pat's outings with certain friends, to Halesowen Town Hall, Johnny comments: "Well Harold Evans would 'egg Pat on'. He'd take Harold anywhere.

"Pat always wore an overcoat, and a muffler around his neck, in those days. My cousin and myself wore smart white macks. But even when he had status, although he was smart, he was always casual." He lost touch with Pat when he did his National Service. By the time Johnny was de-mobbed, Pat was already into boxing. Later, Johnny became an Amateur Coach at *Nechells Community Centre* in Melvina Road.

'Con' Harris is Johnny Harris's brother. Like several others in our book, I met the two brothers at the Jewellery Quarter Memorial Service for Pat, held in November 2004. Con, short for Cornelius, describes his initial meeting with Pat, at the age of twelve. "I remember him coming in the house with my brother, Johnny. What struck me was how tall he was, coming through the door. He seemed pretty slim, but that was probably because of his height. We lived at 19 Ward Street, between Tower Street and New Summer Street.

"I found him outgoing and willing to talk to you. Whether it was because I was a bit younger I'm not sure. When I was older and used to go out for a drink with him I found that he was a brilliant storyteller. He told me different things about the wrestling. How they fixed it. He'd got to go somewhere the next week and he said: 'The next week *he* wins!' Me and John used to 'slag' him, because we were into boxing. We'd say: 'Ah – a load of rubbish!' Pat would say, 'D'you want to try it – when they throw you? I've hurt me back.'

"He told me a story about his dad, when his arm was cut. The surgeons wanted to take Pat's arm off, but his dad said: 'You're not going to. Sew that back on!' He said: 'If it hadn't been for me dad, I'd have lost the arm.'" Dolly confirmed recently that the scar resulted from an accident when four-year-old Pat fell out of a tree, when they were evacuated, for a second time, to Hereford. This resulted in an expensive taxi ride, back to Birmingham. Osteomyelitis developed, which was why amputation was suggested. It hardly bears thinking about, but without Frank's timely intervention, Pat's future sports career would have been non-existent!

Being three years younger than his brother, Con was too young to mix with the Laura Dixon Group. "When Pat visited our house in Ward Street, dad made a great big pile of toast, because there were four of us lads, attending St. Chad's School. Johnny was the oldest, so he was working. Pat used to sit down by our John while we were having breakfast. If they were late for work, Pat would just tap on the door and John would be gone."

He saw Pat a few years later, whilst walking with his future wife, Josie. "We were walking towards Dale End, over Lancaster Bridge, heading towards the Fire Station, when 'beeb-beeb-bib!' People were shouting, out of a car window, but it was the lads, playing me up. Pat was at the steering wheel, with passengers Harold Evans, my brother John and Johnny Mo. They were offering Josie a lift – and I'd got to walk; but I was sixteen – I'd got to protect her!"

Con remembers drinking until four in the morning, with Tom Jones: "We sat with him all night, in the *Cedar Club*, after he'd done his gig. It was before *It's Not Unusual* came out and he became famous. His group was *Tom Jones & The Squires*. They all wore green suits, with a paler green shirt, and dickey-bow. I remember Tom taking his coat off as he sat down and he was wringing wet with sweat. I thought, 'Scruffy sod! At least he could have brought a spare shirt or something,' because we were all conscious of getting 'geared-up'. But he sat with us, drinking all night then. He seemed very nice. Brummies didn't normally like Welsh blokes, at the time. But he came across well. Pat seemed to be getting on with him."

Successful Birmingham businessman Tony Green, one of the original 'Townies', has been a lifelong friend of Pat's. He is from a family of Lithuanian Jews. "My grandfather came over before the Revolution, to escape persecution," he explains. "They came to Birmingham and lived near Holloway Head. My father was one of ten children, who came up the hardest way possible.

"My grandfather's name, originally, was Samuel Katz. I only remember him vaguely, because he died when I was about four years of age. Grandfather became Samuel Green when he arrived in England, and was waiting in the immigration queue. He eventually went into the hardware business." Tony's father, Harry Green, worked in the markets in his youth. "He was a fireman in the war and told me many tales about wartime life. I remember, as a child, he took me up on the automatic ladder, on Stratford Road – right up high. But he was so poor that he went to the market, in the daytime, and was a professional boxer, in the ring, at night.

"Our family lived by Holloway Head, just off the Horsefair, in a kind of ghetto. All Jewish people lived near the Synagogue. They had no transport then. The nearest Synagogue was at Holloway Head; there was also one in Hurst Street, which has been demolished – almost opposite the Hippodrome. That's the one the family went to."

Tony and Pat first met quite informally, when they kept running into each other! "There were very few places to go to, in those days. It was the prelude to the 'Swinging Sixties'," Tony explains. So who exactly *were* the *Townies*? "The Holloway people, in the coffee bars. There was Ken Kilminster, Tony Carr, Michael Brown, Phil Cohn, Don Careless, (deceased), Micki Leigh, Rodney and Malcolm Hearn (both now deceased), and myself. The Fewtrells were on the scene of course: Eddie, Don and Gordon Fewtrell, and Larry Farrington. Some of these guys are alive today, but there are a lot who are deceased."

Tony used to work at the Coventry Great Fair, nicknamed the *Pot Fair*. "Pat would come and see me on the stall, before he went down to the booth. I've known Ronnie Taylor, who ran the booth, since I was a little lad." Ronnie is featured in Chapter Sixteen of our first book, *If – The Pat Roach Story*. "After being in the ring, it could be a freezing cold night, but Pat would be bare-topped. He always had time for a chat or a wave. Our friendship lasted around forty-eight years." Many of Pat's friendships were the kind where he might not see someone for ages, but would then become re-acquainted, as though there hadn't been a gap. But the friendship between Tony and himself was very special, and almost continuous.

Jim Collins, another 'Townie', was five years Pat's senior: Pat was about twenty-two and Jim would have been twenty-seven, when they first met, in 1959 at the *Kardomah Café* in New Street. They were introduced, either by

Larry Rudd or Alan Wilson. Pat used to refer to Alan Wilson as 'Big Al'. Describing his fellow Townies, Jim recalls: "We also used to meet at the *Tow Rope* and *El Sombrero*. There was a lad they called 'The Oxford Kid', and Kit Mancini. They were all different characters; some that fiddled for a living – some that didn't work – at all! Gamblers, con men, thieves."

Jim describes the *Kardomah* as a 'chat-up' place for meeting girls. "I used to meet Pat there, during the 1960s, sometimes as many as two or three times a week. For about seven years I was in and out of that café and scrap yards with Pat; in and out of his life." For the last thirty-four years, Jim has been a chauffeur to many, including several celebrities. He also 'worked out' with Pat, at the *Nechells Community Centre*. "Pat asked me to come down and have a workout – to stop Ron Gray poking him on the nose! Ron was an area boxing champion."

Just after Pat met Jim Collins, he decided to spend nine months up in Manchester, learning to wrestle, and visiting his friend Alfie Evans, whom he'd just helped to move up there. Harold reckons: "After Pat had been away nine or twelve months in Manchester, he came back speaking completely different. So that must have been where he had the lessons. You see, Paddy locked himself away, to do things; for example, when he went on the Coal Wharf, he was lifting great heavy weights and building up his muscles."

Jim Collins recalls an occasion in Plymouth, when Pat persuaded him to wrestle: "I was parked up as a lorry driver, in Plymouth, and saw the poster – 'Wrestling – Pat Roach'. As I walked in, Pat said, 'You're just the bloke. Do you want to wrestle son?' I said: 'I've never done it in my life!' They were one short. I went into the ring with Leon Fortuna, who was about my weight. I copped a right good hiding!"

Jim also spent some time as a Semi-Pro Light-Middleweight boxer. "I'd had seven fights by then. Somebody talked me into doing unlicensed fighting when I was twenty-one, so I lost the chance to become a fully professional fighter. Then I went into Unlicensed Fighting – about four or five times a year. Later, in 1961, I was going to London, to meet my agent. The underground train came in and sitting there was Pat – on the train. So I went into the same carriage and we chatted. He finished up coming to *Milden Hall*, the American Army Base, having just attended a wrestling event. He happened to know the agent I was going to see.

"Pat was leaning on the apron of the ring. I finished up winning. The next thing I knew, Pat grabbed me by the ankles, pulled me underneath the ropes and out of the ring! I hadn't realised how much money was going down on the fight. It was in an aircraft hangar – I'd never seen a crowd like that before. Every other bloke had a fistful of money! I knocked my opponent out, at the beginning of the Fourth Round, although I was well behind on points."

Pat rescued Jim, 'in the nick of time'. "I don't know what would have happened otherwise," acknowledges Jim. "There was a jeep waiting, with a driver, plus me, Pat and the agent, who had already collected the money. I think it was the man who ran the fight who told Pat to get me out as quickly as possible." Although Pat has had a few narrow escapes in his life, *several* other friends and acquaintances have been rescued by him.

"At one time I had a red 1500 Austin," recalls Jim. "I'd only had it for three months. Teddy Edwards borrowed it and offered to drive Pat to Shropshire, for a wrestling match. I hadn't realised that Pat and Giant Haystacks would both be backseat passengers on the journey. It was impossible to use it after that!"

Like Jim, Mick Walker, comedian, raconteur and all-round entertainer, also had his first introduction to Pat, at the *Kardomah,* describing the venue as "...the hangout for a range of people. It was an incongruent situation," Mick remembers. "It had three floors. The ground floor was the old ladies, for afternoon tea and scones; the basement level was the hangout of the slightly nefarious Birmingham characters. It was said at the time that you could get anything you wanted, within half an hour, by speaking to the right people in the basement!

"From about mid-day onwards, the first floor became the meeting place for people who were perhaps in a more elegant situation: maybe on the periphery of villainy or gangsterism. That was where I met Pat. It was considered quite an honour to be invited to go and have a cup of tea upstairs, in the *Kardomah.* At the time I was introduced to him, I was about nineteen years of age and still in a Rock 'n' Roll Band. Pat's physical size was quite impressive and the other noticeable thing was his gentleness and his quietly spoken manner. It was a great pleasure to meet him, albeit on a peripheral level. Subsequently, whenever we met he would nod and say hello and that's how I gradually got to know him.

"In every city there are Townies. The Birmingham Townies could hold their heads up with the best – they were great people. I lived in the East End of London for a while," continues Mick, "and the Birmingham Townies were as good, if not better. There was a wonderful guy in Birmingham, who died some years ago – big Jimmy Workman: he was a great friend of Pat's too. He worked at the *Birmingham Theatre* as a scene-shifter, and did some door work at the old *Rum Runner* club in Birmingham, in the old days. He used to pick phrases up. The lads would stay out late at night, but they'd all be down the markets in the morning, getting a bit of 'swag'. I'm not sure who it was who coined the phrase: 'The Pressburger Jacket with the wooden arm,' but the Townies, in the late 1950s and through the 1960s, bought some of their clothes from a Viennese tailor, Kurt Pressburger, down Bristol Street way. He made what we used to call the 'Bum-freezer Jacket' – slightly exaggerated broad shoulders.

"The Townies had this wonderful way – they always spoke to you as if it was a secret! Slightly out of the side of their mouth, and always looking round. Many of them, as they walked away, would keep their right arm stiff. I think they sometimes had a cigarette in the palm of their hand, in that slightly fey style. If you refer to George Cole, when he played the 'spiv' in St Trinian's films, the way he used to walk – that epitomises, to a large extent, how the Brummies or the Townies were. Pat never had to be like that; he used to walk tall and strong as an oak tree.

"But the ones whom we used to describe as being on the 'hurry-up'; they'd always got a scheme of some kind going on. 'I can't talk for long…' They had a wonderful, slightly – mincing waddle, (without wanting to misinterpret, or to be unkind about it), with the exaggerated broad shoulders, the wooden arm. The right arm looked as though it was absolutely inanimate! Jim Workman coined that phrase once, when I was talking to him. He said, 'Look at him son. Pressburger back, Pressburger Jacket and a wooden arm – proper Townie!'"

On a Saturday morning, Freddie Frost and I met in a Jewellery Quarter pub, to recall his memories of Pat. We had met just a month previously, at Pat's Memorial Service – but then – I'm running ahead of my story! Freddie lived with his family, including younger brother, Johnny, at 4, back of 148, Icknield Port Road, only five minutes from where we're conducting the interview.

Unlike Pat, Freddie wasn't evacuated. "I was only two at the time, but I can recall the front of the house going, in 1944. I told my mom in later years that I could remember a lady throwing herself across me. I can still picture it today – flashes of it. It turns out that it was my mom! The Germans used to come over and bomb all the factories that made 'ammo', which were all around Ladywood."

Freddie and Pat first met in 1951, in the *Market Hall*, at the back end of the Bull Ring. "I was nine when we first met; he was on his own – mooching," Freddie explains. "I had a part-time job in the market, fetching sandwiches and billy-cans of tea. Then I started serving, behind the market pitch, selling pet food, of all things. I worked for *W. Pimm and Sons*. They were famous in

Brum, with shops everywhere, selling budgies, canaries and pet foods. There was one in the Bull Ring next to the *American Bar*, years ago.

"The market had been bombed during the war years: one of the unexploded bombs was still there. It was put on display by the *Birmingham Mail* for the *Christmas Tree Fund* – in the *Market Hall*, by the Ladies' toilets. Our pitches were there. I've seen Pat there, many times. After that, I'd see him down the *Rag Market*, on and off – down Jamaica Row – past all the Barrow Boys. Pat and I would just mooch around down there. If I'd got a shilling in my pocket I'd go down and look round.

"I'd see him there often – especially on a Saturday, but sometimes even mid-week, like a Thursday or a Friday, because he went down there on certain days." Pat was five years older than Freddie. "I grew up faster that way," he explains, "knowing the likes of people like Johnny Farrington, Pat, and John Landon. They used to call me 'Frostie'; Pat was 'Roach'. I worked, as a milkman's assistant in Ladywood, just to earn money, around the houses in Summerfield Crescent, Gillott Road, City Road, and Sandon Road. I was only nine, and I'd still be collecting, out the dustbins, jam jars and paper – like everybody else. We took them up to Monument Road, to Louis, who eventually had a company called *Jaffa Cartons*. He used to give us an old halfpenny, for a one pound jam jar. They'd recycle them, because the jam factory was down in Freeth Street."

Freddie remembers 'Queenie', the Rag Queen. "She just sold clothes. I never got too involved with that; I was looking for more... You get this thing when you're looking for the *fortune* – you know what I mean? I collected stamps. I still do; also crystalware. You buy things, then sell them on.

"There were quite a few strong lads about in those days, (Pat wasn't in on this). We used to have racing, around Ladywood, with three-hundredweight on our shoulders, in bags of sand, and run round the block. We'd show off, especially if there were a few girls about! By the time I was sixteen, Pat and I lost touch, because he was into boxing and judo. I used to watch the boxing at the *College Arms*. Johnny Prescott and Pat worked out there as well." Our story moves forward to 1962, as the dramatic events of our next chapter begin to unfold...

Chapter Five

UNCHAINED MOLODY

We put a 1946 silver sixpence on a doorway, at Snow Hill Station, at a meeting place with a police sergeant, whom we'll call 'J'; that was our proof that we were actually at the meeting point.

Pat Roach

In all of our lives there are peaks and troughs, periods of elation and light, interspersed with dark despair – when it seems as though the sun will never break through.

One evening, in the summer of 1962, Pat and his friend and business colleague George Cullen, visited a popular Birmingham nightspot. With hindsight, they must have wished, a *thousand* times afterwards that they'd never gone near the place!

Pat was twenty-five years old. He and his senior partner, George, were paying a brief visit to the club, for business purposes – to collect some money. Without warning, a fight broke out. In the confusion that followed, a teenage boy was badly wounded.

Eight men attacked George and I. We were fighting for our lives. We fought our way out, in the hallway of a great big old-fashioned house, which is the only reason why we weren't beaten really, because we were sort-of back-to-back, fighting at ten o'clock and two o'clock (if you know what I mean?) Whacking them and smacking them.

They convicted us at the time, firstly because there were eight other guys, in various wounded states, having received thumps on the chin, and punches on the jaw, and also because the young lad got a glass in his face.

Roy O'Neill confirms: "Pat took the blame for that, didn't he?"

Ronnie Callow recalls: "George used to sit in the *Jeweller's Arms*, sucking on his pipe and drinking his pint. He'd always got a polythene bag in his pocket, containing various items of gold jewellery, such as gold rings, necklaces and bracelets. He was around five feet ten, and stocky – he weighed about thirteen stone. George had a beaky nose – and a typically Irish look about him."

But in any event, at the trial, they used the word 'concert'.
Yes, a combined effort; that's why you both got six months.
Bear in mind that case, years ago, when they hung a poor guy who'd been in police custody at the time of a shooting. The man who actually shot the policeman was on the roof. And everyone in the country knew that they hung the guy because he shouted: "Give it to him!" But what was he saying? "Give the officer the gun?" The guy they hung was retarded.
Ronnie explained: "… it was an injustice." There had been another witness who could easily have cleared Pat of the charge, but unfortunately wanted to keep out of the whole affair." Ronnie was given twelve months for GBH, on the same day as Pat, for an offence completely unrelated to this club incident. Shortly before this happened, Georgie James saw Pat in his nightclub, *The Spider's Web*, in Walsall. He recalls: "I was married at the time, and living in Walsall. Once or twice I saw Pat in the area and he said: 'Oh, I'm just out of the way.' That was *before* he went to prison."
So Ronnie and Pat found themselves incarcerated in Winson Green together, for different offences. "What Pat got his six months for was just keeping 'schtum' – just keeping quiet," explains Ronnie. Although Pat and Ronnie were already friends, it was purely coincidental that they were sentenced on the same day and served time in identical prisons.
What's also coincidental about the time we were in Winson Green, is that a few years later, Ronnie had a yard, which was a hundred yards further down Wellington Street from mine, almost opposite the main gates of the prison. So at a later point we both had scrap yards, within a hundred yards of so of the prison. On a Sunday afternoon, from Ronnie's yard, you could hear the prisoners shouting to each other, through the cell windows.
Paddy White recalls: "Funnily enough, I knew Ronnie, prior to Pat having a yard up there – up the road from Ronnie, didn't he?" Pat had a yard on the Queens Head Road, before that. He and Jimmy White subsequently opened *The Budokan*, on the same site, then Pat moved to his Winson Green yard later. Doreen recalls: "Pat used to take Patrick Junior up to his yard, some days; he'd come back 'black as the Ace of Spades', but with a huge grin on his face! Diane used to go mad: 'Oh, look at his clothes!'"
Paddy White recalls visiting Ronnie Callow, at his Winson Green scrapyard, before Pat moved there. "I've done some business with Ronnie – over the years – bits and pieces – and found him to be a really nice guy. Again, it's the breed of person he is. It's like Pat's old man – Ronnie's the same. It's a 'cash' business, and if you're dealing in that sort of business, you don't want to tell everyone about what cash you've got – so you tend to be

private – and a 'loner'. That *makes* them private, secretive – a little bit 'dodgy': you know you're not being told everything! And you don't expect to be, because you, yourself, are probably doing something similar."

I bought my Winson Green yard in 1986 and kept it for many years. A third coincidence is, not only did the prison back onto a canal, (shades of Amelia) but Ronnie Callow's got a water gypsy background too. He didn't realise that we both had, until he read a copy of 'If'.

Ronnie's father, William, was one of eight children, born in 1906, to Romany parents. The family travelled the country in a Bow Top gypsy caravan, which William had been born in. His own father was also named William; they were both known as Billy. Ronnie's grandmother was Emily. In the late 1920s, Ronnie's grandparents abandoned the open road for the canals, becoming 'bargees', or 'boatees'. He explains: "They hauled anything from coal, grain, scrap metal and beer barrels, throughout the country, although the majority of their work, in the early years, was around the Black Country." His father narrowly survived a drowning in the canal. His widowed mother's crippled suitor, Rubin, tried to hold him under the water with his wooden crutch. "Luckily for me, he did not succeed," continues Ronnie, "otherwise I would not be writing this." A few years later, William met Ronnie's mother, Florence, in Birmingham. When the children were born, the family settled down in Clay Lane, South Yardley. "My parents insisted that I went to school and got a proper education, as at this time, my father could not read or write."

Grandmother Emily lived to the ripe old age of eighty-five. "A photograph was taken of her, at the *Lea Hall Tavern* in Kitts Green, Birmingham, by the landlord, Mr. Keenan," recalls Ronnie. "Her black plaited hall went all the way down her back to the floor, touching her size nine shoes!"

From the open-air freedom of the canal behind them, we return to incarceration in Winson Green. It would have been particularly uncomfortable for a man of Pat's stature to share a cell, but fortunately that wasn't the case. Ronnie explains: "I was on the '3s' and then I went down to the '2s'. Pat and I both had a single cell. It wasn't too crowded in those days. But generally speaking, Winson Green was always bad: always three or four to a cell – like a dog kennel." A recently published report showed that overcrowding in the prison is still a problem. So how did Pat manage to get his own cell?

Because I was Mr. Roach – the judo instructor. What helped me a lot was that some of the prison officers used to call me 'sir'. I knew all of them, because I used to teach them judo at my club. They lived in prison officer houses, around the club. They used to call me 'sir' – 'Mr. Roach'. "Have you finished with that potty, Mr. Roach?"

According to Harold Evans: "When he was away on this Holiday Camp – put it that way – he was practicing Pranah Yoga. I've got some nice Yoga books – I like reading them. I meditate sometimes, but Pat was doing it all the time. He was teaching the 'people' there unarmed combat. How to look after themselves and defend themselves. There was a young lad in there at the time, with the nickname 'Ali Baba'. He had a great sense of humour, but had been in and out all his life. He was the biggest shoplifter in Birmingham – always locked away. When Pat first arrived, 'Ali' said, 'Hiyah Roachie. You'll like it in here. You'll need about six of them effing dinners to fill you up!'

"When Pat was in bed, the sheets used to come up to his chest. His legs would be bent up in the bed, because the beds were that small. But Ali played him up terrible when Pat was in there! He was a real character, but sadly he's dead now. He must have drove Pat made, when he went on his 'holidays'! He said, 'You'll never like it in here Roach – you'll never stick it. The grub won't fill you up.' He was never an aggressive person, Pat, but Harry Bubb said to me: 'If he'd have gone all the way, he'd have just killed Ali, because he's too strong!'"

The thing was – when we went to jail, everybody knew why we'd been sent there. Everyone in Town knew: the police knew, the prison officers knew. We were convicted on ten counts of malicious wounding. How can you be convicted on ten counts – a woman, a boy, and eight grown-ups? How could you do that? They were saying that while we were fighting eight men, we also had time to wound a woman and a boy, which is a physical impossibility. But they were determined to make charges like that stick because we were 'Jack-the-Lads', and ran three illegal drinking clubs in Birmingham. Also, because I was a judo instructor, they saw me as a fighting machine – my hands were potential weapons.

During the month Pat spent in Winson Green Prison, he became friendly with master-spy Gordon Lonsdale. Ronnie met him on a couple of occasions, but Pat had more contact with him. "I know he was doing a lot of 'bird'", recalls Ronnie. "He was in for twenty-five years. He had a privileged position, working in Winson Green library, because he was a very well educated man. He was Slavic – a good-looking man, with dark hair and blue eyes: very thickset, square jaw, flat features, high cheekbones, and spoke very good English." In fact, Gordon spoke four languages: Russian, English, Finnish and Polish. He was assigned a librarian's job in the hope that occupying his mind would keep him settled, and he would therefore present no threat. During the two years Gordon spent in Winson Green, he made frequent petitions for his release.

Gordon Lonsdale was an adopted name, for someone who was, in reality, a Russian. According to Ronnie: "I've seen photographs of this man, in books, over the last twenty years, and I've said: 'Yes, I remember him.'" Gordon Arnold Lonsdale was born in Russia, but was sent to live with an aunt, at the age of seven, in California, in 1929. He lived there for nine years, learning to speak English fluently. He returned to Russia in 1938 and immediately joined the *Communist Youth Movement*. After fighting in World War II, he was accepted by the *KGB* and trained as a spy. He was subsequently sent to Canada in 1954 with a forged passport, under the alias, Gordon Lonsdale.

A year later he arrived in London, disguised as a successful Canadian businessman. He opened up substantial bank accounts and rented a luxury apartment, overlooking Regent's Park. Gordon made friends easily and talked of opening a firm to distribute amusements and games in Europe. He was regularly seen in London's best nightclubs in the company of attractive women. This was, however, all a front. Molody, to use his Russian name, had the ability to charm all manner of people; it was part of his stock-in-trade.

Pat recalls that Gordon, (as he was known to the inmates), would sometimes have storytelling sessions, when the mood took him. Truth, as the saying goes, is often stranger than fiction; in reality, this 'teller of tales' had been dispatched to England on a specific *KGB* mission, to learn all he could about British underwater detection devices. During the late 1950s, he contacted Harry Houghton, a Chief Petty Officer in the British Navy. Ethel Gee worked at the Admiralty Underwater Weapons Establishment in Portland. Gee stole naval secrets for her alcoholic boyfriend, Houghton, who passed them on to Lonsdale.

In 1961, British agents pounced on them, arresting Lonsdale, Houghton and Gee, outside the *Old Vic Theatre* in London, and confiscated a shopping bag, which Houghton and Gee had given to Lonsdale. It contained fifty pages of Admiralty Fleet Orders, two hundred and twelve pages of underwater photographs, plus details of war vessels, classified British Navy documents, and drawings of the navy's long ships. The Krogers, a married couple, were also arrested and all five prisoners were placed on trial, convicted and sent to prison.

Pat and Lonsdale, aka Konon Molody, would sometimes have conversations with one another, although at the time, Pat had no way of knowing just how infamous his fellow inmate was.

Gordon was a long way from home and from his family. He reminisced about his wife – how much he was missing her – and how much he loved her. He talked about his dad and how he deserted him – how much he hated him. How he blamed him for being in jail. Because, had he been brought up in a loving and steadfast childhood, he'd never have become a spy, or ended up in jail.

Molody had been in Warsaw, as a young man, just days before the German occupation. His landlord's daughter, Irma, whom he was very close to, was killed. He swore, over her grave, to fight fascism in all its forms, for the rest of his life. Many traumatic events happened to him in the early part of his life; it was a classic case of a young boy becoming embittered and scarred for life.

He found it the ultimate irony that here he was, possibly in the most democratic country in the world, locked up in jail; in an anti-fascist country – when he hated fascists!

Another thing we talked about, was how disgusted he was with the hygiene in jail. He could never get used to using the toilets, and it affected his ablutions. He hated using them – and 'slopping out' – it sickened him. Sometimes you could actually use a proper toilet, but you'd be in full view of everyone anyway! There'd be a whole group of guys, looking over the top of the cubicle saying: "Hurry up you, hurry up you!"

We talked about the fact that young offenders were sometimes put in with recidivists. He was very critical about that. In those day, 'Yps' (Young Prisoners), were by and large, kept separate, although sometimes there wasn't any choice, in cases of over-spill.

Pat was allocated the mind-blowing task of stencilling the word 'mailbag' on the front of sacks. Ronnie was perhaps a little more fortunate, as he worked in the tailor's shop. He and Pat always tried to meet during Recreation, in the prison yard. Konon was particularly noticeable at such times.

He used to walk around in patches: high profile prisoners were obliged to wear them. Patches were for escapees – on your leg – anywhere. Totally incongruous, disproportionate patches. They were for the warders' benefit, so they could see him across the road – if he was near a fence or climbing a wall.

Molody's special set of clothes had three large contrasting patches of colour; one on the left breast, one on his left knee and a third behind his right knee. This meant that he was under 'Special Watch', known as SW, a treatment usually reserved for prisoners who have tried to escape. Other features of SW included his being kept in a special cell, with additional bars. He appealed to the governor but was informed that the decision to categorise him as an SW prisoner had been a direct order from the Home Office, without any specific explanation.

The reason Gordon palled up with us was because we weren't 'tea leaves' you see. And we weren't over-violent. He was far more intellectual than the others – he didn't see himself mixing with thieves.

After a month's acquaintance with the Spymaster, Pat and Ronnie were handcuffed, then 'shipped out' to Preston Jail. Ronnie recalls: "On the A34 to Preston, approaching Congleton, the coach stopped because of a traffic hold-up. We were there for about fifteen or twenty minutes. It was one of the old coaches where you could wind the window down. As it was a hot day, the 'screws' had got their hats off, so the coach appeared to be just full of guys in 'civvies'. Two young women walked past. We said: 'Hi, how are you darling?'– chatting the girls up. They said: 'Where are you going?' 'Oh, we're going to Blackpool – like.' (I told them that, 'cause Preston's near Blackpool!)

"The coach started pulling away. One of the girls asked: 'Are you coming back this way?' 'Yes, in about twelve months' – and I held our handcuffed arms up! Pat said... (mimes Pat hitting him). You think about these things, over the years.

"Pat palled up with an Hungarian acrobat on the exercise yard, because you got out for an hour every day. It got to the stage where this guy would stand on Pat's shoulders. Pat would walk around. Then this guy would slowly turn himself over, and he was on Pat's hands like that – above his head. He was a circus acrobat, doing about twelve – fifteen months, and this was how they used to exercise – in the yard. He was smallish, probably about 5ft 8 inches and 9 stone. But very agile, like circus acrobats are." He and Pat went through this routine quite frequently, not so much for the entertainment of the inmates, but as a practice session for the acrobat. Ronnie comments: "There was no one else in the nick who was strong enough to hold him up.

"I think Pat and I were the closest of how anyone can be, you know? I always remember the centre of the nick, because in any prison you've got four wings, off a centre. And in the centre of this one, there used to be cages and cages of bloody budgerigars! They used to drive you crackers. I always remember the birds in that nick – 'birds doing bird'!"

The fact that Pat and Ronnie had each other for company, helped to make the situation more bearable, as did their combined sense of humour. "Keeps you going love!" comments Ronnie. It's easy to imagine the two of them, trying to keep each other's spirits up, in this way.

Doreen explains that Dolly, herself and three or four-year old Mark would often visit Pat at Winson Green. They also made the long journey up to visit him in Preston jail, after he was transferred. Pat was released from Preston Jail a month or two before his friend. Ronnie remembers the day before that happened. "He came down to my cell and said: 'Here you are, this is for you.' He gave me some tobacco and peanut butter, and a load of goodies that he'd saved his money to buy." Pat mentioned something (tongue-in-cheek) about becoming a 'Tobacco Baron' while he was in there. Ronnie elaborated: "Well he didn't smoke at the time. He used to buy tobacco and lend it to people. He wasn't interested in taking a profit, whereas the Tobacco Barons would lend you a quarter, and take half an ounce back. He used to help people out by just lending a quarter ounce, then taking a quarter back."

In fact, Pat only served four months, as he received two months remission (time taken off for good behaviour). By the same, token, Ronnie had a third of his sentence removed.

George was released at exactly the same time as me, but was met within the gates, which is what they do. They release you from prison, but there's still another door to go through. That's where the police re-arrest you. Can you imagine? George went through his bath, got changed, put his suit on, walked through the gate, only to be met by two policemen, who re-arrested him – a terrible ordeal!

I was very anxious that the police would forget about me and my 'Jack-the-Lad' reputation, and very conscious that if they had me on their mind, in those days, they could have me back in jail, at the drop of a hat. There were, allegedly, some unsavoury police officers about in those days. And I very much wanted to disappear. That's just what I did. I went to London

A newspaper article, written in 1963, when Pat had begun his incognito lifestyle in London, reported, despite strong denials from Lonsdale, that the man who led the Portland Spy ring had written to his wife, telling her to keep her hopes up for his early release. In the event, Lonsdale served less than four years. In 1964, they finally unchained Molody, exchanging him for Greville Wynne, the Englishman accused of passing Russian secrets to the British, during the *Penkovsky Affair*.

On returning to Moscow, Pat's former fellow prisoner was hailed as a hero and awarded two medals – the *Red Star* and the *Red Banner*. He wrote his, propaganda-ridden memoirs, with the help of fellow spy Kim Philby. In a second book, Molody *alleged* that some of the prisoners in Winson Green had been framed... by a certain police sergeant. Unsurprisingly, he didn't name anyone, in case the authorities suppressed his book. Meanwhile, Pat continued with his new lifestyle, safely out of harm's way.

I lived in Harlow and studied judo there, with a guy called Dennis Wynne. Although I was in and around Birmingham shortly after my release, from a business point of view, I 'laid low' for some considerable time.

Former boxer-turned-club-manager, Brendan Breslin, was born in Dublin in January 1934, making him three years older than Pat. He met Pat around the mid-1960s. "It was in the *Bell Public House*, on the corner of

Anderton Street and King Edwards Road, in Ladywood – by the 'rec'. Pat came in with George Cullen, who introduced me to Pat, saying, 'This is a friend of mine, Brendan Breslin. He's mixed up in the boxing game.' I was attached to a *Ladywood Boxing Club* there. Pat was very tall, but slim: not as well built as he later became. My first impression was that he was a very quiet fella. We'd talk about the boxing game; he used to box for *Mitchell's and Butlers*, and in the Jack Solomon's competition too." Doreen recalls that often, when Pat returned from boxing, he'd taken a real bashing. "The ends of his teeth were chipped, and he'd have a big black eye. I said: 'Oh pack it up – it's ridiculous!'"

Brendan Breslin has discovered a photograph of himself, taken around the time when he first met Pat, in the actual pub, *The Bell*, where that meeting took place. Brendan, who is standing in front of the dartboard, was in his early thirties, and Pat would have been in his late twenties – just a year or two after he was released from prison.

In 1970, (when Pat was building a successful wrestling career, and a year before he appeared in *Clockwork Orange*) Gordon Lonsdale collapsed and died of a heart attack, while picking mushrooms in a small garden behind his Moscow apartment. He was just forty-eight years old.

Chapter Six

THE ENTERTAINER

My approach to a part would vary so much, depending on the day, and what I was allowed to do with that particular character. For instance, I always try to speak quietly, as a big man. People misunderstand what I'm trying to do, and ask me to project more. A lot of established actors are allowed to talk quietly – it's all about power.

Pat Roach

This chapter considers certain aspects of Pat's early wrestling experiences, and his film and television career: apart from the four *Auf Wiedersehen Series* and subsequent *Christmas Special*, which are covered separately, and in some detail, from the next chapter onwards. Our first book, *If – The Pat Roach Story*, gives a detailed account of Pat's showbusiness career. Recent research, however, has produced a wealth of additional material – enough to fill at least two more volumes. This chapter and the first half of the next one, give a condensed version of that new material.

We begin with tributes from some of Pat's sportsman friends, combined with memorable spectator moments. Pat and wrestler-turned businessman Ace Allcard first met in 1964. "I was in Lew Phillip's office by the Victoria Law Courts, in Birmingham," Ace recalls. "Lew wanted to introduce me to another wrestler, a guy by the name of Pat Roach. We had a chat about where we aimed to go in life, in our profession. Pat said that he'd like to become the British Heavyweight Champion. I just said that I'd like to wrestle – professionally."

Pat would subsequently visit Lew's City Centre office on many occasions. They became such close friends that Pat kept Lew's prayer shawl after his death, passing it around to Lew's Jewish friends, to use, in his memory, at various synagogues. Judo Pete Roberts, Ray Robinson and Ace are amongst several wrestlers who confirm Pat's opinion, that Lew was a very honest, warm-hearted individual. Pat would have been pleased to know that Doreen has now given Lew's prayer shawl into Tony Green's safekeeping.

Ace's first wrestling show was at the *Cannon Hill Park Festival*, Edgbaston in 1964. "A Yorkshire wrestler and promoter called Cyril Knowles, who died recently, brought me to Birmingham and introduced me to Lew Phillips." Former wrestler Ray Robinson knew Cyril too. Ace moved from Lightweight amateur wrestling, and turned Professional in 1964, increasing his weight and his wages in the process. "I felt my future would be better as a Heavyweight, and became one around 1971."

After the *Cannon Hill Festival*, Ace wrestled at *Digbeth Civic Hall* in the winter of '64. Lew Phillips put on his major wrestling shows at a hall in Sparkbrook, which seated over a thousand people. *Digbeth Civic Hall*, mentioned by Chrissie Doyle in Chapter 3, was only about a five or six-hundred-seater. Pat wrestled in his judo outfit, at that stage.

Although Ray Robinson is thirteen years Pat's junior, their friendship goes back twenty-two years. Ray won the British Cruiserweight Champion title in 1989 and held it until 1993. "I retired undefeated. I didn't lose the belt in the ring. Cruiserweight is between Light Heavyweight and Heavyweight: you had to be under fifteen stone."

Ray and I met initially at the August 2004 Reunion at Bill Bridges' pub in Horton Kirby, Kent. I'd promised Pat that, should he be no longer around, I would go instead. The occasion was a bit of a blur, because, following a rather exhausting trip down there, with other friends of Pat, (including Rob Knight and Bernie Guest), I spent the remainder of a glorious hot summer's day selling Pat's books. Many wrestling celebrities were present that afternoon, including the famous referee Joe D'Orazio, featured in Chapter 10.

Ray observes: "Pat was a proper wrestler. I met him in 1982, when I joined *Joint Promotions* from the Independent Wrestling side. I'd turned Professional in 1970 and had ambitions to become a professional boxer, so I went with another guy, to see these fellas. They gave me a real pasting. I don't like getting beaten, so I kept going back, while they taught me how to fall and things like that. Then they started taking me to gymnasiums and I got into wrestling. Cyril Knowles knew Pat very well too; he gave me my first professional match, at Goole Market Hall, on 12 February 1970. I was nineteen at the time. I'm training a professional boxer, Christian Woollas. I was sparring with him, just before your call!"

Ray appeared on *World of Sport* several times. "I wasn't the British Champion until after it finished on television. The first time I appeared on television was in 1981 or 82, with Alan Kilby, the Light Heavyweight-cum-Cruiserweight. I did TV shots with King Ben, and was Top of the Bill with Skull Murphy, for the Grande Prix Belt. I won in two rounds against Simon

Hurst: that was in Buxton. I also wrestled Bearcat Wright and Ian MacGregor: I had a TV match with him.

"The last time I saw Pat he said, 'Hey, there's one thing boy. They won't spoil your looks, will they?' – it was a playful joke that he had! But Pat was *always* interested in my Strongman stunts. One in particular was about judo – one of Pat's real loves. My son, Mark started judo at about eleven or twelve; he went on to do some wrestling early too. The mat at his local club was becoming unsafe. They needed a thousand pounds for a new one, but hadn't got the funds.

"I devised a stunt, and talked to Pat about it. He said: 'Well, it's going to take some doing,' but I said: 'Well, I'll do it.' I lay down on the floor and I got an eighteen-stone guy, standing on my stomach, doing squats! My idea was that he should do a hundred, before I cried off. On the night, I did a hundred and thirty-two. I was a part-time wrestler, working at the steelworks, and I had the workmen, in the staff breaks, coming with their steel boots on, stood on me stomach, practising. One would do about fifty; another would do another fifty. I picked the biggest fellas I could!

"Pat liked the fact that, as I got older, I never stopped training. I've got a big gymnasium in the back yard. All the local lads come and train: I box and wrestle with them – even to this day. I can just about beat every one of them in strength. The first time I wrestled Pat, in 1989/90, I'd become Cruiserweight Champion. Max Crabtree, Big Daddy's brother, promoted nearly all of my fights. He persuaded me that I'd be suitable for Heavyweight wrestling; although I wasn't as big as some, he convinced me that I'd have good matches with them.

"I'd already met Pat, but when I knew I had to wrestle him, he looked particularly *huge* to me! I'm six foot, nearly, and weighed about fifteen stone three or four, but Pat was about six five and about nineteen seven. I was very nervous! Max Crabtree was the MC. Pat got a fall in the third round. He knew my style of wrestling, which is Strength Wrestling. He wanted it to be a good match, so he maybe eased off a little bit for me. In the fifth round I got a Power Slam in and I actually pinned Pat. Max Crabtree got the MC and he said: 'Nearly twenty stone that, ladies and gentlemen!' I'd picked Pat up, ran and crashed him down, and kept on him all the time. So there was Pat's weight and mine, crashing down. They said afterwards that the ring moved across the floor when we did it!

"He won the match with the Brummagem Bump – and that is a *frightening* experience, because he picks you right above his head – and just drops you. He didn't use it early on in a match, as you were able to keep out of his way, because you're fit. What he did was to slow you up; he deliberately allowed me to 'post' him, then he put his hand down and I thought: 'I can get him again.' So I posted him again, then ran after him, to weaken him, because I'd just got a fall. He came back and 'footed' me, right on the point of the chin! With me running in, it wasn't that he'd kicked me hard, it was because I'd run into it – I hadn't expected that!

"People say it's about rehearsing. That's a load of crap! I've never rehearsed – I ran straight into him. He just stunned me, for about five or six seconds, then picked me up above his head – he was a very powerful fella. He was in *Britain's Strongest Man* at one stage you know? It was a cracker – a six-rounder. When we'd finished, Max Crabtree got into the ring, and did the announcing. Pat got hold of the microphone and said, 'Ladies and gentlemen, I'd just like to say a few words. It beats me why the wrestling promoters spend a fortune bringing foreign competition over for us top Heavyweights, when we've got a guy who works in the steelworks during the daytime, then comes here and wrestles me in such a form as he has done tonight. He's done very well. Ladies and gentlemen... put your hands together for Ray Robinson!' The crowd really took to me, and every time I was in that hall again, I went down really well there."

This is a typical example of the way in which Pat was quick to recognise and promote talent. "He was that kind of a guy," agrees Ray. "Years later, I asked him, 'Can you remember the first time that I wrestled you, and you got the microphone and gave the spiel out?' He just looked at me... and he started to smile... gave me a playful punch on the chest and said: 'Ray – did I lie again?' That was Pat – a really dry sense of humour!"

I wondered about the view, expressed by *some* wrestlers, that wrestling is a partnership: that you work together? "Well, I don't go along with that so much," comments Ray. "We need wrestlers *and* entertainment. Pat agreed with me on this point; we talked in depth about the people who knock wrestling." I reassured him that Pat and I had a long-established agreement: to promote the positive side of the sport.

Ray elaborates: "I have absolutely the same thoughts as Pat did. The wrestlers that 'knock' wrestling, are wrestlers that really couldn't do it. They didn't like us, who *could* work, and it was their way of saying: 'Ah well, we do this, we do that.' Some people think that in wrestling, you get a move, they get a move, but it just doesn't work like that. It certainly didn't in my matches! When you wrestled heavyweights, like Ray Steele, Marty Jones, Finlay, Pat Roach, and even Alan Kilby, the deaf and dumb lad, (who I had two great matches with), you *had* to wrestle, to get the holds; that's what made our matches good matches.

"This other sort of wrestling – you could see through it! I wouldn't have anything to do with it; that's why some wrestlers didn't want to wrestle me. The injuries that I've had, and I've talked to Pat about them. I mean, I'm deaf now, and I think it's because my opponents *had* to wrestle me; because I wasn't going to ease up on anybody. I certainly didn't ease up on Pat Roach – and he didn't ease up on *me*!"

Ray had over seven hundred professional matches. "I can honestly say that I've never come out of that ring without being hurt. You didn't go out there to *kill* one another, it's a skilful art; but the sort of wrestling that I did, Ray Steele did, Jones, Pat Roach and so on, it was hard." Ray sustained a broken leg, at Withensea, near Hull, had a broken collarbone; also broken ribs, courtesy of Honey Boy Zimba! "I've scars over my eyes. Barry Douglas hit me with a Big Knee, but I was supposed to be working at the steelworks the next day. Max Crabtree kept saying: 'You've got to go to hospital.' I got my son, who was about twelve years old then, to put a towel over my head. We got lost, driving out of Scarborough. I said, 'Hang on a minute Mark,' and pulled over, to ask this lady where Staxton Hill was. She nearly fainted, when she saw the blood pumping out of me head!

"It *is* a 'rough-tough' business. But the people that knocked it were the people who picked the opponents that they wanted to go on with; so I totally endorse what Pat said." I wondered if Ray ever fought Judo Pete Roberts? "No, I didn't. I always wanted to, but I never got a match with him. He was a great wrestler – a Super Destroyer – a very fit man."

Ray retired from wrestling in 1993, due to knee problems, and opened his gymnasium about five years ago. Like Tony 'Banger' Walsh, he also runs a Security Firm. "My dogs are trained up to Police Standard. I want to make sure that Christian Woollas, this boxer that I'm training, gets the Midlands Area Belt back again for us. He used to be the Midlands Area Professional Cruiserweight Boxing Champion.

"Pat used to say, 'Tell us what you've been doing Ray.' The latest stunt that I do, I have two hammers tied together, (I've just done it for a policeman here today and he said: 'Wow – that is amazing!') I have a fourteen-pound hammer and a twelve-pound hammer, tied together. I actually put the hammer at arm's length and touch my nose. Pat said: 'That's really good. A lot of the boys would be really envious, if they saw you do that.'

"I've got a photograph, at the Reunion, of me and Pat and Barry Douglas, a mutual opponent, who Pat and I fought on many occasions. It was at the first Reunion of the Northern Boys, at Ellesmere Port, a few years ago. I wrestled Pat again, three to four years after that first match. I think he won: it was just a one-fall match; probably for one of the independent promoters.

"Sometimes Pat was away, wrestling in Germany, so I would maybe see him six or seven times a year. When he came back over here, for a series of matches, I'd probably be on the same bill as him – for lots of them: Manchester – *Belle Vue*, all over the place; we'd get together and have a talk. I walked round Stratford-upon-Avon with him, because he was very interested in the buildings around there. When he came to *Brigg Corn Exchange*, (which has now been pulled down), Pat tried to keep it open, and put a bit in the local paper. I must have wrestled there fifteen times, over the years. It was only a small place, but it was well known for wrestling, and had *character*."

Con Harris, whom we met in Chapter Four, has been an Amateur Boxing Coach since 1972. He and his brother, John, turned Professional, in the 1980s. "I became a Professional Boxing Coach and Manager, with eleven lads on my books. Although they didn't fight for the British titles, some of them *nearly* got there. One of them fought Kostas Patrou, down at *Aston Villa Leisure Centre*: that was on TV. We used to be on *Fight Night*, the television programme, regularly: it was Gary Newbon's show."

Whilst becoming increasingly involved in sport, Pat still found time to run a scrap yard and continued to do so throughout his life. Johnny Harris, Con's brother, recalls visiting Pat at his Winson Green yard. "I'd nip over in the van, to see if he'd got a part, and stop and have a drink with him. He put a gearbox in for me – lovely job, but two days later, it ground to a halt, because they'd forgotten to put any oil in. Pat had it re-done, put a new gearbox in – never charged me a penny." John was an Amateur Coach at *Nechells Community Centre* in Melvina Road.

"I went there to train and finished up holding a stopwatch, timing the lads. I started there in 1970, coaching and amateur boxing. Pat used the Weight Room: that's where I began seeing him again, after a long spell. He'd come into the Bag Room and we'd have a chat. I lived across the road, in Bloomsbury Walk, which was then a new estate." John trained professional boxers, from 1985 – 1990.

Whilst I was visiting Pat's half-brother, Pete Meakin, Dolly phoned, asking me to include a particularly funny wrestling moment! Pete and his wife Shirley retell the story between them. "Years ago, Pat was wrestling 'The Red Scorpion'," begins Shirley. "I think the match was at the *Adelphi*, in West Bromwich," interjects Pete. "The Scorpion, apparently, was giving Pat a right good bashing. Dolly sat there fuming and getting all agitated," Shirley continues. "When the Scorpion was down on the floor, Dolly pulled his mask off and scratched his face." Pete concludes: "I think it was Lew Phillips who commented: 'Pat failed to unmask the Scorpion... but his mother did!'"

Doreen recalls taking their son Mark, his wife, Diane and Patrick Junior, to watch Pat wrestle at a fair, some distance away. "Patrick was only five or six years old. Pat's huge opponent was getting the better of him. Patrick kept rushing backwards and forwards, bashing his little wrists on the side of the ring, shouting: 'You leave me Granddad alone – you!'"

Seated in Johnny King's lounge, former boxers Billy Wooding and Johnny recall early sports experiences with Pat. John explains how Billy and himself started together at the YMCA, on the Soho Road – in the gymnasium. "Then we went to the *Bull's Head,* West Bromwich. Al Lawley advertised: 'Do you want to be the Heavyweight Boxing Champion of Great Britain?' He had posters printed, so Pat approached him."

Pat, Billy, Johnny King and Gordon and Ray Corbett all signed contracts with Al, and trained for boxing together, at the *Bull's Head.* Billy explains: "We'd go down to Salford Bridge, which is Aston Reservoir, and run around the track there. We used the dressing rooms too. Sometimes we'd train with Pat. That's how we got stronger and more knowledgeable about each other and kept together." This four-year training period was between 1954 and 1958. Pat entered an Open event, the *Heavyweight Novices Competition*, run by Jack Solomons.

Billy recalls: "In those days, if you wanted to turn Professional from Amateur, you had a trial bout with a professional boxer, to determine whether you were good enough." "It was very strict, the difference between an Amateur and a Professional," explains Johnny. "If an Amateur was caught, training with a Professional, he was crossed off the Amateur List."

According to Pete Roberts, there is also a world of difference between Amateur and Professional wrestling; the same applies to boxing. "It was almost a crime in those days," recalls Billy. "In fact, I went to get into the ring at Salford Bridge, at a fair called *Hickman's Boxing Booth*. Unbeknown to me, there was a British Amateur Official there who came up to the ringside and said: 'Look, if you go ahead with this fight, you're finished as an Amateur.' I was only seventeen, and decided that it just wasn't worth the sacrifice, so I pulled out of the fight."

Johnny King recalls: "You never had all these head-guards in Amateur Boxing, like they do today. If your gum-shield dropped out of your mouth, in Professional Boxing, the referee used to kick it out of the ring: they'd wash it and put it back in your mouth, at the end of the round. But now, the fight has to be stopped and the referee sends it to the corner to be washed. So it's kidology, because if you're feeling a bit groggy, you just spit it out!"

Pat was a *natural* comedian, particularly his observations about human nature. "I know what you mean," comments Billy. "In the gym he'd say to Johnny, even if he'd just been hit: 'Is that the best you can do?' And Johnny would come back at him again!" They never saw him lose his temper – "and I used to box with him at least three times a week, from when he was about eighteen," adds Johnny. "We both enjoyed each other's company. Billy was a Southpaw – the opposite way round to Pat and me." Billy elaborates: "His trainer would say to Pat: 'Have two rounds with Johnny.' Johnny would really speed him up and push him hard."

Billy and Johnny worked as Bouncers, at dancehalls, in the Banbury, Atherton and Nuneaton areas. A weekly venue was *The Winter Gardens*, in Banbury, a huge place, complete with boxing stadium. "That's what gave us the idea to do occasional work there, as Bouncers. They liked us working there; because there were Yanks stationed there. The dancehall held about six hundred. If one of the others didn't turn up, we'd ask Pat." On their free nights, the extra money would come in handy. Johnny King explains: "We started the 'Bouncing', with Jerry Jeery, now deceased: the biggest wrestling promoter in the Birmingham area. He owned the *Indoor Stadium* on the Pershore Road."

"They rang me up," remembers Billy, "and said, 'Would you be interested in doing a job at the *Cedar Club*? It's for Tom Jones, so we need someone who can handle himself.' Johnny Crowhurst, the Amateur Middleweight Boxing Champion rang me up. I went with him and his wife, Jill, and Maisie, my wife. When we arrived, unbeknown to me, Pat was there. I walked in and suddenly, I'm on the floor; he'd banged me on the back – he didn't know his own strength! I turned round – 'You silly ****!' Maisie stepped back and thought: "Oh God – he's only just got here and he's going to start fighting already!" But it turned out to be a really good reunion.

"We've both been Bouncers at some of the earlier Emile Ford shows. The first show was at the old *Stafford Bridge*, off Tyburn Road. Also, for a *Rolling Stones* concert at *Birmingham Town Hall*, and for Lulu. We were Minders at Dusty Springfield shows." According to Billy, "Dusty used to push us away all of a sudden, and we'd get annoyed about it. We never knew, until she died, that she had problems with her eyesight.

"When we went training, we'd sometimes feel a bit down. Thankfully, Pat would come out and say, 'What's the matter with you, you silly sod? Get a bit of work down you!' (Jokingly, but it would keep you going). I was walking past Pat's gymnasium down by New Street Station one day. I'll never forget it, because I hadn't realised that it was Pat's," continues Billy. "As I was walking down Piccadilly Arcade, I heard someone shout, 'Somebody grab him – quick! Stop that little ginger-haired bastard down there!' I turned around and it was *him*, towering in the doorway of the gym, dressed in his tracksuit. 'Why don't you come in and get a bit of work down you?' – or words to that effect. With me running down the arcade and Pat yelling out, a crowd gathered, because they thought there was going to be a really good fight! He chased me right down the Arcade. I remember jumping down the last three steps. Although we were joking, you never knew with him, because he didn't know his own bloody strength! I suppose in a way he was annoyed. He thought I was snubbing him – but I wasn't. I'd got some business at the station. There was a Heavyweight boxer who was older than Pat, named Billy Conn. They were opposites. Billy had quite a temper, but I often wonder what would have happened if Pat had been matched against him, because they were two of a kind."

Finding good Heavyweight *wrestlers* was an international problem too. In Chapter 11, Bill Bridges and Killer Kowalski recall wrestling trips abroad with Pat. The promoters were keen to hire Pat for extended tours, but he wouldn't leave Britain for more than six months at a time. "A lot of the boxers were like that," Billy observes. "Johnny Prescott was like that too," adds Johnny King.

Former boxer John Crowhurst, whom Billy referred to earlier, recalls: "I'd known Pat, at a distance from boxing and wrestling but we met for the first time when he visited my Balsall Heath scrap yard, around 1974, as Safety Officer for the television series, *Gangsters*. He walked in, looking like an American Film Director, wearing a leather waistcoat a very bright muffler, a bright shirt, jeans, and knee-length boots. He spoke very quietly and gently and asked if he could use my facilities in the yard, while they were making the series. It was for a scene where houses were being knocked down. Some of the actors are inside, so some of the bricks fall on top of them. I believe it was the scene where the gangsters try to get rid of a club owner. Usually, Pat would have been dressed for working in his scrap yard, but these particular clothes he was wearing as the film's Safety Officer were a bit 'loud' for him. I was rather surprised by it. We spoke about the scene for a while.

"Later, I met him at the *Albany Hotel*, where I played squash quite frequently. There was a big social night on Thursdays, where everybody turned up; they had drinks and dancing upstairs, in the bar. Pat would arrive, generally by himself and sit very quietly, at a long table where there were a lot of us, eating, drinking and chatting. Once again, his clothes, compared to what he'd normally wear then, were a little loud: he'd have a green suit, red shirt and a bright dickey-bow tie. But he was never outlandish and he was a gently spoken man. He never imposed himself upon anybody, as I remember him.

"Unlike some reasonably successful men in our company who talked about where they came from, Pat never did; although I believe, he came from quite humble beginnings. Despite having achieved a celebrity status, certainly in Birmingham, he never spoke about it. He'd sit down and join us, very quietly. Whether he was coming for company, I'm not quite sure. But I never saw him with anybody; he was always by himself.

"Thursday night at the *Albany* was well known for a good night out. It was a kind of status symbol – to be seen there. Everyone would play squash, and sweat and exercise quite heavily. Then they'd have a swim, shower, cool down and have middle drinks. Afterwards, they'd watch television, then get dressed in their smartest gear. Then it was upstairs, into the restaurant and bar. The women of the town knew about it so we'd meet there, sit, talk and dance.

"Johnny Prescott was there, plus various other celebrities and business people: including those connected with the jewellery industry. Pat never threw his weight or authority about, never imposed himself on anybody, and seemed to make friends very easily. Not because he went out of his way to do so, it was simply that he was a celebrity and people wanted to know him. They would come and talk to him and he was very easy-going with them. He never gave the impression that he was *above* anything. He always had time for you; even if you were a complete nonentity, and you went up to him, he would spend time talking with you."

Former boxer Brendan Breslin, whom we met in the previous chapter, helped to manage several Birmingham clubs. "The first was the *Limelight Club*, in 1967, which was in Navigation Street. We opened when the pubs closed, at half past two and closed about half five, when the pubs opened again. It was hard to get a license in those days, for afternoon clubs. George Cullen's mother had a club on the Stratford Road. Pat and George used to run it, as *The Oyster Bar*," Brendan recalls.

"*The Windsor* was a famous pub in town, with all the Irish connections. It was in Cannon Street. *The Limelight* was near the centre of town; nicely fitted out – lovely. We opened in 1967. You could get eight pints of Guinness for a pound there, in the old money. I ran it for Jimmy Grogan, for just under three years." After the *Limelight*, Brendan worked for Seamus Dunleavy, at *The Jigsaw*, in Alum Rock for about three years, in the early 1970s.

"I started a boxing club on the top floor of Chetwynd's – the *Birmingham Irish Amateur Boxing Club*. There were four storeys to that building, at number 90 Navigation Street. It was a tailor's at the bottom; the *Limelight Club* was over that; there was another room over that for the dancing and my boxing club was on the fourth floor. That floor had been disused and I just turned it into a boxing club. It was ideal for it." Brendan showed me famous boxer Jack Doyle's signature and message, on the club notepaper.

The *Birmingham Irish Amateur Boxing Club* moved with Brendan, when he went to *The Jigsaw*, and is run nowadays at the *Lea Hall Centre* up in Kitts Green. "It's good to know that I founded it... and it's still going strong.

"In 1983 I opened *PJ'S* in Branston Street, in the Jewellery Quarter. I managed it for Peter Gibbs. His name must have been Peter *John* Gibbs, so that's where we got the name." Ironically, years later, I was to meet Brendan for the first time, at these same premises. As we explain in Chapter 20, the building was later occupied by *Gems Wine and Dine*. Sadly, this wine bar no longer exists, as it was destroyed by fire, on 14 June 2006.

Seamus Dunleavy, who features more prominently in Chapter 10, recalls seeing Pat's first television appearance – a walk-on part in *Crossroads*. Seamus particularly remembers his friend's later performance, as the German Lieutenant in *Raiders of the Lost Ark*. "I thought he was brilliant at that. I can see him still today, backing off and the shadow of the propeller falling across him. He looks up towards it. I thought he was absolutely amazing!"

Brendan Breslin renewed his acquaintance with Pat, when he opened his Gym in the Piccadilly Arcade: "Round about 1980. I was a town man. Nearly every day I'd pass up New Street, and Pat would be at the doorway of his Gym. He was a very good advertisement for it, wasn't he? He'd always wish you the time of the day and ask you how things were going. I was still attached to the boxing game then."

Unfortunately, in Pat's absence the club was mis-managed and after ten years, was declared bankrupt. Pat thought the world of it, and referred to it as his 'baby'. In it's 'hey-day' it was advertised as the largest of its kind in Europe. Pat's film debut, *A Clockwork Orange*, was as early as 1971, but other roles followed, soon afterwards. During the 1980s to 1990s, Brendan doesn't recall seeing Pat in any of the clubs: possibly because he had nine years' total abstinence from drinking, during the 1980s, while he was making the two earlier series of *Auf Wiedersehen Pet*.

Brendan saw Pat at other times, with George Cullen. "He'd be in *The Railway Club* and the *BSA Club* quite a few times. There was me, him, and Councillor Frank Carter, who later became the Lord Mayor of Birmingham. George used to like to get Frank, Pat and some of the others together, because he thought they could help each other; it was good for Frank to be seen with a film star – if you know what I mean?

"I became licensee of the old *Matador*, in September 1998, which became *The Blarney Stone*. I was the very last licensee there: where *Borders Bookshop* is now, in the same premises. It was there just before they started demolishing the old Bull Ring Centre – about five or six years ago. By the time I became licensee it was already called the *Blarney Stone*."

Con Harris and his family ran into Pat again at Birmingham Airport, en route to Portugal. "Pat was visiting a different part of Portugal, but he was on the same plane as us. He was studying a huge script, which he'd got to learn. My granddaughter asked me to get his autograph. She was only about seven then, so that was about nineteen years ago." This would have been the script for *Indiana Jones and the Temple of Doom*, released in 1984.

Vic Armstrong sent the following tribute to Pat, from America, whilst working as Stunt Coordinator on his latest film. The letter, delivered in a honey-coloured envelope, and addressed to the writer in copperplate script, bore the distinctive label, '*Paramount Pictures*, Melrose Avenue, Hollywood'. It takes Pride-of-Place amongst my memorabilia: a reminder of happier times when Pat was alive and well, and the two of us were Vic's guests at *Pinewood Studios*. Vic writes about his good friend with tremendous affection:

*   *   *   *   *

'I was flying to Berlin, to continue my work on *Mission Impossible 3*, when my companion said: "Here – you had better read this." I was shocked to see it was an obituary for Pat, because it seemed like only a few weeks since Pat was one of my star guests on *This Is Your Life*. He had looked so fit and well; we even joked about him picking me up and throwing me, just like we have done several times during our long collaboration together, in some of the best action movies ever made. These include *Raiders of the Lost Ark*, *Never Say Never Again*, *Conan*, et cetera, et cetera.

Memories came flooding back to my first meeting with Pat; it was in Arundel in Sussex, around 1971, wow! Was that really over thirty years ago? I was a young stuntman, just really getting established in the film business. Pat was a famous wrestler, who I recognised immediately. The commercial was for a Whisky and was intended just for Japan. A young Ridley Scott was directing it. Pat was playing a caber-tossing Scotsman, with a big red beard; what was required was for him to pick me up and throw me. Little did we know that this was the start of a routine that would take Pat and myself around the world, from Arundel to Mexico, to the South of France, and more.

The commercial went over a day, which was great for us because we were on a daily rate, and it meant that we would end up with double the money. This was important, because work was tough to come by in the 1970s. Pat and I decided to stay in Arundel for the night, and to save money we shared a room. It was my first experience of the Philosophies of Pat Roach. We had dinner and then Pat regaled me with his theories of life in general, from working abroad, to socialising, to money-making schemes, and a lot of things that I could not put down in this article!! He was a wealth of ideas and I have never forgotten that night.

Another time I remember with Pat was in Alnwick, in Northumberland. We were working on a Disney movie, called *The Spaceman and King Arthur*. It was one of those films that turned out to be a really nice moneymaker. Because it rained and rained nearly every day, which made the schedule go on and on, which of course meant our contracts would get extended.

I had, by this time, elevated my status to Stunt Coordinator, which basically means that I employ all the stunt people and devise the fights and battles et cetera. There were a huge amount of battles in this particular movie. I would always confer with Pat as to different moves I could employ in the fights, to make them different. After work we would go back to the hotel and work out in the gym. This is where Pat and I started our sparring routines. One day I was leaving the hotel and Pat was arriving, having been home for a couple of days. As he got out of his Rolls Royce, I noticed that the rear of the car was really low to the ground. I said to Pat: "Has your suspension on the rear end gone?" He just opened the boot and inside was about a ton of barbells and weights; always the professional, Pat had taken all his weights home with him, even for a couple of days.

A few years later, I had been filming a movie called *Green Ice*, in Mexico. I got a call to go out to Tunisia, to work on a Steven Spielberg movie called *Raiders of the Lost Ark*. I duly turned up in Tunisia and a unit car drove me way out into the desert, to a little town called Nefta, near the Algerian border.

As I walked into the hotel, someone attacked me in a bearhug, from behind. As I looked around, ready to fight for my life, I realised it was Pat. He told me that the call the next day, to leave for work, was 3am.

Apparently, we had to leave that early because it was so hot that no one could work much after 2pm in the afternoon.

When we got to the set the next day, Peter Diamond, who was the stunt coordinator, told me that I was going to be the stunt coordinator on a fight sequence involving Pat playing a giant, bald-headed German, and a new actor, Harrison Ford. I immediately studied the storyboards and started to work it all out with Pat.

Around 12 o'clock I said to Pat: "Let's slope off and have an early lunch, before the rest of the crew break for lunch." As we were walking away, I heard someone shouting "Harrison, Harrison!" I kept walking with Pat and suddenly, someone grabbed me by the shoulder, spun me around, and said: "But you're not Harrison!" It turned out it was Steven Spielberg, who had mistaken me for Harrison. Steven then said: "You look just like Harrison. What do you do?" When I said that I was a stuntman, he called over the First Assistant Director, David Tomblin (another great friend of Pat's). Dave said: "This is the guy I've been telling you about Steven. He has only just become available."

The next day, we were into shooting the fight and I was standing behind the camera, checking that the punches *looked* like good hits, through the camera lens, even though they were intentional misses, in reality. Steven, whom I had not spoken to since the incident the day before, said, after a particular punch: "OK, cut the camera and let's move on; that was perfect." I had seen, from my angle, that it was *not* a good hit – in camera. So I said: "Excuse me sir, but that was a miss." A big silence suddenly descended on the set. Spielberg turned, looked at me, then said: "Oh you again. I thought that was a good hit." I said: "Not from my angle." Pat said: "You had better listen to him Steven. He knows what he's talking about." So Spielberg grudgingly said: "OK, one more." When the take was over, almost mockingly, he said: "How was that one?" I said: "Fine."

About three days later, Pat and I were in the hotel, watching 'dailies', which is the processed film that we have shot previously. Spielberg and everybody was there. Dailies can be a nerve-wracking experience for every department, because any fault or mistake is examined in great detail.

Anyway, the offending shot came up on screen and thankfully, it was perfect. As Pat was nudging me, Spielberg turned and said: "Good call Vic!" After *Raiders*, Pat and I worked on many movies together, invariably fighting each other. One in particular was *Never Say Never Again*, with Sean Connery. The climax of our fight was when Pat had to pick me up and throw me across the room, into a glass cabinet. The end of the fight was Pat drinking a glass of urine and staggering backwards into shards of broken bottles. We had great fun working out the fight and then shooting it.

We then went to Mexico to work with Arnold Schwarzenegger, on *Conan the Destroyer*. We worked out a great fight in a hall of mirrors. Every evening we would gather in the gym, that Arnold had had built in Mexico City. Arnie is a great team player and loves to encourage people to work out. So you would find Arnie, myself, Pat, Grace Jones, Dolph Lundgren and Arnie's other buddies, all working out at night. Then we would go out for a great steak and salad and tons of hilarious stories.

It was on one of these evenings, while Pat and myself were sparring, that Pat just caught me with a good left hook, which brought a swelling up, under my eye. Arnie thought it was very funny. The next day, when I went into the Production Office, I had a great black eye. All the girls in the office were very sympathetic and were fussing over me, saying what a great brute Pat was. I, of course, lapped up the attention. The next night in the gym, Pat said: "Go on – punch me." When I asked him what on earth for, he said: "So I can get some of that sympathy you've been getting all day, from the girls." Needless to say, I did *not* punch him back!

From there, Pat and I went to Italy, as we were considered part of Arnie's gang. Also, the director of *Conan*, Richard Fleischer (he had also directed *Twenty Thousand Leagues Under the Sea*) really liked Pat's acting and he wanted him in his new movie, *Red Sonja*.

While we were shooting Pat's death scene, one of Arnie's buddies, who had a small part in the sequence, had to make a particular sword move. Well, he could *not* get it right. We got to about Take 20 and tempers were getting frayed. This guy was trying to get the move correct and was swishing his great big broad sword around, slashing it downwards for the final blow. Pat meanwhile, who was supposed to be dead, was lying on his great bed and had actually fallen asleep. Suddenly this guy, forgetting Pat was there, because he was so still and quiet, slashed his sword down with a terrific thump, onto the bed.

There was this tremendous roar and Pat leapt bolt upright, because this guy had belted Pat, right where a man doesn't want to be belted!! We all fell about laughing, as Pat chased this poor unfortunate individual around the set. Of course, the guy was so shaken that any nerves he had before were trebled and we never did get the sword move on the film.

After Rome, Pat and I teamed up again on the concluding film to the *Indiana Jones Trilogy*, *The Last Crusade*. Once again, Pat and I did a variation on our trademark throw, when Pat threw me, as Indy, into the mine car, before I succeeded in finishing him off, in the stone-crusher.

These are just a few of the wonderful times I have spent with Pat Roach, and it has nearly involved my whole career. I will miss Pat and his witticisms and observations on life. He was truly a great friend and it was a wonderful feeling, seeing him walk onto the stage, to relive some of our moments, on *This is Your Life*. Little did I know – that would be the last time I would see him...'

Chapter Seven

FILMS, FRIENDS AND AUF WIEDERSEHEN

Through all the 'Auf Wiedersehen' years, I never used to go drinking with the 'Boys', because I wanted to keep out of the smoke. I've always been fussy about not going to pubs, for that reason. My favourite uncle, Charlie, Dolly's brother, had a particularly bad lung condition through smoking, so from my childhood, I was very much aware of the damage that could be done by nicotine... and smoking.

Pat Roach

Over the years, Doreen and Mark, sometimes visited or accompanied Pat, to film and television locations, at home and abroad; special friends, like Tony Green, Sarah and Bill Bridges, Ace Allcard and Bernard Guest were invited to UK film locations.

Pat's close friend, Tony Green, was offered a part, in *Indiana Jones and the Last Crusade*: "Unfortunately, it coincided with a week's fishing that I'd got booked in Scotland, so I couldn't make it. Pat had spoken to Spielberg, and he thought it would be a great idea if, in view of my origins, I appeared in the part where they burn the Jewish books! They thought it would be a great irony." Tony also attended a film premiere and end of film party, for one of the 'Indy' films, and, as we learn in the next chapter, a party celebrating the first *Auf Wiedersehen*.

"The 'Indy' party was at Regent's Park Zoo," recalls Tony. "I can remember tripping on the stairs and bumping into Denholm Elliott," – (like you do!) "I met a lot of the cast. Sean Connery wasn't there, but Harrison Ford was. I just had a brief conversation with him, but the people I met there were very down-to-earth and friendly. George Lucas was quite a serious guy, as I remember." That's interesting, because George seems to have had a more bizarre, often grotesque imagination, compared to Spielberg. Certainly, he wrote the more gory scenes in the films, some of which were censored for the American market.

Ace Allcard relates a funny, but true 'Indy' story. "Around 1989, when I was managing a rehabilitation unit at Kilburn, Pat said: 'Come to lunch at Elstree and I'll introduce you to Steven Spielberg. Sean Connery and Harrison Ford will be there too.' I gave my name at reception and was taken upstairs to the Actors' Restaurant. It was a massive hall, crowded with people, with eight or nine big circular tables, each seating about twenty. They opened up one of the tables, so that I could sit with Pat. Who should be there, but Sean Connery? I couldn't believe that I should have the privilege of sitting next to him! Pat was to my right. He said: 'Steven, this is Ace Allcard.' This chap went: 'Hallo Ace – how are you? Who's the guy sitting next to you?' Of course, that was Sean Connery, so I came away thinking that Steven didn't know who Sean was!

"I was talking with Sean Connery about the prison service. He told me that his son Jason had just done a YOPS Scheme for the Scottish Government. I think he was training to be a carpenter or something." Jason later became a film and television star too.

Pat invited Lynn Perkins, the daughter of his wrestling friend Jack Perkins, (aka Jack Little), plus two additional guests of her choice, as part of the studio audience for a *Central Weekend Live* programme, on 13 March 1987. Pat, who had known Lynn since she was a toddler, was one of the wrestlers present, debating the self-same question that Ray Robinson and I were discussing in the previous chapter: namely, whether or not wrestling was 'fixed'. Jackie Pallo, who sadly is now deceased, was also a guest celebrity, following the recent publication of his controversial autobiography, *You Grunt and I'll Groan*, which *seemed* to suggest that it was. Pat was arguing against the idea. Lynn, who herself contributed to the studio discussion, kindly lent me a video of the programme.

Pat invited Bernie Guest to a TV programme presented by Jim Bowen, marking the 25th Anniversary of *Central TV*, recorded in front of a celebrity audience. Bernard, as Chapter 18 will reveal, would eventually come to his friend's rescue, in a highly dramatic 'life-and-death' scenario, to equal any drama that a screenwriter might produce.

"Jan and I were Pat's guests. We turned up at the TV Studios and he was there to meet us. He was sitting at the front, with some other people. We were seated just behind him – by Lesley Phillips – and right next to *The Krankies*. They had to do 're-takes' for several hours, to get it just right, but most of the audience was used to that. Pat introduced me to *Grottbags, the Witch*: she kissed me on the head, leaving black lipstick marks! It took six or seven hours to record the programme."

During the period when *Auf Wiedersehen* was first televised, Bernie owned a club called *J&Bs*, (*Jan & Bernie's*), in Darlaston. "We had acts from all over the place. From America, we had *The Drifters*, *The Dallas Boys*, Bob Monkhouse – a fantastic man. We had Tommy Trinder, especially for me. We had Marty Wilde, *Freddie and the Dreamers*; many of the comedians: Lee Wilson, off the telly, is Geoff Beards. He comes from just round the corner! He's a friend of mine.

"Pat invited me down to London when they were making *Robin Hood, Prince of Thieves*. I had a great time meeting all of the people who were in it. They had fantastic food – on the film set – lobsters and all sorts of things! The director wore a Stetson; he showed me shots, through the camera. Pat was very much respected by everybody there." A photo, taken on set, shows Bernard laughing – because they'd just put him in the stocks!

I once asked Pat how he varied his performance, between stage, television and films, according to which of the three media he happened to be working in.

It would depend entirely upon the character you were playing, your costume, make-up, and your fellow artists. I might be playing the f*** hunchback, in which case I'd be dragging a foot! That's why, when I was playing Petty Officer Evans, I went to the Gower, to find out as much as I could about him, in order to portray the man as accurately as possible – but put my own interpretation upon it. You have to get down to basics in order to diversify.

Sometimes, directors prefer certain characters not to have a distinctive accent, as with Edgar Evans, particularly when the product has to appeal to the American market. So voice coaching for that part eventually proved redundant. The ability to imitate a range of accents is, naturally, one of the prerequisites for creating authentic characters. It is not widely known that Pat had a particular *talent* for dialects. Sadly, the roles he played, with the exception of 'Bomber', seldom gave him scope to demonstrate this.

Again, what are you playing? (Uses a Northern – Irish/Belfast-type accent). "Are you playing a Northern Irishman who lives in a big council house now?" Or are you (slips into a Welsh accent) "playing a Welsh boy from Glamorgan? Do you like playing cricket?" Or if you're a Scot, you do it in a different way again.

Actor-manager Ian Sandy comments: "Pat was a big star – he had the common touch; he was on the telly every week, and because of that he was very identifiable. He's had the persona of being a bit of a rough diamond; it's almost from the wrestling side, isn't it, that he's Big Bad Pat Roach? And the man is such a pussycat, such a sweet kind man. I will argue with anybody – that's what Pat Roach is. But Joe Public is very demanding. Their expectations of a celebrity are very high. If you are a definitive character, you've got something different to offer. Pat had one because he was a big guy."

Pat always regarded acting as a challenge. "I wasn't an actor and probably still aren't. I'm a total usurper, aren't I?" Being a master of disguise was, for him, " just part of the job."

I enjoy everything I do, because it develops the characters: it's part of making the character work, whether you've got loads of dialogue, or mainly gesticulation and moving around. But early days for me, it was just something new to have a go at. I've tried a lot of things that I haven't been successful at, or that I didn't have time to develop. I've had that silly computer for over a year now – I don't even know how to switch it on! I just haven't got time. It's a thing – you peep around the corner one day, and you think: 'whoops, that looks alright!'

Assuming another identity was one aspect of performing which didn't particularly appeal to Pat. Also, given the choice, he preferred roles requiring the minimum of preparation.

What I enjoy more than anything else is doing parts where I can portray the character without the help – the assistance – of all the make-up, which has always been more demanding upon me. For example, I missed that thing at the Royal Court the other week, playing a homosexual who came out of the closet – the gold medal winner – marvellous! I mean, there would have been no makeup, except sufficient for the audience to pick out your features. I'd have just walked on like this – it would have been marvellous for me – I'd have loved it! Wouldn't it be easier to walk on stage having just changed your trousers, shirt and socks? Bear in mind that I've already done my fair share of the 3½ to 5½ hour makeup sessions and eight other people to work you.

Con Harris spent an enjoyable evening at *Barbarella's Nightclub* with Pat. "We sat at a table on a little raised area. There was Pat, Ken McGibbon and me. Ken was a very good friend of Pat's at the time. Joe Frazier was singing with a group: because he was 'Smoking Joe', we all wanted to go. When he finished singing, he was wringing-wet with sweat! He had a lovely black silk shirt on and all of the girls were clamouring for it. I'll tell you what, me and Pat were in amongst it! And the next thing, an arm went off it, and another, and it was all in shreds. Everybody had a bit of it: the fellas and the girls, because he was so famous. He'd fought Muhammad Ali three times; he was a great fighter.

"It was a really colourful night. That was the night when Pat said, 'What are you drinking whisky, rum or brandy for? It takes ages to get it out of your system. Drink vodka instead, because it's clear – it goes straight through your system.' I thought he was on pop, but he was drinking vodka and tonic.

Mind you, with his size, Pat could quite easily put several vodkas away, couldn't he? I had plenty of those with him after."

Jim Collins, Pat's wrestler-turned chauffeur friend, particularly admired him in the role of Hephaestus, in *Clash of the Titans*. "I couldn't keep my eyes off him when I saw him in that. I was watching him ever so closely and reading his mind. I think he might have had a couple of lines to say." Jim frequented a nightclub in the Piccadilly Arcade. "Pat's gym was upstairs and he would sometimes pop down to the club. I used to go there with Alan Wilson, Gordon Thomas, or whoever was around. In certain situations when myself or others might have had a go, Pat never did: he was very controlled; nothing would bother him – unless a bloke was drunk."

Several of his friends have mentioned the closeness that they felt to Pat. Jim is no exception. "It was as if you were sitting or standing with your brother; it was *that* kind of feeling. I only saw him use physical violence in the ring, but sometimes, although he controlled it very well, I could tell if he was angry."

Jim witnessed a fight between Pat and his father, at Pat's Cuckoo Bridge yard in Aston. "Pat was on one side of a car and Frank was on the other. I walked straight up to the car. Pat grabbed me and said: 'See to him!' I thought they were just gaming, so I put my fists up to Frank and he hit me! He caught me the once, because I thought: 'It's a joke – a game.' Pat ran into the caravan and called to another kid, who got between me and the old man. In the end, Frank ended up bathing my eye for me and apologising."

Jim has chauffeured many celebrities: "Some of the England cricketers – David Gower's nice to drive. He's very well spoken. I've driven David Hasselhoff – the chap out of *Knight Rider* and *Baywatch*. I drove David Niven – what a nice fella. He was meeting friends at a pub in Chipping Campden. Some of my clients go to sleep, because they work all bloody night! I drove Richard Todd. I think he'd finished filming then. He'd got freezer vans and a frozen food business."

Vic Armstrong, the celebrity stunt coordinator, featured in the previous chapter, told me that his father trained racehorses for Richard Todd, many years ago. Vic would watch Richard's movies, as a boy. Jim has also chauffeured for James Nesbitt; my favourite advert is the one where he mistakenly wears an elf costume, at an Elvis Party!

"I drove James last year, when he won the actor's award," explains Jim. "He's a nice fella too. I sat in his kitchen and played there with his two girls – Peggy and Mary. I like the advert where he's chopped his daughter's hair off and he pays the hairdresser to pretend that it's her mistake! It was done for *Yellow Pages*. I drove him while he was doing that."

Businessman Tony Walsh, at one time Big Daddy's regular TV opponent, observes: "Even after *Auf Wiedersehen* had been on some time, I don't think Pat realised how big it had become. People would stop him in the street. In the wrestling he was Pat Roach the wrestler, but I don't think he ever got to grips with being a Superstar."

Chrissie Doyle recalls that at Dolly's eightieth birthday party, some people came in from the bar and asked for Pat's autograph. He said: "If you don't mind, I'm out here socially. I'm not here to autograph anything. My private life is my private life. If you want an autograph I'll be at so-and-so.'"

"I got my Equity Card about the same time as Pat," explains Tony Walsh. "I can understand where he was coming from. I've done the same. I did a programme called *Out of Order*, in the late 1970s, with people like Don Henderson, and Sue Hanson, (who was Diane), in *Crossroads*, and a lot of accomplished actors. Deep down, you're still a professional wrestler and you think: 'Well, what am I doing here?' Don was a great bloke, Ricky Tomlinson was in it too: Frank Windsor from *Z Cars*, Jill Gasgcoine, from *Gentle Touch*. It went to the *Birmingham Film Festival*."

Ed Doolan's opening comment, for *The Other Side of Pat Roach*, remains particularly apposite. "I'd like to start by my putting to you, something which has always disturbed me about you sir – that you have done so much, you have appeared in so many things, and yet it's never *recognised* as such. They never talk about you as one of the great film stars – and yet you are."

I couldn't agree more! People have frequently said that they simply hadn't realised the full extent of Pat's film and television career. As he was such a modest man and so often in disguise, perhaps that's hardly surprising! Ed held him in high regard, and rebroadcast the programme on two occasions, following Pat's death.

On a television set, depending on which angles you were working, the boom mike would follow you around anyway. Invariably, depending upon the other actor you were working with, some directors would film on the back of your head – which isn't very nice for you. That means that they don't give a damn about you – only the lead actor.

To illustrate the point further, Pat recalled an occasion at the *Birmingham Hippodrome*, when the lead artist used a 'throw-away' word to the audience, to make them laugh. Then one of the actors, whom Pat described as "brilliant", walked on the stage and did the same. Everybody laughed, but after the show he was told to "cut the 'ad-libbing'."

There's a film called 'Far and Away', which I auditioned for – the part of the gang boss. At the audition, I played him as a shillelagh-in-hand, straw-hatted Irishman, which is exactly as I thought the Americans wanted him. But I made the mistake of doing it in front of an Irish casting director. He said: "What the *** is that?" I thought I knew what the Americans wanted, but he didn't want an Irishman to be played that way, you know what I mean? I think that's how I lost the part, because the guy who played it hardly had an accent at all. Imagine an American gang boss, when the immigrants arrive in America, he's in charge of putting them into this and that, changing their names. First of all, he would be a big man – and if he wasn't, he'd make up for it with gestures and diatribe.

William Forsythe, who played Al Capone, wasn't particularly big, but was allowed to make his presence felt. Because when he talked they shot on him – single, single, single. That's why – to answer your question – "I'm the man to have on yer side in a foight!" That's how I played him. But the guy who played him understated it.

They needed an actor who wouldn't overshadow the main character, because the star, Tom Cruise adopted a very quietly spoken Irish accent. He dropped his voice, so that the camera, and everybody else, had to come to him. Pat stressed the importance of having 'insider knowledge' before an audition: who's playing the leading roles, and who mustn't be upstaged, the preferences of various directors, and so on. Pat acknowledges, "I lost a lot of my parts that way."

I can remember Timmy Spall being interviewed by an American for a job – and it went something like this: Tim was sat there. (Takes both parts, with appropriate accents – absolutely hilarious 'send-up')! American Director: "Hi Tim, you know this film, it's all about necrophiliacs. You know what a necrophiliac is, don't you? Do you like necrophiliacs Tim?"

Tim said, "Well let's put it this way: my old dad died last year. If somebody dug him up and f*** him, I wouldn't be very pleased!" He didn't get the part.

Tim provides his *own* view of the differences between acting techniques required for stage, film, television and radio. "I don't think that you've got to be larger than life – you've got to be a bit louder! Obviously on stage you have to present the performance more. In television and film, the cameraman will come to you," he explains.

"You have to speak the way that human beings speak, instead of projecting your voice and moving your arms about a bit more, as you do on the stage. They're all the same things, you know? You've always got to try to be believable. There's no mystery – in a sense. It's only difficult to do if you can't do it. It's pretty difficult if you can! All you're trying to do is tell a story, and hopefully make the audience relate to it somehow. I don't think there's a great deal of difference."

Peter Charlesworth became Pat's agent in the early 1980s. Val Hastings met Pat in 1976, as an *Equity* member. "It was the first meeting that I attended, when Pat was Chairman. I had seen him on television, because my husband, Brian, followed the wrestling." In 1977 Val became Branch Secretary of the Birmingham Branch of *Equity* and held the post for six years.

Their daughter, Karen, was only eleven when she first met Pat. "My first impressions were of a tiny Mini pulling up, and Pat extricating himself from it," recalls Karen. "I think my Dad made some comment about an octopus! He was almost *stuck* behind the steering wheel! The door came open and one leg came out, then another leg, followed by his arm. When he stood up, there was this huge guy who was instantly recognisable.

"I remember thinking, particularly as I watched the Saturday afternoon wrestling with my Dad, about how imposing Pat was. He came in and stood next to me. I'm only about five-foot now, but I was well under that at the time. So here was this great big character, with gingery blond hair, towering above me. But as soon as he opened his mouth, it was a complete contrast, because although he'd got a booming, deep voice, he was softly spoken and he didn't talk down to you. I remember him trying to put me on his shoulders, in the lounge and my dad said: 'Watch out for the lights!' Once he actually spoke, you forgot how big he was and what he looked like, because he was really approachable and with his jokes et cetera, he made you feel really comfortable in his presence."

Val recalls that before *High and Mighty* stores opened, Pat had to have his clothes specially made – even casual wear. Also, he wore an impressive identity bracelet. "Pat had relatives in the Jewellery Trade. Obviously, now I know he lived in Hockley and that his cousin, John, made it for him. It had PAT inset into it in diamonds. He wore it at one particular *Equity* meeting. Everybody was a bit dumbstruck: 'Oh my God! How on earth can you lift your arm up Pat, with all those diamonds and gold – and aren't you worried about being mugged when you leave?' He just laughed and said, 'Well, I can afford it. Why not?' If he went on holiday, he could never get a comfortable bed, because they were always too short. I suppose he had trouble on aeroplanes as well – like a lot of big people."

Val's husband, Brian recalls: "We saw one or two films that Pat was in. For *Raiders of The Lost Ark*, he got us all a Family Ticket. It was very exciting, especially when he came up on the screen and we instantly recognised him.

It was a bit unbelievable that you knew him, in front of that whole cinema audience, all waiting to see what happens. He looked like a big thug!"

Pete Roberts and Pat were on the same bill in 1981, around the time Pat was making *Raiders*. "He'd shaved his beard off, which was unusual for Pat, and he'd shaved his head – which was even more unusual! I asked him what was going on. I thought that maybe he'd changed his image or something. But he didn't explain that it was for the film."

By chance, Pete's son was one of the Marines who played the German soldiers, marching in the background, and just happened to 'bump into' Pat, on location. Pete explains, "Pat must have just been sitting on the set somewhere and Mark went over and introduced himself. Mark is the same as me – he's quite 'laid back', so he just said: 'Oh yes, I met Pat.' When Mark left the Marines he wanted to be a stuntman, but later decided against it. Pat gave him a few pointers about how to get started."

"We went to see Pat when he was in *Clash of the Titans*," continues Val Hastings, "with Sir Laurence Olivier, playing Zeus and Ursula Andress and Claire Bloom. Pat was the blacksmith god. I always remember the clockwork owl, which flew round. I think of that when I see Harry Potter, with his owl. Hephaestus's owl predates the Harry Potter one!

"You forgot that it was Pat, because all of his roles were quite exciting. The comedy in *Auf Wiedersehen* was completely different to anything he'd done before. Sometimes it spoils it if you know too much of what goes on behind the scenes. Because both Karen and I have been involved in television drama, at one time I couldn't watch a lot of programmes, because I was looking at all of my friends who were playing 'Extras' and 'Walk-ons'. Sometimes, it spoilt your concentration on the actual story. You need to keep the mystery. I don't like these programmes that tell you about how films are made, because you never see them in the same way again."

Entertainer Mick Walker, featured previously in the 'Townies' chapter, saw Pat quite often, in *The Rum Runner*, from 1966 onwards. "He was well known by then as a wrestler and he was performing on television quite frequently. He was a celebrity, in his own way, but always a 'Gentle Giant'.

"I worked at the *Rum Runner* originally, from 1966 - 1969, and booked quite a few big-name cabaret acts. I also took the responsibility for running the door, which was basically to keep the bad people out and to encourage nice people to come in. There was a driveway of about fifty yards between the big gates on Broad Street and the club door. One night, in the wintertime, a big fella came down, wearing a vest and a cap. He had a very broad Black Country accent, was built like a tank and was trying to talk his way into the club. We persuaded him that he couldn't come in, because he wasn't a member. Then one of the other doormen let some people in who obviously weren't members. This guy saw it, took umbrage and came over. It was quite obvious that he was prepared to fight his way into the club!

"I looked up and saw, coming down the drive, the unmistakable figure of Pat Roach. He leaned over and in his quiet way said: 'Everything alright Mick?' I said: 'Yes.' He said: 'Are you sure?' I said: 'Well, we might have a bit of trouble with this one.' This chap was probably only six inches shorter than Pat, but certainly as broad across the shoulders.

"He was just a guy who had come in on a Friday night, which was not uncommon; the kids came in from as far afield as Coventry, Leicester and certainly the Black Country. If you kept a nice club, you just couldn't risk letting them through the door.

"So Pat spoke to this guy as quietly as possible, but he obviously didn't realise who he was, immediately. To cut a long story short, we had a brightly coloured fenced off area about six feet six high, around the dustbins; separating them from the main door of the club. After a few quiet words with him, Pat lifted the guy up and sat him on top of the fence; he had never in his life been treated like a six-year-old child before!

"The guy then immediately said (Black Country accent): 'Eh – yo're that Roach the wrestler ai' yer?' He said: 'Yes.' He said: 'Oh, I've always wanted your autograph!' It completely diffused the situation, from this guy who wanted to fight his way in, to someone who, within a few minutes, thanks to quiet ministrations by Pat, was an adoring fan and just wanted the autograph.

"Prior to that I was with a Birmingham band called *The Redcaps*. We made records for *Decca* Records. We were quite well known. We did all of the old TV Rock 'n' Roll shows, like *Thank Your Lucky Stars, Ready, Steady, Go* – and things like that. We were minor celebrities, I suppose, in my latter teens. But when the act finished I moved to London for a year, and worked as an agent, and was then asked to book shows at the *Rum Runner Club*. I eventually moved back to Birmingham, to work at the club full time.

"Pat was a great character. The one night we had a Fancy Dress Party. In those days everyone participated – all the *Townie* guys rented costumes. Pat came as the Pantomime Giant, in a splendid costume, together with leather jerkin and knee boots: he looked fantastic! But because of his interest in Yoga he was able to do body piercing – before it was fashionable! In his beard, under his chin, he had secreted, running straight under his chin, and through the skin of his neck, a huge kilt pin. His particular party piece that night was to very quietly invite ladies to dance with him. We didn't do all that 'dance of the burning witch' – waving your arms about; in those days, the gentlemen did a smooch. Halfway through the dance, Pat said something to the girl that caused her to look up. Then he'd lift his head up, to expose this bloody big kilt pin, going through his neck! I think we had two or three girls faint and one or two scream! But that was typical of Pat.

"I moved away from Birmingham subsequently, to London, as a musician; where I had a comedy-jazz trio for ten months, then went overseas. The act broke up and I stayed in London for quite a few years. I kept in touch with Pat, after working for Elton John, in the Wine Bar business. I became Head of Security for Elton John's Management Company, Elton John, *Queen,* and Kiki Dee. Then I went back into the Wine Bar business – (the *Brahms & Liszt* in Great Russell Street, Covent Garden). Pat used to pop in for lunch, whenever he was able to.

"When I moved back to the Midlands in 1984, after working in Spain for *Pontinental* for a couple of years, I moved back to Birmingham, and Pat and I got back in touch. I became a member of his gymnasium, by his invitation, and would see him three or four days a week, in the gym. By then, I was working as a comedian and doing some TV work. Pat said: "You specialise in accents don't you Mick?" I thought he wanted me to help him with an accent for one of his roles. But he explained to me that he'd got a lovely E-Type Jaguar – a yellow 'Drop-Head'. It was in good shape, but needed re-upholstering. He sent it to a specialist in the restoration of Jaguar cars. The restoration on the upholstery had been completed. A mechanic, however, had drained the fluids, then someone else had taken the car for a spin and the engine seized up!

"Now Pat was furious and he insisted that this engine be rebuilt, with completely original Jaguar parts et cetera. But the owner of the company was dragging his heels. So Pat said, 'I want this guy to be frightened into getting my car ready quickly. I've told him that I've sold this car to a Scottish gangster, who's just done six years in Barlinnie Prison in Glasgow.' He was asking me to assume a fictitious role, put a Scots accent on and go and see this man. At the time I was lifting weights. I was six foot two and fifteen stone – big chest, arms, shoulders and all that. So I greased my hair back, to make me look like an ageing Teddy Boy, I was about forty-two at the time. We went over in Pat's car, to this place in Coventry, and I had to put this face on, of a disgruntled, slightly furious Scot. Pat went over and said a few words to this guy: 'Listen, you'd better get this together. This guy's really angry!'

"Then I went over, and in a cross between Billy Connolly and Gregor Fisher, said: 'Look here Jimmy. My bloody car – Roachie's had the money for this. I've been sitting in Barlinnie, waiting for this, looking forward to driving this motor!' I had to 'put the arm' on this guy. But as I'm going through this routine, trying to keep a straight face, (because the proprietor of the restoration company by now, is quivering in his shoes), I glance across. Pat had turned away from us, for obvious reasons, was leaning on the bonnet of his car with one hand, and shaking, almost uncontrollably, with laughter. It *did* pay off. The car was ready within a week. But all I remember from that episode, is that all the way back to Birmingham we could hardly speak, because we were cracking up!"

Mick then provided a further example of how thin a dividing line there is, between having a full-scale fight and turning a situation into a positive one. In both examples Mick's common sense played a part, but it was also helped by the fact that: "Pat commanded tremendous respect, with all sorts of people."

Like Pat, Mick lives in a world that is 'poles apart' from his more humble Birmingham origins. In early February, he flew to Rio de Janeiro, sailing from Rio to Buenos Aires, to entertain multi-millionaire Americans on a Cruise Liner. "It's a two hundred-passenger ship and they've all got suites. Oh it's wonderful. But I never forget my roots. I might get back to Birmingham and go and do a show at the *East 57*, King Heath!

"Pat never ever suffered from a star complex. He still kept in touch with his roots. I remember an incident during the late 1970s, involving a dear friend of mine, Mike Smith, who played keyboards with *The Dave Clarke Five*. He was the writer of the hit record *Bits and Pieces* and *Glad All Over*. He was in the *Brahms & Liszt* one lunchtime when Pat came in to see me. I introduced him to Mike, (who knew everyone – he'd been on the *Palladium*, he'd done American tours). He just stood open-mouthed, because Pat *filled* this doorframe.

"I had the downstairs section in the Wine Bar – I was a partner with two other guys. Pat completely shut all the light out of the basement. Mike Smith referred to it several times subsequently. He said: 'I couldn't believe it when I met your big pal – that Big Pat, but also what a nice quiet gentle guy he was!' He was that kind of guy: if you didn't know you were going to meet him and you turned the corner and bumped into him, it was like bumping into an oak tree! But what impressed a lot of people was that with this huge and slightly ferocious-looking guy, in a way, he was so quiet and gentle, and he never raised his voice. I never heard Pat Roach shout, or speak loudly.

"Pat always wore smart clothes – tweeds and things: nice suits and lovely tweeds with waistcoats." That's in *total* contrast to what so many people, Pat included, have said about his scruffy appearance; although he *could* dress smartly when he chose to, for public appearances, including our joint book signings.

Mick recounts a conversation in a crowded club, between Pat and an acquaintance of his called 'Farmer Freddie'. "Freddie said, (rural accent): 'Ow you be Roachie? I've seen you. I think it's all bloody tricks, isn't it – all them things that you do? You pick them up and throw them about!' Pat wasn't a show-off but he'd reached the point where he had to do something to shut this guy up. Because people used to centre-in on Pat: they wanted to be in a position to say: 'I was talking to Pat Roach.' Freddie was probably six foot three and seventeen or eighteen stone, but Pat put an armlock on him, so that he couldn't bend it. Then he lifted him up, in a wrestling hold, until his head touched the ceiling! It wasn't a very high ceiling in the club. Pat said, very quietly: 'I think you mean something like this don't you?' He slowly lowered him down... and it went very quiet! And that was how Pat was."

Auf Wiedersehen Pet was first televised in November 1983, and undoubtedly changed the lives of all the leading actors, making household names of them almost overnight. Pat's character, Brian 'Bomber' Busbridge, was a married West Country bricklayer, with an older daughter and two sons – in reality, the sons of Ronald Lacey, a fellow actor in *Raiders of the Lost Ark*. One of them, David, is now a television producer in America. Although Pat has had a tremendously varied sports, film and television career, he still regards the series as one of his most significant achievements. The media obviously agreed with him, and often referred to the programme in subsequent articles.

The fateful first meeting between writer Ian La Frenais and the creator of the *Aufpet* series, Franc Roddam took place at *Café Moustache*, Melrose Avenue, in Los Angeles. Before discovering his writing talent, Ian had been a cigarette salesman, When Ian and Dick write new scenes, they read through them, dividing up the lines and speaking with the characters' accents. The only problem is that Ian can't do an Aussie accent, so Dick has to do it for him!

The Principal Cast List, for the first two series, was as follows:

Barry Taylor: Timothy Spall
Neville Hope: Kevin Whately
Dennis Patterson: Tim Healy

Leonard 'Oz' Osbourne: Jimmy Nail
Bomber Busbridge: Pat Roach
Albert Arthur 'Moxey' Moxall
(aka Brendan in Series Two): Christopher Fairbank
Wayne Winston Norris: Gary Holton
Brenda Hope: Julia Tobin

Series 2 featured Ally Fraser, played by Bill Paterson and Kenny Ames, alias James Booth. The scriptwriters were, and still remain, Ian La Frenais and Dick Clement, although two episodes were eventually written for Series 1, by Stan Hey. Martin McKeand and Allan McKeown were the Producers; the Director was Roger Bamford. The Floor Manager was David McDonald; Casting was by Barry Ford, and the music was composed by David Mackay and Joe Fagin

I have been in lots of films, but usually in disguise. It was only after 'Auf Wiedersehen Pet' that people started to know my face. I enjoyed filming the series, but found that getting the timing right for comedy is an art, and the schedule was demanding.

Filming for the first series began in August 1982, although only scripts for five or six episodes were complete. Dick and Ian had written the first three together, but when Dick became otherwise engaged, directing a comedy called *Bullshot*, Stan Hey was invited to write. He produced two episodes, one being Episode Five, which featured Bomber's runaway daughter, paying a visit to the lads. This became one of Tim Spall's favourite episodes from that series, and enabled Pat to portray Bomber as a more rounded, three-dimensional character.

Chapter Eight

BREAKING NEW GROUND

There were times in 'Auf Wiedersehen Pet' when I couldn't quite believe it was Pat. Because Bomber's quite quiet and very polite – and in all the years I've known him, Pat was never that way at all!

Billy Wooding

The *Birmingham Mail* reported that from 11 November 1983, Series 1: '…had viewers glued to their seats every Friday evening. Ratings soared from single figures in the second week to nearly 14 million 12 weeks later. It was voted the tops by viewers and television critics alike, in Britain, Australia and New Zealand – where it was repeated within 12 months.'

Con Harris echoes the majority view of those interviewed by the writer: "I preferred the first two series, because they seemed more down-to-earth. A lot of builders had gone to Germany. A few of the people off this estate had gone over there to work. You could believe that, couldn't you? Kevin Whately acted that part: he was really missing his wife, and ringing home." Describing the differences between the real Pat and Bomber, Con comments: "He's something *like* he is because Pat would sooner stop a fight than cause one. But I wish they'd have given Pat the rougher part of Oz that they gave to Jimmy Nail." Thomas Felkin, a friend of Pat's since the age of ten, also prefers the first two series: "They were more action-packed and much livelier."

Val Hastings reveals that Pat had additional coaching, to perfect his Bristol accent, before auditioning for *Auf Wiedersehen*. "He rang up to say that he'd got this audition for a TV series, that might run for more than one; he was really excited. He said, 'But they don't want me to play a Brummie. They want me to play a man from Bristol. Do you know anybody who could help me with the accent?' So I rang the *Birmingham School of Dramatic Art*; they recommended somebody who gave him private tuition. When he got the part he was really pleased. He rang me and said: 'I've got the job!' But we didn't realise then, what a success *Auf Wiedersehen* was going to be and that it would run for four series!"

In the *Foreword* to *Pat Roach's Birmingham*, Timmy Spall talks about swapping identities with Pat: a Brummie, rather than someone living further south – (in Tim's case, London). Pat was certainly more dynamic than Bomber. In *Willow*, for example, he played the much fiercer character of General Kael. Although Kael was rather obnoxious, his fighting spirit was much closer to Pat's true nature. "Bomber was rougher, and plainer, comments Chrissie Doyle, "whereas Paddy was a very colourful character.

"If you met Paddy for the first time, it would take a long time to get to know him. He'd keep his real personality hidden. But once you knew him you'd realise that he had a great sense of humour. He didn't trust everybody. When he wasn't working he didn't want people to come up to him, asking if he was going to make another *Auf Wiedersehen Pet*, or for his autograph. If he was out with his family, he wasn't looking for publicity."

Freddie Frost recalls *Auf Wiedersehen's* popularity. "It would be the talk of the town on a Saturday, when it had been on the night before. Bomber was sometimes bombastic, but I've never seen Pat on the rough side. He was more forward with people he knew. He'd got a charm about him; he wasn't big-headed. Not being rude, but I sometimes used to think that he was a little docile, at times." It became crystal-clear however, from numerous conversations with Pat, that being so physically powerful, he *consciously* held himself back, on many occasions, to avoid hurting anyone.

Pat has *always* been a practical joker. According to Bill Bridges, when he and Pat travelled with a group of other wrestlers to various venues, the one thing they all tried to avoid was taking a nap. Because invariably, when you woke up, you'd find he'd snipped off the end of your tie, or blancoed the tips of your shoes. Another favourite trick was, in the restaurant car: he'd tie the end of the tablecloth to someone's clothes. When that person stood up, the whole table setting would come crashing down onto the floor. Pat would always pay for any breakage afterwards, so it was all taken in good part.

Wherever I go, I travel first class, but I don't even have a drink. Just because you're first class, doesn't mean you drink champagne. I'd been there anyway – did it wrestling. When we did the three-week shoot in Hamburg, though the series was meant to be set in Düsseldorf, the boys couldn't wait to get into the big casinos, go down to the main street, San Pauli,... and when we were in Berlin; but I'd done it all – twenty years before!

When we did the brothel scene, in Hamburg, there were fifteen girls lined up, who were real prostitutes, by the way. When they took them to Wardrobe, they found out that three of them were guys!

In the 2003 BBC publication, *That's Living Alright (The Auf Wiedersehen Pet Story)*, written by Franc Roddam and Dan Waddell, Julia Tobin describes the very first cast meeting:

'I remember us reading all the episodes and everyone being there, all the actors. We sat in one gigantic circle and everyone introduced themselves. I think a few people knew each other already, but for everyone else it was quite a new, quite nerve-wracking. Kev Whately and I had been at the same drama school, so we knew each other. He was in his last year when I joined. That made it a bit easier considering I was playing his screen wife. But we started reading and within seconds people were laughing, really, really laughing and it was fabulous.'

During a subsequent interview with Julia, I explained that our new book is based upon the four series, but with particular emphasis upon the more recent two, because Pat was trying to combat cancer, whilst making them. Julia has been involved in all four series. Pat was particularly keen that she should be featured in this, his last book. I began by asking how she originally became involved with the series.

"I got a call from a friend of mine, who was in the RSC with me – (the *Royal Shakespeare Company*). We'd just finished doing a Solzhenitsyn play. My friend heard that *Central* were thinking of doing this particular series and were looking for Geordie actors. She said: 'If I were you, I'd send your photograph in and give them a call.' So I did exactly that. I got a call the next day, asking me to come in for a meeting with Roger Bamford. So I went in and met Roger. He said: 'Yes, that's great!' Then they called me a week later, saying: 'Could you come in and meet the writers?' So I went in and met Dick and Ian. Then I got a call, a couple of days later, saying: 'Yes, we'd like you to do the part.'"

Did she realise at the time, what an the impact the series would have? "Didn't have a clue. I mean, we knew that the scripts were really good. When we all sat down for the first read-through, we were *genuinely* in hysterics! We all got on really well, but we hadn't a clue that it was going to be so successful."

Across the four series, which locations did you actually go on? "I went to Germany: that was for a few days. Although it's in the dim and distant past, I remember quite vividly that we all got together – Kevin and Tim Healy. I don't think Jimmy or Gary were there. There were a couple of others, including Pat, and we all went to the fair, in Germany. I remember particularly, going for a ride; nobody would go on them, but I like to.

"I coaxed Tim Healy into going on this ride, where you were locked in a cage, and you were flung around like a mad thing. I remember him sitting behind me, going: 'Oh my God!' That was one of the abiding moments for me, in Germany. The fair was in the middle of the city. It was a typical German city, in that everything was very organised. It wasn't a travelling fair, but more like a permanent fixture. I dare say Tim's never been on one since either!"

Did she experience any particular difficulties in being the foremost female member of the *Auf pet* cast, and, in fact, the only remaining 'Pet' – from amongst the initial female cast members? "I expected all sorts of problems, when we first embarked on this production, way back in the 1980s. I expected – Oh, it's going to be full of male ego. But it was never *ever* directed at me – *never*. All I had was the most tremendous respect from *all* of them; they were all *extra* nice. You hear stories that Jimmy Nail was difficult to deal with; Gary Holton was difficult to deal with. I never found that with any of them, they were always very nice to me. It's strange," comments Julia. "You would think that with seven guys thrown together like that, there would be tremendous ego fights, et cetera, but there weren't any."

Tim Healy recalls: "When we made the first two series, Pat was really strong. I was pushing him down a hospital corridor, because, in one particular episode, Jimmy had dropped this big concrete block on his foot, and I'm taking him to hospital." There's a photograph of that scene in our first book, *If – The Pat Roach Story*. "In my role as Dennis I said, 'Don't you worry Bomber. We'll catch you up later pal. We'll sort you out.' And I had to drop him off. This 'extra' just had to walk past us. Of course, she didn't know any of us, because none of us except Pat had been on the telly much, so none of us were famous. She was a very Middle Class sort of person. She said: 'What were you saying?' I said: 'I'm just saying to Bomber, "don't worry, I'll catch you later." She said: 'I can't understand a word you're saying!' I thought, 'What am I telling you this for anyway? I'm trying to do the scene!'

"About ten minutes later, I heard her phoning her husband: 'No there aren't any stars in this, so I shan't bring the script home.' I thought: "What a prat!" I told this story to Pat and we just thought it was hilarious. But those were the kind of conceited types that he'd be likely to play a trick on." Pat disliked any pretension or arrogance in people. Chris Millard comments: "Pat was a very shrewd businessman in reality. That's the only difference between Bomber and the real Pat, I think."

None of the boys had excelled in anything at that time; they were unknown. I was on television every three weeks, and was fortunate to have been in a film or two. So I was quite well known. Nowadays they're more famous than I am, but in those days it was quite the reverse. I was thrown into the deep end with six tremendous actors

*and was able to learn off them all. I was no actor – I'd never been to acting school
in my life. I hadn't done any dialogue until then, but rubbed shoulders with these
great actors – it was wonderful!*

Pat firmly believed that it was the quality of the acting and scripts
combined, which produced the winning formula: "Wherever I am at this
stage, I owe it to them."

Roger Bamford acknowledges that, had he been selecting the actors
today, he would probably have been *told* who to cast. "I don't know how
people find actors today. But the whole show might not have been made
today; there certainly wouldn't be thirteen episodes, and it wouldn't have
had a chance to build. It wouldn't have set new ground, which it did."

Of all his television performances, *Auf Wiedersehen* was undeniably the
one that gave Pat the most satisfaction.

*Because we became a family – all of us. It had such a long run, and a bundle of
wonderful stories came out of it. While I was doing that I did the Bond and Indiana
Jones. I wrestled all the way through it, as well!*

Like all successful scriptwriters, Ian La Frenais and Dick Clement are
astute and sympathetic observers of human nature; the *Foreword* to our book
provides yet another example of this. They wrote most of it at least a year
before Pat's eventual demise, suggesting that we should include a paragraph
about Pat's bravery and stoic professionalism. Naturally, Pat didn't want his
cancer made public until he had passed away. So Dick and Ian kindly agreed
to wait until an appropriate time, before sending the missing paragraph.

As the two scriptwriters became more familiar with the leading actors,
they incorporated more of their *true* characteristics into the scripts, thereby
making the roles even more believable. In some cases they adapted story
lines, according to the direction that each was taking, with his particular
part. "The scripts were fantastic and the characters were great. Certainly, in
the first period of filming, Ian was around all the time," recalls Chris
Fairbank. "His head was a tape recorder. He listened to what we were all
saying, then incorporated it into the characters. Moxey is the sort of bloke
who's wonderfully out of touch with mainstream life.

"I had a few wild years, and met the person I base Moxey on – in a police
cell, as a matter of fact! I was just in overnight, for 'drunk and incapable'.
This guy was in because his ex-wife had called the police, saying that he'd
tried to burn the house down. He was only knocking on the door, she wasn't
letting him in and it was a freezing cold night in Liverpool. So he set fire to
the dustbin, to keep warm; he had no intention of burning the house down
at all. But his wife saw the flames, called the police, and he was arrested on

criminal damage/arson charges. It was ironic – at the time. I don't think they'd decided *what* Moxey's shady past was. All I can remember from the interview is that he had a permanent cold. That was the running gag – no pun intended! I *might* have mentioned that character and maybe that was how the whole arsonist scenario occurred? But I'm not a hundred per cent sure on that: we are talking over twenty years!"

Mick Walker comments: "I watched as many episodes as I could. When I got back from Spain the first time, he'd done them while I was away. Someone told me: 'Roachie has got this wonderful TV programme; he's acting in it.' I said: 'Oh, great.' But I never understood why they got Pat to do a West Country accent. He could do it, but at times he obviously wasn't very comfortable with it. Having said that, Tim Spall did the Brummie character very well." Tim's portrayal was enhanced by the fact that his wife Shane's family is from the Cannock and Wolverhampton areas.

I didn't want to play a Brummie anyway, because they're often portrayed as 'thick' characters. By playing someone from an entirely different region, I at least avoided criticism from other Birmingham people, about the way I would have been portraying a local character, from a home region that I love so much.

"I was very proud of Pat in *Auf Wiedersehen*, because, with all due respect to him, to make the transition from wrestling, which is showmanship, to acting, isn't easy," Mick observes. Brian Glover, who wrestled under the name of Leon Ariss, appears to have been the only *other* British wrestler to make that transition successfully, over a prolonged period

"Pat was a bit like Bomber, but he wasn't limited," continues Mick. "It's difficult to describe a character in a book. Obviously they wanted him for his physical appearance and that was absolutely appropriate to the role. But it's difficult to make comparisons, because they didn't give Bomber *that* much to do. He was a bit like 'Hoss' Cartwright in *Bonanza*, who was the big strong guy at the back, who was there – you know – 'in case of emergencies, break glass'!

"It was a great idea, and quite credible to have groups of British builders going to Germany. I think the two earlier series were more refreshing." The majority opinion seems to be that this was because they were all younger, full of hope and raring to go!

"I only ever experienced generosity of spirit from Pat," continues Mick. "And the only time I was ever able to reciprocate, was that if he came down to the Wine Bar in London I wouldn't charge him anything. But he wouldn't take advantage of the situation. I'd say to him: 'Would you like something to eat?' But he'd say: 'No, I'm alright.' If he decided you were OK, and you were his friend, he would do *everything* for you: he was generous of spirit." Conversely, he was nobody's fool. I would have hated to upset him. "I never witnessed him being caustic with anyone," replies Mick, "but you knew that he didn't *need* to. In his background, before I knew him, there were things going on, which were possibly to do with the other side of him."

I did the Bond when Sean made his comeback. He'd retired from it and Moore had taken over, and done a very good, quite different job. It was funny how it happened really, because we were doing 'Auf Wiedersehen', just across the road, in Borehamwood. David Tomblin rang me up and said: "Come across – I've got something that might be interesting for you."

I had time off the 'Auf Wiedersehen' set to do 'Indiana Jones 2', and to do the first few shots of 'Never Say Never Again'. After we finished, I went back later, to do more filming. Roger Bamford, the 'Aufpet' Producer, wangled me a day off to film at Luton Ho, at a beautiful old house. When I arrived who should be there but Ian La Frenais and Dick Clement. I walked straight into them, because they were doing re-writes for the film – so I was exposed straight away!

Pat had the distinct advantage of being a character in his own right, before he even opened his mouth! But he deliberately understated Bomber – making him quietly spoken, rather like Burt Lancaster. Although this approach was unexpected for a character of his size, he 'stuck to his guns'.

I once remember Timmy Spall talking about 'grown-up acting', and it always struck a chord with me, inasmuch as I could be guilty of some grown-up acting in Auf Wiedersehen, but before that, it was very much bits and pieces. I was very fortunate about that. There is lots of stuff that people don't know I've done.

Chris Fairbank recalls: "When I met Dick, Martin Mckeand and Roger Bamford, it was a case of just getting a job. I desperately needed to work in order to prove to myself that I was still employable. The problem was that Moxey, as a character, was originally created for a friend of Ian La Frenais, who was a musician and hadn't done any acting. As Ian and Dick weren't too sure about the acting of whoever this person was, not very much was written, and Moxey didn't feature strongly." It was Chris's suggestion that Moxey should be a Scouser. In total contrast, Chris's own voice is that of a classical actor: he trained at RADA for a while. He acknowledges: "That does tend to raise the proverbial eyebrow, every now and again!"

He reveals that his agent, Pippa, had doubts about him accepting the role, simply because there wasn't enough to interest him. To this day, Chris has a very low boredom threshold. "But I was frankly, all for it, my rationale being that there were only four episodes written and another nine to go. So if I showed them I was good at what I do, then more would be written. She quite rightly observed, 'Look, there are seven characters on the go here. The three Geordies are the main characters. There is just no way, in terms of screen time, that they can devote equal attention to all the characters.' But she also understood my reasons for wanting to do it, so we went ahead.

"The high points were most definitely the cast – no question about that! The chemistry of the *characters* worked, as well as the chemistry of our individual *personalities*. There was such a fantastic range of experience that each one of us brought to it. Tim Spall, Kev and myself came through Drama School and the 'Rep' system, and bits of telly and what-have-you. Tim Healy came through the northeast club circuit. I mean – talk about an 'ordeal by fire'!" Chris had spent a year, working as a deckhand, but was shipwrecked! On returning to England, he joined the *RSC*, before landing the starring role.

"Pat, as you know, came through wrestling, and had subsequently worked in feature films. Up until that point, he hadn't really acted in a long-running TV series. Jimmy, of course, is the classic story. He was a singer, and in those days you had to be a member of *Equity* in order to work in Drama." Jimmy was also a bricklayer, and the last of the Geordies to be auditioned for the part. According to Kevin Whately, they originally had Tim Healy in mind, for the part of Oz. At that point, Jimmy was in a band called *The Crabs* and used to dress in hobnailed boots for the performance. His girlfriend, Miriam, who later became his wife, suggested that Jimmy should try for a part as an extra, having heard about the auditions.

"Basically what happened was that we had something like a two-month filming session," continues Chris, "and then we were off for a couple of months, while they had a look at what they'd got. We resumed, I think, after Christmas. I know there was definitely something like a six-week or two-month gap, while they had a look at stuff."

Chris attributes the success of the series to a combination of factors. "I think certainly with the first series, (which was the most successful out of the first two), it was timing. Thatcher was closing all the loopholes that allowed builders to go off to Germany and work for tax-free money, and so on. All of this was happening just at the time the first series was screened. There was a massive identification with the situation, on top of which, in those days, television was a nationalistic industry: programmes were made for here, whereas nowadays they're made with a view to overseas sales. Because of that, there are certain things that have to occur, in the casting, the way stories are scripted: it's all geared to viewers and overseas sales. But it seemed in the early 80s, that wasn't the case; ratings were always important, but nothing *like* as crucial as they are today. The terms of reference were completely different.

"There isn't one particular episode that stands out. I think all of them were really good; that is one of the success factors in it – the consistency. The characters were all very real, and people could identify with them." The series was born out of realism – where all great humour comes from.

"The filming of the first series was the absolute antithesis of what most people perceive the making of a TV series to be about," continues Chris. "You know – the glitz and the glamour and all that. Nobody really knew what we were all up to. We'd troop into the canteen for lunch every day and were just looked upon as these 'Herberts' who were pratting about on a pretend building site – or maybe it was real? They didn't really know what was going on! We went to the studio occasionally for non-hut scenes, but by and large, we were in the hut for nine months. These days, you don't get things running as long as they did; they took about nine months a-piece, those two series. There just isn't the luxury of that time any more.

"We were a gang – a team – and we all got on unbelievably well. I think Pat was kind of on his own – just because of the age gap. He seemed to be of the older generation, with traditional views and principles. I suppose, politically, we were opposite ends of the spectrum; although I'm not a political animal in any way, shape or form. But Pat would read the *Daily Express*, whereas I'd read something like the *Independent*. It was more that if Pat were the 'traditionalist' – then I would be the 'anarchist'.

"But that was many years ago, and now, particularly being a father, my traditionalist roots are well and truly to the fore. Basically, Pat was responsible for an off-screen soap opera, centered around his health club. Pat's generation didn't show their feelings – their vulnerability – their pain – and they certainly didn't cry! He embodied all of that. He was quite mysterious. The thing was, nobody even knew how old he was. In many ways, off camera, he was as big a catalyst as Jimmy – or anybody else was."

Aufpet 1 was on television one particular Saturday afternoon; I think Big Daddy was wrestling too, when Liverpool and Everton played each together in the Cup Final, all those years ago. Tommy Cannon gave me his tickets. I walked down to the twin towers of Wembley, and found this little scraggy-arsed kid, who was about twelve years old, from Liverpool. He'd thumbed a lift down there. He was standing outside the game, without a 'snowball's chance in hell' of getting in, and I actually gave him a ticket; bear in mind that I could have got a tidy sum for it. When I gave it to him, he snatched it and ran.

I then looked for another person to give a ticket to. I found a woman who had come from Canada, to see the Cup Final, but couldn't get a ticket. She was stood there, with tears in her eyes, because she couldn't get in. I gave her Tommy Cannon's other ticket. She was absolutely 'over-the-moon'.

Pat's mother, Dolly Roach, ready to take on the world! Taken in the back yard of 92 Belgrave Road, Balsall Heath c. 1955. By permission of Chrissie Doyle.

The same location as the previous photograph. From L-R: Dolly, Jimmy Doyle and his mother, Bridie (Bridget) Doyle. By permission of Chrissie Doyle.

Seated from left to right, in the kitchen of their home at 92 Belgrave Road, Pete Meakin, Pat's stepbrother, Pat's infant son, Mark, and Pat's other brother, Rickie. A horse was kept there, until it kicked the cooker up in the air! By permission of Pete Meakin.

Pat's brothers, Rickie Meakin and Pete on either side of him, with his Mark 10 Jaguar in the background. Pete recalls: "The Jag was parked in Varna Road. It was 1967, and I was on leave from the army." By permission of Pat Roach.

Chrissie Doyle and her daughter, Debra, on the pavement outside Dolly's house, in Belgrave Road, c. 1961/62. By permission of Chrissie Doyle.

Basement bar at Digbeth Civic Hall, *following Pat's wrestling match. Front row, standing, from L-R: Kim Mohammed, Dolly & Chrissie. Middle row: Auntie Mary and Freda, (a friend). Back row: Pat and Pete Meakin. By permission of Chrissie Doyle.*

Wedding Day of Francis and Alfie Evans, at St. Chad's Church, Snow Hill, 1957. Lily Evans is second from the right. To her left is Sylvia Evans, Harold and Alfie's sister. All of the adults in the photo were market traders. By permission of Alfie Evans.

Judo Club in Burlington Hall, *Blews Street, Aston, Birmingham 1955. Frank Ryder has his back to us. Wilf Ryder is in the far left-hand corner. Harold Evans is fifth from the left. By permission of Harold Evans.*

Chrissie Fewtrell, waving, on the right of a photograph taken in Denia, during a Spanish holiday with his brother, Don, (seated next to him). Don had invited Chrissie and his wife, Lisa, (left foreground) and their son, to spend time in Spain with him. By permission of Don Fewtrell.

Evening Mail newspaper article about Chrissie's funeral, held on 24 August 1999. Pat paid his respects to a very dear friend. Kindly loaned to us by his brother, Gordon Fewtrell, from his private cuttings collection. By permission of the Birmingham Evening Mail

Johnnie Prescott opening the Surfside Stop, *in 1966. From L-R: Tony Green, Johnnie Prescott and Michael Brown. By permission of Tony Green.*

Pat, completing the Birmingham Centenary Marathon, in 1989. His friend Tony Green, was slightly ahead, having run the ten miles in a hundred minutes. By permission of Tony Green.

Pat at Josie Rudge's son's wedding, 1984. He is holding Darren, one of her two grandsons, and has his arm around a second one, Carl. By permission of Josie Rudge, featured in Pat Roach's Birmingham.

Dolly Roach's 80th Birthday Celebrations in 1995, at the Majors Public House, *Warwick Road, Sparkhill, Birmingham. Pat's sister-in-law's daughters are seated either side of him; Denise on the left and Susan on the right. By permission of Shirley Meakin, Pete's wife.*

Four generations of Roaches: Pat's wife, Doreen, Dolly, Diane and her son, Patrick Junior, Pat's grandson. By permission of Doreen Roach.

On holiday in Goa. I wonder why he's looking so pleased with himself? By permission of Doreen Roach.

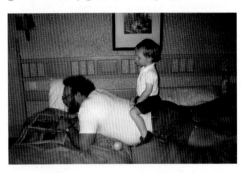

The two Patricks catch up with the latest news. By permission of Doreen Roach.

Pat and Ronnie Callow, friends since their twenties, 'joined at the wrist'! Photographed at Pat's Erdington Gym, by Shirley Thompson.

Pat with Ronnie Callow's youngest son, Adam, at Pat's Winson Green premises c.1999. Photographer Mark Roach, Pat's son. By permission of Ronnie Callow.

Brendan Breslin, c. 1964 at the Bell Public House, *around the time when he was first introduced to Pat, by George Cullen. By permission of Brendan Breslin.*

The signature and good wishes of famous boxer, Jack Doyle, which he gave to Brendan, many years ago, on Birmingham Irish Amateur Boxing Club *notepaper. By permission of Brendan Breslin.*

Grays Promotions *Celebrity Tribute Dinner for Sir Henry Cooper, organised by Pat's good friend, Ron Gray, and his son Steve, featured in our book. The ex-boxer celebrities are front row: Sir Henry Cooper, Billy Walker, Jim Pridding, Shane Silvester, Brian Cartwright, Ronnie Brown and Richard Carter. Second row: George O'Neill, Tony 'Banger' Walsh, John Thomas, Ron Gray, Charles Giles, Deka Williams, Nick Allen. Back row: Billy Gray, Teddy Hayes, John Allen, Alex Mason, Nigel Rafferty, Scott Murray and Steve Gray. Photographer: Graham Beckley. By permission of* Grays Promotions.

Pat hangs on to the toe hold as he comes down for a knee drop, to the leg of Mike Marino. Photographer: H.G. Stevens. By permission of Bill (Wayne) Bridges.

Photograph by internationally-renowned photographer Rolf Konow, of Copenhagen: André the Giant, flanked by husband-and-wife friends of Arnie Schwarzenegger. Pat's wife Doreen is on the far right. Published by permission of Rolf Konow.

Charity Darts Match at The Walnut Tree, *Leamington Spa, in March 1978. From L-R: Jackie Turpin, Pat, Knollys Daley, Roger Draper, 'Banger' Walsh and Ahmed Khalli (from* Gangsters)*. By permission of 'Banger' Walsh.*

Wrestling in Venice: from L-R: Pat, in an unusually despondent mood, John Cortez, Ian 'Bully Boy' Muir. Chris Adams, in the foreground, with John England to his right. By permission of 'Banger' Walsh.

L-R: Pat Roach, Albert 'Roccy' Wall - (former British Heavyweight Champion). 'Mighty' John Cox and Mick McManus. By permission of Joe D'Orazio.

L-R: Joe D'Orazio, co-founder of Wrestlers' Reunion; *elected Lifetime Chairman 2003. The great Northern Heavyweight Colin Joynson. Mark 'Rollerball' Rocco, 'Jumping' Jim Hussey. By permission of Joe D'Orazio.*

Joe Cornelius' pub, The Tanners Arms. *The third* Annual Reunion. *L-R: Joe 'Dazzler' Cornelius, Joe D'Orazio, the late Pat Roach. The late Brian Glover. The late Kent Walton.*

Pat Roach, Lyn and Kent Walton, Big John Kowalski. By permission of Joe D'Orazio.

Banger Walsh and Alan Kilby, at the Sheffield United *football ground, for a* Showbiz Eleven *match, c. 1983. Alan is a former wrestling opponent of Ray Robinson. By permission of Banger Walsh.*

From L-R: Banger, David Essex and well known actor, Tony Selby. By permission of Banger Walsh.

From L-R: Vic and Peter Stewart (father and son Tag Team) versus brothers Mick and Seamus Dunleavy. By permission of Seamus Dunleavy.

Ray Robinson performing his latest Hammer Stunt, just one of his Strongman feats. By permission of Ray Robinson.

Darren Walsh, aka Thunder, *having just won the EWP* Championship, *for 2003. By permission of Darren Walsh.*

Northern Wrestlers Reunion, *2001. From L-R: Ray Robinson, Pat Roach and Barry Douglas, a mutual opponent, whom Pat and Ray fought on many occasions. By permission of Ray Robinson.*

Mick Walker, comedian, raconteur, and all-round entertainer, was a great friend of Pat's and shared a similar sense of humour. By permission of Mick Walker.

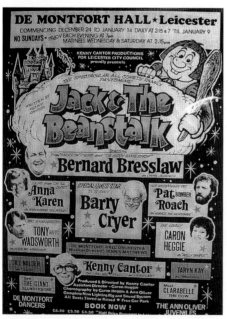

Tony Wadsworth and Pat were a comedy duo 'Horace and Boris', in the 1988/89 pantomime, Jack and the Beanstalk. *Unbelievably, Pat was the 'meek-and-mild' half of the act! By permission of Tony Wadsworth.*

Posing in the dressing room: Bernard Bresslaw, Pat, Tony Wadsworth and Barry Cryer. Pat was interviewed by Tony, for the Late Show, *in January 2004. By permission of Tony Wadsworth.*

On location in Rome, for
Raiders of the Lost Ark.
Doreen, with Ronald Lacey.
By permission of Doreen Roach.

Pat takes a break with Ronald Lacey, in Tunisia, during the filming of Raiders.
The photograph was taken by Mark Roach, Pat's son, who was on location with
them. By permission of Doreen Roach.

From L-R: Pat's agent, Peter Charlesworth, Steven Spielberg and Pat having a relaxing drink at the Camden Palace, London. By permission of Peter Charlesworth.

Pat, at his Erdington Gym, looking remarkably fit and healthy, despite his battle with cancer. The Indiana Jones *jacket was awarded to him, in recognition of the fact that he has been in all three of the movies. Photograph by Shirley Thompson.*

Left: Pat as Little John, in Robin Hood. *By permission of Doreen Roach.*
Right: "Where's the front door?" Pat as Jarn Saxa, the Giant. By permission of
Doreen Roach.

"As if one Celtic Chieftain wasn't enough!" Bernie Guest thinks he's seeing double,
on the set of Robin Hood, Prince of Thieves. *By permission of Bernard Guest.*

Left: An early Northern Wrestlers' Reunion, in Seamus' pub, the Royal George, *in 1994, before the venue moved to Ellesmere Port. L-R: Pat Roach, Seamus, referee Max Ward, and Sparkety Clarkety - who'd gate-crashed! By permission of Seamus Dunleavy.*
Right: Seamus and Pete Roberts at a Wrestling Reunion, outside Bill Bridges Greenwich pub, the Prince of Orange. *By permission of Seamus Dunleavy.*

Probably the last photograph of Pat, to be taken at a social event: Pete Evans' 60th Birthday Party, at the Redwood Club, Bristol Road, Birmingham in March 2004. From L-R: Eddie Richards (Ronnie Taylor's 'right-hand man'), Pat, Ronnie Taylor (now deceased) and Pete Evans. By permission of Pete Evans.

Pat invited Tony Green to the end of filming party for *Auf Wiedersehen Pet 1*. "I've met Timmy Healy a few times," Tony comments. I explained that he has written a whole chapter for this new book. He also did a joint book-signing with me at W.H. Smith's Birmingham store in early December 2004: two acts of kindness that are typical of Tim, and a mark of the close friendship between himself and Pat.

"I had a Bank Holiday Monday party, many years ago, at my boathouse on the Thames. Tim Healy came to it," recalls Tony. "I met him out in Mauritius, when he was one of the celebrities in the *Marlin World Cup*. He was in this televised fishing competition, and he caught a marlin. We laughed and had a joke about it. He's a tremendous singer too."

At the time of writing, May 2005, Tim's playing the father in the musical version of Billy Elliott. Playing at the Victoria Theatre, the show is currently breaking all West End box office records, since *The Sound of Music* – (as I was reliably informed by Tim, during a telephone conversation today). I was aware that he was a folk singer, from the photographs on his farmhouse wall. "His singing is tremendous," observes Tony. "He sang at a Gala Dinner, in Mauritius, after the fishing competition. He sings like Louis Armstrong."

*   *   *   *   *

The *Birmingham Mail* announced that work was about to begin at *Central's* Nottingham studios on a new, 13-part series of *Auf Wiedersehen Pet*. It was due for transmission in Spring 1986, and would feature all the old cast – (despite all the scares during the summer) and would have the same backroom team. Producer, Martin McKeand explained that there would be some location work in Spain.

Although the second series was filmed over twenty years ago, each of the cast retains vivid memories of the experience. It went into production in the spring of 1985 and finished in January 1986. But it proved to be an extremely problematic eleven months. *Central Television* had moved studios from London to Nottingham the previous year, so most of the actors, and Roger Bamford, stayed at the *George* in Nottingham, rather than driving home.

Pete Roberts' appearance in the second series was only for a split-second! "In the introduction, they show you a shot of two wrestlers," he explains, "because there are shots of what the characters have been doing in between series. Well, that was me wrestling Pat – you can just see my arse – (to be quite honest with you!)"

Tim Healy and Kevin's wife, Madelaine Newton, have been friends since their *Live Theatre* days in Newcastle. She played Tim's girlfriend, Christine Chadwick, in the second series. Kevin explained that Madelaine had originally been short-listed to play Dennis' wife, but in the end the part was given to Caroline Hutchinson. Shortly after filming for Series 2 began, the scriptwriters had to do a hasty re-write, as Caroline Hutchinson, who played Vera, Dennis's soon-to-be ex-wife in the first series, was diagnosed with cancer; she recovered for a while, but eventually died.

The script was re-written to include Dennis' sister and also a girlfriend. Kevin explains: "Madelaine only had two day's notice before she took the part of his girlfriend." He described their experiences working on location, while making the series. "Endless laughs; we all had a different sense of humour. It was very funny all the way through. We had the same crew for both series. Everybody got on so well – the chemistry was good. So often it's the luck of the draw – it's 90% luck."

Filming for *Aufpet 2* involved six weeks in Spain, then working on location in the Peak District. Tim Spall's character, Barry, asks the boys to help rebuild his house, in time for his wedding to Hazel Redfern, played by Melanie Hill . They congregate in Birmingham, for that purpose.

Tim Spall observes: "The wonderful thing about the character of Bomber, especially in the writing, is that they do give him a kind of nobility." Whenever Bomber was around, the 'boys' always felt safe. The same went for being with Pat, especially in tricky locations.

The 'Magnificent Seven' are employed converting a large country house called Thornley Manor, into an old people's home. The landlord in the local village takes an immediate dislike to them. As the Manor is a listed building they are forced to down tools. Wayne's dalliance with the landlord's daughter results in eviction from their hotel. Forced to 'sleep rough' in the old manor, they find a set of videos, implicating local dignitaries, one of whom is Arthur, the landlord, played by Brian Pringle. Oz sings a Merle Haggard song in Episode Six. The lads refuse to cut corners on converting the manor, so Ally Fraser sends in his henchman, but the lads eventually win the day.

Later, the action moves to Spain, where they are mistaken for a criminal gang. Barry and Hazel subsequently marry on Kenny Ames' yacht. Ally brings a briefcase of cash, but Customs give chase, by boat. As Episode Thirteen closes, the 'boys' head for Tangiers. Bomber suggests they might find work in North Africa. Moxey replies that there's a good chance...they built the pyramids!

Once the show became successful, the lives of all the principal cast members changed irrevocably. Overnight, they became public property; no longer able to pop down to the local supermarket or slip out for a pint. Jimmy Nail, in particular, had difficulty adjusting to the notoriety of his new screen image. Life as an entertainer has generally been a very positive, often lucrative experience for Pat. Nevertheless, he has always taken great care to guard his privacy, and his family, from any unwanted attention on the part of the media, the public at large, and from those who presume to know him, simply by virtue of his being a celebrity.

Coping with this new celebrity status seemed to bring the cast closer together, at events such as christenings and birthday parties. In our penultimate chapter, they all rally together for an occasion that they could never have foreseen, in those more halcyon days.

To outward appearances, Gary Holton seemed to be the only one comfortable with the Press; the remainder of the cast being fiercely protective of their privacy. However, in the following chapter, two of the people closest to him explain how Gary's problems were simmering, just below the surface.

In all well-observed situation comedies, the delight – rather than the devil – is in the detail. Who can forget Wayne's 'shades' and dangling ear-rings? Or Oz, fixing a treasured photo of Arthur Scargill in the gap between curling wallpaper, alongside a topless pin-up; filching strawberries from a sweet trolley, and talking about Wayne's need for moderation while loading his thousandth can of lager into a supermarket trolley. I can still picture him: casually cleaning his toenails with a trowel, during a conversation with Bomber! Barry's apologetic domesticity, philosophical outpourings and mud-splattered van after trout-tickling.

Moxey, wearing his woolly hat, in every *conceivable* situation. Bomber's solid, reassuring presence, and his favourite saying: "Bomber's away!" when he was ready to go out. Neville's plastic apron with a bottle of beer on the front, when he returns home, and the Rupert Bear poster on his kitchen door. The seedy, off-white underwear of the 'lads', as they emerge from their sleeping bags, in stark contrast to the affluent Spanish lifestyle of their boss, Ally Fraser. Bill Paterson played this Scottish role with panache, in company with fellow 'shady-dealing' entrepreneur, cockney Kenny Ames, alias James Booth.

Tim Spall attributes *Aufpet's* success to a variety of factors. "I think it appealed to the older generation. It was a classic army situation: seven guys in an enclosed space, who wouldn't, given normal opportunities, be anywhere near each other. It was also about guys who were trying to make a living because things were bad at home. They're missing their loved ones and they're also 'out on the razz' a bit, because they're away from home."

Tim Healy recalls: "There were 30,000 Brits working out there in Germany. So it was a statement too: 'How dare you send these people abroad because they haven't any work here?' It had that wonderful truth underneath." Kevin believes that a significant factor is the chemistry that Roger Bamford created on set. He and Pat enjoyed working together and remained close friends. He describes Pat as "… a 'driven' man, with a very strong work ethic and more energy than anyone I've ever met. We had totally opposing political views. He had a huge laugh; we'd be helpless with giggles for a lot of the time."

According to Chris Fairbank: "When we were doing the second series, we ended up filming in a scrap metal yard, not far from the East Midlands Airport. Pat was like a kid in a sweetshop, with all this scrap metal, plant and what-have-you. At the end of the day he said: "I've found the owner – fantastic! I've got a propeller-starter, off an aeroplane." So I thought, 'OK I suppose. If that's what you want, good-on-you Pat.' He said: 'I've got this scrap metal yard, and I'll be knocking this out for scrap, and I'll make a hundred quid on it.'

"Then about two or three years later, I was coming down the M1 and stopped off at the Watford Gap Service Station – where I literally bumped into Pat. He was coming out of the restaurant, as I was going in. Pat and cars are not a marriage made in heaven – I'm sure you know that. He'd stopped there because yet another car had given up the ghost – three hundred yards down the M1! He was waiting for a replacement car, to get him off to Bristol; he was appearing in an episode of *Casualty*. We had a coffee, and the usual 'Hi, how are you, what have you been up to?' kind of conversation. He said, 'I've got the VAT people on me back – inspecting. It's f*** murder! Do you remember the day we were at the scrap metal place near East Midlands Airport and I was after the aeroplane machine? Well I couldn't shift it, so I've had it in my yard. The VAT people found this fr*** propeller starter, and they want to know where the rest of the f*** plane is!' They wouldn't believe that he hadn't got it stashed away somewhere!"

The making of *Auf Wiedersehen Pet 2* coincided with Pat's nine-year abstinence from drink, so when the rest of the cast went to the pub, he pursued his training programme. Tim Healy confirmed, "He did that all the time. This was after the first series had gone out. He used to be a 'baddie' and all of a sudden he was a 'goodie', because he was Bomber. Audiences changed towards him, because he was a lovable fella in the series." The highest recorded audience for any series was 16, 017,000 for Episode 8, in which Oz returns to Newcastle, to stop his son moving to Italy.

Tim and Pat are both car enthusiasts, a fact that brought them to the edge of disaster! In Chapter 19 Tim describes a potentially fatal accident, which occurred whilst he and Pat were travelling in his Porsche 911.

Val Hastings' daughter, Karen, played a hotel receptionist in the second series. "I had to go over to *Carlton Studios* in Nottingham," Karen explains. Unfortunately, Pat wasn't filming that day. "Timothy Spall was there. I was a receptionist at a Conference Centre. Timothy was quite affable, approachable and talkative," continues Karen. "I remember them talking about the way that Pat played jokes on the cast and crew and how they would retaliate. The Conference Centre was supposed to be back in England and Barry had come to find his girlfriend. At the time I was very young, compared to everybody else. Melanie Hill, the actress playing Barry's girlfriend, was very friendly and gave me advice. I'd not long got my *Equity* Card – and to do things like that, with people who were really famous! They made me feel really welcome."

"I'd become an Agent in 1989 and resigned from being Branch Secretary of *Equity*, so people thought that I was pulling strings to get Karen's *Equity* Card," explains Val. Pat arranged for a Committee member to watch Karen on stage in Birmingham, then chat to her backstage. At the next meeting Pat said: 'That's it. She's entitled to be a member. We'll all vote.' So she got her *Equity* Card and carried on filming for the BBC, Central and Carlton, using her stage name, Karen Karlsen.

"I met Jimmy's sister, Val MacLean, before *Auf Wiedersehen* had started," Val recalls. "By coincidence, when I was Branch Secretary of *Equity*, I attended six-weekly *Variety* meetings down in London, for the Branch Secretaries. We all met in Harley Street and Val MacLean was Secretary for the Newcastle-upon-Tyne Branch: years later, I realised that she was Jimmy Nail's sister. She played Tim Healy's sister in the very first *Auf Wiedersehen*. She is a wonderful actress, and has played a lot of Geordie parts."

Julia Tobin was in Spain for about four to five weeks, "...because the girls were used quite a lot in Spain. But we lost Caroline, prior to that. She had cancer, so she couldn't go and she had to be written out. We'd already done that. She hadn't done any filming, so Madelaine Newton and Melanie Hill were put into it. We rented an apartment block and we all practically lived together, for a long period of time. We had some marvellous times. The apartment block was in Marbella. We all used to go out together to Puerto

Banus. A couple of us went to the local 'feria', which is another fair. I probably dragged everybody there!

"As we were all living together, we used to organise things like a barbecue and then on another occasion there was a first birthday party for Kevin and Madelaine's son, Kieran. Also, a table tennis tournament – Tim Healy won that; he used to be County Champion.

"Pat was always a person who looked after everyone – almost like a father figure. That's not to say that he was imposing in any way. I've always felt that Pat was a marvellous gentleman. He had tremendous respect for everyone – especially female members. Pat would always open a door for you and make sure that you were attended to first."

Pat was very funny, in his own right – and a great practical joker. "Yes, he was. Thankfully, I wasn't the butt of any of them! I think he possibly thought that it wouldn't be a good idea to play any practical jokes on me!" Julia provides further insights in later chapters. We are also most grateful to her for providing a unique set of *Auf Wiedersehen* photos, from her private collection.

Gary Holton was becoming increasingly isolated during location work in Spain. He and Pat had become the closest of friends, as the next chapter reveals. Before his own death, Pat stipulated that we should devote an entire chapter to his friend. He arranged for me to visit Gary's mother, Joan, over five years ago; in the event, Pat had more time left than he imagined. Gary's manager and friend, John Harwood-Bee *also* reveals what happened to a young man who, at first glance, seemed to have everything going for him....

Chapter Nine

GARY

Wayne was a character of fiction. Gary was very real. I think what Gary put into the character of Wayne, was a lot of his cockiness: by that I don't mean conceit. It was the way he carried himself. It was this 'Jack-the-Lad' swagger. Gary Holton was like that, and took that into Wayne as well. I suppose, to a degree, there was a lot of Gary in the character.

John Harwood-Bee

In March 2001, I spent a day with Gary Holton's mother, Joan Pugh, at her Shropshire bungalow; the surname change resulted from her second marriage. Before my visit, I knew relatively little about her son; by the time I left, several misconceptions had flown right out of the window!

Joan and Gary's manager and friend, John Harwood-Bee, have maintained contact, throughout the years. John kindly visited me, in October 2004, providing additional insights into what actually happened to Gary. These two interviews, plus observations from some of the *Auf pet* cast, combine to produce, at Pat's *particular* request, a re-examination of his friend's life – and untimely death. It's notoriously difficult to present an accurate, unbiased picture of someone, without first spending time in his company, but hopefully, we have achieved some degree of success.

Joan, who is now in her late seventies, has two other sons, Tony and Nigel, from her first marriage to Ernie Holton. Gary and his partner, Sue Harrison had a son named Red, although it was Donna who actually became Mrs. Holton.

"He never divorced her you see," explains Joan. "Susie claimed that being with him for six years, she was legally entitled to everything, and Donna claimed that being Mrs. Holton, *she* was. They're both married again now. I've not seen Red since he was a baby, although I looked after him from when he first came out of hospital.

"I love everybody's children; they call me 'nanny', because I'm old. Red would be about twenty-four now. Sue had another son, Max, before she met

89

Gary. My second son, Tony is in his forties now; he's got his own business; doing very well – he goes skiing. He's full of life, in a different sort of way to Gary. My youngest son, Nigel, is in partnership with Tony. They have three businesses, operating from Shrewsbury, Manchester and London. The company's called *ARH Electrical Services Ltd.*"

Gary was the eldest son, born on 22 September 1952. He and Tony were born in Clapham Common – so they're both Cockneys: the speaking voice he used for the role of Wayne was close to his normal speaking voice. "Yes, he wasn't acting!" confirms Joan. "But unlike Wayne, Gary was a hardworking person, and also went on charity walks with Jimmy Saville – he had blisters on his feet." John elaborates: "Gary was very discreet and quiet about anything of that nature, but he made quite a few personal appearances for fund raising." Gary also worked with organisations connected with disadvantaged children (in terms of mentally handicapped).

"It was surprising, the rapport he had with these children; it touched the heart, because he had a great ability to communicate with them. In realising that, he went on to make personal appearances, whenever requested." John has interacted with disadvantaged children himself, from childhood onwards. "One of the first things that you realise is that to communicate with these people, the nicest thing possible is to come down to their level." Gary needed no such prior instruction. From the minute he entered the room, he instinctively got down to eye level. "He didn't say: 'Here I am. I'm the big star of this new TV Show.' He just walked in there as someone they already knew, because many of them watched TV," explains John. "Then down he went – talking on a one-to-one, in an effort to understand." John received a heartfelt letter, from a mother whose daughter had mental health problems; Gary had been her hero, through *Auf Wiedersehen*. Her mother requested a signed photograph, which, unbeknown to John, Gary had delivered personally.

So what was Gary like, as a boy? "Beautiful, clever, brainy," Joan remembers. "He went to grammar school, when we lived in London: that was where his life *really* started. Before that, we went ballroom dancing and won lots of trophies. He'd got a very good sense of rhythm: Latin American, and so on. When he went to grammar school his music teacher, Peter something; (I can't remember his surname), liked Gary very much, and could see that he was gifted. Talent-spotters visited the school, auditioning children for parts in *Quatermass and the Pit*. They picked Gary out for that, when he was about twelve.

"When he was thirteen, he was picked from 400 schoolboys to audition for *Love for Love*. He got the part – three seasons. Sir Laurence Olivier was in that, with the *Old Vic Theatre Company*." This was an experience that Gary and Pat had in common, as sixteen years later Pat was in *Clash of the Titans*, with Sir Laurence; he describes the experience in *If – The Pat Roach Story*.

Gary had private tuition, and Joan was paid to chaperone him. He went on tour with *Love for Love* playing a rogue, and sang in it, although it wasn't a musical. "Then one day his voice broke," explains Joan, (imitates a gruff voice) "so that was that." He performed in *Much Ado About Nothing*, still with Olivier's company. "Gary used to play lots of instruments: you name it, he done it – piano, xylophone, clarinet! He had lessons at the same London school, with his music teacher, Peter, and he got top stars: it was top, top, top, all the time. On the programme it said: 'all instruments played by Gary'."

This was followed by *A Girl In My Soup*, starring John Stride. "He got four standing ovations for that," recalls Joan. "He played the drunken brother-in-law, and stood on the edge of the stage, leaning over, with a bucket on his head. The audience just *screamed* – because he had to lean right over!"

Gary's Rock n' Roll career began when he was in *Hair* in 1970. "It was his 18th birthday, and he asked me to go. I had no idea what sort of show it was. He said: 'I've got my mummy here tonight – and she's going to come up on the stage – aren't you darling?' I went up and he said: 'All you do now, is take your clothes off!' Well I'd got a cardigan on, so he goes: 'dah-dah-dah,' ('Stripper' tune). So there I was, up on stage, with all the little willies flying about! I didn't undress! But my God, he was good: all dressed up, like a general, with a sword. Being younger he was in the Chorus, as in shows like *Hansel & Gretel*. In *Les Enfants:* he was in the front row, dancing and singing. He'd also been the Milky Bar Kid, on the TV adverts, but he wore a blond wig and glasses. As he got older, it was all speaking parts."

Gary decided on a career change when he finished *Hair*. "One of his big breaks," explains John, "came with the formation of a band, which he fronted as lead singer and the front man – a band called *The Heavy Metal Kids*. It was one of the first Punk Bands, precursors of *The Sex Pistols*. They were signed to *WEA Records*, which as part of *Warner Brothers* was one of the main international labels. They recorded for *Warners*. That's when I first came to know Gary, reasonably well, because I was a Director of Warner's Advertising Agency, at the time. We were handling the marketing and promotion for the *Heavy Metal Kids* Campaign.

"*Warner Brothers* sold the contract on to Mickey Most of *Rak Records*. Mickey recognised where the style of music was going, and was determined to make it a Mega Band: before the *Sex Pistols*, or any of those bands. Unfortunately, there was a falling out and disagreement and Gary walked out on the project."

In 1977 Gary's girlfriend Tracy Boyle died tragically, aged nineteen. He seemed to bounce back from this crisis, returned to acting, and appeared in the rock music feature films *Breaking Glass* and *Quadrophenia*. He played Eddie Hairstyle in the television feature film about London cabbies called *The Knowledge* and guested on several TV shows, including *Shoestring, Minder, Gentle Touch* and the controversial feature film *Bloody Kids*.

"After the break-up of *The Heavy Metal Kids*, and the contractual problems with *Rak*, Gary carried on acting in this country," John continues. "During the time of *The Heavy Metal Kids*, he had met up, at *The Marquee*, with a Norwegian singer called Casino Steel. 'Cas' had worked with *The Ramones* in New York and with various other bands. He was with a quite notorious band called *The Boys*. Gary and Cas got on very well together."

In 1979, in a whirlwind romance, Gary met and married Donna. "That same year," remembers John, "Cas invited him to Norway. On arrival, he found that, contrary to the popular opinion of Norwegian music, there was a thriving Rock Music industry over there. Cas was already well known, particularly in Norway, as a solo artiste and through the various bands that he'd performed in; he'd been around for several years.

"Both of them had been writing songs. They got together, with Cas's manager, and record company boss, Barry Matheson. Barry put the two of them into a studio where they recorded a 'demo' – a variety of songs, some cover versions, some original. When Barry heard it he realised the commercial potential. They formed a duo, called *Holton, Steel* and signed to *Polydor* in Scandinavia, subsequently creating 'Rigrock': the Norwegian oil industry was booming; they wanted an umbrella for it, so they called it Rigrock. At other times it's been described as 'Punk-country'.

"They took a classic song, *Ruby*, (a hit for Kenny Rogers over here), and made it into a more raw, rock version, with a Punk element to it. That and others were released in Norway, and the album went to Number One. Subsequently, they had a total of four Number One consecutive albums in Norway, between 1979 and 1984 – the year before Gary died." They were awarded gold and silver discs for *Ruby, Don't Take Your Love To Town, Catch A Falling Star* and *Blackberry Way*.

"He went on *Top Of The Pops*," recalls Joan, "with a Hit Record – and all the *Early Morning Breakfast* TV programmes – I've got the little eggcup they give you. He was on the telly all the time."

Extensive Scandinavian tours put a fatal strain upon married life: Gary and Donna separated in 1981. Returning to London, he performed in the regional tour of *Once A Catholic*, appeared in David Anderson's rock play *His*

Master's Voice and starred with Paul Jones, Kiki Dee, Carlene Carter and others, in the original cast of *Pump Boys* and *Dinettes*.

In the same year, 1983, Gary began work on *Auf Wiedersehen Pet*, for *Central TV*. It is as the crafty cockney, Wayne, that Gary will undoubtedly be best remembered. His laid-back style made him a hit with fans; some actually believed that he really was Wayne! He'd go backwards and forwards to *Holton, Steel* concerts, even while he was recording *Auf Wiedersehen*.

An accident, during a Spanish holiday in 1984, left Gary temporarily paralysed. However, that same year he secured a licensing deal for his record to be released in the UK on *Magnet* records. He recorded *Holiday Romance* and *Catch A Falling Star*, the latter arranged and produced by Jim Lea of *Slade*, without either of them being the hits they'd been abroad. He wrote the words and music for quite a number of songs and records, composed a broad range of music, starting with Rock n' Roll, but he ended up singing ballads. One of his main ambitions was to write film music. It was while he was preparing a concerted effort to bolster his British recording career that he died.

"We were in the London studio one evening, during the time that he'd been working on the second series of *Auf Wiedersehen*. The producer was also there. Gary came up with an alternative, catchy theme tune, with a backing group of four friends," John remembers. "He had some help from the other guys, but it was predominantly Gary who sang and wrote a track called *Auf Wiedersehen*. Unfortunately, it wasn't accepted by *Central Television*, but was released on one of the albums, in Scandinavia."

"Gary sent me photos of himself and Pat," Joan says, wistfully. "In Gary's eyes he was just wonderful. He looked upon him as a big brother. I don't really know how to explain it – he was so close to him. Before he died, Gary was offered a film part, and he said that Pat was going to be in a film involving snow." This was *The Last Place On Earth*; Pat's role was heroic Edgar Evans, originally played by James Robertson Justice. It was actually filmed at the North Pole: logistically speaking the South Pole was impractical. Martin Shaw took the role of Captain Scott.

"Gary liked everybody – he didn't run anybody down, but he just praised and praised Pat; he never spoke about the others as much as he spoke about Pat," Joan explains. "They were all good 'buddy-buddies', but Pat was Number One, in his book. They used to get up to little tricks and Gary would phone me and tell me about them... but it's a long time ago." Both men shared a common bond of having to cope with being in the Limelight, plus occasional adverse publicity.

Describing the near-disaster with the *Aufpet* hut scene, Joan recalls: "His legs caught light, but they got him out. They took him to hospital on another occasion, because of a scene where Gary falls flat in a mud puddle, outside. We were *so* close, you wouldn't *believe* how close! He always said: 'If you weren't my mum I'd marry you!' An ornamental black tea service edged with gold retains pride-of-place in her lounge. "They were Gary's: he collected it, so I made sure that I looked after it for him." When Gary came to visit, in Houndwood, he preferred to catch up on family news, and just relax. "He loved to curl up in a chair and go to sleep, or 'pootle' about in the garden: 'What time's dinner?' and that sort of thing." "Yes, he loved the occasions that he went home to mum," agrees John. "There's no question; we would work round that – if he had a couple of days when he could get home to see her."

Joan and first husband, Ernie, Gary's father, ran pubs together: no wonder he seemed so much at ease during the *Aufpet* pub scenes! "Gary was accustomed to socialising and mixing with customers, from a fairly early age," Joan recalls."When we were at Welshpool, he had his photo over the bar. They all sent him birthday cards when he was eighteen. He'd sit with the customers and play dominoes."

In *Auf Wiedersehen Pet* Gary was 'Jack-the-Lad'. "He was lovely; he just wanted cuddling. But he was going around with two people who were like gypsies and tried to 'con' him out of money," Joan reveals. "They had nowhere to live, and Gary was a 'soft touch'. He paid for them to go out to Spain; he couldn't get rid of them. That started just a few months before he died, during the second series. He used to say, 'They're weird mum. As soon as they know I'm going away, they take over the house.' I'd say: 'Oh Gary!' 'Oh don't you worry yourself,' he'd say." The police couldn't help, and it would have been bad publicity, especially with the drugs. Joan agrees that he probably decided to 'ride with it'.

"I think with Gary," reflects John, "he was picked out at such an early age and given that recognition – and perhaps that formed *how* he was. Although generally children can handle the element of fame, they play up to it. It is that recognition: it may be that in later years, he found he actually *liked* that." It is common knowledge that some actors seek audience approval, for security; one reads that certain actors are at their happiest when playing other people, rather than as themselves. "You do get extraverts," elaborates John, "but there are so many introverts who put on this extravert persona, to gain that recognition, and the reason that they act or perform, is their way of gaining approval.

"One of the things that the Arts, in general, (I'm not sure whether it encourages it, or is a result of it, or whether it is just synonymous with it), is Excess. Whether that's excess in drink or sex, or drugs or behaviour, it's there. It's like a vein that runs through the whole profession: through music, acting and television. What they're doing is delivering to *their* public this imaginary world, which has to be larger than life, to take it away from the mundane. Gary knew *exactly* where the line between reality and fantasy was, and chose which side of that line he wanted to be. Unfortunately, there are an awful lot of people who do *not* know where reality stops. Gary was in control of where he wanted to be at that time, but I'm not sure that he was always in control of his behaviour.

"He *loved* doing the *Auf Wiedersehen* series, and had tremendous fun, from his perspective. The first series, in particular, was a big break for *him*. Although he'd done quite a lot of good quality television, this was taking him into a different league. I don't think any of them anticipated the impact it would have; although Gary realised that it had 'legs', because he fought so hard to get the part.

"Gary was living with his partner, Susan, who had a son, Max, from her previous marriage. That son's godfather was Ian La Frenais. Gary heard about the series at a party and persuaded Ian to let him read for the part. Of course, the part was him – I don't think there's any question. There has been comment that Ian actually rewrote the part for Gary, but I don't know whether there was any substance to that. As with any actor, he took the character and moulded it, but the lines were those of a cocky, almost cockney lad."

The *Auf Wiedersehen* book mentions a friendly rivalry between the Cockney and Geordie elements. "Within all of those things you will find that rivalry – I don't think you would describe it as friction," comments John. "It would be wrong to say that all was 'sweetness and light', because without question, you're talking about really talented Journeyman Actors: they'd paid their dues. Then into that, they brought somebody who had little or no acting experience, for example, Jimmy and Pat. Pat was one of these people who endeared himself to people, because of his nature. Jimmy, by his nature, is more reserved; he was a little more reticent and hadn't had *that* much experience."

At the beginning of the first series Pat was the celebrity amongst the cast, through wrestling and films. "Over the years, the situation was somewhat reversed, certainly in the case of both Tims, Jimmy and Kevin, although Pat could never fade into the background! The British public really took to Jimmy Nail's performance, despite his relative lack of experience. So the 'bad boy', was the one who came shining through. He created that character.

"I was up at Elstree, when they were filming the first series. Everybody seemed to get on well. I was managing Gary, so I had discussions with him, to see that everything was going well, and watched while they were filming the building site, on the Back Lot." It was there that Gary first introduced John to Pat. "It was as if I'd known him for a tremendously long time. Pat was his usual, informal self – 'Hello John.' There was no Prima Donna about him whatsoever. What you saw was what you got, and the same when we were out in Spain. Whenever we were relaxing, even when we were recording up in Nottingham, when production of the second series was moved up to *Central*, he always had a big smile on his face. The only time I ever saw Pat without either a smile or a grin, even though I'd met him in numerous occasions, was at Gary's funeral. He *was* an incredibly positive person."

Gary responded to Pat's 'Gentle Giant' nature. "Here was somebody who didn't judge, who didn't feel threatened by him," John remembers. "When he first went into *Auf Wiedersehen* Gary was already a well-known actor, (although obviously there were others too). But there was no friction, with Pat. He could talk to him, about anything to do with the series, or about life in general. Totally laid-back – they created this rapport. Gary found a *true* friend in Pat – and possibly a cross between an older brother and a father figure. During the first series I'm sure there were no problems, or Gary wouldn't have been invited to take part in the second.

"There was none of the rivalry, which is automatic in any situation like that. Here you have seven characters, brought into a brand new series: every one of them on an equal footing, (contract-wise too). Each one of them is trying to establish himself, so there are *bound* to be professional rivalries. Pat didn't need to be like that – he'd already created his own 'giant' on the screen, so Gary's reaction would have been: 'Here's someone I can relax with and relate to – a really nice guy;' there was no hidden agenda."

When filming on the second series began in spring 1985, Gary's problems had already begun to emerge. In September 1984 he'd admitted the seriousness of his heroine addiction, and with the support of *Narcotics Anonymous*, spent the following year trying to beat his habit; treatment was paid for and prompted by the Management Company, who were determined that he should 'clean up his act'. "Despite having worked around the Entertainment and Music Industries for most of my life, I hadn't recognised prior to that, that he had a problem," reflects John. "It hadn't become extreme, but it was heading that way. We'd called him to London, to a business meeting, knowing that he and his partner were using drugs. Gary agreed to receive treatment, and to seek help, backed by us, and others around him.

"We were not aware of their being any further problem until around August 1985, when we were contacted by *Central Television*. They were having problems with Gary in Nottingham: people who were accompanying him were having a bad influence on him; we had absolutely no control over them. On one occasion, there was a woman on set with Gary." An argument ensued, leading to erratic behaviour, on Gary's part. "After that, *Central* asked for a meeting, which I attended. Gary had this distraction, and was late onto set a couple of times. Everybody was moving to Spain, and *Central* wanted Gary to have Representation out there, so I went out myself, for the first ten days of filming.

"At the time, the request appeared to be, perhaps a little bit Draconian. But on reflection I think perhaps it wasn't. For whatever reason, (and I'm still not convinced it was drugs in Spain), he was having a rebellious period. Playing, perhaps, a larger part than he was entitled to...in small things, like taking the car, and as you say, in refusing to comply with an instruction: 'Don't get a suntan,' which is basic professionalism. Until that point he had always been the *ultimate* professional, so there had to be something that was causing the problem, but I never found any direct evidence that it was drugs.

"Whilst in Spain, we were in negotiations with a major national newspaper, to cover Gary's life story and to tell the story of his battle with drugs, as Gary had become more of a public figure." Gary stuck to the agreement, that whilst filming in Spain, none of the cast would have anything to do with the Press. "I think that the Spanish episode was something totally different again Shirley. As we discovered afterwards, he was in another relationship, following the breakdown of the one with his long-time partner, Sue. Gary had been trying desperately to kick his heroin habit; we'd had him in clinics and so forth. He'd given an undertaking to Barry Matheson, the boss of *Continental*, that he would kick the habit completely and as far as we were aware, through most of that year, all the evidence pointed to the fact that he had done so.

"Throughout the early part and mid-1985, without *question* he stayed clean, worked hard, and things were going well. Unfortunately, his partner chose not to accept the same backing and assistance, and this had put some strain upon the relationship. Sometime during 1985, they split up." John stayed in Marbella with the crew. On his return, Dave Green, one of the management team replaced him. Gary was well aware that John and Dave were in Spain because of his behaviour: refusing to avoid a suntan, confusing his lines and 'appropriating' a Bentley!

Describing the latter, John comments: "I suppose it was very irritating to the Production Team, but it seemed to amuse everybody else. A beautiful soft-topped Bentley had been hired for a day's shoot. Everybody was on set waiting, but nobody was ready to go, because the producer hadn't turned up and the director wasn't there; but the car arrived. Gary and the person he was with wanted some cigarettes, so he walked over to the chauffeur and said, 'Run me down the hill. I need to get some fags.' That was the last we saw of the car, for about an hour and a half. It was typical of Gary. They weren't supposed to get suntanned, but up until I left, that wasn't a problem."

I asked Julia Tobin if she'd been aware that Gary was having difficulties, during *Series Two*. "I remember one point, when we were doing a scene; it was in the studio, with Gary," she recalls. "We were filming in the afternoon, and it had obviously been a particularly trying day for him. In the morning he was fine – there were no problems. But then, in the afternoon, we had to do about ten or twelve different takes, before we got the scene correct, because Gary couldn't remember his words. I'd never witnessed him *taking* any drugs – obviously – but I was aware at the time that there were problems. And certainly, he did sometimes appear to be a different personality. He was never *nasty* to me, but perhaps a little *happier* than you would expect!"

"One of the things about this memory business is that when he'd had his accident in either Spain or Portugal, he banged his head quite badly, and there were odd occasions when he found it difficult learning lines," explains John. "Now whether or not that was exacerbated by having a couple of drinks… But certainly he didn't drink to the extent that a *lot* of other people drank – nowhere near. But he did get drunk, quite *easily*, on just two or three drinks.

"My experience of Gary was that he never let anything put him off. It didn't matter what the adversity was, whether it was a van breaking down on its way to a gig, or whether the lighting wasn't working. Even to the extent of being told: 'You've been put forward for this part, but we'll let you know,' he never gave up: whatever it was, he went for it."

In the Recording Studio, if he felt that there was something wrong with a track, even if everyone else thought it was excellent, he'd continue until it was absolutely 'spot-on'.

"To a degree, he was a perfectionist," observes John, "but sadly, towards the end, he lost that will for perfection. He'd always been a true professional. There were two sides to him: a very serious side, but also a very light-hearted, 'Jack-the-Lad' side, which he put on for his public." Gary constantly courted new experiences and was always on the lookout for new projects. Ironically, this penchant for challenging situations sometimes got him into scrapes that were plastered across the media, at various points in his career.

Pat tried to reassure Gary when he was feeling depressed: 'What's the matter? You've got everything going for you. You're very talented, you're an attractive fella, and you've got your whole future ahead of you.'

"On reflection, explains John, "it wasn't Depression in the clinical sense. It was probably when he was being put under pressure, by us, or the TV Company – to curtail behaviour or spending. It is a recorded document that, sadly, when Gary died he was deeply in debt to the Management Company. Within those last couple of years, we had taken a much stronger line with his spending."

One particular evening, after a day's filming, "Gary and I were having dinner in the hotel, when a bottle of champagne landed in the middle of the table, and a 'character' was pointed out by the waiter, saying: 'This gentleman wishes to buy you a drink.' We just nodded and said thank you, thinking that it was one of the numerous 'well-wishers': the British holiday contingent in Southern Spain. Seconds later, a chap introduced himself as Jeff Baker, from the *Daily Star*, and asked if we could we talk afterwards. Gary didn't wish to talk to anybody and we were religiously sticking to the cast agreement, so he went to bed and I joined Baker at the bar. He said that he wanted to negotiate Gary's life story, for the *Daily Star*. I informed him that we were already in discussions with a national newspaper, but would be quite happy to discuss it further, once we'd returned to England."

The next day, when they were filming on the beach, Baker and a photographer attempted to take candid shots of Gary, which John tried to block. "Unfortunately, one of them appeared in the National Press, the following day, showing Gary, in my presence, together with somebody else; who had accompanied us to Spain. It was considered to be innocent, because Gary and myself were maintaining the no publicity rule.

"Arriving back in London, we discovered that, far from Baker being in Spain to negotiate Gary's story, he was there because Gary's ex-partner, Susan, had sold the drugs story to the Press. Baker was looking for further salacious stories. I received a telephone call in my office on the Monday evening, to say that they were going with the story and did I have any comment to make? I said: 'No comment.' I contacted our lawyers, who suggested that it was probably not worth them trying to get an injunction. We let Gary know that the story was going to appear.

"Unfortunately, when the story appeared, it was far worse than we had anticipated. It was also a bit of a shock to Gary, because he had actually wanted to tell the true story – his side of it – to *The News of the World*, with whom we were already in discussion." The business about journalists being good friends, probably arose from his previous good relationship with *The Sun*. "Gary would laugh when his wife, Donna, sold stories to the press: 'She's making herself a few bob, so she's not going to be asking me for anything!' What shook him *this* time was the *nastiness* of the reporting: he felt badly betrayed, that he'd been lied to."

This could have been overcome with evidence showing that he'd been cleaning up his act. But, according to John, "What *really* finished it, I think, in terms of him perhaps giving up the fight against the drugs, was being harassed even further by a reporter and photographer, and the press headline that came out the next day: *Heroin Hoodlum*. That really knocked him sideways – and the rest is history."

Gary was unable to visit Joan to reassure her about the article, because of the filming schedule. Kevin Whately found him sitting with his head in his hands. "We watched him go into a tailspin that week; it all just got to him." Joan cites previous occasions, when she'd had a drink with Gary in a pub, but the following day he'd be reported as being somewhere entirely different, with a certain woman; they were simply looking for another story. "I'm absolutely sure that that had happened," agrees John.

"It didn't matter who it was or what it was. We'd been to *Stringfellows* one evening, in London, and had a couple of Gary's male friends with us. As we were leaving the club, there was a very pretty lady coming out behind us. Two of the press tried to push her forward, between us. It was only the fact that I had my arm on his shoulder, guiding him towards a waiting car, which prevented them from getting their photograph. I still have no idea, to this day, who the photographer was!

"I said: 'What the hell are you playing at?' 'I'm only trying to get a decent picture guv'.' It was fair game – to the Press, but Gary didn't mind *that*. Whereas the drugs may have been a problem, he did not have a serious *drink* problem, other than he could not take his drink: two or three, and he was very merry indeed. I never saw him drunk, but I understand there was one situation, where they were filming in a pub, just outside Nottingham, and they probably had a few drinks at lunchtime.

"Gary had been living in a large flat, in Maida Vale, with Susan, which they jointly owned. When they split up, Gary moved out. Because filming for the second series was centered on Nottingham, we rented a flat for him in

Nottingham, which was his main base, although when he was in London, he stayed with friends, close to Maida Vale.

"I'd been due to meet Gary on the Thursday evening, on his return from Nottingham, but he postponed our meeting until around 9pm He was due to call me back again, to confirm a meeting place. I never got the call and I couldn't get hold of him. On Friday morning, just after nine o'clock, I was sitting in my office, when I received a telephone call from friends of his in Wembley, to say that he'd died at their flat. Gary was there, with another woman, with whom he had a relationship. I immediately left my office and went to Wembley. We assisted with the phone calls – and obviously, the police had to be called. It wasn't until later that morning that I was able to contact *Central* to inform them of Gary's death."

A national newspaper, eager for an unusual story angle, interviewed Pat about his friend. Prior to attending Gary's funeral, Pat put his funeral suit in the back of his Rolls Royce. On trying to open the boot to access the suit, part of the key broke off. He made an off-the-cuff remark: "If Gary's up there, he's probably laughing!" Unfortunately the journalist fabricated the rest of the article, implying a psychic link between the two of them. Pat was subsequently invited to appear on a television programme about the paranormal, but was never given the chance to put things right; he felt badly that the public could be deceived by someone else's account of what he was supposed to have said. Gary was only thirty-three when he died.

"I had heard that, almost immediately after Gary's death, the medium, Doris Stokes, claimed to have been in contact with Gary," comments John. "Certainly, there was some speculation that she had made contact with him. I've read the elements in her book relating to it, some of which are understandable, and some of which could have been gleaned from newspaper articles or radio conversations that I had, at the time of his death."

According to Joan: "There was an article in the paper about Doris Stokes, that she was doing a séance and that as she was talking, Gary appeared. She said: 'What are you doing here Gary?' He was saying that he wanted to get in touch with his mum. She said: 'But I can't help you: you're on the wrong side!' She didn't know that he was already dead. Doris was adamant all the time – that she wasn't lying. Ernie said she was money making, but she offered to donate any money to charity."

Pat and I discussed the discrepancy between Doris' version: that Gary died of a heart attack, and the official cause of death. Ostensibly, this *was* a possibility. Joan confirms: "Gary had a series of minor heart attacks before that, and I've seen him go on stage in a wheelchair, when he'd hurt his ankle, but it didn't stop him appearing." "I haven't had any direct approaches, either to us or to the office, to suggest that anybody had any Supernatural contact with Gary," comments John, "other than the conversations which went on immediately after his death, regarding Doris Stokes.

"I was in close contact with the Coroner, throughout the period immediately after Gary's death. The Coroner spoke to me on at least three occasions. As far as I am concerned, there was an Open Verdict, but the Medical Report was that Gary died from an overdose of drugs and drink. What I *would* comment on that, is that I attended the Coroner's Court – the Inquest – and there was absolutely no question that there was only *one* new needle mark, in Gary's arm. What Gary had been saying all year, that he had been cleaning up his act and trying very hard to stay off the drugs was certainly, as far as heroin was concerned, borne out by the Coroner's Report."

According to the BBC *Auf Wiedersehen* Book an Open Verdict was recorded because there were too many unanswered questions about Gary's death. Levels of alcohol and morphine were discovered in his blood. He'd visited a pub after returning to London from Nottingham, then turned up at a friend's house in Wembley, in the early hours of the morning. He had a cup of tea before going to bed, but was alone when he left the room before going to sleep. No syringes or any other drug abuse materials were discovered, and no witnesses came forward to testify that he had taken a fix of heroin.

The Coroner was therefore uncertain about what killed him, but of course, there's Press harassment, to add to the extenuating circumstances, especially as there was just the one needle mark. "It's a sad reality," John reflects, "that we were unable to bury Gary for some time after his death, because of the extensive tests that were done. I had several telephone calls from the Coroner's Office, asking for information, which we were able to give. Obviously, they were checking for other drugs and for any evidence of major drug abuse – but they found none. All the other needle marks were over a year old."

"I was devastated when I heard what had happened: I was in a 'fog'," Joan recalls. "I just didn't want to know, and went my own sweet way. I didn't want to do anything, or speak to anyone – for years. I'm getting better now, but if I play his records, I cry my eyes out. He's just with me! When you love your children and they've grown up and been good and worked hard – and then they print all that trash!

"Gary was a real 'trouper'. I suppose he got his strength from me. After the stroke, they said I would never walk, or do anything again. I was in

Intensive Care, but somehow Gary *spoke* to me: 'Walk mum – I'm willing you to walk! I want you to be walking before I come next time.' I suppose it could have been that I just *dreamt* it, and he simply said, 'I'm here mummy darling. I'm watching you. You'll be well soon!' But the point is that it gave me something to fight for. The nurses came over, and they couldn't believe that I was conscious and wanted a drink!"

John recalls: "Immediately after Gary's death, and for a couple of years, we were in contact with Susan because of debates and discussions over Gary's Estate. Red was still a very young boy then. Unfortunately, we then had no further contact, as Susan chose to remove herself from London, until last year when Susan contacted Cas, in response to something that she'd seen or read. It would appear that she has found happiness and chose to take herself out of the scene altogether.

"We are trying to put together a new official website, which goes over what he did; we're in the middle of doing that. It's a slow process because it takes time to talk to people, to get permission for photographs and so on. But there is every intention that, by 2005, the twentieth anniversary of his death, we will have a new website that features not only what he did as an actor, but also as a very talented musician. There are a series of excellent music videos that were shot: these will be re-done and re-released, as time permits." The unofficial website is www.garyholtonsite.tripod.com.

"Obviously I was there as Management, although we were also close friends. He got on incredibly well with my wife and I, personally, outside of the business sphere. But you can never *really* tell, because actors and entertainers tend to band together; they let themselves go mostly with their peers. But certainly from what I perceived, he was happy. He knew what the drugs had cost him in financial terms, over the years. I'm not sure whether he knew in physical terms. I don't think we will ever know. He would have been very wealthy, had it not been for all these other problems. Which is incredibly sad."

Joan description: "He was lovely. He just wanted a cuddle," made me wonder. Could it be that, essentially, Gary was a relatively normal, good-hearted person, who every now and then just needed reassurance? Or is that too simplistic?

"There's no question that he *gave* a lot more than he took," replies John. "He was very generous with his giving spirit and rarely asked anything in return. He was remarkable like that, but away from the spotlight and the glare of publicity, if you happened to put your arm around him and be chatting away and going: 'Yeah!' the reaction that you got was quite surprising.

"For the majority of 1985, Gary had been back in the studio, recording: supported by the team and everybody around him. We found new songs. He had been produced by Joe McGann and by Jim Lea of *Slade* and everything was being done for him to go forward.

There were negotiations in hand, for new advertising contracts, he'd had an incredibly successful advertising series with a lager company, and everything was looking positive.

For all of this to fall apart, as it did, in October of 1985, was nothing short of a tragedy. There is absolutely no question in my mind, that whatever the cause of Gary's death, and it is still not totally clear, the one thing that I will argue again and again, is that he had absolutely *no* intention of taking his life. I think that the Open Verdict was absolutely correct."

Chris Fairbank comments: "Over the course of the time-span of the two series, Gary had deteriorated – become more isolated. By the end, he'd surrounded himself with 'allies': people who aided his habits or addictions, but also protected him from the reality of what he was becoming. Fame – as I discovered – is a 'many-splintered thing'! You just don't have that sort of *protection*. There seems to be some sort of unwritten rule that you're up for whatever people choose to do to you." Pat was fortunate in this respect: the type of questions he tended to be asked were about wrestling, having already established a separate persona from 'Bomber'.

The pressures of the show, and Gary's untimely death exhausted the cast. Tim Spall describes Gary as: "...being more *lost* than really in trouble." Only the previous night they'd been filming in the Nottingham studio. The following day they were required in London, rehearsing for location shots, scheduled for the following week. "The logistic problem," explain Chris, "was that we'd actually filmed the end of the second series in Spain, so it wasn't a case of being able to write him out, so-to-speak. It was infinitely more complicated than that. We were quite used to dividing up his dialogue. There was a lot of behind-the-scenes commotion over Gary, although he had rendered himself indispensable by that time. But sadly, he's not the last, nor will he be. The whole game is *littered* with Gary Holton stories."

In the event, the series was saved, following hasty re-writes by Dick and Ian. A body double only had to be used once: in the casino scene, where Bomber removes Wayne as he attempts to chat up Ally Fraser's girlfriend. And – the supreme irony of all – it was Pat who was required to lift Gary's body double above his head. Inevitably, the weeks following Gary's death were difficult for everyone, but they coped as best they could. In January

1986, filming of the second series ended, followed by transmission of Episode One on 21 February.

For more than twenty years, Gary has been at peace, his ashes interred in a Welshpool plot, alongside his maternal grandparents. According to John, Gary's son, Red is a DJ somewhere, "... according to information that we received through the office."

Joan and the family were keen to honour Gary's heartfelt wish, to help others with drug problems. With their blessing, a record was released called *People in Love*, the Royalties of which were donated to the Pete Townsend *Double O Charity*. The album's cover features a large portrait photo of Gary; he sings on all of the tracks.

In summarising his life and not his death, John Harwood-Bee concludes: "Gary was somebody who, if he befriended you, was a friend for life – absolutely loyal. He lived life 150% and he lived it at 150 miles per hour! It didn't matter what he did, he went into it with the greatest of enthusiasm – for himself – and with the intent of delivering pleasure to those who were watching him. On occasion, other things got in the way, but in those short years, he packed his life with more than most people would put into a seventy-year lifetime. It is a *tragedy* that circumstances led to him dying so young."

Chapter Ten

AN EVERLASTING CANDLE

I didn't really choose sport as a career, or decide one day that I was going to be a wrestler on the telly: I drifted into it. I was always very tall and somewhat swarthy, so people would comment: "Oh, you should be a rugby football player, a boxer, or a wrestler. I suppose it's all part of my nature: I've been described as a 'driven' man, and had all this energy to expend. It got rid of inhibitions too, although I must confess, I didn't think of it that way at the time – it just happened. If you're a man you are usually interested in combat sports. I saw a little niche there where I could earn a few quid.

Pat Roach

This chapter continues the tributes and recollections from Pat's Sports World, begun in Chapter 6. So who better to begin, than his lifelong wrestling friend, Bill Bridges, aka Wayne Bridges. The following 'Tribute to the Passing of a Friend', (with just one interruption from Pat!), contains *most* of Wayne's heartwarming eulogy, delivered during the July 2004 Thanksgiving Service for Pat, at St John's Church, in Bromsgrove, Worcestershire. The ceremony is described in greater detail, in Chapter 20:

'Ladies and Gentlemen, my name is Wayne Bridges and I have come here today with many of my wrestling colleagues, not to mourn the loss of yet another grappling buddy, but to celebrate a lifelong friendship and association with a giant among men: the 'Bomber', Pat Roach. At six foot five and weighing in at twenty stone, Pat was obviously a huge man, but it is not his stature that I refer to, when I call him a giant. The friend that we all knew was as tough and strong as a lion, had the tenacity and stubbornness of a bulldog, did not know the meaning of fear, or submission; yet was as softly spoken as a new born lamb, with the gentle ways of a woman.

His love of poems such as *If*, his beloved family, especially his son, and the finer, elegant things in life, like his Bentley, were legendary. He could beat any man mercilessly, who faced him in combat, yet cradle a fragile butterfly in his enormous hands, with all the love of a child. I have personally seen him rage in temper like a rampant bull, over some trivial misdemeanour, and yet cry uncontrollably, following the death of my own beloved son. These are the qualities that mark a truly great man. Such men rarely pass our way; when they do, they should be treasured... as we did him.

Pat started his phenomenal path to fame, with an early interest in Judo, becoming the youngest exponent to ever win a Black Belt and Dan, in the quickest possible time ever known. It was during the early sixties, however, that his greatest love affair started, an association that was to endure for forty-four years, changing his life forever, and culminating in Pat becoming an international film and TV star, author, celebrity and international icon, surpassing even his wildest dreams. That love was Professional Wrestling.

I had the privilege to first meet him in 1964, when I was wrestling for *Paul Lincoln Promotions*, where stars like Mike Marino, 'Judo' Al Hayes and Ray Hunter were barnstorming the Halls in the UK, carving out major reputations for themselves. The young, unknown athlete, with a big mop of hair, had tasted success with Jack Taylor in Leicester and came down to London's Soho Headquarters, to sign as an apprentice grappler. He had his first contest against me in Aston and within a few weeks was topping the bills, all over the country, wowing the audiences with his agility and skills. Nobody had ever seen a man so huge, who could move as fast as a Lightweight. In 1966, Lincoln amalgamated with the legendary stars such as Prince Kumali, 'Judo' Pete Roberts, Colin Joynson, Steve Veidor et cetera, all of whom are here today, to page homage to their pal. For the next twenty-three years, we all trod the boards together, working six nights a week, visiting every Hall and venue across the length and breadth of Great Britain. Those glory-ridden, halcyon days seemed to go on forever, with regular TV appearances and so on. Of course, with the media exposure came a little fame and a certain amount of fortune.

Pat and I gelled immediately, forming an unholy alliance and bond, sharing a perverse sense of humour and fun, which endured across the globe and through the years, until his premature demise. We spoke on the phone almost daily and shared a platonic intimacy usually reserved for couples.

Another saga between us went on for twenty-five unbelievable years. I am known to be conservative with money, and asked Pat to get me some tyres for my Volvo, which I then drove in the seventies. Being in the scrap business, he not only got the tyres, but wheels as well, charging me only a hundred pounds for the lot. I gave him a cheque, reluctantly, but kept moaning about the cost. It was never banked and a few weeks later I received it back in the post. Being an 'honest injun', I thought it was a mistake and returned it to him. Well, this went backwards and forwards for the next quarter of a century, finally resting with him, when he passed away. Which reminds me that I do not want to see interest charged by the family, and whilst not being mean, should be grateful if we could now tear it up!

Every time someone sends photos from the annual wrestling meetings, I'm wearing a blue and white striped shirt. So every now and then Bill Bridges sends me a photo with a note: 'That shirt's turned up again!' What he did, nine months later, was send me another photograph of me wearing the identical shirt; I think he must hate it actually! But he also returned the money that I sent him for selling the vitamins. I've still got that money. So I'll probably give it to you to keep, Shirley. We'll buy a registered envelope, with a note inside saying: 'Gotcha!' And send it at the appropriate time, so that he can't return it! We'll put that in the third book.

Such was Pat's humour, that many of his most famous quips were reserved for the boys in the business. It was no secret that he loved his Bentley car, which he used when travelling to the shows. One evening, a wrestler passed him at the traffic lights and later, in the dressing room, knowing how mean the Promoters were with expenses, remarked to him, "That's a bit flash Pat, turning up in a Bentley; what mileage does it do?" Always quick-witted, he replied: "Sixty-five miles to the gallon mate, at least, with *my* expenses it needs to do that."

We travelled the world together; Japan, Canada, America, Europe, India and Africa, but he always wanted to return home to Blighty. When we drove across from appearing in Spain, Germany or France et cetera, no matter how choppy the sea, he would always stand on the bow of the ferry, just to see the White Cliffs appear.

The Canadians and Yanks wanted him to remain permanently in the *WWF*, and offered to make him a superstar, but he refused to leave home. In Germany, where he was Heavyweight Champion, they offered the world, but to no avail. Pretty soon, he became British Heavyweight Champion and defended the Title many times on TV, even topping the bill at the *Royal Albert Hall*, in front of the Duke of Edinburgh and Her Majesty the Queen, who was an ardent wrestling fan. His great move was the 'Brummy Bump' and such was the respect that he commanded, no other wrestler has ever tried to emulate it.

He had also been signed up for Mel Gibson's new blockbuster, *Alexander the Great*, but was sadly too ill to appear. He struggled through the last series of Pet; being forced to miss filming the *Christmas Special* in Thailand, from which his dear colleagues have flown back, especially for today.

Despite all this success, he never lost touch with reality and remained with his feet firmly on the ground. He ran a scrap yard for many years, a health studio and owned various rented properties, all expertly run by his friend and mainstay, Bernie Guest, who has organised this event today, in conjunction with his biographer, Shirley Thompson. Pat always told us that Bernie was his anchor, and the man that he trusted above all others. I should like to thank him, on behalf of all the wrestlers, for the loyalty and devotion that he always showed our friend.

Pat never gave up wrestling and in 1989, when ITV decided to cancel the contract after thirty-two memorable years, it was Big Pat who fought the last bout and closed it with a speech in the ring, thanking the folks for allowing us all into their "parlours".

Along with his humour, Pat was also known for retaining his links with all of his buddies from the wrestling world. He was an Organiser and Committee member for the *British Wrestlers Reunion Association*, along with founders Tony Scarlo, who is here today, Bob Bell, a fellow cancer sufferer, myself and Joe D'Orazio, who has contributed to the following chapter. In the twelve years since its inception, Pat never missed the annual gatherings at either the Northern or the Southern venues.

As Joe will later confirm, Pat took great pride in reading from our obituary lists, the individual names of over two hundred wrestling associates. To this list we must now sadly add his own name. In memory of his immense contribution to the wrestling fraternity, the organisers have introduced the *Pat Roach Memorial Trophy*, which will be awarded to the best young wrestler in the UK, every year. Two years ago, on the 8 August 2004, we honoured the Big Guy with a *Lifetime Achievement Award* and everlasting candle. This now takes pride of place in my public house, *The Bridges*, in Horton Kirby, to ensure that the memory of this legendary fighter will always live on.

His bravery, courage and dignity were an inspiration to us all. At the 2003 reunion, even with an obvious weight loss and his voice badly affected by his illness, he still insisted on performing his duties. Rather than harp on about his own problems, he spent time worrying about the welfare of his less fortunate former colleagues, even insisting on paying for a minibus, to bring some of them down from the North. This meant that young wrestlers could meet their heroes, like Dynamite Kid, Bert Royal, Vic Faulkner and the like.

He would regularly donate monies to the sick or infirm wrestlers, never letting them know the source.

In spite of terrible suffering and pain, over the last six years, he never told the boys, preferring to keep his distress to just his closest allies, like myself. We were all sworn to the utmost secrecy, which was very difficult when everyone could see that he was not himself. None of us here today could possibly imagine what was going through his mind, having no one to share the torture of radiotherapy, or the uncertainty of its outcome. Yet his incredible love of life and quick Brummy humour always shone through.

At the 2003 Reunion, he was enjoying a beer on the pavement, during a lull in the proceedings, obviously feeling the strain of 101 degrees of heat, when a fan walked up and said: "I saw you on TV last night Pat, in *Robin Hood, Prince of Thieves*. Didn't say much, did you?" Quick as a flash the old Roach temporarily appeared and he replied: "At five grand a word I didn't need to pal!"

Later in life, he turned his attention to writing, with his biographer, Shirley Thompson, tackling his books with the same gusto as he did his wrestling. He wasn't seeking more fame, but just wanted to let the world know, on paper, how much he loved his mother, family, beloved son and grandson; how his thirst for life had spurred him on to achieve greater things; the *Foreword* for this first book was written by Arnold Schwarzenegger. Messages were also sent by Ryan O'Neal and Harrison Ford, all paying homage to his professionalism. But it was his love of his mates from "Pet" that he treasured the most, often saying that it was they who had accepted him and taught him the skills of acting, beyond all others.

He called his first book *If*, after the Kipling poem that he loved so much. Following its success, after the Launch, he and Shirley set about writing a sequel. Yet again, he set about selling copies signed copies of *If* at the wrestling shows and Reunions. He donated a quarter of the proceeds to the Reunion itself, in order to buy wreaths and flowers for other deceased wrestlers and their families, such as the late broadcaster Kent Walton, to whom he was particularly close.

Ironically, he was too ill to see his second book *Pat Roach's Birmingham* launched. As a mark of our love for Pat, my wife, Sarah, to whom he was devoted, stepped into the breach, in her role as the *Women's British Heavyweight Champion* for 2004, to promote the launch, nationwide. With typical foresight, having realised that he would no longer be with us, he asked Shirley to attend the August 2004 and subsequent reunions in his place, signing copies of his books; helping to support the organisation, as on previous occasions.

His influence as a great ambassador for our sport was so great that he became the only wrestler from the *World of Sport* era, to be offered the role of Commissioner by the *FWA*, who are today's market leaders in TV wrestling. Pat gave tremendous moral support to young student wrestlers, from the *Dropkixx Academy*, which is run by Reunion Secretary and former wrestler, Frank Rimer, who was unable to attend today. Along with Tony Scarlo, Pat delighted in tackling all the twelve-year-old hopefuls, and would roll around with them in the ring, much to the delight of their doting parents.

Speaking of *If*, during my last ever conversation with Pat, on the phone, just hours before his passing, he asked two things of me. One was that six wrestlers would act as pallbearers of his coffin, to carry him into the church and secondly, that I would read the poem *If*. Much as I loved that man, I am only a punch-drunk old fighter, not a natural orator, as you can see by the way I am reading this tribute. So I am highly relieved that the honour will be accepted by Kevin Whately and the other professional speakers who are here today – the actors and friends that he admired so much.

Bravery was a byword to this great man, and even eighteen months ago, following a throat operation, during which his gullet was removed, and with failing eyesight, along with his voice, he still accepted a wrestling job, which most men half his age and in good health wouldn't attempt. The Promoters were spellbound by his professionalism.

Every once in a while, Ladies and Gentlemen, someone very special passes through this world. Thank God that we were all privileged to know this very special and awesome man, whom we could call friend.

I am humbled and honoured to be allowed to take up so much of your time, paying tribute to him, on behalf of both myself, my wife, and the whole wrestling fraternity. He has left a legacy to the world, far beyond his obvious talents, that if you dream enough and are dedicated enough, and have enough guts, then an ordinary boy from a plain background can achieve any goal he desires, just as Pat did.

May God keep you next to him, 'Bomber' Pat Roach, because with you there beside him, he need never worry. You have left the world a better place for being in it. Your courage, dignity, bravery, generosity and humour will live on in us forever.

No more for you the pain and suffering that you secretly endured for the last six years. Sleep in peace my friend. You have earned it. You really were a GIANT among men. A SUPERSTAR.'

The following are just a few of the many tributes received from other wrestlers:

Adrian Street and Miss Linda
Pat was a great man, and having had cancer of the throat myself, I have some idea of the suffering he went through. I am inconsolable at his passing.

Jackie Mr. TV Pallo
He was so tough that it is hard to imagine him gone. He was the backbone of wrestling.

Mick McManus
I knew the Bomber for forty years and had the highest regard for both his professionalism and for Pat as a man. I was proud to call him friend.

Spencer Churchill
Pat was the hardest man I ever met, but also the loveliest, gentlest fella in the world.

Bobby Barnes
Pat Roach was the ultimate epitome of what a man should be. We shall miss him.

Mel Stuart
I worked with the Bomber all over the world and each bout I had, taught me a little more. I liked and respected him – the ultimate Pro.

Frank Rimer – Reunion Secretary
Most of us looked up to him because of his size, but I just looked up him.

Vince McMahon – owner of the WWE
The British always were the best wrestlers in the world, and Pat Roach was the best of the best!

Tony St Clair
Man should not be measured in feet and inches, but by the size of his heart. There, Pat was a true giant.

Bill is on the far left of Sarah and Pat; Billy Barber is on the right.

This poetic tribute by Bill's wife, Sarah Bridges, says it all:

Sarah Bridges is my name
Bodybuilding was and is my game.
Now there are many strings to my bow
Because someone special showed me the way to go.

He finished up being my dearest friend
And helped me to the very end.
I once, in a picture, sat upon his knee
And he said TV and films are where I should be.

For film work he became my coach
This man, of course, was dear Pat Roach.
He took me on to many a set
Where I met the stars of Auf Wiedersehen Pet.

Film parts he did get for me
And I finished up acting with Nick Nolte.
Now whenever I'm on film or TV
I know my friend Pat is there with me.
Also when I'm training in the gym
Those soft words of wisdom I can hear from him.

Now my world is a sadder place
As no more will I see his smiling face.
I always listened to what he had to say
And I know we'll all meet again one glorious day.
Heaven's where I know Pat will be
So please continue to look down and guide me.
You left so many broken hearts behind
Because, my friend, you were one of a kind.
Thinking of you always
My love as always,
Sarah

Tony 'Banger' Walsh first met Pat around 1970: "I 'seconded' Pat, many times. He was a very approachable bloke and talked to me about Amateur Wrestling and judo. I followed him into the profession and once I got into it we became close friends, really, because there's not been many lads from the Midlands make it big on the TV – on *World of Sport*. The big Midland names in the 1970s and 80s were me and Pat. Then Jackie Turpin came along – I got him into the business. I worked in the boxing and wrestling booths with Ronnie Taylor and young Jackie Turpin: his Uncle Randolph had been in the business, years before us. Like Pat, I was also 'Man on Top', taking on punters who didn't know what it was all about."

Banger's life ran parallel with Pat's in several ways, although Tony didn't have a scrap yard. "We both came from humble beginnings, and both had businesses, in addition to our wrestling careers. We needed to, because no matter whether you were Pat Roach or 'Banger' Walsh, the only guys in the business who were making the money were the promoters and possibly Big Daddy.

"I began as an Amateur, then turned Professional. In 1974, I was the doorman at the *Maverick Club*, which was a central part of *Gangsters*. It was Klein's club. Klein was played by Maurice Colbourne. The other main lead was an Indian guy, called Ahmed Khalli, who became friends with me, my family and Pat. Pat and I did *Gangsters* together and had loads of conversations, between takes, over a cup of tea. He gave me his long suede red cloak, when he got his new one; later, Pat wore a long purple cloak, which was down to his ankles. I was wrestling then. I'd made my television debut in '74, against Bobby Graham, from *World of Sport*. Then I was on television constantly until 1985/86.

"I knew Kent Walton very well, because he'd come into the dressing room before any TV show, for any news that he could include in the show.

Kent was a good ambassador for the business; he believed in it and tried to convince the spectators to believe in it." Pat once explained to his co-writer that Kent's philosophy was "Don't just tell the viewers what they're seeing; they want as much extra detail as possible – make a real performance out of it." "He had a better saying than that," observes Tony. "Every week, he always finished on a Saturday at a quarter to four, before the football results came on, with: 'Have a good week until next week!'

"When Pat started, he worked with Alf Kent, Reg Yates and Harry Yardley: all the good old names who I knew when I started. Birmingham had a little nucleus of wrestlers, at that time. But there was only Pat who really shone out and possibly 'Lucky Gordon', (real name Billy Jordan), who also got onto television. The minute he appeared in *Auf Wiedersehen*, Pat became Bomber Roach, because it put backsides on seats. He was not such much of the villain, but a sort of 'hard-case' type. I found him a very hard guy to wrestle with, but of course, he was a lot bigger.

"At the peak of my career, I wrestled seven nights a week, doing other jobs as well. I was Big Daddy's Fall Guy, for most of my top years in the job. Giant Haystacks was my Tag Partner for a long time, along with Mark 'Roller Ball' Rocco, who was also my partner. I partnered villains, because I was a villain. My biggest claim-to-fame was probably that whenever Big Daddy was on television, then I'd be in the match – doing the stuff.

"There's no wrestler in Britain who's made money out of wrestling, apart from probably Big Daddy, because his brother was a promoter and he could pay him what he wanted. Now, whether you're Pat Roach, Giant Haystacks, whoever; Mick McManus was the same – if you speak to him. I don't think he ever made a lot of money out of wrestling. None of them did."

Banger saw Pat regularly until 1985, "…until I packed the business in. Then he fell out with me, over what I did in *The Sun*, because Pat loved the business, and he hated anybody knocking it – he had that persona. Pat said: 'I don't think you should have done it Banger.' I said: 'But Pat, you know what my reasons were. I didn't knock the profession as such: just those who were exploiting us.' I think Time was the healer. We hadn't seen each other for a long time, when *Carlton* did the *Millionaires* Show on me. He was on the bill, with Darren, although he didn't wrestle him. We had a chat and it was like old times. Once or twice he's been 'offish' with me – but that was Pat. I didn't like it, because you don't, when your friends fall out with you.

"Luckily, it healed itself. I think a lot of that's down to my lad. Pat took him under his wing and protected him. I didn't want him to go into the business, with people taking it out on him, because of what I did to the bloody hierarchy, who were *running* it. Pat also spoke to me about Mal Kirk. When Mal died in the ring with Big Daddy, he was on £25 a night. They kept it very quiet that Tony Walsh gave his wife over a thousand pounds. Pat knew, because Pat and Mal were quite close. They'd been to Germany together.

"Pat was always quiet. When I first started wrestling we travelled together quite a bit, because we were the only two from the Midlands, (before Jackie Turpin and Ringo Rigby got into the business). Pat started way before me. I'd meet him at his house in Northfield. Obviously I met his wife, and his son Mark, who was deaf and dumb."

Martini's Restaurant on the Brixton Road was a favourite lodging place. "It was six quid a night in those days. So you'd have Pat Roach, Banger Walsh, Tony St Clair, Mark Rocco, Kung Fu – (Eddie Hamill), Johnny Saint – all in rooms like dormitories, on six quid a night; that included a 'fry-up' in the morning. The owner, an Italian guy called Martini, tried to protect his daughter from the wrestlers: he was *convinced* that we were after her. I remember one particular story about Roachie, when they terrified Haystacks one night, that the place was haunted!

"We both worked for ITV, on *World of Sport.* Pat was very generous: he spent a lot of time helping Darren." Pat helped several others too; Sarah Bridges, Bill's wife being a prime example. Arnold Schwarzenegger confirms, in the *Foreword* to our first book, that Pat helped people to realise their ambitions, provided they were prepared to work hard themselves. By sheer coincidence, Tony had met Arnie in Vegas, only the week before our conversation.

Banger has some witty sayings, for example: 'Famous faces, empty bank balance.' "We would all have been the same, except for those like Pat and myself, who started their own businesses. He had the scrap yard up Queen's Head Road. Despite being the nice fella that he was," adds Banger, "Pat didn't suffer fools lightly." Tony completed a TV comedy script, *Back On Top*, with Barrie Tracey and Giant Haystacks, just before Haystacks passed away.

Tony's son, Darren Walsh, won the *Dubai Desert Classic* in 2004. He remains the current EWP World Heavyweight Wrestling Champion, having recently re-defended the title, against former *WWF* star Rick Steiner. "There's a move called a Backdrop," explains Darren, "where you bend over so that your opponent flies over the top. But Pat used the Brummagem Bump, which was side on, as opposed to a straight on move. With a normal Backdrop, when you stand up, I can push off your shoulders and get the height off it. But Pat used to come that way – and tip you over – just awkward." Banger was also on the receiving end of the move: "You cross your legs when you're up in the air; we knew what we were doing, but it was very impressive. I don't think anyone will 'nick' it, because it was his." Pete Roberts recalls: "He just used to scoop you up somehow. When you were up there and he's dropped you, there *was* no certain angle! It's the way *he* did – whatever; for a big man, he'd do it so *quickly*, the next thing you knew, you were up there!"

Darren Walsh continues: "My first job, at the age of fifteen, was with Klondyke Jake, around 1990. I'd been brought up in the wrestling world. You looked up to Pat because of his wrestling abroad and his film and television work. When I came into wrestling, because of the business with the newspaper, there was quite a bit of animosity, but a handful of the older guys, including Pat, looked after me. They pulled me to one side to avoid other guys hurting me, because I wasn't as muscular as I am now. I was a young kid of fifteen or sixteen years old."

"Darren didn't tell me what was happening, because he knew I'd probably stop him from wrestling," interjects Tony. Darren explains, "I wasn't a *great* friend of Pat's – more like an Associate. The last time I saw him was at the *Film Memorabilia Fair,* he was signing autographs at the *NEC.* We talked for maybe half an hour about the old times and about wrestling."

Darren had quite a few Tag Matches with Pat: one such match was described by both of them, in Chapter 2. "I did a lot of travelling with him," Darren continues, "because we were Midlands based; we'd meet on the M6 or the M40 if we were going down South. He'd drive me there, in a little blue Metro, and wedge a round pillow, next to his knee, to stop the door handle digging into it, when he changed gear!"

Jack Taylor has said, (present company excepted of course), that there are no longer the characters in wrestling that there were in Pat's day. Would Darren agree?

"The English wrestling industry these days is rife with young guys who have never learnt wrestling skills. The older wrestlers had done an apprenticeship and were taught *in* the job, the right way. Over recent years, *certain* people, who couldn't cope with the apprenticeship, started wrestling schools, saying that they'd teach youngsters to become wrestlers. These kids weren't really good enough to get a job on the major circuits. The only way these guys running the schools could justify taking the money was to put on local shows. So they'd book local town halls; the guys wouldn't be paid for it, because it would be part of their education. Unfortunately, more people began to jump on the bandwagon. There's lots of wrestling schools now; there's one in Coventry and two or three in Birmingham. But, in some cases, they're being taught by guys who've never worked as wrestlers."

Others *are* bona fide, for example, the *Dropkixx Academy* in Kent, which Bill Bridges mentioned earlier in this chapter. "There *are* wrestling schools where they're being taught by professional wrestlers: it's the only way to learn," Darren confirms. "But if these guys I mentioned before, put on a show in Birmingham, the audience has to watch young people who can't wrestle; understandably, the audience may not return. So we go there and only have small audiences to play to. It's killed the industry completely."

According to Jack Taylor, there's a tendency for young wrestlers to repeat the same moves, so they no longer 'tell a story' within their performance. "It's all down to psychology," Darren explains. "If the first match did everything and immediately took the crowd that high, you can only come down from that. So you would have quite different *types* of matches, to take them up to the Main Event. You have to take them back down too, so that they don't go home irate or over-excited.

"Pat was a consummate professional. A bloke of his size could always use real wrestling moves such as arm-locks, reversals, et cetera. Nowadays we have young guys doing back-flips and so on. The referee's got not control. They just hit each other with chairs. There's no 'Good Guy-Bad Guy', because they're *both* breaking rules. So unfortunately the industry has really suffered because of this."

"Pat believed in that wrestling business one hundred per cent," interjects Tony. "But I'm glad that now he's gone to his resting-place, he didn't go, thinking that he was my enemy. In the latter years when he saw Darren, he'd say: 'Oh, give your dad my best.' And for that – I'll be eternally grateful to Pat, because he left me with a clear conscience – that he was still my friend – deep down."

Tony has a wealth of wrestling stories at his fingertips: "There's a book there in itself – if you talk to all the old wrestlers – the guys who've got stories from the old days. But the Big Fella was a bit special. I don't want to patronise him – because he didn't like that – but he *was* a 'one-off' – he really was. He was also a very private person," concludes Banger.

Pete Roberts and Pat met around 1961. "I first went to *Severn Street Amateur Club*, in Birmingham, as an amateur, between 1958 – 1960, while Pat was learning judo, then touring the country with Jimmy White. Pat joined afterwards, and attended the club between 1960 – 1962. It was held on Sunday mornings. There'd be people like Gordon Corbett, John Treadwell who wrestled as Tommy Walsh, and a couple of others. There were just judo mats –no ring – no anything. We learned holds and moves.

"There was an Irish guy who turned to professional wrestling, named Jimmy 'Tiger' Ryan; certain members, myself included, looked up to him. Occasionally he would show us some holds and moves, and basically train us – as did Reg Yates, who turned professional. Reg came down on a Sunday morning, to the Pro-wrestling. His amateur background was fantastic: he went to the *Empire Games*, around 1958, and became a Middleweight Amateur Wrestling Champion. Then there was Tony Charles, who was a similar age to Pat."

Despite his wrestling title, Pete was never actually into Judo! He left Birmingham in the 1970s, moved to Worcester, but spent an increasing amount of time working away from home, so eventually moved to London and the South, working continually for *Dale Martin's*: a member of *Joint Promotions*, the company that arranged television wrestling.

"Colin Joynson was the first professional wrestler that I met. I got hooked on it. Judo Al Hayes was my favourite," explains Pete. "Mike Marino – those guys; Francis St Clair Gregory, the father of Roy and Tony St Clair. I'd watch live Professional Wrestling at Pershore Road – the Pershore Stadium, around 1958/59."

Thomas Felkin, a friend of Pat's from his Jewellery Quarter childhood, was another regular at the Pershore Stadium. Thomas recalls: "From when I was about ten, Pat used to come up the road and have a chat. I'd go down Newtown – Perry Barr with him. About half a dozen of us guys used to hang around together. Between about eighteen and twenty we'd dress up smartly and go out – to Halesowen too and Wolverhampton. We'd have fights in the road. If another gang came up, Pat would stick up for you, so they'd run away! He was a good guy. In Summer Lane there was a pub where we all used to meet, between the ages of eighteen to twenty. If there *was* any trouble, he'd get up and the guys concerned would walk out. Pat liked films: we'd visit some of the local picture houses. There was a ring inside the *MEB* Building. You'd also go to the *Waldorf* and the *Pershore Stadium* to see Mick McManus wrestling and Big Daddy."

Pete Roberts continues: "England came to a standstill didn't it, when the wrestling was on? It was the first big sport that got through like it did: programmes like Saturday afternoon's *World of Sport*, for example: it was the ten or twelve years after the War when it came out." Pete's neighbour suggested he should contact a promoter and even provided the address. Pete wrote to him, somewhat reluctantly, explaining that he'd won an Amateur Championship. "I started Professional Wrestling in 1961, with *Wyton Promotions*; they were Manchester based, but did all the shows around the Midlands – Wolverhampton and all those places. I also worked for Lew Phillips." Like Pat, "We all had a soft spot for Lew," observes Pete. "He was good to you and had done it himself, so he had our respect.

"Fame wasn't really that important to me. What it really meant was extra money. I've never consciously thought: 'Right, I'm going on television and I'm going to become a big star.' For years I didn't tape or watch any of it." Pete wrestled Pat many times. He was particularly skilful, so Pat's strength and Pete's skill produced a fairly even balance. "I could hold him off for a while, but then, a good big one will always beat a good little one! He'd wear you down. Pat was very serious with his wrestling. *Whatever* he decided to do, he was quite serious and dedicated about it, and would do it to the best of his ability. You didn't *know* one another's moves, because you both had so many. Our matches were hard because we were always trying to out-do one another. They were entertaining for us – we didn't bother about the other people!

"Southampton and the *Albert Hall* come particularly to mind, because Pat phoned and asked, 'Do you want to go to Southampton mate?' – whereas normally he'd go on his own. As you've probably found out, he was always coming from somewhere or going to somewhere – or doing something." (Never stopping actually Pete – I think he was in perpetual motion!) "There was all kinds of entertainment, if you wanted to be bothered. There are girls that follow any form of entertainer– and fellas too. In the 1970s there was a big 'gay' community that followed wrestling; so it was either way.

"I bumped into Pat one time, when we were wrestling in Croydon. He had the scruffiest pair of jeans on, old boots and an old woollen hat, with his beard. I mean, he was a fearsome sight anyway. Six foot four – and he would have something like a five-thousand-pound bracelet around his wrist! That was Pat – he was eccentric.

"There were a couple of brothers: Seamus Dunleavy – he was as strong as an ox – and Michael. Both brothers became Professional wrestlers: Michael wrestled as a Light Heavyweight and Seamus, as a Heavyweight." Michael now has a large house over in Ireland. Seamus and the co-writer have recently launched Seamus' own biography, *Finally Meeting Princess Maud*. It is a highly entertaining book, and is selling extremely well.

Pete Roberts has known Seamus for as long as he's known Pat. "The Dunleavy brothers were into everything and rented out loads of property. Gordon Corbett worked in a factory that made pots and pans, which they were always running out of, in the Dunleavy's 'lets'; they had houses all over Sparkbrook, back in the late 50s and 60s. Some of the Irish tenants would come back drunk; kick the door down. I was, and still am, a carpenter.

That's how we enticed the Dunleavy brothers down to train us! They'd have a load of pots and pans off Gordon and perhaps half a dozen locks off me. Thinking about it, *they* prepared us for professional wrestling as much as anybody. Mike and Seamus were stars, who us guys used to look up to. To get then to come down to show us moves was a really big deal! They were television stars, back in the late 1950s/early 60s, having formed a Tag Team together, and were featured regularly on *World of Sport*.

"Seamus was the 'Shooter' of the two," continues Pete. "'Shooter' is a term for wrestlers who have a good amateur background. He came from a gym in Wigan, which taught Submission Wrestling. He learned how to wrestle there and was *very* good."

Seamus arrived in Liverpool aged seventeen, having left Charlestown, County Mayo, on Ireland's West Coast, with a burning ambition to be a boxer: "I was going to make a lot of money, win big fights, and look after me parents very well." He started boxing three nights a week, at *Duffy's Boxing Club*, in Litherland. *The Pegasus Wrestling Club*, held on different nights, was in the same building. Being stocky, Seamus would fight lads who were much taller. "So I always had a 'straight-left' in my face, which wasn't very good. I wasn't a very good boxer. I would always grab people and lift them up in the air!"

So he switched to *The Pegasus Wrestling Club*, and learned the art of Amateur Wrestling. As subsequent runner-up in the *Northern Counties Championships*, Seamus was selected to enter the *All England Championships*, which included Commonwealth wrestlers too, at the vast *Empress Hall* in London. Despite being defeated in the Finals, by the reigning champion, Harry Kendal, a deaf-mute, thus terminating his chances for an English title, Seamus maintained a very successful wrestling career, for several years.

"The *English Championships* were absolutely brilliant; there were wrestlers from all over the country. I had great admiration for Ken Richmond, who was the Heavyweight Champion of England, for perhaps five or six years: the man who used to strike the gong for the Rank Organisation." Seamus also met one of his childhood heroes, Georges Hackenschmidt, the famous Russian champion. "Georges was a very old man when I met him, but he was one of the 'Greats'.

"In Submission Wrestling, you kept going until your opponent had had enough. It was totally different from normal wrestling. You couldn't use it in a 'Pro' game. I enjoyed it and we had some good times. Most northern wrestlers either come from Wigan in Lancashire or Bradford in Yorkshire. When I was very young, maybe twenty, I was wrestling on bombsites, in Wigan. There'd be about half a dozen of us from Lancashire, wrestling fellas from Yorkshire: a bit like the Wars of the Roses! There'd be 'side-betting' on it. They'd take me along, like. There'd be about fifty wrestlers there and we'd see who was the best. There was *terrific* rivalry.

"There was a move called 'The Hook-in'. Once they'd got that hold on you, that 'Half Nelson', you were beat – you couldn't move. They had one of your legs trapped too. They put this grip on me and all of a sudden, I stood up, with a wrestler on my back! They said: 'We have never ever seen that happen before!' The word went round: 'Seamus Dunleavy got up with the Hook-in on.' 'No – he didn't!' "

They took him to a bombsite, where he wrestled a coal-miner from Bradford. "There was a bet on of between seventy to a hundred quid. My opponent said: 'Is that the strong Irish fella who gets up with the Hook on?' They said: 'Yes.' He said: 'Bloody Hell – you should have told us!' Anyway, I beat the fella that day and got a few quid for us.

"When I married Mary Griffin, in 1962, we'd eight houses in Sparkhill." At the age of twenty-seven, that was a considerable achievement! Seamus was doorman at the *Shamrock Club* in Hurst Street for ten years, eventually owning five clubs of his own, over a ten-to-twelve-year period. These included *"The Talk of the Town*, on the Stratford Road, Sparkbrook – a 'stone's throw from Pat and George's illegal club – *The Oyster Bar*. Pat's club, described in detail, in *Pat Roach's Birmingham* was much rougher that Seamus', with crates of beer stacked up and a clientele of mainly Dubliners, just standing around drinking.

Seamus' other clubs were *The Liffey*, in Navigation Street, catering *totally* for Birmingham's large nucleus of Dubliners; the *Peter Rabbit* in Broad Street, a successful Strip Club; *The Jigsaw*, at Alum Rock, which was a very busy club; the fifth was *The Speak-Easy* in Stratford Place. "That was a small little place. It was two shops knocked together. It was open, round the clock." He bought his first club in the early 1960s but had sold all five by the early 1970s. "We got so busy with the properties during the 1970s and I didn't want the kids involved with the clubs. Mary hated the clubs all of her life – she detested them." Seamus stopped wrestling when he was thirty-five, except for the odd match now and again.

Pat and Seamus first met at a Handsworth Gym on the Soho Road. "Gordon Corbett used to come with me; he was the mainstay for getting me out there. Pat and I got to be friends and mates. He was bloody huge, wasn't he? There was a hold called 'The Figure of Four', where you've hooked a man and you can turn and lift him up on your shoulder. But not Pat Roach – none of us could shift him! I was very strong then – but I couldn't pick Pat up.

"Pat was always 'quietish'. In our game, in the dance halls, you get involved in lots of fights, but I never heard of Pat being involved in any fights, except a bit of business. This applied with the Fewtrells' clubs too; we all knew, around the town, who the troublemakers were; there was a nucleus of villains. You'd want a squad of lads with you, to see that they didn't get 'out of hand', or to stop them at the door. But I've never heard Pat's name linked with anything like that: although he'd got the size and the weight, if he'd wanted to. I found him 'sound as a bell' Shirley. I couldn't say a bad word about Pat."

Seamus' brother, Mickey, was the first man to teach Pat to do the 'Roll-up' "Pat couldn't do it at first, but Mickey spent time showing him; it's a throw, where you end up on your feet. Pat was very flexible from the judo. At the time we didn't recognise judo, so I didn't know much about Pat's involvement with that until later."

Seamus would also meet Pat around the various clubs, such as the *Cedar Club,* the *Rum Runner* and *Barbarella's*. "We'd sit together, chatting. I was well known at the time, to the wrestling and so was he." According to Seamus, from a technical point of view, Pat was an even better boxer than he was a wrestler. "I saw him box a few times and thought that he should have given it a good go. But obviously, his heart wasn't in it." He decided that it was a bit too dangerous; also, once he got into films, he didn't want to disfigure his face. "Yes," agrees Seamus, "because you get Heavyweights with a punch that could knock an ox down!"

Pete Evans, the original 'Balsall Heath Basher', was a good friend of Pat's. "Pete was– a very good wrestler – a very hard lad," Seamus explains. "He worked with myself on the doors for years and wrestled all over the West Midlands. We taught him from Day One. A great man to have beside you. He was a good Light Heavyweight – about thirteen stone." He was called the Balsall Heath Basher because part of Ombersley Road, where he lived, is in Sparkbrook, and the other part is in Balsall Heath. Pat also knew him through the scrap business. He still has a wagon – he's still going. Peter was sixty-two, a few months back.

"This is one of the embarrassing things that I've got to say, but it can be authenticated. I wrestled Pat in Brierley Hill, on a Jack Hatherton Promotion (somewhere in the early 1960s). I beat him, two falls to one, but he wasn't long in the wrestling game. I had shown him most of his moves, so it was only fitting that I should have beaten him. It was a few years after we were in the amateur gym, over in Handsworth. So we wrestled just the once in a match and I won. And Pat, if he were here, would tell you that too. I wished to God that I'd kept the Bill!

"After that, I was very busy with the houses and the clubs and Pat was coming in strong. He became very good, and went abroad. So had we met a few years on, the tale might have been different. But anyway, a win is a win Shirley!" Pat used to half-joke about the fact that, although he won the majority of his matches, photographers preferred a shot of him in the losing position. But at least one photo in this book redresses the balance!

It's interesting how many successful sportsmen have become entrepreneurs. "Many of them have that sort of a mind," comments Pete Roberts. "I tried it and hated it. Wayne Bridges tried to show me how to run a pub. I was a longtime friend of Bill's, before I moved down – from the early 1970s. He's always been one of those people who will help you; as you know, there are a lot of people who aren't like that. But he's the same as Pat: he's always got his head down – doing something."

"Pat was probably the first of the really agile Heavyweights – a Super Heavyweight, who wrestled like a Middleweight," Pete explains. "He did all those moves; people in this country had never seen that done before, by a guy of almost six foot five and nineteen stone. In the States, they bred that sort of athlete later on. In England, Pat was probably the first of the really big *agile* guys, who had the speed of people several weights lighter than themselves. That's what made him a Star. He shot up really quickly; he passed all of us."

Chapter Eleven

'STAGE' AND THE
FINAL REUNION

We all had nicknames for each other. Pat used to call me 'Gas', which stood for Gas Meter – Peter – rhyming slang. I always called him 'Stage', which is 'Stage Coach' – Roach! Whenever we met, he always used to say: "How's things Gas?" And I'd say: "OK Stage." That's how we used to talk to one another. I think it was Johnny Kowalski who first nicknamed him 'Stage', but always, from an early stage, he called me 'Gas'.

'Judo' Pete Roberts

Pat's previous two books contain detailed chapters about his foreign sports career. This chapter includes some of the stories that 'got away'! But before we head for foreign parts, it's worth taking a few more pages, to take a closer look at the quintessential Pat. For nine years, as Pat's Personal Assistant, Rob Knight not only ran the Erdington Gym, but became one of his closest and most supportive friends, during his final days. Pat trusted him implicitly to manage the gym, plus other business interests, in his absence. The two men first met, for an interview, on the 25 March 1996.

"He greeted me with a hearty handshake, pulling himself up to his full height, and looking me straight in the eye – and I tried to do the same," Rob remembers. "After an interview that probably lasted half an hour, he said he was confident that he'd found the right person. I started the following Monday, the 4 April, but it wasn't until a week after that that we actually opened. The gym did fairly well, but although Pat was always very optimistic, it never really came to any kind of fruition, as a business.

"From the very beginning, he made it clear to me that his involvement in it would be very minimal. He was aware of how foreboding his presence could be to some people, so he made a point of being very sociable, so that they felt welcome and relaxed. The Bond Machine was already there when I arrived.

"My first impression of Pat was that he was very down-to-earth; there didn't seem to be any airs and graces about him. He was very forthright, open and friendly. Everything was very laid-back and informal. The situation from the very beginning was very much a partnership. As we've mentioned before, that was one of Pat's skills: he always made people feel that they were on an equal level with him. He gave people a chance to show how good they were, so that he could judge, very quickly, how useful they would be to him.

"The two of us had a meeting with a Birmingham City Council official, who was supposed to advise us about making successful applications for grants. So Pat was quite keen to meet him and explore the possibilities, but this chap was very dismissive. After ten or fifteen minutes of listening to his negative comments, Pat leant forward, looked him straight in the eye, and said: 'Have you ever been body-slammed? Because I'd really like to you show you what it's like to be dropped from nine feet! I've got a marquee out the back, with a wrestling ring set up.' Needless-to-say, the meeting ended quite soon afterwards! You could see that Pat had lost all patience with him, but he didn't loose his cool. That was Pat, down to a 'T'. How to take charge of a situation. Not being affected in any way, but putting his foot down firmly, 'That's enough of that!'

"Working with Pat was a very relaxed situation. He trusted me a great deal and allowed me an awful lot of freedom, to express myself, if you like; to put my own stamp upon the Fitness Centre." Whilst Rob was dealing with a telephone inquiry from a prospective lady client, Pat bellowed down from the floor above, not realising that he was on the phone. "The lady on the phone could hear Pat very clearly – and asked who it was!

"There seemed to be a very common bond between us generally. We would talk for hours about fitness and the body and things like that. I think there was a lot of mutual respect and trust. He realised, over a long period of time, that I had a lot of respect for him and a willingness to work, under my own initiative, without expecting a lot in return.

"He was always telling me about how impressive his City Centre club had been, and how terrible it had been that it had to close, and that he'd 'needed somebody to love it'. He told me on many occasions that he wished he'd known me at the time, because that would have been ideal. There were many times when Pat was relieved that the Fitness Centre was one business that he didn't have to worry about, as he had other business problems, which were very stressful. He also trusted me to take good care of the flats and properties that he took on, at a later date.

"Inevitably, when we were out and about in public, people would recognise Pat. They'd come up and want to shake his hand, or ask for his autograph. He was always friendly and made them feel very welcome. He allowed them as long as they wanted to talk," Rob concludes.

Pete Roberts explains that although most of his memories of Pat relate to tournaments or being on tour together, "I've known him all that time, and I always felt I was quite close to him. Even after five years or so of not seeing him we could just pick up our friendship again." Pat inspired that kind of feeling, because he was so warmhearted, and had a special talent for drawing people close to him.

Tony Green and Pat used to run a few laps around Edgbaston Reservoir, and train in a gym over Tony's business premises. "When he gave up the premises in Town, around 1990 it suited both of us to do it here." The two friends also participated in a ten-mile *Fun Run* – "which proved to be hard work for me," recalls Tony, "because I'd played Rugby, the afternoon before. The final run into Birmingham was great: I left Pat for about half a mile. We were all given our times and a medal." The event started at Perry Barr Stadium and finished at Birmingham Town Hall.

"Pat would never let you in on exactly what was going to happen," Tony continues. "I changed into my 'whites', at his request, and put a towel over my arm. He said, 'Be outside the dressing room in twenty minutes,' so I stood there, waiting. Then I had a ten-feet-high flag pushed into my hand, and walked out to the ring with him. He was wearing an elaborate purple dressing gown, which I had to take off him. I moved out of the way and tried to find a home for this Union Jack: various people suggested where I should shove it! By the time I'd parked the flag it was the end of the round and I was mopping his brow, with a bucket in my hand. It lasted four or five rounds."

Pat won that championship, against a Nottingham opponent. "I had to jump in the ring with the Lonsdale Belt," continues Tony. "Pat whispered, 'Show it to the crowd.' I had to walk around the ring, holding his arm in the air, feeling generally embarrassed about the whole thing! That was part of being a friend of Pat's: you never knew what was coming next! I also saw him wrestle at *Hyde Town Hall* and Stratford-on-Avon, where he wrestled a Russian guy, who came rushing out, before the bell. I got stuck, in the corner, between him and Pat. He was raining blows down on us and I was ducking, trying to get out of the way!

"I was at *Wembley Conference Centre* with him. They started off with about twenty wrestlers, all in the ring together, and they had to reduce it to two. I sat on a corner chair, but a Second said: 'I'd move if I were you.' The next thing I knew, Haystacks would have ended up on top of me! Pat was well respected by the rest of the wrestling fraternity. I was introduced to the guys, and they accepted me as a friend of his."

Bernard Guest recalls one particular *Annual Wrestlers' Meeting*, hosted as usual, by Bill Bridges. Unbeknown to Bernard, Pat had already told everyone that he was Kendo Nagasaki. "I'm sitting at a table. They were doing a raffle with these paintings. This fella comes over to me and says, 'Can you tell me something? Why don't you ever take your mask off?' I thought: 'He's heading for a smack' – (do you know what I mean?) "This is my normal face!" Then Pat came over, laughing. I won second prize in the raffle. Pat said, 'The man's won it. You know who the man is, don't you?!' (There was tremendous applause and cheering)."

Pat also invited Bernard to the *Special Olympics* at Kirby; he wore his tracksuit for the occasion. "Until that time, I never realised how famous he was, because to me he's always been Pat. I've never bothered with the other side. We walked through this stadium entrance, into the ground itself, and the crowd were all yelling and shouting for him. There were five mayors there and civic dignitaries."

Pat met Ron Gray round about 1963, at a gym previously mentioned in Chapter 6, *The Bull's Head*, in West Bromwich. Ron recalls. "Pat would come and spar with me. He was a bit 'dirty' – always hitting you low, when he could. He wasn't like me – a gentleman!" Nick Owen presented a special 30th Anniversary television feature on Ron, in 2004, celebrating his thirtieth year as a Promoter. His two sons, Steven and Jason, are also involved in the business. "Nick was the first person to interview me, when he was with *Radio Birmingham*, (or *Radio West Midlands*), in 1974; when I'd taken my first show on, at the *Civic Hall*, Wolverhampton." Another good friend of Pat's, Billy Sutton, also worked with Nick, who was his producer, when Billy presented a Saturday morning *Little League Football* programme, from Pebble Mill.

Recalling the Jack Solomons Competition, Ron explains: "Pat was an amateur boxer at the time, but he hadn't done any for ages, because he was concentrating a hundred per cent upon wrestling. He'd got no kit; the competition was at the *Grosvenor Hotel* in London. He borrowed my gear to go down, saying: 'I'm not going to turn professional or anything, even if I win it.' I was twenty-one then, so he'd be about twenty-six. He had my dressing gown too. I said: 'If something disastrous happens and Pat gets knocked out, they'll think it's Ron Gray lying on the floor!' Pat did very well: he got to the semi-final."

Ron married in 1963 and his wife, Sylvia, bought a café in Winson Green, called *Bob's Café*. "Pat came in the café occasionally – at the time he'd already got a scrapyard. When Ronnie Williams opened the *Tow Rope* in Broad Street, I'd see Pat down there a lot. I also had three ice-cream vans. We kept them at Robert Road in Handsworth. Pat always wanted to know if I'd got any broken cornets! I could never get him to buy an ice cream. I said: 'Do you remember when I gave you that ice-cream? Well, you ought to give me a car!'

"We arranged to meet at the *Minerva Centre*, for a training session, a week in advance. In the meantime it had snowed – probably a couple of inches. The main road soon cleared, but it was still treacherous. I said: 'Pat we can't do this.' He said: 'Come along, we can do the roadwork.' So he took me to this sixteen-storey block of flats in Nechells. We must have run up and down all sixteen storeys, about twenty times! I think it was harder than the five-mile run. To make it harder I said: 'Pat, get on me shoulders.' But I was always good coming down!"

Ron boxed for eleven years, retired at the age of twenty-seven, then became a Midlands Promoter. After five or six years, Mickey Duff invited Ron to work for him at Wembley, the *Café Royal*, the *Albert Hall*, and the *Grosvenor Hotel* in London. "Fantastic venues! When Jack Solomons died, Mickey took over and became England's top Promoter. He put more World Titles on than anybody. I became his main Matchmaker – on the Frank Bruno - Witherspoon World Title Fight at Wembley, in 1987; Alan Minter and Tony Simpson, for the European Title at Wembley and for Lloyd Honeyghan the World Welterweight Champion. As well as London fights, we did shows in Wales and Scotland and internationally: we staged fights in Spain – in Marbella." Ron also managed Pat Cowdell, the former British and European Featherweight Champion.

"If ever Pat or I had any problems, and there was something we could do for each other, we were only a phone call away; that's how we've always been. Although we weren't in each other's pockets, when we saw each other, we carried on as if we'd seen each other two nights earlier." Steve Gray, Ron's son, met Pat for the first time at the *2003 Summer Ball* for their company, *Gray's Promotions*: "He came over as a very genuine and warm person. I could see the rapport, between dad and himself, and felt very relaxed in his company. He was fun to be with." But Ron remarked to Steve: 'There's something wrong with him.' "I looked at him a couple of times and I could see a certain expression in his eyes. I said to Steven: 'If you'd known Pat, twenty years ago, you'd have really seen what I mean.' It wasn't until a few weeks ago, that someone told me. I phoned Pat straight away and said: 'Is there anything that I can do?' But he didn't really want to talk about it. That made it worse really, because you can't do anything really then, can you?" Pat attended a promotion for Ron, in the early part of 2004, at the *Holly Bush Garden Centre*, in Cannock. "He made a personal appearance and he went down ever so well there. It's one of the biggest Garden Centres around. They thought he was great."

Ace Allcard was wrestling in Stirling, during the late 1960s. An Edinburgh newspaper subsequently reported: 'Ron Allcard was the only one who won on the night, at the *El Dorado*.' "Based on that, and the fact that they described me as an 'Ace Performer', the promoter, Max Crabtree, said: 'Ace Allcard eh?' And that's stuck with me ever since."

After retiring from wrestling, Ace became an Electronics Engineer. He was also a part-time Theatrical Agent in the 60s, for acts such as *Yes, The Searchers*, Joe Cocker, Dave Berry, and *The Fortunes. You've Got Your Troubles, I've Got Mine* was a big hit for them. They found fame on *Opportunity Knocks*, with Hughie Greene.

His friendship with Pat goes back over forty years. "Pat was a very honest person and would never try to mislead you. He was always there to talk to you, if you'd got any problems – he'd help you look for solutions, and give you his own personal telephone number. He had that number, right from the 1970s, and used to carry a battery around that was almost as big as a small suitcase, calling it his portable phone!

"I'm a friend of longstanding, and being a Virgo, we don't like criticism. The only thing I didn't like about Pat was that if I was wrong, he'd give me a lecture about it, and he'd often go below the belt – he was very capable of 'dishing it out' to you. Because he was a friend you see, I took it very seriously. It was almost like your dad telling you off. He could be quite cutting. I'm a sensitive person, so I'd think: 'How could he say that to me?' But the next day he'd apologise. It wasn't until Pat left this planet that I realised how successful and knowledgeable he'd been in other areas. When I was trying to raise money for one of my ventures, he was very supportive. I never knew or cared about Pat's wealth, because I never saw Pat as a wealthy person anyway. His Rolls Royce was an old one – like the car he drove. He wore scruffy old clothes. When we went out to a restaurant, he'd have a sandwich, rather than a dinner. There were many things that led you to believe that he wasn't wealthy. He often used to say: 'It depends upon what it costs Ace.'" In *Pat Roach's Birmingham*, we reveal how his early background produced this entrenched attitude to money.

"Pat always seemed to have money on him. I did a big job for him, on his boat. He'd be looking all over his pockets and finding two hundred quid

– in bits and bobs, rather than in a big wad of money! But it wouldn't have made a scrap of difference to me either way – because I am what I am. We used to have some laughs; I've had that man in stitches! He used to ring me up about his barge." In 1988 Ace offered him £8,000 for it. A short while later, Pat phoned: "Have you got any pumping equipment? Because the barge is sinking!" When Ace mentioned this to one of Pat's friends, he was told: "Oh, it's been down there *many* times!"

*   *   *   *   *

"We wrestled in a lot of tournaments abroad – Kowalski, myself... I was in Germany with Johnny Kincaid in Berlin – in *that* tournament," continues Pete Roberts. "They were going to fire Johnny, but Pat stood up for him."

The following Table of Events, is the revised edition of an earlier chart, published in *Pat Roach's Birmingham*, to provide an overview of Pat's foreign tours. The co-writers apologise in advance, for any omissions. Countries are listed alphabetically, rather than in chronological order:

Pat's wrestling tours abroad:

Country/Continent	Approximate Date	Wrestling/other Companions
Africa (South)		Pat defeated in South Africa. Toured Cape Town, Durban, Johannesburg and Pretoria; became good friends – Willie Grové (Groovay) and family.
America/Canada	Los Angeles 1971 & 1974/75	Wayne already in Canada on a different circuit. Pat touring alone.
Austria	c. 1965	Billy Sutton
Germany	1970s 1976 – Cup in Hanover	Pete Roberts, Johnny Kincaid, Killer Kowalski, Johnny Lees & Ace Allcard
India	early 1970s	Wrestled Singh brothers: Dara & Randhawa
Italy (Venice)	1970s	Tony Walsh, Yasi Fuji, Ian Muir, John England, Chris Adams, John Cortez & Jackie Turpin
Japan	1971 & 1975	Killer Kowalski, Wayne Bridges & Pete Roberts

Whether at home or abroad, Pat always had schemes 'on the go'. "Half the time you'd be thinking: 'Oh Christ – here he goes again!' – (some scatterbrained thing). He was always up to something, and *very* versatile, whereas I wasn't," continues Pete. "I wasted a lot of time in my life, just doing wrestling. Pat, on the other hand, *used* his time."

Ace wrestled with Pat, in Germany and all over Europe, but not in South Africa. He never wrestled Pat for an English show. 1976 was the first occasion when he accompanied Pat to Hanover. "I'd known Pat for a number of years, since that first meeting with Lew Phillips. Pat told me that the German Tournaments were where the real money could be made. They began around June, starting off in Bochum. He said: 'I know the promoter and I might be able to get you in there.' Which meant, in simple terms that he would be my introduction – and the promoter took me on."

During a typical Hanover wrestling tour, there would be a set route. "It would begin in Bochum, usually in a large marquee, as opposed to a proper building. The one at Bochum would last about three days. The next stage was at Bielefeld, a British Military Base, near Dortmund, and lasted three days We moved on from there to Hanover, which was the longest part of the tour, lasting forty-six days."

Ace confirmed that Pat won the Cup, twice, at Hanover. "From there we moved on to Siegen and stayed there for three or four days. The wrestling at Siegen was held in a hall, whereas the previous three were in marquees; it was halls for all those that followed. At Kiel it was held in the Osteseehalle – the East View Hall, or something like that."

From there they moved to Braunsweig – (Brunswick in English). It was like the Town Hall – the Rathaus, in Brunswick – a three-day event, from Friday to Sunday. "Then the seventh and final destination was the Phillipshalle in Dusseldorf. That was a 10,000-seater. They closed half of the stadium, reducing it to five thousand by using an automatic door system."

Ace remembers travelling to Germany in Pat's Rolls Royce. Somebody scratched the car; there was a big line down it, which looked as if it had been made with a file. "They did it all over the boot and the side doors – about £3,000 worth of damage. He never lost his temper, he just said: 'Well, this is what people do, when they see this sort of car.' He just had it re-sprayed, and that was it."

Pat would sometimes fly home, before the end of the tour. "There were three or four promoters who he worked for," Ace remembers. "Pat would come back, probably to do a Guest Visit for Otto Vance, or Eugene Wiesberger, Georges Blemenshutz in Vienna, or Niklaus Selenkowitz. He was with all the top people at that time. Pat was the best Heavyweight *ever* to come out of this country."

According to Bill Bridges, Pat was the highest paid wrestler *ever*, in Germany. Ace recalls: "The Germans used to fly in other big names than Pat, from overseas; from America, Japan and so forth. We'd be back home by Christmas. Sometimes Pat would decide to go to Vienna, to work for Georges Blemenshutz.

"Don Leo Jonathan had told Pat, in an earlier meeting in the States, that one of the best 'ribs' they could play was the 'Sister Gag'. So they played one on me. The idea was that I would be training in the gym, with a person who was a lot bigger than myself. Eventually I'd be asking a very poignant question about the guy's sister, although in my mind, it wouldn't be poignant at all."

Ace had already been 'fed' false information, that the sister was just a normal person. "But the outcome was that the big guy would have me by the throat, up against a gymnasium wall, in a rage, saying: 'How dare you!' – leaving me wondering what I'd said wrong. The following day, Pat said that I should be careful what I asked people. All I'd done was to ask a wrestler named Bob Ufo De la Sierra, if I could look at some photos of his sister, dancing 'A-Go-go', (which I'd been asked to look at, by Colin Joynson). Colin had mentioned that Bob's sister was a 'Go-go' dancer. I was told later by a friend that this sister had actually been very badly mutilated, had lost the use of both legs, was paralysed and in a wheelchair! It was all fabrication, but nevertheless, they kept it going for another week."

Ace felt dreadful: "I'd either have to commit suicide or leave!" His first wife, Carol, was due to visit him, at any moment. "I was so upset about what I'd allegedly said, I decided that when she *did* arrive, I would ask her to go back to England, as I'd heard that Bob De La Sierra was resigning from the tournament – because of what I'd said. He was the biggest name, and I was just an ordinary wrestler! So I eventually went to Bob and told him that I was about to leave and that if he wanted to fight me on the street, he could do, because I couldn't put up with any more. He said: 'Hey Ace – this is just a big 'wind up' Man!' It was a well executed trick – and Pat had organised the whole thing! He had a very clever way of getting everyone involved. I'm sure even the janitor of the halls would have been included!"

Ace and Pat had planned a trip to Germany, for 2002 but postponed it, until September 2003. "We were going to be using Bernard Guest's Winnebago Camper Van." Bernard explains that this original plan had to be aborted, because Pat was too ill to travel. Ace hadn't realised that Pat's condition had worsened considerably: "I thought that he was going to make a dramatic recovery.

"Four years ago, in 2001, I'd asked him to be the godfather to our child, Roisin, which he'd agreed to do. He then told me at the Wrestling Meeting in 2002, that unfortunately he was unable to keep his promise. We were outside the Bridges Pub, in Horton Kirby. I couldn't believe it. A good friend of mine and Pat's, Jean Tranter, remembers my face turning ashen-white!"

In September 2003, Pat had recovered sufficiently to accompany Ace, by ferry, from Harwich to the Hook of Holland, arriving there about 5pm. Then they set off for Hanover – getting lost several times on the way. "We eventually arrived at the Schutenplatze in Hanover at about 11.45 at night. The bar was still open but it was an unbelievably small hall! We hadn't been there since about 1984. The problem wasn't simply finding the hall. No, the first problem was that we couldn't find Hanover!

"Pat said, 'Every time I see you Ace you're asleep.' We took it in turns to drive. Pat was very determined to share all duties." During Pat's final visit to Germany, in 2004, Bernard Guest was obliged to be the sole driver, because Pat had reached a stage where he was totally incapable of assisting. But that story must wait... until Chapter 18.

Ace and Pat met Peter William, (the man who had invited Pat to go over there), whilst they were in Hanover. Ace recalls Pat's disappointment: "I think Pat expected Peter to give us more of his time, but Peter was very busy. We met Tony St Clair there too, who was the promoter; he ran the show with Iggi Steinbeck. It was the *Glide Wrestling Festival*."

Pat's good friend Killer Kowalski, aka John Hayles, is featured in Pat's previous two books, and was one of the principal speakers at the Launch of *Pat Roach's Birmingham*.

John recalls: "During our many visits to Hamburg, we would often go to one of the many jazz clubs after the wrestling. These were free entry, but the drinks were exorbitant prices. So we told them we would just have water, which we would then ditch and drink the vodka, which we would take in, in a couple of small bottles. We had told them that, being athletes, we couldn't drink alcohol. It always worked! For me, trips abroad were always great when in the company of the likes of Pat, Pete Roberts, John Kincaid et cetera."

According to Tony Walsh: "Italy was a great trip. The only thing that spoiled it was that one of the other wrestlers tried to pull an Italian bird in this nightclub and they were all devout Catholics. It was a local area and we had to get him out of the club pretty quickly! I've got some nice pictures of Pat in Venice. We did a couple of shows there. There was myself, the late Chris Adams and Ian 'Bully Boy' Muir. The Japanese guy, Yasi Fuji: a big Japanese guy – he came over here to wrestle. John England and John Cortez were also there and Jackie Turpin. We had loads of conversations, basically about business. At the time I was trying to start a business, whereas Pat had already had several."

Other wrestling companions, such as Killer, Pete, and Bill Bridges, have explained how they never tired of Pat's company, when they were abroad. Tony agrees: "People like Pat are like Hans Christian Andersen, because they've always got a tale to tell. But that's what's missing from wrestling today – the characters – Ricky Starr – the Ballet Dancer, Billy Two Rivers. My son is the best wrestler in this country at the moment. You can talk to any wrestling enthusiast. He's now thirty and he's had a good career already. He's been in Dubai, won the World Title in Germany – he's just defended it. He's got it all going for him. He earns good money. He goes abroad for thousands – not like the Big Fella and me."

Wayne Bridges recalls: "On one occasion, while touring in Japan, we were accosted by the statutory suit vendors. Pat ordered plain blue serge. I noticed that the samples included a cloth containing twelve different coloured stripes, such as purple, yellow and red – all a quarter-inch wide, just like a technicolour rainbow. Having ordered my own outfit, I informed the tailor that Mr. Roach was so impressed with this material, that he wanted to change his order to the multi-colour. I shall leave to your imagination, the range of expletives he used when they delivered his new three-piece! He never forgave me for that joke and even on his deathbed mentioned it, when I rang to inquire how he was feeling."

On page 160 of *Pat Roach's Birmingham*, we describe a 'pack of cards and press-ups' routine, which Pat used to great effect in Japan. Pat thought that Pete Roberts was the originator of the routine, but Pete explained more recently, that although he introduced the card routine, his friend, Karl Gotch invented it: "As far as I know, but he may have got it from someone else! We all get things from somebody, don't we?" Killer, aka John Hayles, used to visit the Jazz Clubs with Pat. "I wasn't into jazz," explains Pete. "Those two spent a *lot* of time travelling together; they went to Japan and India together." Seamus Dunleavy points out that Pat would have met the top Indian officials when he was wrestling in India. His rather dramatic tournaments there, with Dara and Randhawa Singh are described in previous books.

Timmy Spall and Chris Fairbank have previously discussed the problems of being in the public eye. Tim makes the point that quite often, people feel as if they own you, because they see you on their TV screens. You become the centre of attention. Did Pete find that?

"Yes, I did – and they were quite personal at times," Pete recalls. "I very rarely drank in the bar, because people thought that because they'd paid to see you, they owned you – and they want to know your life story! Really, I suppose, I was an introvert, doing an extrovert's job, and I found it quite difficult, for a long time – to be honest. I was happy in the ring, but not very happy with the other stuff that surrounds it.

"Pat and I would bump into one another, particularly at tournaments, but the nature of the business was that everybody went their separate ways. Johnny Kincaid I know very well.

"I retired in 1993, after returning from Japan. When I came back for the nineteenth time I thought: 'This is it.' My body was tired and I thought, 'It's time to pack up'.

"I was a Grande Prix Television Champion. I was always wrestling the champions. Apart from the Grande Prix, I was the one always knocking at the door. I was in the final in Hamburg, but came sixth. So I never quite figured out how it all worked!

"I never took any of it too seriously. My friend Karl Gotch came to my house years ago. (Bill Bridges will tell you this). There's a Japanese wrestler called Sammy Lee, who came to this country, from Florida. He stayed with me for the first two weeks, when he came to London – and then with Bill. I was the one who brought him over from Florida. His real name was Setora Siema. I went from Tokyo, Japan, to Tampa in Florida, where I spent a week with Karl. Setora was already at Karl's place – and he was coming back with me."

Val and Brian Hastings recall Pat's German tours. "It was the time when they would buy anything," explains Brian. "He once said to me: 'I could sell anything to the Germans. If I fill a flask with tea and take it over, I guarantee I'd flog it!'"

"He would go to Germany, for several weeks at a time, and live there – to wrestle. I said: 'What's it like, living there? I've never been to Germany,' Val remembers. He said: 'You wouldn't want to got to the places I go to – like Hamburg. It's a bit naughty. It's not the sort of place you'd take your wife or girlfriend to! You have to be careful while you're there – and keep your wits about you.' They had a lot of Black Market trading going on after the war. They were short of fresh fruit and consumer goods."

Dave Prowse aka Darth Vader, also a former British Weightlifting Champion writes:

'One could not wish to meet a more down-to-earth and gentle man, and it was always a pleasure to be in his company – he is sorely missed by us all. I have known Pat for many years, from the time when we both auditioned for Stanley Kubrick's *Barry Lyndon* (a part that he got), through gym ownership, wrestling and hosting the annual wrestlers' reunions. I am also proud to say that I introduced him to the convention scene, when I arranged for him to do a show in Paris in 2003.'

Time to jump on a plane from Charles De Gaulle, heading back via Heathrow… to the South London home of famous referee, Joe D'Orazio.

Joe D'Orazio was born on 27 July 1922 in Bermondsey, South London, of Italian parents. He was brought up in a very tough, working-class environment. In fact, two of his classmates were later hanged for murder, and five others became professional wrestlers. He was educated at English Martyrs Roman Catholic School in Walworth, attending school with Tony Scarlo's father, and Harry Geohegan, who went on to become a fine wrestling referee. Joe's best friend, until his untimely death in 2003, was the South London Iron Man, and for many years Mick McManus's tag partner, Steve Logan. Joe became a professional wrestler in 1948. This was followed by a very distinguished international career as a referee, most notably at London's *Albert Hall*, where he was resident referee for twenty years. He and Pat became good friends, as he recalls, in the following tribute:

'It must have been some time in the very late 1960s; I had gone to work full time in the offices of *Dale Martin Promotions Ltd*. One of the very first jobs I was given, after taking over from the great Charles 'Spider' Mascall, was to handle all the wrestling write-ups to the press. There was a National Newspaper reporter who wrote a weekly column in *Tit-Bits* – a magazine of the day. Charles was his go-between, between the journalist and the wrestlers. He would give the chap any information that was required and then fix up a meet for the two of them to get together and the article would then evolve. Pat was next in line for such an interview.

I made an appointment for the three of us to meet one day at *Roses Café*, just on the other side of Brixton Road; a few minutes walk from D.M's office and gymnasium. A couple of hours before the appointed time there was a gentle tap on my office door and Pat presented himself. He had come early because he had some photos of himself to sort out and take across to Brixton Post Office, to send off to some German promoter. When he had sorted them out from our files, we both walked across to the post office, with the intention that, when the packet had been weighed and stamped, we would then walk down to *Roses Café*. There we would have a chat over a cup of tea, and wait for the journalist to show up.

No sooner had we taken our place in the queue, when a very portly lady, who looked as if she had just stepped off a boat from Jamaica, shuffled through the door, aided by two walking sticks. She was carrying two large carrier bags, full of what looked like a week's shopping. She finally stood, panting heavily behind us. I asked her if she wanted to take our place in the queue, but she said she didn't want to cause us any trouble.

Pat said it was no trouble; in fact, he had a better idea. Giving me one of the carrier bags, and taking the other himself, he began to lead her further along the queue, asking the people in front if they minded the lady going in front of them. "No problem at all," they all said. We were about halfway down the queue, when we came to a big fellow (not as big as Pat mind) who was puffing out clouds of cigarette smoke and coughing all over everyone. "I ain't giving up my place for no one," he said to Pat's polite request. "I'm too tired and I've been waiting a long time. I ain't letting no one in front of me – so there!"

Pat looked at me with a puzzled, hurt expression on his face. He put the old lady's hand in mine. He then placed one of his hands (in a very fatherly sort of way) on the man's shoulder and spoke very softly in his ear. The man coughed (more smoke came out). Pat then took the old lady's hand again and we deposited her at the front of the queue.

As Pat and I then walked back to our former position at the back, I noticed, in passing, that the man with the cough was no longer there. I mentioned the fact to Pat and he said, "He's probably gone to buy some fags." As the old lady left, she thanked Pat and again said that she didn't want to cause any trouble. "No trouble at all," Pat said. "No trouble at all."

We still arrived at *Roses Café* ahead of the journalist, so I took the opportunity to ask Pat what it was that he had said to the man, just in case I ever found myself in a similar situation. He leaned across the table and placed one of his great big hands on top of mine, in that fatherly way he had with him. "Joseph, what I said is not for your ears. Let's consider the matter closed shall we?" It was at this moment the journalist arrived. He was seven minutes late.

During the first two years of the *Wrestlers' Reunion* there had been no such thing as an Obituary List of wrestlers being read out. It was as if we were afraid that if such a list existed, it would only be a matter of time before our own names would be added to it.

On this occasion, however, the venue was at the *Prince of Orange* public house, Wayne Bridges' previous public house, and things were about to change.

Pat Roach, who had attended all of the previous reunions, asked Tony Scarlo and myself, as the co-founders, if it would be in order for him to say a few words to the assembled revellers. Pat said how pleased he was to see so many of the 'old faces' from the past, who had turned up to relive old times et cetera, et cetera. He then went on to say that we should remember those who were no longer with us, but had departed to what "Joe D'Orazio always calls, that great dressing room in the sky." He suggested that all the wrestlers present should call out the name of someone they knew had died. Well, the names came thick and fast and every name was greeted with applause, by the crowd. I took the opportunity to scribble most of them down and thus, the Obituary List was born.

Tony and I got together, after a week or so, and we finally ended up with a list of well over one hundred names. The next year, we handed the complete list to dear old Pat and told him that he had been voted in to read out the list each year, 'ad infinitum'. What a magnificent job he made of it, over the years. To me, personally, it was always the highlight of the day.

On one occasion, when Pat was reading the names of our dear departed, he read out the name of "Our dear friend Jumping Jim Hussey." No sooner had the words left his lips than a commotion broke out in the crowd. A man at the back was jumping up and down, frantically waving his arms about and shouting at the top of his voice: "Pat – look it's me – Jim Hussey. I'm not dead – I'm here – look!" Sure enough, it was 'Jumping Jim', making us all aware of his presence.

After quite a while, the laughter died down, and another voice came on the scene. "Don't take any notice of him Pat – he's lying. Read his name out again." After another five minutes' laughter, Pat called us all to order, to continue the job. I asked people nearby at the time, whom the other voice belonged to, but they all claimed not to know. Myself, I think it was Jumping Jim's son, Mark 'Rollerball' Rocco; he couldn't stop laughing for the rest of the afternoon. Furthermore, we never found out how Jumping Jim's name got on our list. When Pat returned the list to me, Jumping Jim's name wasn't on it. So you 'pays your penny and you takes your choice', as they say!

Pat continued to read the Obituary List at subsequent reunions. Now he is no longer with us, we the Committee, have decided that the reading of the full list will be discontinued; it will be replaced with one minute's silence. For who could we possibly get to replace dear old Pat? It is my one regret that I was not able to attend Pat's funeral. When I went out into my garden on the day, I thought of Pat, and came up with the following:

I have walked with Giants
(A tribute to Bomber)
I have walked with Giants,
High, wide and handsome, broad and tall.
So I shall say but this of thee Pat Roach.
You were the gentlest Giant of them all.'

Across Pat's three books, we have done our utmost to include as many of the Big Fella's *numerous* friends and colleagues as possible, from the International Sports World. I only wish there had been the time and the space to include *everyone* concerned.

Ace accompanied Pat to his last ever Wrestlers' Reunion – the Northern one, in Ellesmere Port. "He rang me up two days before, saying that as his eyesight wasn't so good, one of his friends was going to drive him down, in his red Mondeo. On the Sunday morning of the Reunion, he rang me again when I was on the M6 and said that he'd see me there. Then he rang me up an hour later and asked me if I was passing anywhere near Knutsford. I said yes. So he said: 'Well, you'd better pull in here, because I've broken down!' I said: 'Bloody hell!' The Big End – the engine had blown up – which wasn't surprising.

"Every car that I ever travelled in with Pat broke down. I'd always take an AA Card with me, and enough money to stay in a local hotel: you would never get home – ever! In all the time I've known Pat, I must have been in car with him at least half-a-dozen times, where I've had to make alternative arrangements – spend the night away from home. And to think that he could have bought a fleet of cars! Although the Mondeo should have been scrapped, he had an engine from another car put into it.

"At that last reunion, when we reached the Labour Club in Ellesmere Port Cheshire, he said: 'I don't want you to tell anybody here that I've got cancer.' I said: 'Pat, most of them probably already know.' He said: 'Well, they won't know unless you've told them.' I said: 'I haven't told them.' He said: 'I think I can get up those stairs.' As soon as we opened the door, there was a tremendous roar! He was wearing his baseball cap, trying to hide the scars on the back of his head, where they'd had to drill, to try to get rid of his brain tumours. There were *many* people there to wish him well. Some guys were in tears. I could see that they were turning away. But overall, he had a marvellous day and he was so pleased to see everybody. He gave a little bit of a speech; he said: 'Thank you guys, for turning up.'"

Ray Robinson was also there. "It was in June 2004, only a few weeks before he died," recalls Ray. "I had my meal, sat next to him. He told me that he'd had this operation; he was all bandaged up, behind his ear. I said, 'I'll see you at Wayne Bridges' Pat.' And he said, 'I hope so Ray… I hope so.' I didn't see him again, because he died before then. We talked in depth, for the best part of a half an hour, but didn't have a photo taken, because he was ill. He said, 'Ray, I sometimes have to just pause, with my words. I have to think what I'm saying, because I've been lying on my back, for a couple of weeks.'"

Ace telephoned me on his mobile, in a very sombre mood, shortly after dropping me in a side road, adjacent to Marylebone Station, London, that evening. I'd spent the day in London, interviewing him. It had suddenly dawned on him that I'd left the car at the identical spot where he'd dropped Pat off, for *his* return railway journey... the very last time that he saw him alive. And, as I began my return journey into the darkness, I realised that, with one exception, the stations that I was about to travel through, were *precisely* those that Pat had travelled through, after taking his final leave of Ace. Pat's parting comment, as his friend dropped him off, was still ringing in my ears: "I don't say this to many people Ace, but I really *do* love you."

Chapter Twelve

HEART OF THE MATTER

You can live with cancer – you don't have to be dying with it. That's what Frank does – he lives with cancer and gets on with his life.

Chemotherapy Sister, Jayne Illsley

It was Pat's particular wish, to share his experiences of coping with cancer, over what eventually became a record period. By providing a first-hand account, through our third book, he hoped to provide some degree of hope to other patients and their partners, who find themselves confronted by a terminal illness. His message is simply this: "Don't give up, following diagnosis, but strive for as reasonable a quality of life as possible, for *whatever* time remains." Pat's Consultant, Dr. Geh, confirms later in this chapter, that a positive attitude can, in certain cases, prolong life.

Everyone's experience of cancer is different. Our two opening chapters describe how Pat was diagnosed with Oesophageal Cancer, towards the end of February 1998. Major surgery followed, a fortnight later, in March. Originally treated by Professor Casson, Pat made a rapid recovery and was discharged from hospital within a week. He was told he had a seven per cent chance of lasting five years. Mr. Steyn then took over as Pat's Consultant. Pat received conventional treatment, but turned, progressively, to alternative treatments, during the final two years, as he felt hope slipping away, and realised that the conventional methods were simply buying him a little extra time.

Rob Knight remembers: "When Pat was first diagnosed, there were only two other people who knew. He hadn't even told his family. He told me, because I was running the business for him. The only other people who knew at that time, were Ted, aka Paul, at the yard and his agent, Peter Charlesworth. He decided not to tell his family straight away, but was scheduled for an operation, to remove the oesophagus." According to Pat, he told Doreen the day before the operation.

"The news was a complete and utter shock to me. His son Mark was working with me, two or three weeks later," continues Rob. "Pat had asked

Mark to take him to hospital, but I hadn't realised it was that particular morning. I remember working with Mark, when there was a knock on the door. Pat and I were the only people who had keys to the front door, so normally Pat would let himself in. I wasn't expecting anybody, but opened the door and Pat was standing there, in his long wax coat. As he was going for an operation where they had to make an incision in his neck, he'd shaved his beard and his moustache off. I looked at him and I didn't recognise him! I had to look twice, to realise that it was him. He said: 'It's alright Rob. It's only me!'

"There was a noticeable difference in him; within that short space of time, the deterioration was obvious. I know from personal experience, with my own father, how critical it was for Pat to go in at that time. If it had been even a week later, they wouldn't have been able to operate on him. My father went into hospital on the Monday and died on the Saturday. It was that quick; he had exactly the same type of cancer."

According to Alfie Evans: "Pat called me in 1998, when it first happened. He said: 'I've got the 'Big 'C. I'm going into East Birmingham Hospital, but I don't want you to come and see me.' A couple of days afterwards he'd had the operation, I arrived in there. He looked bad. I saw him a lot of times after that."

In August 1999, Chrissie Fewtrell, a close friend of Pat's, died of cancer. Chapter 2 described how Pat has previously told Chris, in confidence, that he *also* had the disease.

Chrissie was a handsome young lad. Although he was never a big man, he came across as a strong character. He was as game as a pebble and would put up a fight when he had to, with anyone who was a nuisance at the club door. His lovely character – with his strength and his philosophy of life: 'if you don't get off your behind, you'll never get anywhere', continued throughout his life. We took him for granted, like we all take each other for granted over the years.

I kept in touch by phone and on two occasions he came over to see me. I was happy to see him. I threw my arms around him and gave him a hug – kept a smile on my face. But when he left I completely broke down. I phoned his brother, Gordon: God knows how I must have sounded on the phone! So sad, having seen all the weight he'd lost – the fact that he was still there – fighting. I'd ring him up periodically: ten days, two weeks. I'd have a chat with him and he was always in good spirits. As things got worse I didn't ring him so often.

Bernard Guest recalls: "Pat phoned me up and said: 'I'd like to see you.' I said: 'Yes – no problem come down.' Pat's grandson went to the same school as my grandson, and his son lived just round the corner. He came and had a cup of tea and we talked. He brought me a statue, actually. We went outside and he broke down. He told me he was terminally ill, which upset me of course. I said, 'Don't be stupid. You've beaten it before.' A week later, we went over to have a meal with him and he said, 'I've just got one wish – that we can do this again next year' – which we did.

"He was fighter wasn't he? Smaller men would have given in a long time ago. I'm not talking about his size," continues Bernard, "I'm talking about him as a man. He exuded strength. He was a Gentle Giant: a fair man – an honest man. If you'd got him as a friend, you'd got a *good* friend."

Pete Meakin, Pat's step-brother, remembers: "Pat absolutely *doted* on his grandson, Patrick. I remember when Pat had major surgery, and he wasn't very well, he brought Patrick down to mom's. Pat had a bad turn: he sat in a chair and closed his eyes; I thought: 'He's not well.' So me and Patrick went out into mom's hallway and we just had a game of Pennies: chuck the pennies and whichever lands nearest to the penny wins the money. I didn't know what else to do with him and I wanted to give Pat a bit of time, just to come round. Patrick loved this Penny Game. There was only about ten or twenty pence to be won, but afterwards, any time that he came down to mom's, when I was there, he'd say: 'Can we have a game of Pennies?'"

Our second book, *Pat Roach's Birmingham*, was dedicated to Patrick Junior. "I feel sure that if Pat had lived longer, he'd have really brought Patrick on," observes Pete. On several occasions, Pat spoke of his regret that he wouldn't be around to see him grow up…to actually be *there* for him. According to Pete's wife, Shirley Meakin, "We found out that Pat had got this cancer, around Valentine's Day. He told us the next time we met at his mom's house, which was just after that. Obviously, he asked us to keep it quiet – which we did, until it came out in the papers recently." He told his co-writer at our second meeting in 1999, in case I suddenly had to write his first biography on my own. But thankfully, we were able to publish two books, before his death.

The following is a private tape that Pat made with me in March 2001, when he had met his new Consultant for the first time. He wanted to share his thoughts, as he didn't know how much longer he would live. In the event, it was a further three years and four months, but he had no way of knowing that. If he had, the recording may have been somewhat different!

I suppose things are starting to look a bit grim, by now – if that's the right word. I was with the doctor yesterday; of all names, his name is Doctor Geh (pronounced Gay). I said to him, "Doc, can you keep me alive until Christmas 2001?" He shook his head and said: "I really don't know." The idea being that it's now the end of

March and it would have been nice to have been alive for Christmas, because that would have been the end of the filming for the third 'Auf Wiedersehen' series. And it would have meant that I'd got some money in the bank, for the family.

On Tuesday, I start a chemotherapy course. I start it with the strongest of treatments. I'll be hooked to it permanently; I'll have a 'bumbag' around my waist and I'll be hooked up through my arm – hopefully – otherwise if they can't find a vein in my arm they'll got through my neck, which seem a little more inconvenient. But I'll be grateful for whatever they can do for me. The main thing is that I'd like to stay alive for a while, in order to get rid of my 'bits and pieces'. I don't really look forward to 'chemo', as far as the side effects are concerned – although I'm very grateful to have my life prolonged. Going bald – well, I've been there before! I suppose losing my eyelashes doesn't appeal to me too much, and my eyebrows. And then of course, there's the devastation – can you imagine? I've got to lose my bloody beard!

I'll look like a billiard ball won't I? The last time, I got well paid for it, (in 'Raiders of the Lost Ark') – which stood me in good stead. They tell me that even to this day, they still do some of my stunts at the MGM Film Studio. So I'm destined to going back to being an 'Old Baldy' again! They say that after a very short time your hair all grows back. As I pointed out to the nurse, without sounding too negative, it might not have time to grow back with me, But it would be nice to be able to do the full circle, where you have the treatment, lose your hair, and you're still there when it grows back. But we won't complain at anything… because it won't do us any good.

During a later meeting with Pat and myself, Dr. Geh explained that the despondency, which Pat has just been expressing, was due to the fact that he'd had a 'local recurrence' within the oesophagus. There was also evidence, in the scans, that it had spread to the lungs as well. The cancer in his lung and brain were both secondary cancers. Treatment for this new situation had already commenced and was as follows:

Initial treatment – a course of radiotherapy.

Eight cycles of Chemotherapy, until Autumn 2001. According to Dr. Geh, Pat responded very well to this treatment and the disease had significantly reduced in size.

There was a planned break in treatment, so that Pat could film *AWP 3*, from summer until November 2002.

When Pat was transferred to Doctor Geh, three Chemotherapy Sisters, Christina Hughes, Jayne Illsley and Clare Horrobin, were, at the same time, given the responsibility of administering his treatment.

During November 2002, Pat arranged for me to interview his nurses. In the interests of confidentiality, Pat is referred to throughout as 'Frank'. All three nursing sisters had been administering medical care to Pat, in cycles, since March 2001. Conducting the interview felt rather surreal, because even as we were talking, Pat was in a nearby cubicle, undergoing treatment, whilst I was discussing his condition, in relative comfort. He was actually completing his chemotherapy that day, which included having his line removed and the last pump taken off. His previous six courses of 'chemo' took six months to administer (one per month) and had lasted just over one year. The photograph of Pat, with his nurses, which we have included in this book, was taken that same day, following treatment.

The following, is an edited version of that four-way discussion, which took place, with Pat's permission, in the Staff Room, of Ward 37, Heartlands Hospital, Birmingham, between Chemotherapy Sisters, Christina Hughes, Jayne Illsley, Clare Horrobin, and myself.

Christina Hughes began, by explaining: "We're all members of the same team, we're all Chemotherapy Sisters, so we are seeing the patient, right from the beginning of the cancer journey, right from the time of diagnosis, speaking to them initially about the chemotherapy." Three years later, in 2005, Christina and Jayne have become Macmillan Nurses and Clare is a Research Nurse.

According to Chemotherapy Sister, Jayne Illsley: "When Frank first came to us, he needed to have some chemotherapy. For the type of chemotherapy that Frank has, he has to have a special line inserted called a PICC, which stands for 'peripherally inserted central catheter'. Basically, that's a line that goes into his arm, but is actually fed through the veins, so that it sits at the top of the main vein into the heart. We, as chemotherapy nurses, are trained to put these lines in. Once his line went in, he started his chemotherapy within the same week – and we continued with it. It was probably a little under two years ago when he first came to us. He had eight cycles of chemotherapy, which is 8x3. Over a longer period of time his case was delayed, because Frank's blood results were sometimes low and we also had to plan a lot of his chemotherapy around his filming for the new series of *Auf Wiedersehen Pet*.

"He started his treatment in March 2001. It's a three-weekly cycle, from start to finish. He comes here right at the beginning of every cycle and has a full day's course of treatment. Then he attends the next couple of weeks and just has a pump change each time."

So he had to be there *all* day, for the first day. "Then the following next two weeks he comes in for a pump change. He's on that chemotherapy continuously for 24 hours a day, 7 days a week, for the whole three weeks. Then if his blood counts are OK, he'll start his second cycle, the week after. So he's continually on chemotherapy."

Jayne continues: "With any kind on cancer like this, you always want it to be operable, so he had the surgery then. Unfortunately, when he came back to us for chemotherapy, it was because the cancer had, what we call, 'recurred'. He had the surgery first, but couldn't have another operation, so chemotherapy is the second line, after surgery. Because chemotherapy is 'systemic', (it works all over the body), it was the treatment of choice. The cancer in his lung and his brain are both secondary cancers – what's called 'metastasis' – from the original cancer that was in his gullet. The chemotherapy is given because it will work all over the body, whether it's a local re-occurrence in where the cancer was removed, or in the lungs. Radiotherapy can only target one spot. It can be given in cases like brain metastasis, because of it being in one area."

Christina outlined the benefits of the treatment: "Commonly, when patients present before having chemotherapy, they may be having problems swallowing, certainly with eating; sometimes difficulty eating even soft foods – sometimes even fluids. So chemotherapy can help greatly in that sense, because it helps to reduce the tumour size, therefore opening the tube and allowing food and fluid to go down. When Frank came initially, he didn't really have too many problems with that; he was still managing to eat. He hadn't a great deal of weight loss or anything. So from *his* point of view, looking at his symptoms, there wasn't a lot to measure it against, because he was still eating and drinking and things were generally quite good.

"The most common side effects with chemotherapy are nausea and vomiting. This *can* sometimes be a problem. We tend to have very powerful anti-emetics now, which control these problems very well. But there is always the potential for that as well."

Chemotherapy Sister Clare Horrobin explains: "On the day that Frank came for his all-day treatment, he would have chemotherapy injected into him and he would also have anti-sickness drugs injected into his vein. When he went home, he would be given oral anti-emetics – oral tablets – to take for a period of about five days afterwards: usually it's a combination of a steroid tablet and another tablet, which you take together. On the whole, the combination of the two tablets controls sickness very well. But Frank has never really had any vomiting to speak of – perhaps the occasional nausea, but other than that he has done very well."

Christina elaborates: "On the whole, with his chemotherapy, Frank's been very lucky and he's not really had many side effects at all. He's managed to maintain his weight very well; eating and drinking has never really been a problem for him – right from the start."

I understand that tumours often eat up a substantial amount of the body's nutrients and that's therefore one of the main causes of weight loss in cancer patients? So, as Frank has tumours on his brain, and some spores remain in his lungs, (which can spread almost anywhere), why hasn't he lost more weight?

"It's a very difficult thing to explain – there's not really a reason *why*. Some people lose weight very rapidly – even those who are eating," Christina replies. "It's a very individual thing – but it's just never really been a problem for Frank."

Clare observes: "Initially, Frank came across as a very frightened man. I think it was an unusual experience for him. I get the impression that he's a man who's used to being in *control* of everything. Then all of a sudden, someone's ripped the carpet from underneath him. As far as he's concerned, he's having palliative treatment. He was always very open with us – that this is *palliative* treatment – and who knows how long it's going to be? I think he was just completely scared. Initially, I hadn't seen him so much as the other two. But you quickly get to know Frank. He's a man who initially always wanted to know: 'What does this do? What does that do?' Was it going to be the same every week? His confidence grew – once he knew, he could cope with it; that's *my* perception He's always been quite open with us. Once he got to grips with what was happening, then he relaxed, as any patient does really.

"One thing that particularly struck me, was that he was able to turn his experience into something positive," Clare continues. "He knew he was going to lose his hair – he was obviously aware of that fact. So he did something positive by making it into a fundraising issue."

This was an occasion when Pat raised £1,000, in May 2001, for the *City of Birmingham Special Olympics*, which he subsequently presented, at the start of the regional athletics championships, at the *Alexandra Stadium*, in Birmingham. "It kept it private and personal to him," observes Clare, "but he was keen to take it further and say: 'Well it's happened to me, it's awful, but let's see how it can be of benefit.'"

According to Jayne, "One of the other reasons that Frank's coped so well with his chemotherapy has been his attitude. Right from Day One, he's continued to work all the time. He wants to be able to go to work, to start his training, which he's done from time to time, while he's been on the treatment. I think that has an awful lot to do with how few side effects he has – the fact that life goes on as normal, despite having to cope with this."

Christina comments: "In terms of prognosis, when patients are told that their cancer's not going to be cured, they're then referred to as being 'palliative'. But there's no way of anyone giving any time limit on a person's life – from that point of view. Death can occur at any time, whether patients are having radiotherapy, chemotherapy, or actually at home, having a period of no treatment at all. So it's not possible to predict whether someone's time will be short or not: it's a totally individual experience. There are no comparisons to be made between people."

Jayne summarised Frank's positive response to treatment: "It's probably down to two things: one is that he's responded very well to the treatment he's been given; he responded to it the first and second time around, when he's been re-challenged, if you like, with chemotherapy. Also, because of his positive attitude: the fact that he just gets on with life. You can live with cancer – you don't have to be dying with it. That's what Frank does – he lives with cancer and gets on with his life."

Clare concludes: "Basically, I agree with Jayne. If the drugs work and you have a positive state of mind…" Christina adds: "Another thing that helped him initially, was that he was in great physical shape. He's always looked after his body; he knows what to eat. As he's a very *private* man, the fact that a lot of people don't actually know that he's ill, has helped him to feel more positive and to feel healthy. He doesn't actually get sympathy or pity from anybody. That helps a great deal with his mental attitude and the way he feels.

"Frank has now *completed* chemotherapy," Christina explains. "This afternoon he's having his line removed and the last pump taken off. When Frank came the first time round, in March 2001, he had his first course of treatment. He completed six courses of treatment, which took us, roughly, over six months. That is the full cycle of the treatment. Luckily, he's lasted just over a year."

At one stage, he wasn't even sure if he was going to make it to Christmas 2001. "That very much depends on the individual symptoms – whether there's been any further growth. Obviously, the doctor reviews the patient and if he thinks chemotherapy is going to be effective again, then they'll give it again. At the end of the day, he's probably just a little tired from being here, but he doesn't have any symptoms. He doesn't go out feeling unwell or anything," adds Christina.

When Pat was linked to the PICC line, he could sit up, or wander around. It didn't restrict him in any way. He was also attached to a drip, but he could take that with him. So he could function fairly normally, and read the paper, for example. He was able to take his mind off the chemotherapy, rather than being too focused on the situation. The fact that his nurses described his cancer treatment as a 'journey' seemed a very positive approach.

"Yes, it just seems to individualise it really – everybody's experience will be *so* different, from when they're initially told, to how they respond to treatment – and the side effects," Clare observes.

So it's a *journey* – and although you don't really know what's going to happen along the way – you're being positive?

"I think you have to take it as it comes – and Frank's attitude has been very positive – right from the start," Christina concludes.

Yes, I think he's been exceptionally brave about it. Thank you all very much for your time – and your understanding. We both appreciate it *very* much.

*   *   *   *   *

Shortly afterwards, on Thursday 28 November 2002, I interviewed Dr. Geh, in Pat's presence. Pat was again referred to throughout as 'Frank'. Dr. Geh stipulated: "The main thing is that I'm telling you this in Frank's presence, so that there's no issue about confidentiality and no one can be accused of giving out confidential details, without Frank's permission. You're the only one who is responsible for whether or not it leaks out." I explained that one of our book's principal aims was to convey a message of hope; because Frank has responded well to treatment so far, he wants to convey his own positive outlook to other patients.

Some sort of message that people can relate to.

Frank would also like to include in the book, his appreciation of the way in which you and your staff have enabled him to maintain his anonymity throughout. The fact that most people don't know that he's ill has been crucial in helping him to maintain a very positive and healthy attitude towards the situation. Has preserving anonymity presented any particular difficulties?

"I have to say, that's mainly the work of the nurses and the rest of the staff. Obviously I see Frank when he's having treatment," Dr. Geh explained, "but the rest of the time it's been the responsibility of the nurses, to tuck him away in a corner, and out of sight. It certainly hasn't caused me any problems."

I must just tell you this funny story – quickly. You remember the day you had me up here for my treatment for a brain tumour? They'd got me all ready to go. There were about eight trainees there and about eight members of staff: about sixteen or seventeen people altogether. A message came: "Could you keep Mr. Roach there for a while please?" It was all very official – we were all stood there waiting – until suddenly there's a nurse there – wanting a bloody autograph! Can you believe it?

150

It was all very efficient. We thought Doctor Geh was going to turn up with some last minute information: "The laser's broken – you've got to go home again!" And there I was – looking like Frankenstein's monster!

I asked the doctor to summarise Frank's treatment, since he took over his case – and the way in which he's responded to that treatment.

"Frank was referred to me by Mr. Steyn, who had taken over from Professor Casson. At that time he had what we call a 'local recurrence', within the oesophagus. Also, in the scans, there was evidence that it had spread to the lungs as well. The initial treatment that I gave you was a course of radiotherapy, to the local recurrence, to try and reduce the pain and get you feeling a little more comfortable. Following the radiotherapy treatment, you went on to chemotherapy treatment and you had that until the autumn of last year.

I think what was important was that you responded extremely well to the treatment – and the disease, which was present on the scan, significantly reduced in size. That meant that you were fit in yourself and able to have a break in treatment, to film another series of *Auf Wiedersehen Pet* and enjoy what we would call a 'good quality of life'.

"Frank came back with new symptoms, and a scan of the brain showed that there were two deposits in the brain. In addition, a scan of the chest showed that some of the metastases had also returned. So we then went on to offer Frank a treatment known as stereotactic radio-surgery, which is a highly accurate means of delivering high doses of radiotherapy, to the deposits in the brain. That went very smoothly, and in fact, a subsequent scan, several months later, showed that those two deposits had completely disappeared and that there was a complete response to treatment. In the meantime, he continued on a few further cycles of chemotherapy; the same chemotherapy that he had last year. He has made a reasonably good response to that as well. Not quite as good as last time, but certainly, there's no evidence that the cancer has got any worse, during this time."

Did Frank's case present you with any particular problems or concerns?

"I think the main problem was when he came back with the brain metastases, because in that situation, the majority of patients would have a rather poor outlook. Quite often, treatment would have left them in a difficult situation, and new problems were quite likely to have occurred. But this wasn't the case and in fact, his treatment went extremely smoothly; he didn't develop any problems, either from the treatment, or from the metastases. So that was a very positive result."

How much importance do you place upon the patient's attitude?

"It's *extremely* important. A patient who hasn't got the will to live, or the will to do well, is extremely difficult to treat, because they are more likely to suffer psychologically, as well as physically, from the side effects of treatment. We, as professionals, always find it easier to work with patients who are positive. When we are faced with patients who are negative, we do our best, but it's probably harder work."

Has any research been done into the correlation between a patient's attitude and his likely recovery rate?

"I'm pretty certain it has been tried, although I'm not able to quote exact references. Anecdotally, most of us would say that positive patients tend to do better. But there could be other confounding factors, including the fact that negative patients may be in a worse physical condition, or have more symptoms."

I understand that Frank has completed his course of chemotherapy, for the present?

"Yes, the main thing is to see how he is in himself – and whether he reports any new symptoms or not. If there are any new symptoms, we need to establish what these could be due to. At some stage I may repeat his scans, to see what's going on, within his chest. But to some degree, we are already in un-chartered territory with Frank, anyway, with this ECF Chemotherapy treatment, which he's already received."

What does ECF stand for?

"There are three drugs called epirubicin, cisplatin and fluorouracil. The epirubicin and cisplatin are given every three weeks; the fluorouracil is given as a continuous treatment, for 24 hours, 7 days a week. The data on ECF Chemotherapy, in this situation, in three large randomised trials, is what we call the 'median survival', that's the time in which 50% of the patients will still be alive, and 50% will have died.

"The median survival rate is around nine months, from the start of treatment. Obviously, Frank has done twice as well as that and therefore is already an exception, rather than the rule.

"The second thing is that there is no data in the medical literature of patients receiving a second course of ECF Chemotherapy, following the first course, because there are usually very few patients who are fit enough to receive a second course of treatment after the first. Therefore, that's in un-chartered waters.

"But on the whole, if patients respond well to the first course and remain well, there's a reasonable chance of them responding to a second course; maybe not quite as well as the first time, but it's better than if they hadn't responded well in the first place. So that's the reason for giving him the same treatment, all over again."

We would prefer to be really positive – but am I right in thinking that the more courses of treatment a patient has, the more it weakens him?

"Not necessarily. I think that what we are concerned about is the progression of the cancer, rather than the treatment."

So one has always to think of the treatment as being essentially beneficial to the patient, rather than taking the other point of view?

"Yes, exactly. So quite often, patients get weaker with the cancer, they respond to treatment, but the effect of responding to the treatment is greater than the effect of chemotherapy on the body. Therefore, the total sum of that is that they feel better, rather than worse."

I must just tell you, doctor. When I was wrestling, some time ago, I pulled up at the stage door of the hall. I looked up and there was this large, full-sized poster of me – the main event on the bill. I put my invalidity card in the window of my car, parked on the double yellow lines, went in and wrestled – top of the bill!

I sent Professor Casson my poster, and I wrote across the stomach, because it showed me bare, from the middle upwards, 'I never thought I'd have the stomach for it – P.S. I'm over 21!' (I was sixty-four years of age). And just last Christmas, I was back up to nineteen-stone again. I was doing a thousand 'free-reps', every lunchtime. At six o'clock in the morning, I was doing 500 free squats – you know how the Japanese do the free squats?

I put an additional arm movement to it, which was rather hard work. I was weight-training three nights a week – training the whole Auf Wiedersehen production/film team, and got absolutely as fit as a fiddle. On a scale of 1-10, as a non-patient, I would have been at 9, let alone a patient who had just finished a 'chemo' course.

All being well, apart from this water retention I've got, I'm ready to go back and start training again. And if I get back a few months – I only need about five or six weeks to get back – because I 'blow up' normally. It's like getting a balloon; the first time you try to blow it up, it's difficult. But once you've blown air into it, then let it down, then it's easy; that's exactly how my body responds. As soon as I start training, it will all come back to me – straight away. With just a little bit of luck – not much at all – I'll actually get back fit again, for a second time, and that will be quite unusual, won't it?

My chest, my arms, my legs, will come back; I'll be doing a thousand squats – or whatever. I want to get to that stage, obviously for my own benefit, but also to enhance the story of how well the Health Service has done. Having had an oesophagus removal, two courses of chemotherapy, the resurgence of a disease, and to still get back a second time to eighteen or nineteen stone.

You see, always on my mind was the fact that I would be dead, when the book came out, especially the second book. So if I write The Joke's On Me, and I die of lung cancer, I would have been telling people all my life – "Definitely don't smoke – do anything else that you want to do, but do it in moderation." And I will have died of lung cancer.

"Well, it's not really lung cancer – it's oesophageal cancer, with secondary cancer in the lung."

But the point is that I've been telling people all my life: "Don't smoke, but do everything else in moderation. So the book will be subtitled, 'The Joke's On Me'. But I need to die – to do that.

"Not yet!" concludes Dr. Geh.

*   *   *   *   *

A conversation, between Seamus Dunleavy and myself, draws our chapter to it's close: "It's funny Shirley, I heard the rumours that he was sick, but he never spoke to me about his illness. Obviously he didn't want it out – although it did come out. But you know, I'd have gone to see him more often if I'd known that he was sick."

When was the last time you actually saw him? "Well, I looked round Pat's three houses, at Gravelly Hill, with a view to buying them, but there were sitting tenants and they're difficult to get out sometimes. So we didn't go through with the deal. I saw Pat three or four months before he died. He instructed me to go up there and Rob Knight showed me round." Seamus subsequently told me that on 7 February 2005, he'd seen those same properties for auction in the papers. However, at the time of writing, I believe they still haven't been resold.

"He said to me the one day: 'I'm selling the scrapyard Seamus.' I said: 'God Pat, that's a big thing; you've been there a good while!' He said: 'Yes, I'm getting out now.' And then I *still* didn't think there was anything that wrong; that was fairly recently – not long before he died; he told me a while later that the deed had been done with the yard and he was off." As he had no idea when he was actually going to die, Pat had been going around, on and off, for at least two years, saying goodbye to many of his friends. Sadly, when he gave them a big hug, they just thought that he was pleased to see them. Most of them didn't realise that he was living on borrowed time. But that was the way he wanted it. There were a few who knew – but not many. Seamus wondered: "Did he ever get depressed Shirley? Why has this happened to me?"

Only occasionally – which is amazing. There was a time when one of his boxing friends visited him at his yard and caught him in a depressed mood. He was talking about having a cardboard box for a coffin and a removal van for a hearse, but happily he changed his mind and gave me a totally different, relatively normal set of instructions! It was absolutely amazing how cheerful and brave he was, for most of the time, throughout a period of over six years. To a large extent it was his state of mind and strength of character that kept him going.

Seamus observes: "Normally you'd reach a stage where you say: 'That's it. I've had the symptoms and I don't want to see anyone.'" But Pat was so tenacious and so determined to keep going, trying every possible remedy. "And you never know, he *might* have found a way through it, by doing that," Seamus adds. "He was riding on the crest of a wave with the parts still coming in."

And, as our following chapters show, he still managed to make two further series of *Auf Wiedersehen Pet*, supported magnificently by the BBC. For that was the nature of the man... he just *wouldn't* give up.

Chapter Thirteen

DEEP BLUE SKY AND RED-ROCK CANYONS

Filming in Arizona was a very good time really. Certainly we were all relieved that Pat was there and that he had the back up. But the most striking thing about it was the way that his health kind of recovered. He hadn't been too well in Middlesbrough, but as soon as we got to the States, you could see him visibly growing. My over-riding picture of the Grand Canyon was of Pat standing in front of the mountains, doing his press-squats and just getting stronger and stronger. It suited him down to the ground. It was dry and warm – and that landscape is so inspiring anyway. We were all on such a 'high' to be back together – and working with the Navajo tribe was very exciting for all of us.

Kevin Whately

The third series of *Auf Wiedersehen Pet*, first broadcast on 28 April 2002, might never have materialised, had it not been for two *seemingly* unrelated events. Franc Roddam had returned from Hollywood to London by 1999, and was working as producer on various projects. He then discovered that the rights for *Aufpet* had reverted to him. The idea of resurrecting the series appealed to him, so he put the proposal to Allan McKeown and then to Dick Clement and Ian La Frenais. They in turn contacted Roger Bamford, who 'sounded out' the cast. To rally them all round, at this stage in their careers, could well have proved impossible. But the second, even more decisive factor, turned out to be the death of Sammy Johnson, that same year, in Malaga. He was Tim Healy's best friend, and a much-respected actor, perhaps best known for his role as 'Stick' in the *Spender* series, starring Jimmy Nail. I visited Tim at his Alderley Edge home, in August 2004. As articulate and sociable as ever, he provided a detailed account of making the two latest *Aufpet* Series – *3 and 4*, and the *Christmas Special*.

156

"Sammy and I started off together at the *Live Theatre Company*," recalls Tim. "He was only forty-nine when he died; he was training for the Great Northern Run. It was such a shock! He was out in Spain, running up a hill, and he dropped down dead. So we brought his body back to England. Jimmy Nail said: 'Why don't we do something?' So we set up the *Sammy Johnson Memorial Fund*. We do a concert every two years – all the famous Geordie Mafia: *Lindisfarne*, Brendan Healy, John Miles, and Brian Johnson.

"We did this first one, and Ian and Dick wrote sketches for Dennis, Neville and Oz. We hadn't played these characters for fifteen years, and we'd never done them live on stage before. Jimmy had never worked on stage before as an actor. There were two thousand people in the audience. They went absolutely mad – they laughed and laughed! We came off and that gave us the thought: 'Shall we do another series?' – because of the audience response.

"So we phoned Dick and Ian, and we had a chat with Franc Roddam. He lived next door to the Head of BBC Light Entertainment, Alan Yentob. So that conversation started and bang! Within six months we were up and running. But it took Ronnie to die. That was his real name; his stage name was Sammy Johnson. We've done three concerts up to now and we've raised more then £120,000. All that money goes back to young people, in the Northeast, who want to become involved in the Performing Arts. We have meetings three times a year and we give out grants to these people. So that's why *Auf Wiedersehen* happened again. Sammy knew Pat. They worked together. He was in the second series of *Auf Wiedersehen* and had a fight scene with Pat, in a bar!"

People asked me, many times, "Would you ever do another one?" And I said: "Absolutely not!" The reason being that Jimmy Nail has now sold eight million records, done so many wonderful things – multi-millionaire. Kevin, with his Morse – millionaire twice over. Tim Spall – tremendous artiste – very wealthy. Tim Healy – wonderful actor. I didn't know sugar from salt, did I? All of these guys have been so successful; you would never get them all together. So when Jimmy Nail asked: "Pat, would you do another Auf Wiedersehen?" I said I'd be game for it, but I thought: 'No, they'll never do it.' But they all put big deals on one side – to do it again.

After six months of negotiations all six principal actors were contracted for the new series, including Noel Clarke, the new cast member, who was to play Wayne's mixed race son, Wyman. He'd only been eight years old, when the first series went out. Noel and Pat developed a special rapport, as we explain in the next chapter.

Tim Spall was completing work on a feature film, but would join them later, in Middlesbrough. Although Julia Tobin had retired from acting, she had no hesitation in taking the role of Brenda again, saying, "it was like seeing an old friend."

The initial meeting for *Aufpet 3*, was at *Mirabelle's Restaurant*, in October 2000.

They threw a lunch for us at the Mirabelle, in Curzon Street, London, in a private room. I suppose the lunch bill must have been somewhere between £1500 and £2,000 – the most amazing thing! I had the privilege of sitting there, as they all walked in. And they hugged each other, and kissed each other – in a very masculine way – of course. They were so happy to be together. I just swelled up inside.

Chris Fairbank recalls: "At the *Mirabelle*, it was as much to do with the excitement of getting the whole thing going again. I didn't really notice any difference in Pat at all. He looked a little bit older, as we all did! But beyond that, there was absolutely no indication that he was ill." There was a subsequent meeting at Franc Roddam's house.

"This particular evening, at Franc's, was ten months after the *Mirabelle* meeting," continues Chris. "Pat was just stood in the street, before the meeting, and I was waiting, in the car. When I looked at him I thought: 'Cor, you look like you've been through something!' At that point, Pat came over and told me that he'd had cancer of the oesophagus, without explaining that it was terminal. Then he suddenly added: 'You know kid, it's not going to be long now before people realise what a terrific actor you are.' I said: 'Oh, come on – you big lug!' It was mainly his hair that was different, because it used to be curly, but it had become really straight – like a brush."

Work on *Aufpet 3* began in August 2002 and finished in December. They began with some location shots in London, then went on to Middlesbrough, and other areas of the Northeast; from there they flew to Arizona, and finally back to Bray Studios. Pat's cancer treatment had been modified, to enable him to stay the course.

I was so lucky to have such a professional group of people around me, who were able to cope with my handicap, and just carry on with their jobs as well, even though the pressure from me was on their heads. They weren't condescending with me in any way at all. They helped me in every way they could, and left me alone to do my thing. Occasionally, when they could see me in pain, they left me alone. From time to time, they asked how I was. Just about everyone bent over backwards to help me – all of the boys – and my driver, Steve.

Julia Tobin recalls: "There'd been a gap of about fifteen-plus years. Walking back in to see them, it was as if we'd never been away. I missed the initial read-through, so I went on to the second one, which was just *our* scene, in a room in Regent's Park; it was always in an echoing type of room. Seeing all the 'boys' again, after such a length of time and just not really noticing any gap at all – that was my most memorable moment."

I asked Kevin about his memories of working with Julia, the only remaining 'Pet' on all four series. "It's difficult to say, because I didn't work with her at all on the final one – the *Christmas Special*, and she did frighteningly little on the most recent two. We were trying to get them to write some more for her, but basically I think I did about two scenes with her, in both series. So it was pretty minuscule."

For insurance purposes, each principal cast member was required to have a medical examination, so Pat was a little apprehensive... to say the least!

When I went to London, although I didn't set out to deceive them, they asked me these medical questions, and I answered: "Yes, I had suffered from cancer, and yes, I was having on-going treatment" – which was entirely true. What I didn't tell them was that I had a needle stuck in my arm. The doctor took my blood pressure in my right arm, instead of my left. I don't think he thought about it, because I was wearing long sleeves. I looked too fit to be a walking dead man. When they sent for a medical report, they would then have been told that I was terminal.

The doctor would subsequently have told the insurance company. This is where they all leapt to my defence. Franc Roddam, Joy Spink and Jim obviously had a lot to say, and put pressure on the BBC. They probably said something like: "Look, Pat trains every day – a thousand laps a day, he's looking really good. He's got a very positive attitude." Although they were very serious about the story line: Bomber's very ill, and could drop dead at any moment.

The basic plot was that Oz reunites the 'lads' in Middlesbrough, by inviting them to his own, fictitious funeral. He then persuades his old mates to take down the old Transporter Bridge, and eventually ship it to Arizona. A company called *Men from Mars* created the special effects for this. It was so convincing that Middlesbrough Council had to issue a press release, assuring the town's inhabitants that the bridge wasn't really being moved. One couple actually drove from Portsmouth, to see if the bridge was still there!

Plot-wise, the lads have fallen on hard times, in the interim, with the exception of Barry, who has become a millionaire. Bill Nighy plays the sleazy but suave MP Jeffrey Grainger to perfection. Although the roles are somewhat different, his 'suave-joker' approach to the role, is not unlike Roger Moore's 'tongue-in-cheek' portrayal of James Bond. Although Oz previously met Grainger in prison, the MP has secured a potentially lucrative book deal, so Oz doesn't anticipate that he will try to renege on the bridge scheme.

Jimmy Nail and Franc Roddam put a tremendous amount of effort into planning and developing the concept beforehand, including a ten-day road trip across Arizona, and prepared the show's 160-page bible, outlining all the characters and plot lines. Their research provided a great 'starter motor' for scriptwriters Dick Clement and Ian La Frenais, who met up with them in Arizona, halfway through the trip. At first Dick and Ian didn't think it was worth the risk, but they slowly gained interest, being particularly impressed by the scale of the project. Franc Roddam had the inspirational idea of contrasting the relative drabness of Middlesbrough with the American Indian culture and vivid landscape colours of Arizona.

Joy Spink, the producer of the series, gave me a first-hand account, in February 2003, about how Pat was able to continue filming, despite his potentially terminal condition. Joy was responsible for the day-to-day running of the production. "It's a logistical and creative input," she explains. "The producer is also responsible for the smooth running of the production – and for the budget. So basically, it's a day-to-day involvement: you're there to oversee all of those aspects, in conjunction with everybody else. It's one of those things where you try and keep the whole thing together."

The production team was unaware that Pat was terminally ill, until about three weeks into the shoot, whilst filming in the Northeast, from a Middlesbrough base. "There were two things to consider," Joy remembers. "Principally, all of our minds were on Pat's well being. Whenever we discussed the situation, it was of paramount importance, that whatever we decided, should be right for Pat." Describing the situation facing Joy at that stage, Pat said, with great feeling, "God bless her – what *would* I have done without her?"

"We were concerned to make sure that Pat didn't end up doing too much. He obviously wasn't terribly well, at some times more than others, because, of course, he was undergoing treatment. People don't usually work when they're having that kind of treatment – but Pat did! The hours of filming are very long," continues Joy "although it's not always particularly physical work, just the mere fact of being there, is physically tiring – for such long hours. You need to concentrate, and also, in Pat's case, he didn't want to let anyone down."

As a general rule, filming began at about 8am. and finished at 7pm. Sometimes, they filmed at night, so the hours would change. The actors would arrive half an hour or so earlier, usually for make-up and costume. "If they were there a whole day," Joy explains, "they might be leaving half an hour after we finished. So it was actually 7.30am. to 7.30pm. – a twelve-hour working day. We worked what we call an 'Eleven-day Fortnight', so we'd do five days one week, and six days the next week: that would be six days a week, for Pat."

Even when they were filming in England, the tight schedule allowed little opportunity for actors to return home, but there *were* times when Pat had to disappear for treatment. "Apart from Pat's health, it was a huge undertaking for the BBC: many millions of pounds were involved. So we had to discuss two things: firstly, Pat's health and secondly, the implications for the production – which was a secondary thing on our mind," recalls Joy. "We obviously sought medical advice about what we should be doing, and about what we thought was best for Pat." She confirms that the BBC sent for a report, from Pat's consultant. "Any production carries insurance. Your leading cast would be insured and obviously, for something like that, it would be excluded by the insurers."

Pat cleared it with 'the boys' too. "There were times when some of the actors would talk to me about it: 'How's Pat doing today?' Because, having known each other for twenty years, they'd know more than I would. So he'd feel free to talk to them, rather than me, who he'd not known for very long," observes Joy.

Kevin Whately recalls: "Normally he was such a fit guy. He looked very grey-faced, but then Middlesbrough was so cold anyway. We were aware that he was going back to Birmingham periodically, for various chemotherapy treatment and what-have-you."

Pat's chauffeur, Steve Gibson, made those trips with him. It was Steve, also, who escorted me across to the set at Bray Studios in Windsor, where I was a guest for the day, (as described in the next chapter). Pat's medical absences meant changing things round and re-scheduling – "...taking Pat out of some things, or shooting them in such a way that Pat could go, and we could shoot the remainder of the scene." So it was rather complicated at times.

According to Pat, everyone on the production was very supportive. They also needed to be aware that his condition could worsen. "We were concerned on both fronts: from Pat's health point of view and also, what would happen to the production really. It was a tricky situation," Joy explains, " but if Pat was prepared to make it work, then so were we. We wouldn't entertain the idea of him *not* being in it: that would have been soul-destroying!"

Script changes were an on-going process, as this wasn't a straightforward situation. By the time the production team realised the extent of Pat's illness, they were well into filming, and Dick and Ian had returned to Los Angeles.

Joy describes *Auf pet* as a "fantastic series to work on. It was so successful – both critically – and in terms of viewing numbers. There isn't anything else like this. Pat was always extremely professional: he really cared about what he was doing. If I had to sum him up, it would be as a 'gentleman' – in all senses – of the word: 'a gentle man'. He was always incredibly polite and really caring. The spirit that he had, in working while he was receiving this treatment, and the worry that he must have had, about how the treatment was going… There were lots of people on set who didn't know about it – and *wouldn't* have known. I think what's amazing is his inner strength, as well as his physical strength." Pat told me that he felt as concerned about the problems Joy was presented with, as he was about his own predicament. "He was always saying how grateful he was to me – when it was common decency really," she observes.

Why, in Joy's opinion, had the series been so successful? "Well, it's appeal – the characters feel very real; the script is superb: Dick and Ian write such fabulous scripts, that are very funny and tragic – an incredible blend. Also, because the six original actors are fantastic in their roles. It's the script and the actors. I think that the public recognise these characters – and they like that; they're well rounded… you can believe in them."

Joy has been a producer for several years. "Before *Auf Wiedersehen,* I did the first series of *Waking the Dead.* I'm currently doing a two-part serial for the BBC called *Final Demand,* based on a book by Deborah Moggach. I started in commercials, and then moved on to television." Little did I realise that my next conversation with Joy would be seventeen months later… from a remote region of Thailand!

During filming I actually went from strength to strength and got my weight back up to nineteen stone. My legs, chest and arms came back. I was out at six o'clock every morning – training; watching the dawn come up, in Arizona. At least three evenings a week, I was in the gym, training with the First and Second and Third Assistant, and with Timmy Spall's wife Shane – and other people. Without the help of those people, I most certainly wouldn't have got through, and wouldn't have been allowed to.

My latest CT Examination has shown that the cancer has flared up inside me again. But they haven't just filled me up with painkillers and told me to go home and die. They are treating me once again, and telling me that if my cancer returns again, they'll treat me with radiotherapy on my brain. We're talking about the middle of June 2002, as we speak now. My grandson's birthday's coming up now – and who knows?

They got eighteen months out of me. I have to say that I'm eternally grateful that I have that extra time – that bonus. I don't feel bitter about anything. If I pop off tomorrow, I'm already in front. It's given me time to sort things out and get rid of my bits and pieces, and do everything I've got to do.

I asked Pat how making *Aufpet 3* had differed from making the earlier two series. Were there certain things that he could no longer do?

There was nothing I didn't do. There's no doubt that I had a lot of pain – although I didn't admit it. My medication didn't help me with my concentration – with my lines and things. I was having chemotherapy. In the middle of that lot, I also had an attack of kidney stones. The day we had the photograph taken for the cover of 'If', I was in terrible pain. I think it showed, in the photograph. I actually passed a kidney stone that day!

For the first time in my life, I sent out for paracetamol. Don' forget, during my course of chemotherapy, I handed back all of my painkillers, and just took my steroids, and was fortunate enough not to suffer any of the side effects. I didn't have diarrhoea, or the skin problems I was told about. I had no hair loss. I shaved my hair off, to get a thousand pounds for the kid. My hair grew back stronger than it was; albeit, I'm a bit thin on top anyway. Who knows, if I have chemotherapy again, I may lose it all. But hey – all that matters is that they're keeping me alive!

Pat had vivid memories of making *Auf pet 3*, but every single day that he survived, was a bonus in itself.

Like alcoholics say: "Taking one day at a time – being a winner." You arise from your bed, and do a day's work, having been under sentence of death from Valentine's Day 2000. So, waking up every day, and getting through it, was a tremendous bonus.

You know that you're not going to die overnight. But you know that you are dying, so you wonder how far through that particular day you're going to make it. But you ignore it – you just carry on. I was different, but I tried not to think about it. It would have been grossly unfair to other people. Ironically it wasn't so long ago that Timmy Spall was out of action for a year, but he managed to survive leukaemia and continue with a highly successful career.

At the rehearsal, we found ourselves in Middlesbrough, in the northeast of England, which has never been looked upon as a holiday resort type of place, to say the least! In fact, it was very cold and grim, and open, with a cold wind. In my situation, with a tube linked up to my heart…. We stayed in a beautiful hotel in Middlesbrough, and travelled from there, to the location on the bridge and the river, every day, having always been picked up. Having got through that, I used to do my exercise – a thousand free squats and 500 press-ups, before my lunch. Even the guy who looked after the caravans, if it had been raining, said, "I've put the caravan steps out for you Pat." Good as gold – they looked after me so well!

According to Chris Fairbank, "'9/11' happened, a few weeks after we started filming, so at that time, for about five days, there were no aircraft flying out of or into America at all. The schedule was five or six weeks of filming in the UK, followed by five weeks in Arizona, then returning to the UK for another three or four weeks of filming, to finish it all off. After 9/11, it looked as though Arizona could well be in jeopardy: there was talk of maybe having to go to the South of Spain, all of which was pretty depressing. But the most important thing was to keep the show going and get it done. As we all know, aircraft started flying again and – hurrah, hurrah! Arizona was back on."

Although Arizona was a spectacular location, the work schedule was particularly demanding. "The way they work you nowadays," explains Tim Healy, "we're doing seventy-two hours a week normally, in my part. I'm in just about every scene. The main thing I remember was that the scenery and the light were fantastic."

Moving from England to Arizona was a tremendous adventure in itself. I wouldn't fly the very last leg, because it was a light aircraft and I don't like them. They reminded me of previous experiences in New Zealand and South Africa. Sure enough, Jimmy Nail, Tim Healy and Kevin were travelling in the plane, and the undercarriage wouldn't come down. They had to pump it down with a hand-jack – oh yes – on the same small aircraft that I would have been travelling in! I drove down for nearly eight hours to Vegas, instead, – four hours each way. I'd had a couple of days there before. I'm not a gambler, but it was quite interesting, seeing those locations. We got into Navajo country, which was quite an experience – being up at six o'clock in the morning… wonderful views.

In one particular episode, we see Kevin, sitting cross-legged on a rock – exactly the sort of thing I could imagine Pat doing (as opposed to Bomber).

Yes – that was as a result of a conversation I had with Kevin – within the story – which they cut out; because I used to go down and do that – and contemplate. Bomber said something like: "I know it sounds funny, coming from an old codger like myself, but I like to go down and sit on a rock and contemplate the sunset." The name of the tribe in the series was fictitious, whereas the Native Americans they actually filmed with were Navajo.

I remember sitting chatting to the Medicine Man one day. Gordon, the other Indian guy came up and sat the other side of me. I made a joke – used a profanity. I said: "F*** hell, I'm surrounded by Indians!" Saginaw Grant looked at me and never changed the expression on his face at all. By now, people will know about Saginaw's face: it's very much a face you don't forget. Without moving at all, and with a deadpan expression, he said: "Now you know how Custer felt!"

Joe Saugus, played by Gordon Tootoosis, is a well-established film actor. According to Chris, "He was in a really good show, back in the 1980s, which was set in Alaska." Kevin explains that he had a scene with Gordon, "… up on the moors in Middlesbrough, but it was odd for him, because he was coming over, not knowing what he was doing. He was mostly in films in the States, and to end up in Middlesbrough… in the winter! It was difficult for him, because we were staying in a hotel up in Seaham – *Seaham Hall*. He only had a couple of scenes in Middlesbrough, but he had to be over there. His scenes were quite a long way apart, so he was a bit stuck, because it was difficult to get from Seaham to any of the metropolis. Although it was a delightful hotel, I think he felt rather stranded there, whilst we were out filming all day every day."

You'd see them taking the part of Native Americans, but if you closed your eyes, and just heard them talking, they were ordinary Americans anyway. I was talking to Gordon one day, at some length, about different things, and he said: "Of course, you guys are out of touch with your ancestors, aren't you?" And he stopped me dead in my tracks – because you're talking about a very intelligent, educated, very 'normal' person. I said: "What do you mean?" He said: "Well, we're still in touch with our ancestors; we talk to them every day." I have to say that I'm the biggest 'Doubting Thomas' in the world: I don't believe in a heaven and an earth, and I don't believe in a better place; I don't believe in any of that stuff – but I believed every word Gordon said. He said that he still keeps in touch with his ancestors, and that he talks to them all of the time. If I think about it, my earliest childhood memories about spiritualism, is that there was always an Indian Spirit Guide. When I was a child, America seemed a million miles away; it wasn't a plane ride or a phone call away – (well I suppose it was – but a difficult phone call away). But when you think about it, America was so far away, and so removed. When Gordon said: "We're still in touch with our ancestors," it took me back in the same way as you would, when you were a very young girl, if you ever heard of anyone being in touch with their Spirit Guide, it was an Indian guide.

Pat asked Saginaw: "What are your earliest memories of speaking to your oldest relative?" It turned out that he *did* have a very old grandfather.

So when you put the two ages together; let's say, in puberty, he was thirteen, so going back 150 years in time, to his grandfather's childhood, you're talking about the time of the Indian tribes, General Custer – and so forth. Saginaw was telling me that at that time, the Whites, allegedly, put smallpox in the blankets of the native Indians, to kill them off. Gordon was pulled out of his tribe and put through a strict school – he couldn't speak a word of English; told about Jesus Christ, and was whacked and smacked if he tried to use his own language. Taken away from his tribe... it must have been terrible for these people.

So what you've got there is first-hand information about what happened, and it's endorsed by a person, by myself, who isn't relating it, simply to sell a book, but merely to remind ourselves about man's inhumanity to man.

There's also the point that Whites had a built-in immunity against certain illnesses, whereas the Indians hadn't. The Native Americans would have been very susceptible to diseases, which the White Man may have, inadvertently, brought with him.

You could say: "Why would Pat want to tell a lie? He doesn't need to make money, he doesn't need to impress me, so the chances are, that under the circumstances, and in view of who was giving him the information, it's true." And that's what's important: that the information is true – it's not exaggerated.

Kevin explains: "Several of the Native American guys were talking about their tribes. I was asking them how the language thing worked. They were tracing Native American words, right down from Canada, where Saginaw was from, down through the North, then through to Arizona, south to New Mexico, and Mexico; how certain words were common to all the Indian tribes and others weren't common at all. How some tribes got on well with others, and others not. It had come about through different things. Some of them had formed alliances with white settlers, others hadn't. It depended. Obviously, there'd been a lot of politics going on, by white settlers, trying to set tribes against each other, I would suspect… a couple of hundred years ago."

Some of the filming took place in Page, Arizona, at the up-market Marriott Hotel, one of the larger ones, where the cast and crew were staying. The town was built in 1957, to house builders working on the Lake Powell Dam.

They filmed all of the gambling scenes in the hotel – the foyer with the fruit machines, and the swimming pool scenes. The people were very friendly. There was this very close link with the British, over the September 11th business – which was very much to the fore. They appreciated that. The local guys used to go out on the shooting range. They shot the bar fight in a local pub. It was really interesting to meet what they called cowboys, and also Indians, in there. As one of the guys was doing a bit of direction in there, telling people where to stand, one of the 'cowboys' said: "We don't want no fighters in here – you'll have to move!" It was ever so funny.

The guy I went shooting with was one of the drivers – but he actually ran the shooting club. In a small town like that, everybody knows everyone else. Under normal circumstances, there wouldn't be much for the local inhabitants to do. Naturally, once the film crew had departed, there would be far less. I was very privileged to fire a real old buffalo gun, at the shooting club, which had actually been used to shoot buffalo. The driver I went shooting with saved me the pelt – he'd put four shots in it, within close proximity. He bought the buffalo from a Buffalo Farm: he paid two thousand dollars for it. The pelt was worth about 1500 dollars. He bought about eight of the buffalo altogether, but reckoned he'd get his money back.

At the Buffalo Farms, hunters were invited to go and kill the animals: they have to be culled anyway. I then shot a very up-to-date sniper's rifle. I would lay claim to never having shot a rifle in my life (although in strictest terms, that's not quite true).

But to all intents and purposes, I'm a hundred per cent amateur. However, at a hundred yards, with this particular rifle, I could take a man's eye out. Unbelievable! You could just point the gun at the target, put the cross on the thing and fire.

Pat explained that even though I've never fired a rifle in my life, he could take me out there, and at five hundred yards, with that particular weapon, I could do the same thing myself! In the series, Bomber quotes from a book of Native American Poetry. Pat admired the way the local authorities protected the land in Arizona. We're talking about thousands of miles of open desert!

We were issued with handouts: 'Do not do this, do not do that.' It was lovely that they took such a pride in the environment. The interesting thing is that we were taken to where John Ford used to film; we saw John Wayne's cabin – the family cabin – and so on. The most amazing thing was that, wherever we went, they'd got these bloody airstrips. We saw a very famous bird that you see in the cartoons – the 'roadrunner'.

It usually has a coyote chasing it. What did it do – shoot by?!

There were loads of coyotes there; we saw them every day. No, it just walked past; it hadn't got anyone chasing it! When we visited the Grand Canyon, as we approached it, we went into the roadside café or bar. We were sitting there when two hunters walked in, with all the hunting paraphernalia.

They didn't sling their guns across the table, did they?

Yes, the guns were just there, in front of them. And we suddenly realised, it was like being in a scene from a western movie – but this was for real! They were out there for three or four days, hunting in the wild – shooting deer. They were talking about, "I've just shot a big one," and so on – city people who'd gone out for a spot of shooting; they bought a license for shooting a certain number of beasts.

I started training again, a couple of weeks ago. I do free squats. But the moment I decided to do it, bang, crash, wallop – my CT turned out bad again. But I shall carry on training, through my medication. I'm continuing to carry the extra weight around my middle, that's my yardstick; while I've still got that, I'm OK. Hopefully, it will stay on, and we shall carry on.

Tim Healy recalls: "I knew about Pat's condition some time before everybody else. The rest of the guys didn't know. He told me, one night. This was the sort of guy that he was. We went to his hotel room, he lifted his T-shirt up and he showed me these drips – one on either side. He said, 'Look, this is me 'chemo'. What I'll do is, I'll tell everybody it's vodka. I'll say, 'What do you say to a vodka? I'm an alcoholic. I've brought me drinks!' If anybody sees it I'll just say it's me drink – because I drink vodka!' He said, 'When I pull my T-shirt down like that, you can't see them, can you? Don't tell the lads yet – don't mention it to the lads. Because when I'm set up with my gear, you can't see it.'

So I knew for a while, until eventually, all of a sudden, the cast knew. It must have been Joy – or Pat, who told them himself. So it then became common knowledge: we all knew that he had terminal cancer. But he hadn't shown anybody his drips, is what I'm saying... only me."

Chris remembers: "The time that it became public was a day when Jimmy had a later call than the rest of us. He showed up and his chin was on his chest, which was a very bad sign. A couple of us saw him, as he got out of his car. He said: 'Look, at some point we've all got to sit down, because I've been given some news, which I wish I didn't know – and we've got to talk about it.' This was approximately two weeks before we were due to go to Arizona.

"It transpired that, the previous night, Jimmy had a call from Franc Roddam, quite late in the evening. Franc was a little bit concerned, to say the very least, because there'd been a 'problem with Pat's medical'. With every job that you do, you have to fill in a 'tick-in-the-box' – type medical form. There is a section with questions that allude to illness or any condition that is on-going – requiring treatment. I believe – although I obviously don't know for certain – that Pat just conveniently left those blank. In effect, he 'lied by omission'."

During Pat's original cancer operation his stomach was raised to chest level, so he was obliged to eat small amounts of food all the time. " I thought that was the main thing that was wrong with him and he was on the mend," recalls Tim Healy. "Because he told me a story about (I'll never forget this), that when he had this first operation, most people are 'knackered' for weeks afterwards. But Pat was on a walking treadmill the day after. And he had these stitches in here (indicates). Then two weeks later, he drove to *Fairfield Hall*, Croydon and wrestled a guy! Like Superman, wasn't he?"

Until Joy told the cast, only Doreen, Pete and Shirley Meakin, Pat's agent, Tim Healy and a handful of his friends, back home knew too. "Well, he was a very private man, wasn't he? He never used to tell you anything," observes Tim. "You used to have to draw things out of him – you know? I thought he'd been given three months to live, three years before. Then I found out from Doreen that no – he'd been given six months to live six years ago.

"But he just did the job – like he always did. I'd be lying around the pool and he'd be in the gym every day still – training – like nothing had changed. As far as the work was concerned, he had his lines up, and he was 'on the ball'." Tim confirms that, had he not known the true situation, there would have been no way of telling that anything was amiss.

"Pat made not one single mention of his condition," confirms Chris. "The only clue to his not being as fit as he would like to be – and certainly has been – was the fact that you'd see him sat there, in a completely alert position, but he'd have his eyes closed, having a little nap. But as soon as he was called to do whatever scene, or somebody asked him a question, or said, 'Oh sorry Pat. Were you asleep there?' He'd say: 'No, no. What d'you mean?' It was just extraordinary really."

Tim Healy points out that location work in Arizona was one of the few jobs where Doreen came out, although she was in Spain for *Series Two*. "I used to see Pat during the day – at work. On every job that I've done with Pat, because he lived in Birmingham and I lived in Cheshire and Newcastle, we would spend the evenings together – in hotels and things. But of course, when Doreen came out to Arizona, I didn't see so much of Pat in the evenings. Obviously, because he wasn't well, they were spending quite a bit of private time together. We saw each other, down for dinner, two or three times, but other than that I just spent time with him on the set. So that was a first for me, because, as you'll discover in Chapter 19, during the filming of *Aufpet 4*, we spent a *long* time together, in the *Meridian Hotel*, in London."

Returning to *Aufpet 3*, Tim was sparring with Pat, one particular evening. "Afterwards, he banged his head somehow and ended up with a black eye. So when he came in on the set the next morning, the lads asked: 'What's happened to your eye?' He said, 'Timmy blacked me eye – he's bloody vicious! He hit me with a bloody right hook, sparring last night. Don't go near bloody Timmy, I tell you!' Afterwards he said, 'Don't tell them kid. Just let them think it's you.' He wanted the lads to think that I'd blacked his eye... they still do!"

Chris Fairbank remembers: "There's one incredibly memorable time. Pat and I had a day off. I think he wanted a bit more company than just him and Doreen." So Chris, Steve Gibson, Doreen and Pat took a day trip out to Monument Valley. En route, they visited John Wayne's cabin, as Pat mentioned earlier. It must have been absolutely marvellous – like stepping back into an old Wild West film set.

"It was absolutely fantastic... and deeply moving, actually," Chris continues. "I subsequently returned to Monument Valley, with Kev, Tim Healy and Paul Weston, who was Second Unit Director. We actually went right round all of the monuments, but it was about an hour-and-a-half – two-hour drive, from where we were staying. The day I went with Pat, he wasn't really 'up for it'. He just wanted something to eat, which, believe-it-or-not, (I found this extraordinary – being America), was really difficult to do. It was out of season, so an awful lot of places that would normally be open for business, were shut, on top of which it was still the post-9/11 'I'm not leaving my house' situation, for fear of terrorists. So it was just deserted. It was great if you were there, because you virtually had the entire place to yourself! But it wasn't so great if you were hungry!"

In the event, they didn't kill a rattlesnake and roast it over a slow-burning fire! "Pat decided that I'd scored the best choice, with an ordinary sandwich I had, with everything in it. Then we drove back and Pat fell asleep, just at the point when we passed one of the largest scrap metal plants in South-west America. I asked Doreen: 'Do you think we should wake him up, because he'd love this?' But she said: 'No, no. Just let him sleep.' Within about five minutes he woke up and of course, we told him that he'd missed all this plant. We had an ironic chuckle about that! But he was *very* tired and actually slept for most of the journey," continues Chris. "Although he didn't really benefit from seeing the sights, Pat was simply glad of the company. The over-riding memory I have of Pat, out there, was that he was in the gym every morning, training the Accounts people and doing all of his exercises."

Although Tim Healy's filming schedule was particularly hectic, he found time to take a day trip on his own, to the Grand Canyon. "Being in the series kept Pat alive – you know? It was *so* important to him," Tim explains. "When Jimmy phoned Pat up about the third series, Pat said: 'It's given me a reason to live.'"

Chris's description of Arizona reminded me of a constantly changing artist's canvas; the sunsets wouldn't be the same, within half an hour of each other. "They were *incredible*," agrees Tim. "I always remember, in the morning, because we used to start so early – at dawn. I've got one shot of the sun coming up, on *one* side of the desert and I've come up the dark cliff, across blue sky, to the moon, and then down to an orange cliff on this side – all in the one shot! That's the way it would change!"

I asked Tim about the light aircraft flight down to Vegas. "Well, as we started descending, the wheels didn't come down. I know a bit about this, because I've flown in the 'Paras'." Pat's friend, Bernie Guest was in the Paratroopers too, so they have that in common. "So, when you put the wheels down, it's an electronic device you see? You press a button. There's a motor that brings the wheels down. Now, if this thing doesn't work, for some reason, you use a mechanical handle. So that's all that happens. But this guy, all of a sudden, he realises that the wheels weren't down, so he's doing this, (mimes him winding them down). I'm filming along the front – the nose of the plane, as we're coming into land, and Kevin's filming from the back. If we put the two films together it would be great! I was doing a running commentary, 'Well it seems ladies and gentlemen, that we've got a bit of a *problem* here – he hasn't got the wheels down! So we've got to go round again. If he doesn't get them down this time, I think we're going to have a bit of a problem!' But when we came in the second time, we just landed."

Kevin comments: "I think it's fairly common for them to wind the wheels down manually, but it's quite 'hairy', because you don't know what's happening! The port wheel had come down, but the starboard one hadn't, so this guy was pumping away with his arm, without actually telling us what was going on! I've had a flying lesson myself too. Tim was in the co-pilot's seat, Jimmy was in the middle and I was at the back. It was funny, because Tim had his own video camera and I'd borrowed one from the Director. We were both busily filming from our own ends, as a kind of distraction.

"None of us were due to go to Vegas. There was a scene where we go there, to find Joe's son, who works on a High Rise building. But there wasn't time in the schedule. So we said: 'Well, look, this is going to be a nonsense; if we just have a Second Unit taking out POV – it will be just so obvious. Is there no way we can go down there?' Joy said: 'Well the only time is such-and-such a weekend, but that's your weekend off.' We said: 'Well, we'd rather be in the shot, so if you get us a decent hotel, we'll fly down and film the thing, 'buckshee', and not worry about overtime or anything like that.' We'd get a weekend in Vegas and do a bit of filming at the same time. It seemed like a good idea to me – flying down Grand Canyon, to Vegas.

"Pat may have driven there and back, but not that same weekend, because he had time off with his Steve, his driver. He couldn't fly directly into Phoenix. They flew into Los Angeles and Steve picked him up from there, so they may have driven through Las Vegas and the Grand Canyon that way."

One of the experiences, which increased Pat's fear of flying in light aircraft, occurred whilst filming *Willow* in New Zealand. Pat insisted on making the long drive back to base, from a mountain top location, but his makeup artists, plus certain crewmembers, narrowly avoided being killed – in the same aircraft that Pat was meant to have taken! Noel Clarke wasn't keen, either. Having made the trip to Arizona in a small plane, he made the return trip by road, saying, "Planes in this day and age shouldn't have propellers!"

Despite getting up around 6.15am for filming in Arizona, they returned earlier in the evenings, in comparison with DR, because of the light. According to Pat, traffic-wise, the evening return trip was much longer in DR compared with Arizona, and travelling in Arizona was much easier. "Yes – because you wouldn't see a car," agrees Tim. "They had these fantastic roads, which went on forever. You can't really describe them – they were *awesome*.

You'd think: 'Oh – there's a car coming.' Then it would be gone and you'd not see another one, for half an hour. You'd be driving towards a mountain, for twenty minutes and you'd think: 'Well, I'm still no nearer to it!'"

I wondered how much contact Tim had with Gordon Tootoosis, or with Saginaw? "Well, I worked with them every day. Saginaw blessed us all one day, which was fantastic. Then I asked him to wave to my son Matthew, on my video. Saginaw made a necklace for my Denise as well, out of buffalo horn: obviously, a dead one; they don't kill the animal to make these things. That was one of his specialities – making this beautiful jewellery. Saginaw and I took a great boat out on the lake. He was an extraordinary man – a proper Medicine Man – a fully-fledged Shaman."

In the series, he appears to be a man of very few words. Was he like that in real life? "Yes, he *was* really – and a very generous man. I remember after I paid to hire the boat for the day, he bought us all a T-shirt afterwards to say thanks for the boat trip. He was a nice guy." Pat emphasised how grateful he was to the cast, and the BBC, for being so supportive, throughout both of the latest series. By not giving him any great story lines, they allowed him to continue working.

As he and Pat were such close friends, Tim has written an entire chapter for our book, as a special tribute. Chapter 19, which he referred to earlier, is entitled *There's A Statue In My Garden*, and is based on a poem that Tim wrote for Pat's funeral. He also did a joint book signing with me, in Pat's place, at *W.H. Smith's* bookstore in Union Street, Birmingham, in December 2004, just under five months after his friend's demise.

Pat described filming in Arizona as 'an adventure in itself'. Chris agrees: "It was awesome. Out of all the shows that we've subsequently done, since the original two series, Arizona was, without doubt, the most incredible experience, from Day One until the last. It was just jaw-droppingly brilliant! It was a combination of everything. The location was absolutely stunning. The fact that we were there, doing this show, with this extraordinary backdrop – of just the different positions of the sun, each day. It would give you a completely different vista from the one you'd had, half an hour ago. It was like that every *single* day."

Chapter Fourteen

RETURN TO BRAY

I particularly remember Marble Canyon in Arizona. Pat and I stood on the edge of a high canyon, looking down on the Colorado River – just the two of us. Everything looked emerald green. He said: "It makes you glad to be alive!" There wasn't a day when he didn't remark: "Kid, look at the mountains!" He seemed to have an 'eye' for that sort of thing. Pat's outlook brought me down to earth, reminding me about the importance of appreciating simple things and the beauty of Nature. Also the importance of not losing sight of such things... which it would be very easy to do.

Noel Clarke, Bray Studios, December 2001

It was a cold and grey Monday morning, on the 17 December 2001, when I made the six-hour return journey to Bray Studios, in Water Oakley, Windsor, Berkshire, at Pat's invitation. Being unfamiliar with the exact location of the studios, I missed the rather nondescript entrance, making a U-turn a few yards further up the road. Panicking a little, (the last thing I wanted to do was to be late for such an important engagement), I eventually parked my Volvo on a gravelled area, at the far end of the long and winding drive. Reception was in the Old House, some distance to the right, from the studios. After I'd sipped a reviving cup of tea in the studio canteen, Pat's driver, Steve arrived, to escort me to the Studio Lot, having checked, via his mobile phone, that it was an opportune moment.

As our shoes scrunched on the gravelled pathways, I felt as though I was about to be reunited with old friends. My interviews with Tim Spall, Chris Fairbank and Kevin Whately in 2000, for Pat's first biography – *If – The Pat Roach Story*, albeit by telephone, had been both friendly and helpful. I felt doubly at home with Tim Healy, having previously interviewed him in person, the day he moved into his new countryside home, on Alderley Edge; a pleasure which I was to repeat in August 2004, for this book.

Each of the principal actors working on *Aufpet 3* had his own designated chair. I felt particularly welcome when a cast member, (I forget which one), suggested that I should seat myself in the chair marked 'Artiste: Pat Roach' – (well, he couldn't throw me out, because he was on set!) The studio lot resembled a huge corrugated aircraft hangar, or warehouse, with a grey concrete floor and an area to the right, sectioned off like a small room, from which echoing voices emanated… the 'lads' were rehearsing a scene. In the area where I was seated, various members of the production team went about their business.

According to the Callsheet for the day – Sheet Number 86, some of those present had breakfasted from 0700h, then begun work at 0800h, with an estimated Wrap time of 1900h – a long day! Listed on the Callsheet were Executive Producers Laura Mackie and Franc Roddam, Producer Joy Spink and Director, Paul Seed. Also, details of the day's pickup schedule for the principal cast, and the news that the Wrap Party would be in two days' time on Wednesday 19 December, in the West End.

They were filming five scenes that day in 'INT – THE HUT' – even I could work that one out! The first scene read: 'The lads are off for a night out in a bar, hatless,' (as opposed to 'legless', I suppose?). This was followed by 'the lads discuss their police problems'; Oz stops Wyman spending all his money'; 'Barry gives them the good news, but he has to do polygraph'; then, finally ''The cradle is missing'. No doubt readers will recall some of those scenes.

Each actor had his own number from 1-7: Tim Healy was 1, then Kevin, Jimmy, Tim Spall, Chris, Pat and Noel; Pat was number 6. The numbers were shown alongside the relevant scenes, so it was immediately obvious which actors were involved. I sat in the *total* silence required, each time filming began, listening to the dialogue for an hour or so, as crew and actors worked diligently.

If there are only two things that remain, fixed in perpetuity in my memory from that morning, they will be: Neville, dressed in shorts, summer shirt and sandals, with a bandanna around his head – Sergeant Lewis he definitely wasn't! Also, the sheer amount of patience required by the actors, to retake the same shots and repeat the dialogue, over and over again; even for simple things like entering and exiting a set; if the lighting or any *other* detail wasn't perfect, it had to be re-done. By the end of an hour, I was word-perfect!

Kevin will soon star in his own ITV series, *Lewis*, the sequel to Morse. The pilot episode was broadcast on Sunday 29 January 2006. Kevin is filming the new series as this book goes to print.

Around 11.30am, the man himself, in 'Bomber' mode, emerged from behind the screens, and introduced me to the cast, plus some of the production team. As he wasn't needed for the next two scenes, we took a break, to discuss what was then our current project, *Pat Roach's Birmingham*. Pat and Jimmy Nail were staying at a rather grand hotel, just a few hundred yards up the road from the studios. The village of Water Oakley, where the studios are located, is the quintessential English village, complete with Norman Church. According to Kevin Whately, when there were access problems in Oxford, certain scenes from *Morse* were filmed in this actual village.

Noel Clarke and I ate our lunch on trays, whilst he kindly gave me a short, pre-arranged interview, to be followed, six days later, once filming was complete, by a more detailed telephone interview. The two photographs of Pat and Noel, with myself, were taken by those two gentlemen, in the room where we ate lunch.

Noel explained that he grew up in West London. Both parents had been born in Trinidad, but his mother emigrated to England in 1969. Noel has an older brother, who lives in America. Whilst taking a three-year college course, resulting in three A Levels, in Media Studies, Theatre Studies and Physical Education, Noel worked as a lifeguard, and a gym fitness instructor/ assistant manager. During the course, he played the title role in a play – *Superman – the Pantomime*, written and produced by the students. He has always been interested in acting, although his mother was unable to help, or offer any advice.

Writer/director Rikki Beadle-Blair was running a course, where Noel happened to be working, so he and Noel knew one other by sight. A friend of Noel's told Rikki that he was interested in acting. Rikki subsequently wrote, directed and acted in a pilot programme for Channel 4 – *Hetrosexuality*. Noel played his son. This later became a series – *Metrosexuality,* in which Noel played a young straight boy, with two gay fathers! The series featured about thirty characters, whose stories were interwoven throughout six episodes. It was broadcast on Channel 4 in February and March 2001. According to Noel, it was the kind of series that certainly had an impact on viewers: you either loved it or hated it! It had one-and-a-half million viewers per episode, and sufficient impact to get him an audition for *Auf pet*.

Between the pilot and the series he made two short films: *Native*, about a Jamaican immigrant, and *Take 2* – about a student. He also played roles in *The Bill*, three episodes of *Casualty* and *Waking the Dead*, a detective series, which also happened to be produced by Joy Spink. Noel plays both comedy and straight roles.

He observes: "Pat finds good in everything, even in the grimiest settings. He'll look at a thing and say: 'Isn't it lovely?'" Speaking of his relationship with Pat, he said that he felt like 'Uncle Pat' – a favourite uncle, and that Pat has a great sense of humour. Noel used to watch him wrestle on Saturday afternoons. Pat was very encouraging and supportive during the making of the series. In this way he had perhaps "paid him back in kind." (Noel made this comment after I explained how 'the boys' helped Pat in the early days of the first *Aufpet* series). Pat predicted that Noel would be a star in his own right, in a few years time.

Joining the group as a new person could have been difficult enough, but there was also the age gap to consider. However, all the cast made Noel feel at home in a very demonstrative way (hugs, etc). The Director, Paul Seed, and the Producer, Joy Spink, were both present at his audition, earlier that summer. He was somewhat confused; thinking initially that it was, perhaps, a low budget reprise, with an entirely new and younger cast. When he realised that it was the original cast, he became uncharacteristically nervous.

Noel found himself on a very fast learning curve: from doing a mini series he's moved quickly to a really well established one, in a very short space of time. By watching the other actors at work, he picked up some useful tips, particularly from Tim Spall. People sometimes refer to an actor as having 'it'. In Noel's opinion, Tim Spall certainly has!

The most difficult aspect of making the series was the pressure of not wanting to let the boys down. Gary Holton's character, Wayne, is mentioned a few times in the dialogue. "The storyline is that he had an affair with a coloured girl in Camberwell: Wyman, my character, was the result! There are a few jokes about the colour thing. They refer to it, but don't dwell on it." Four years later, Noel has become an integral member of the cast.

Noel remembers a time in Middlesbrough when three of them were looking at the River Tees. "There were power plants, it was cold and wet, the scenery was grim; it's quite a wide river. There was a seal in the water. Pat remarked on that too. He can see beauty in the grimmest of situations."

In a subsequent interview, on Sunday 23 December 2001, Noel explained: "The story starts in Middlesbrough, where the guys meet Oz, and he tells them of a plan he has, about a bridge. I get into to it because I'm just Wayne's son – who turns up – and meets up with the rest of the guys. When I read the script. It said 'Gary met Wyman's mum in a concert in Camberwell' – and there was no real reference as to where she was from. Wyman likes to think he's a strong character. He's a young guy who's basically left everything in London, to travel around with these older guys; there is an element of 'cool' there too. He comes over exactly as what he is – the young character who says silly things sometimes, and gets treated with the respect that he earns – basically. If he does something smart, they think he's a smart kid; if he does something stupid then... They treat him like a younger member of the group. I think if he wasn't Wayne's boy, they wouldn't have taken him under their wing."

Noel has a favourite expression: "Oki-dokey!" – which he uses from time to time, but my overall impression is of an easy-going charm, underpinned by an understated shrewdness and perception; a young man who definitely knows where he's going! One of the conditions of the role was that he should pass a driving test, which he managed to do with great alacrity, at the first attempt.

"Wyman is into his music," explains Noel. "A lot of the time he has his headphones on. He pretty much does what he's told. There are a few times when he gets a bit irate, but not with any of the other guys. He tends to speak his mind, and that might get him into trouble. He looks up to them all: they're his dad's mates. In this third series, you won't see him befriend any particular one, but he has his moments with all of them. The character that he interacts with most would be Oz – which was down to the writers. The character of Oz didn't get on well with Wyman's father, Wayne; the Londoner and the Geordie didn't quite get on; the theme is continued – through Wyman – his son.

"There's a specific scene with Bomber, when I'm driving a boat up the river – up the Tees – in Middlesbrough. Wyman's talking about what it's like for him, hanging around with the six of them, and how he's enjoying it. Bomber says: 'I don't understand why you hooked up with us old farts!' Wyman tells Bomber that he's having the time of his life; he's driving a boat down the river, and he's enjoying himself. He feels like an action hero! It's just the two of us in the boat – a good scene." Thanks to Doreen, we've included a photograph of preparations for this actual scene.

I asked about other, favourite moments. "The entrance of Wyman, I think, plus the boat scene with Bomber which is a good one. I do like that, because I had to qualify to drive the boat. It was a two-day course: that was really cool! But the first entrance of Wyman, when all the guys are together for the first time – and then he walks in; it's that first episode that sticks out in my mind. Not particularly when I was doing it, but since I've watched it. It's not that I thought that I did it quite well, it was – like – seeing the six of them together for the first time. As I walk in, there's a shot of all six of them. It just felt so good – to see them all back together again. And then, even though I'm Wyman, not Wayne, when all seven of them are together – it's like – the group's back again. Even though they're the group and I'm the extra – the London element is back again."

Do you know why they chose the name Wyman? Was there any particular reason?

"He says in the script that he thinks his mum wanted it to be close to 'Wayne', without actually *being* Wayne. That's a line in the script. Just to see them all together again is quite something, because I used to watch the programme when I was a kid."

Did it feel quite strange – that here you were – actually *in* the series with them?

"I don't really get nervous or frightened about much, because they're actors and I'm just an actor, doing a job. But there was a time when I was at dinner with them. I was sitting down and I just thought to myself: my goodness! I looked up and I thought: 'Oh my God! I'm in America with Kevin Whately, Tim Spall, Tim Healy et cetera!' It was a social occasion, so you have to try to just be yourself. There *were* moments when it hit me and I thought: 'Wow – hold on!' I'd been watching these guys from about the age of five years old!"

Were they as you imagined them at all – as people?

"Yeah. They're great – all of them. They made me feel so welcome. Each one of them is so different from the other, in his own way." Kevin makes that point about casting: "...chemistry is so much a matter of luck: it's 90% luck really!"

Pat was saying there's a possibility of doing a further series next year. Would you say there's still plenty of scope for developing the characters?

"The series has, inadvertently become about some form of travel, hasn't it? The first series was Germany, then Spain, now America. So they always seem to travel. So, if you put that element in there, there's always scope for a great story."

You could go on forever really, couldn't you?

"Yes, because there are so many new places. Character-wise, I think it would be good to tackle the subject of them getting older. I'd like to see maybe one of the tough characters realising he's not so tough any more. Or maybe one of the cute characters realising that he's not so cute any more. You know what I mean?" The characters are so true-to-life anyway, but that would add an extra dimension, and extend the plot even further.

Tell me about Dick Clement and Ian La Frenais. What sort of contact have you had with them? They were in our first book and they've written the *Foreword* for this one.

"I met them about three times: at the 'read-through', which was three weeks before we started filming, somewhere just off Kensington High Street; we just said "hello" – and so forth. I'm sure they had something to do with the casting. They may have seen the tape – although I don't know that for certain. Since then I've met them a couple of times – at the hotels in Middlesbrough. Then they came to America as well. They're two great guys – and both so different. Whenever I see Ian, if I didn't know who he was, I'd think, 'That's a rock star': his hair – the way he walks! I mean, I love them to bits. I've only met them a few times, but they're great. Dick Clement, to me, seems like the perfect English gentleman: quiet and reserved. They're so different and yet they seem to connect. They just write brilliantly, don't they?"

Yes – their characters are so believable. Were you able to discuss Wyman's character with them in any depth?

"Not really. At this stage I'm just grateful to have the job. Everybody got his say at the beginning – in rehearsal week. So I put a few points across. But I was just grateful to take whatever brilliant writing they wrote – and do what I do with it. In the opening scene, Wyman's described as slim and polite."

And good-looking! (I'd read one of his script sheets).

"I don't remember that! They wrote it, and I tried to play it as best I could."

It's easier actually isn't it, if they don't give you much detail? Because it gives you more scope?

"Yes, the thing is that if they do go again, now he's established, there'll have to be more to it, won't there? But for the moment, I did all right, and I was just thankful for that."

We discussed Paul Seed's input as Director: "Whenever he thought I should do something a certain way, he did what he's supposed to do – directed me. I didn't want to make him as South London as Wayne."

No, because Gary was actually born a Cockney.

"Mainly because I didn't think he would come over. I'm not saying I can't do it, but it's many years on, and Wayne certainly wasn't that close to his son: he used to come up and see him every now and again. I though of Wyman as more of a West Londoner.

"I remember Pat was always giving me advice – when we were in the car together – or something like that. 'Cause I don't *really* drink, (although I do sometimes), and he was telling me how that was a good thing – and stuff like that. He said, 'You're not one of those people who never drink, and say it's a bad thing. You do *sometimes*, so you know what it's all about. You just *choose* not to do it.' He appreciated that – and *I* appreciated that he did. He was always giving me that sort of advice.

"Oh, I've got a good one! I used to be a fitness instructor, I still am qualified – and still do it sometimes. There was one day in Middlesbrough when we were training together, and there's me – twenty-something – like:

'Yeah, I'm going to do this!' And Pat's doing the squats, and he out–squatted me, by about 150 – he *completely* out-squatted me. My legs were killing me. But he just kept going! So that was a good moment. We always ate fish for lunch, instead of greasy, fatty meat. After lunch he'd come up to me, and he'd say: 'What did you have? Did you have the fish?' This became a tradition with us. And I'd nod: 'Yeah.' And he'd say: 'Good lad!'"

I can imagine him saying that! You mentioned his sense of humour. People often refer to it, in our books. Were there other occasions when you particularly noticed it?

"He was just funny most of the time. It's a *different* kind of funny though; it's not the Tim Spall and Tim Healy kind of 'funny'. He's got this look – whenever something happened – like we were arriving late or something. I'd look over and he'd look at me, and we'd give each other a kind of *look*."

I'd say that he's got a *sardonic* sense of humour – his mum's got the same type. It's half-sarcastic and half-ironic. But as you say, it's not straight humour – it's his own particular brand isn't it?

"Yes, and one I could completely *get*. I was really in tune with it. We've had a hectic filming schedule on this third series, without much leisure time. We had a week off before we went to America, but once we arrived there, it was all go: we only had one full weekend off."

I know the hours were really long, because when I needed to contact Pat about our book, while he was over there, the combination of Trans-Atlantic time differences and long hours of filming, made any communication very difficult. What were the actual hours of filming?

"It depended upon your call. Usually the call for the crew was about 6 in the morning and we'd be called at 6.30/7am. – or something like that. Then you'd work right through the twelve hours."

They were in Marble Canyon for quite some time, for the Native American scenes, which Noel particularly enjoyed. I asked Noel to clarify the various locations. Filming started in London, the read-through was in Kensington, and there was somewhere else apart from Bray wasn't there?

"Yes, we did some scenes just outside London. We also did some filming in a club called *Subterranea*, in Ladbroke Grove. It's about five minutes away from where I live. I wanted to walk to the set, but they wouldn't allow me to. I didn't have a hand in choosing the club as a setting – it was a complete coincidence. It was very strange that it was just a few minutes away, and I already knew the nightclub quite well. It was a pretty good for what we were doing down there. It was supposed to be the club in Middlesbrough, in Episode Three, where Oz goes with a few of the guys, to watch his son sing

Dusty Springfield – to his horror – in drag! Middlesbrough, of course, was cold and grim, but I enjoyed the whole thing. Arizona was a complete contrast to that – the opposite end of the scale – hot... with blue skies."

At Bray Studios the other day, you mentioned the mountains in connection with Pat – the stars, the mountains; the wide-open spaces in Arizona, and the Colorado River. "Oh man – yes! I can't describe it – it's just amazing!"

It's probably similar to the way I felt when I saw the Canadian Rockies for the first time. I went on a two-week tour of them; so huge and magnificent.

"And they're red in Arizona. The people were just great – really friendly – in Middlesbrough *and* Arizona. We met lots of Native Americans, because we filmed on a reservation. All the ones who had lines were professional actors: those who were really established – like Gordon. The dances were amazing. The extras were just real live Native Americans who were helping out."

The dances and the music made quite an impression on Pat too. In fact we wrote a Native American song together, which was quite rhythmical. What type of dances did they do? Was there a Rain Dance, for example?

"They did their traditional dances in the story. In the film they were actually doing it 'live' for us. There were guys beating the drums, and a range of other instruments. They did a *Celebration Dance* and a *Peace Dance*. They were Navajo, in Marble Canyon."

Returning to Bray, did you do any location work for the series there? I noticed several scenic locations in and around the studios last Monday.

"I didn't see any of that, because I didn't stay at the hotel. They picked me up from home every day. All I saw was the inside of the warehouses! I believe there *was* some location filming there, but I wasn't involved in it. It was a pleasurable experience for me, as a newcomer. They all treated me really well, from the producer down to the caterers."

Where do you go from here? What are your plans?

"Well, I'm trying to get one of my short films made – that I've written. It's about four friends who, after a party, discuss the discipline they used to get as children. It makes a humorous story. Nowadays, you can't get that kind of discipline because it's thought of as 'abuse'. It's not geared to one particular race – black, white or whatever. So they reminisce – talk about it – the beatings they used to get. Back then it was the norm."

Is there an underlying message?

"That in the end you can look back and laugh about it, but it could be mentally damaging.

I'm showing various aspects of it and trying to present a balanced picture; there are different kinds of abuse. It's called *Licks*."

Noel explained that *Licks* is a West Indian term for: "You're going to get beaten (get licks) when you get home." It could also be thought of in terms of the licks or 'blows' that life deals us. As far as long-term plans are concerned, Noel simply says, "I'd like to have a good career and get good jobs. Eventually I'd like to do films. I'm into writing too, but I'll just see where it takes me. I don't want to jinx myself by saying that. I'd just like it to go well." Noel has more recently been playing Billie Piper's boyfriend, Mickey Smith, in the *Doctor Who* series. His new film, *Kidulthood*, which he's written himself, was scheduled for release at the end of 2005. During a June 2006 visit to London there were posters in the Underground, advertising it.

Before *Aufpet 3* ended, discussions were already under way about making a fourth series. The idea of setting it in Cuba came to Ian while he was at a hotel bar, filming the third series. Having gone to the trouble of getting everyone together again, they decided it was the least they could do. Whilst on a recce trip to Cuba, before the third series had even been screened, Dick, Ian, Franc and Jimmy discovered that there was a special Foreign Office department which, for security reasons, employs building companies to work exclusively on British government buildings. And so the seeds of a new idea began to take root...

Around the period when Pat was working on *Aufpet 3*, one of his boxer friends, Johnny King, caught him in an unusually despondent mood; normally he was always cheerful. "I was at his Winson Green scrap yard and he was talking about his funeral," explains Johnny. "He said that he was thinking about being buried in a cardboard box! I always remember that. I said: 'Blimey Pat – you're planning it a bit early aren't you?' He said: 'I just want to get it out of the road, because this business is going to pot.'"

Johnny's friend, Billy Wooding adds: "I can honestly say, I never *ever* saw him like that, in all the years that I've known him, Pat was the one who would bring you out of a depressed mood – if anything. He'd liven you up, straight away." Thankfully Pat changed his mind about the cardboard box!

As I sit here on Saint Valentine's Day, February 2002, the second anniversary of my 'death sentence', I've had eighteen months extra time. So I'm doing very well, after not knowing whether I was going to make it to Christmas 2001. We started filming 'Aufpet 3' in August 2001 and finished on the 18 December. Having initial thoughts about anything these days, and any form of projection into the future, is very difficult. But I have to be positive about things, so I think to myself: 'Well, with a bit of luck, we'll be doing 'Aufpet 4'.

Pat's ultimate dream, about taking part in the revival of the series, had been realised; no drama scriptwriter could have devised a better plot!

Episode One of *Aufpet 3* was first transmitted on Sunday 28 April 2002 and was seen by over 12 million viewers. It was a resounding success, subsequently scoring a 'hat-trick' by receiving three awards for 2002: *Best New Drama* at the TV *Quick Awards* in September 2002, the *National Television Award* for *Most Popular Drama* and *Best TV Comedy Drama* at the *Comedy Awards*. Furthermore, on 11 March 2003, it was announced that the programme was one of four nominees for a BAFTA award for 'Best Drama Series'. Members of the cast duly attended the ceremony at the London Palladium, in April 2003, but the award went to *Shackleton* (Firstsight Films, Channel 4)... 'You can't win 'em all!'

Julia Tobin recalls: "One memory that really stands out about Pat, involves the *National Television Awards*. I wasn't invited, as the BBC has taken over this series now. Because it's a 'guy' thing and places were limited, the guys were invited, but I had to ask if I could go. The only way I could do it, was to go as Tim Healy's guest. I *did* say to all of the guys: 'If you win the award, you go up and I'll stay.' But Pat said: 'No you won't. You'll come up with everybody else.' So I said, 'OK – fine. If that's alright with you, I'll do that.'

"So I went up and I was hanging to the back so that the guys could take the credit. But I felt this enormous hand in the small of my back and he pushed me right to the front – and would *not* let me stay at the back. And that really sums Pat up: he will always put you to the front – he won't let you hide in the background."

Pat had an instinctive ability for 'wearing the other person's hat'. 'Empathy' is a very overworked word these days, but he undoubtedly had a gift for feeling what other people were feeling: it was one of his outstanding qualities.

Having already been asked if I'll do 'Aufpet 4', I've worked out that if I go on another course of treatment and it works, I'll be about ready to start the next series, as I come out of it. Because the BBC, during the last series, arranged for my driver to take me back to Birmingham, paying for all my expenses, his overnight stay, petrol and so on. Hats off to the BBC. They were absolutely as good as gold... First Class.

Chapter Fifteen

THE AMBASSADOR...
AND THE JUNGLE

Today is 14 February 2003... and I'm doing very well. Whenever I do things nowadays, I say: "This is not a criticism, but an observation." I have no criticisms about my well being, or being, or whatever, of late, because every day's a bonus: I'm just around – and that will do. Having said that, I'm going for a CT in a few days' time, and the outcome of that will determine whether or not I go to the West Indies.

They may decide, after the CT, that things are very bad for me, and I'm going to die, but they can keep me alive with chemotherapy again, or even radiotherapy. If that happens, I really wouldn't be able to do 'Aufpet 4'. Because once I start a course of 'chemo', it takes about four months or so to complete. It might well be that I never get around to doing it. But I'm sure that, at some stage, I will be in it. Because quite frankly, if I do start to go downhill, I'll make sure that the programme benefits from it, if they consider it beneficial, by mentioning my demise, and the fact that they had me down as having Hepatitis B, which commonly develops into cancer. They've been very clever in the way they've written the series, because if I were to die, it wouldn't present them with any problems. They did the same thing, of course, in the third 'Aufpet'. It was very commendable that they decided to do it that way, rather than just giving me the sack.

Pat was fairly confident that a story line could be fashioned, explaining that Bomber was too ill to travel with them to the West Indies.

At this stage, at the Awards Ceremony, one of the BBC production people explained that Castro's office said that we would be welcome over there (obviously they want the money), but that if Britain went to war with the Americans, against Iraq, then we wouldn't be. So it may well be, that with or without me, they may not go to Cuba. I'm sure they will film somewhere in the South-American continent, because they want the authenticity of the trip.

As things turned out, contracts were signed for April 2003. Then on 14 April 2003, a week prior to their departure for Central America, the cast assembled at Brompton Oratory in South Kensington, London for a read-through of the fourth series. Most of *Aufpet 4* was filmed in the Dominican Republic. Chris Fairbank described the scripts, as among the best he'd ever read.

Kevin Whately recalls: "It was a strange time, because it was just after 9/11, so America was really quite defensive; they were all flying the flag in their gardens. It was a time when Americans were pulling together. They were *hugely* friendly towards us – they were delighted that we were there, because Blair had been so supportive; they really appreciated that. I remember a guy getting into the lift with me, at our hotel, the *Ambassador*, in DR, and saying: 'Oh, you're British. It's great to have you as an allay!'"

As not only Pat's biographer, but also his friend, I always took an optimistic view of his illness. So I said: "Let's just imagine that you were fine. Do you know much about your proposed role in *Aufpet 4?*"

Yes, Bomber's still with Lainie, played by actress, Georgina Lightning. He's still got her and the boy very much at heart – and loves them both dearly. His home is in Arizona – on the reservation. He refers to it, a few times, in the dialogue. He says: "My home is in Arizona. I've got a new family, and I feel like a man who's been given a second chance in life. I wake up every morning and thank God and the angels, for my blessings." That's the sort of thing that he says – on more than one occasion.

Bomber is, as usual, the older person. In a very funny way, he's very stalwart. In Series 3, Tim Healy said: "Poor old Bomber eh? I always thought Bomber was indestructible." And in actual fact, when the writers wrote that, it was probably because they thought that I was – indestructible – being this biggish, powerful person. As always, it's very skilfully written – like art imitating life. I exercised every day, even during lunchtime, and they just saw me as being invincible. Of course, the dreaded 'Big C' just brings everybody down to size. So that's been 'ghosted in' – if you'll pardon the pun!

Brian 'Bomber' Busbridge leaves Arizona for a while, to join the 'boys' in Russia; finishing off a job, through Barry's *former* links with Tatiana, (played by Branka Katic), although he's no longer married to her. But unbeknown to them, they're actually working for the Russian Mafia!

The result is that Barry ends up in jail again – through no fault of his own. Bomber suggests that they gather outside for the inevitable 'group photograph', in front of the big house, but it blows up behind them – with all the money and passports inside! Then the boys finish up in the British Embassy in Russia, trying to get a bacon sandwich, and the fare home. Neville says: "Can I ring my wife? I'll reverse the charges" – whereupon he does!

Before returning to Britain, they meet up with an old comrade of Oz's, named Gus, who worked with him, a few years previously.

Through Gus they discover that there's a gang of Brits working there, in Russia, almost alongside them, who they'd never bumped into, because the other group had not been round the pubs in the normal way; they'd been going to embassy parties. Whereupon the boys say: "What Embassy parties?" They discover that there's an organisation called 'OED', (Moxey re-christens it the 'Odds-and-Ends Department), which takes building workers abroad, to work in their embassies; because of the bugging situation, they take their own workers, and the boys decide to 'get on board' – "We'll try that."

A clever ploy, because it introduces a completely different scenario. During the interview, they're asked if any of them have skeletons in the cupboard. Bomber and Dennis look at Oz (because the other boys aren't there). Moxey would normally be an obvious suspect.

Oz says: "Well, I might as well tell you, because you're going to find out at a later stage, I do have a skeleton in my cupboard." Bomber and Dennis think: 'Oh my God!' The guys from the Embassy look at him. Oz lowers his eyes and mutters: "I've got a son who's 'gay'." In fact, because of Oz's record, they really don't want him to go. Somewhere along the line, at the diplomat's house, it's revealed that they need a new spy – a fresh face – someone who isn't painfully obvious, so they pick on poor old Neville, don't they – to be a spy?

Oh – he's the 'Patsy'? Imagine him as a spy! He's initially approached by M16 recruitment officer, Heather Lane (Sara Stewart), who reassures him: "You're not Piers Brosnan, Neville!" He signs the *Official Secrets Act*.

When MI6 first suggest that Neville should spy for them, he says: "Oh, I don't think so!" But then suddenly he realises that if they want him, they're going to have to solve the problem about Oz, who's now on his way to Bangkok. So he says: "Well, I'll do it for you, but you've got to include Oz." Meanwhile, Oz is boarding an aircraft, bound for Bangkok. The 'suits' get on board and say: "Mr. Osbourne, would you please disembark?" And you can imagine what goes on there, can't you? All sorts of things!

By this time, the boys are about ready to depart for Cuba. So the only way they can get Oz back in time to join the boys, is by helicopter. So there's Oz, dramatically flown back to the boys. You can't believe that this miscreant is flown back 'On Her Majesty's Secret Service', by helicopter! But of course, what Oz doesn't realise is that it's because Neville has agreed to become a spy. Nobody knows.

Alec Guinness played a spy in *Our Man in Havana*, the 1959 film version of Graham Greene's novel, so Kevin is following in famous footsteps! Franc Roddam commented: "I think these are the best scripts so far. Dick and Ian have excelled themselves." When Neville becomes more demanding, on Oz's behalf, Heather refers to him sarcastically, as '00Geordie'!

At the earlier stage, when it's put to the boys that Oz can't go, they naturally have to think about the situation. Well, Oz of course, being totally unreasonable, thinks that they should have said: "Well, if Oz can't go, we're not going." So he took it that they'd just abandoned him, and he's fallen out with Dennis; he's not very pleased with the rest of the boys either.

Eventually, without disclosing exactly why, Neville gets the credit for having got Oz back on board. Barry delivers one of my favourite lines ('corn' not withstanding): "It's good that Britannia waved the rules!" So they finish up in Cuba, (which is really DR). As the boys enter Havana, in a long yellow bus, Bomber comments: "It's a builders' paradise – everything looks as if it's about to fall down!" A fellow woman passenger quotes a saying about Cuba, "Nothing to lose, but everything you could ever want!"

Oz takes every opportunity to rub Dennis' nose in the fact that he'd abandoned him.

Eventually Dennis finishes up in a Cuban jail. Oz finishes up falling in love: the word 'l-o-v-e' never having been mentioned in his life before. Neville carries on with his spying. The biggest and most awful thing in his life is not being a spy, but while he's being one, having to pretend that he's a member of the 'Manchester United Football Supporters' Club'! At one stage, Neville has to don a Manchester United football shirt. Whereupon he looks up to the skies and says: "Forgive me, Sir Bobby!" He wears the Manchester United football shirt to attract the attention of a Chinese man, because the British are trying to find out what's going on in the Chinese Embassy. The Chinese man has befriended Neville, because in China, everyone is a Manchester United fan – apparently.

It's a great part for Kevin. His embassy contact, Tarquin, (Alexander Hanson), the Press Liaison Officer, is not all that he appears to be! Meanwhile, there are additional sub-plots, involving other Embassy staff. Pru Scott-Johns, the Embassy Welfare Officer, (Caroline Harker), fancies Neville. Barry finds himself locked up in jail again. Bomber just ploughs on and does his normal thing.

The boys are invited to the British Embassy, to make the numbers up, and are fresh faces. Oz falls in love with a member of the touring ballet, then goes to her home and gets treated to some rice and beans. There are some rather funny stories about that! He proceeds to follow the Cuban National Ballet around. At one stage, Moxey says: "You've been acting a bit strange lately Oz." Bomber says: "Well, he's been to the ballet three times this week – there's a clue for you!" Whereupon we say: "Are you in love Oz?" He says: "Bollocks!" And they say: "He is!" And that's the end of that scene.

Mick Walker, whom we met in earlier chapters, was in Havana, by sheer coincidence, around the same time that Pat was on the neighbouring island.

"I was working on a cruise ship. I go to Havana periodically, on ships. There are parts of that fourth series that were shot in Havana, because I know the English Hotel, next to the theatre, in Havana. The scene outside the *Opera House* – where Jimmy Nail falls in love with the ballerina, and goes to see her in the ballet, for example. I know the Dominican Republic too, but not so well as Havana. Havana is my favourite place in the Caribbean. But the credibility was stretched a bit, for a group of guys coming over, to rebuild the British Embassy!" Various scenarios follow, involving Neville in clandestine manoeuvres, to obtain information from his Chinese friend. Despite being 'undercover' he doesn't disguise himself...

...Apart from his Manchester United shirt, which he promptly gives away to someone, as quickly as he can. Despite the apparent seriousness of Neville's situation, it's essentially a 'tongue-in-cheek' type of spy scenario, in keeping with the series. The inevitable sleeping tablets come into it, and doping somebody, and taking advantage of them while they're doped – I don't mean sexually – but in an exposure-type situation.

Oz has decided to help Ofelia Ortiz's Cuban family out (his girlfriend) by decorating the place, so they filch some material off the site – even an old bath! Josefina Gabrielle plays the ballerina.

They avoid Dennis; although he's not the foreman, he's the main, Head Honcho, because the original guy didn't make it, but Dennis refuses to take any extra money, because they're on equal 'dibs' all round. They try to keep the fact that they're doing this extra bit of décor from Dennis, although he 'susses' it very quickly, because they're all arriving back very late at night, covered in muck and dust. But he thinks they're 'moonlighting', which is against Embassy rules. There's a showdown again, between Oz and him, but in the end, Dennis joins up, and helps the family.

The ambassador, whose house they're renovating, has been given a very beautiful old bath, by Castro, and the lads have to go and fetch it, from about seventy miles away. They eventually reach the grandiose house where the bath is, only to realise that it's very heavily guarded. Bomber observes to the boys: "I think *he's* here." They say: "Who?" He replies: "El Presidente – look at the security!"

This smart guy comes over and all the guards stand to attention when they see him. He's quite polite – speaks good English. They get back on board. There's some mention about Neville having to get back to a baseball game and the guy says: "Baseball's the number one sport over here." They go off, and on the way back from the big house, they come across a hearse in a ditch, with a coffin hanging out of the back of it. They try to get past it, but they stop, and through interpreters, find out that this old lady is trying to bury her husband.

Bomber quickly discovers that the fan belt on the hearse has gone and suggests: "What we do is put the bath on the side of the road, load up the coffin, help them to the cemetery, and we'll be back in no time." Barry volunteers to stay with the bath and the hearse, because someone has to stand guard. So the boys throw the coffin in the back of the Toyota, jump in the back, and away they go to the cemetery. When they get there, they have to help bury the coffin, because there are no gravediggers. The cemetery situation goes from bad to worse.

Barry's left with the hearse and we find him, later on, looking up and seeing three guys walking towards him with machetes – and of course, he nearly craps himself. There are two little kids there, staring, from the beginning of the scene. Barry says to them at one stage: "I wouldn't like to be in their shoes," then he looks at their feet and realises that they're not wearing shoes, so he adds: "... if you had any!" Which is funny – the way it's written.

When the boys return to the ditch, Barry's gone and they think: 'Oh my God – where is he?' So now they're worried about Barry, and the bath, which is a gift from Castro to the ambassador. When they finally return to Havana, Barry's there, as 'pissed as a rat', and it turns out that the guys with the machetes are the original hearse driver and two mechanics! They repair the hearse and Barry explains that the boys have helped the local woman with the funeral. Tim Spall's references to his 'psychoanalyst in Solihull' and séances in Edgbaston, are hilarious!

The three guys are pleased that they've taken the time to help, and have reciprocated by putting the bath in the hearse, and taking it back to Havana. Barry invited them for a drink, got pissed, and by the time the boys arrive back, the three men had gone. It goes on from there, with Oz's relationship with Ofelia, he and Dennis sorting out their differences, Neville getting deeper and deeper into the spying.

Bill Nighy played a fantastic 'con-man' in the last series, at *least* the equal of Bill Paterson's Ally Fraser, in *Aufpet 2*; but in *Aufpet 4* there are one or two 'suspicious or unpleasant characters', rather than an obvious villain.

There's a situation where the boys are having a drink. Someone who they think is a Cuban woman comes up, grabs hold of Wyman and does the sexiest dance you ever saw, bites his ear, says: "Adios," and leaves. The next night, at the Embassy party, they find out that it's one of the Embassy guys' wives. It's no fault of Wyman's. She thought they were Cubans and they thought she was a Cuban. She says: "Oh dear, dear, this is embarrassing," but the boys say: "We won't tell anybody."

Evan Trasker, employed by the Embassy to oversee the building project, sends a fax back to England, to discredit the lads; attempting to get rid of them, because the woman Wyman danced with is his wife, Erica.

It wasn't the lady's fault. Because Neville's spying for them, they don't want to get rid of the boys do they? The embassy takes the view that her husband's being silly – so that over-rides his importance. This combines with the fact that his wife is having an affair with another guy at the embassy. She's getting a bit strung up: "I don't want this anyway." So this all adds to their reason for getting rid of her husband. They plant a key, or some plans on him, and send him back.

The plot, which Pat and I have jointly described, takes us to the end of Episode 5. Pat was waiting for Episode 6, the final one, at that point. Meanwhile, Barry's in trouble again, Neville's getting deeper into spying; Moxey continues to be ultra-observant, with far more dialogue to deliver – all good, hilarious material. As usual, Ian and Dick have been meticulous with their location research, which gives the series its accustomed authenticity.

Yes, they've got to know what they're writing about. I mean, they're so well travelled. These bloody guys flew over for lunch on Friday. They do other things while they're here, but basically, they came for lunch! It was lunch, re-familiarisation and a general chat about the whole thing. If any of us had got anything quite serious that we didn't like, we were to air our views. Everyone was thrilled to bits with the script.

No doubt, Jimmy will have a lot to say about things. He was already saying: "Oh well, I'll talk to you about this and that." Ian's already conscious that Jimmy's 'blowing down his ear' – although I think that he loves Jimmy to bits. Jimmy said: "Right, whatever happens now I've got to behave myself – I haven't got to be overbearing!" But already he's going: "Well, I'll think about so-and-so – and I'll think about so-and-so."

On 8 April 2003, six days before filming began, I asked Pat: "Is there anything else you'd like me to do, while you're away? Because we're talking about at least two or three months, aren't we?"

Well, not really. Hopefully, I'll have some stories to tell when I come back, won't I – hopefully. What's gone out of the window now, is the fact that we're timing our second book, to coincide with the beginning of the series, unless of course, they don't bring it out until the New Year – but who knows?

But certainly I'll have something to talk about after being in the Dominican Republic. The fact that Castro has made such a dramatic thing about stopping us from going to Cuba because of the Iraqi war. While we're away, who knows what will develop? I'll try to exploit anything I can – along those lines. I will try and get into Cuba if I can – from the Dominican Republic. I'll also visit Haiti, which is the Voodoo capitol of the world. So out of all of that – I'm sure there's going to be an experience where someone's going to be kidnapped – or something – by the bloody Haitians or the Cubans! So the good news will be that Pat hasn't died of cancer – he's been f**kin' shot dead (by the Cubans)!

Readers may be relieved to know that, in the event, Pat didn't attempt Haiti, and the Cubans remain totally innocent of all the aforementioned charges!

So hopefully out of the fourth series of 'Aufpet', we'll have even more to talk about. Unfortunately, at the moment, we don't know what's going to happen...or whether I'll even survive.

According to the BBC's commissioning editor, Ben Dunn, Jimmy's autobiography may be due for publication. I need your advice, to keep me 'on course', while you're away for the eight weeks – and beyond that – when you return to filming in London afterwards.

Depending on the physical health situation, what I'll do, if there's anything needs to be got back quickly to you, because of my deteriorating situation, I'll get it back to you. Hopefully, while I'm away, I'll be getting fitter and fitter, and begin training again. I'm having my shoulder done today; I haven't had a drink in two weeks. Having not had a drink in two weeks, and behaved myself, I've got the worst cold in the bleeding world! It's always the same when I get fit – I get terrible colds and things.

I'm on course mentally; I've been down the doctor's. I've had my shoulder done for the second *time – it didn't work first time. I've started my health foods again now, which I couldn't eat before, because they were creamy, and were upsetting my stomach. Doctor. Geh was good enough to give me a course of radiotherapy – five sessions, on a very active tumour that I have in my lungs – that doubles in size about every three months.*

Doctor Geh had arranged this latest course within the last ten days, bearing in mind that Pat and I were discussing the situation, on 8 April 2003.

The other tumour doesn't seem to be activating too much. So from what the technicians say, it would seem possible that from the point when I get my next CT, (which would be about eight weeks after my radiotherapy), I won't get any more tumours activating in my system – my brains – or my balls, my big toe –or whatever. If I don't get any more, and we are fortunate enough that the one that is doubling in size has been blown away. If we're that fortunate, then it may very well blow the other one away – the smaller one.

I've got two tumours in my lungs, at present: the one that they've blasted away: hopefully – or certainly stopped it growing for a while – which will enable me to do 'Aufpet 4', without any weekly hospital attendance – i.e. chemotherapy. So the doctor pulled out all the stops, to enable me to go to work. He knows that if I'm working, my head's in the right place (I've got a positive mental attitude to the illness – as before). That enables me to go forward and think positively. So it's reciprocal: he gets me right for work. I respond well to work and therefore get well. It's a circular process. Once again, I have to take my hat off to the hospital staff, for pulling out all the stops.

Pat's brain tumour, at this stage, appeared to be either dormant, or had disappeared.

We don't know. At the moment it's not causing me any trouble. We hope that it's gone – we presume that it has, and we hope that no more come. What we do know, is that my body has billions, not millions, of cancer spores. If one of those activates again, then I'm in trouble again. I'm taking my new medicine. Whether that's doing some good we don't know. But desperate people do desperate things – and I'm a desperate person – so there we are!

I did that thing up in Scotland, involving stunts, three months ago, in January 2003. The stunt team wanted to do all of my movie stunts, but they couldn't because it was too hard. So they did other things. It was up there, for my approval or disapproval. It was on one of the satellite channels, but I disapproved of everything that they did, because it wasn't safe. Although I was there, I couldn't stop it, because it was their business, not mine. But I voiced my opinion. They cut everything out, so that in the end I'm there saying: "Ooh, I didn't like that!" (Repeats this). So I end up sounding like an old grouch (winger). In the end, they exploited that situation, so that I was complaining all the time! It became funny afterwards.

Then I went to 'Blandford Forum', in Bournemouth, to see Ronnie Taylor, who'd put a boxing booth up. It brought back many memories. I sat in the boxing ring, in the booth, and reminisced with Ronnie, about the things that happened all those years ago. I told the story about Big Paddy Hallett from Newcastle. How we had the fight at the 'Cedar Club' – and how we had the return fight. It's going to be part of a whole series about fairgrounds. I imagine they might update me – out of courtesy, or Ronnie might tell me. When we hear about it, we'll know to tune into it – on a weekly basis. So we can video it at that point – and make something of it.

Jeff Dowsen, (based in Bristol) – the TV Producer of the six-part series, which was made for Harlech Television, contacted me later, in June, asking to be put in touch with 'Big Paddy'. He offered to keep me informed about the programme, and Pat's part in it. There was also the Ed Doolan broadcast, *The Other Side of Pat Roach*, in March 2004; parts of this are included, with Ed's kind permission, in various chapters.

That went off quite well – the Production Office rang me up and said that they had a tremendous response, i.e. telephone calls. People kept ringing them up, to say that it was really great. They want me back, and eventually, I suppose, I will go back. Who knows? We'll save it for another day. And that's about it, really. What we're looking forward to now, is my getting rid of this bloody cold, and my lip-sores. We're starting' Aufpet 4', this coming Friday: having a week's rehearsals in London.

Then a week on Sunday, (20 April 2003), we fly off to what is probably going to be the Dominican Republic. Because in the first place, Castro decided he wouldn't have us in Cuba, because we went into Iraq, with the Americans. But he's later changed his tune and said it's because of the dancing girls. Well, I don't know about that, because I don't think there are any in it! I think he said, allegedly, that he didn't mind the dancing girls – but there were *conditions – they'd all got to have big tits!*

Six weeks later, the cast returned with fascinating tales about the experience. Pat had some amazing stories about bizarre vehicles on the so-called motorways. There were people travelling in the wrong direction – all kinds of things.

Tim Healy comments: "Oh, it was unbelievable – I saw some horrendous things! You'd see a family on a 50cc motorbike. I mean, a baby on the handlebars, then the mother, then dad driving it and a kid on the back, and a half a ton of bananas. The most ridiculous thing I saw was also on the motorway. There was a guy, on a horse, galloping down the fast lane! While they're doing that, motorbikes are coming up the motorway – the wrong way, on the hard shoulder. I saw two kids get knocked off and killed. They just went right into the side of a van – no helmets on – just bang! That was it – gone! It's probably the worst driving and the worst roads in the world. I took some pictures of taxis. You know that advert for a Peugeot 306, where the guy beats this car to bits, then smiles when he'd got it the right shape? Well, that looks like a taxi out there! I'm not kidding you – you just wouldn't get in it. It's a joke – you know?"

Pat made a point of mentioning the stark contrast between the luxury hotel where you were staying – I believe it was the *Ambassador*, (spelt with a double J instead of S), and the primitive villages you drove through daily, to reach the set, in the jungle clearing.

"Yes – it was the *Ambassador Inn*, a five star hotel, with air conditioning," recalls Tim. "You used to walk outside and it was like walking into a furnace: it was ninety degrees, at six o'clock in the morning! They cleared an entire area in the jungle and constructed the Ambassador's house. We used to drive right out – into the Third World really, where people live on mangos and bananas. You'd see them having a disco – in the road, and a basketball post – on the road – never mind the cars!

"The kids were playing in the street, like we did I suppose, forty years ago, when we didn't have any televisions. They had no 'mod cons', but they were very happy people. They'd see us arriving with the big trucks and all that and you'd just see these heads, peering out of these little shacks like. What on earth is this? Within two days we were using them as 'extras' and got to know them – and they loved it – the fact that we were there."

Pat said that he only saw *one* happy dog, the whole time that he was there. They all looked really miserable, because the locals would throw stones at them, any time they approached, for fear of rabies. "That's right.

If you saw a dog running around the streets in the town, people would shoot them. So they're not like dogs are here."

Pat gave a graphic account of the Tropical Rainforest: the mosquitoes, the heat. Hygiene seems to have been rather a problem, partly due to the many flies buzzing around the food. But Chris sees it from a different perspective. He said that the locals had a healthy fruit diet and looked healthy, and it was just a matter of cast and crew adjusting to a different diet. Tim agrees, adding, "It was a happy time and I thought Pat was on the mend, I really did."

Julia Tobin describes Chris Fairbank as "a great raconteur, full of stories." But Tim Healy falls easily into that category too, as substantiated by both of their invaluable contributions to all three of Pat's books. Chris explains: "You could tell that Pat was suffering really. His demeanour had changed. By the end of each day he was *so* tired; he was on a short fuse comparatively speaking. I remember him 'banging on' about getting CT scans; apparently, they're relatively cheap in the Dominican Republic.

"Doctor Amos, our Medic, was probably the busiest person there; virtually everybody got something, on that shoot. He arranged for Pat to have a scan. I particularly remember the day he was due to get the results of that. On the outside, he was as 'cool as a cucumber', but knowing him as I do, I could tell that he was worried. Amos was due to show up at about lunchtime with the x-rays and he asked Kev to go with him. We were filming in Santo Domingo. They'd got this little hotel, where we'd all got a dressing room each. Kev and Pat disappeared up to his room and about half an hour later I saw Kev again and he said: "Oh, no he's fine," and this is when I heard that he'd got tumours in his brain.

"I knew some of the details, because Pat told me in Arizona. When the Medical thing occurred and it became public knowledge, it was good that it happened, because it then opened things up. I remember him out there in Arizona, saying that he'd got secondary cancer in his lungs and on his spine. But seeing him in the gym and doing all his other exercises, I just couldn't believe how he was managing it – it was amazing!"

Pat gave me a funny account of an occasion when Dick and Ian took the *Auf Wiedersehen* cast out for a meal. He said that service was so slow, you decided to return to your hotel for dinner! Is that true? I thought, 'I must ask Chris about that!'

"No, well, I'll tell you where that was – it was in Santo Domingo and he was absolutely right. But it wasn't a meal that Dick and Ian had taken us all out to. The service was so appallingly slow that I came back to the hotel and got some Room Service. It was a *different* meal that we went out for, as a group: just me, Healy and Spall, and a couple of the guest artists as well. It would have been too late for Pat, because he couldn't eat anything after about eight o'clock in the evening, and he certainly couldn't have eaten anything heavy, at that time, because of having to sit up to digest it all. So by the time we got to the fourth series, Pat was just really frazzled, and there were times when his tiredness, the illness, the heat and humidity really got to him; the conditions got to everybody."

Under normal circumstances the climate and conditions in DR would have taken their toll, but with Pat's illness added to the equation, it makes you wonder how he managed it at all. "Well, absolutely! This is what I constantly thought – every single day. It was quite extraordinary and as time has passed, it was an amazing experience. But the conditions of heat and humidity made every day really, really tough.

"It was a curious thing because I suppose, to all intents and purposes, it really is Third World. And you thought: 'My God – the level of deprivation and poverty!' But actually, when you looked a bit *closer*, you saw that the people who lived there had the most fantastic skin, the most incredibly bright eyes. They were bursting with health, because their diet was so good. You had fantastic fresh fruit and vegetables, which grew everywhere; it wasn't like Africa or North Korea, where people starve to death. It wasn't that sort of poverty.

"The shacks *were* shacks and I doubt if any of them are standing now, because there were terrible floods soon afterwards. It was awful – thousands have died. I believe that they were a little bit further into the interior, but I can't believe that Santo Domingo wasn't affected, in some way. There were so many of these places, built, literally, on mountainsides, which would have been swept away. But it *is* like a kind of climatic condition of the area, so it would happen quite regularly, albeit not to that extent. So if you're in danger of having something swept away, what's the point of building anything permanent? Far better to have sticks and a bit of corrugated iron, then that's all you've got to put back together again."

Kevin Whately observes: "We all thought that Pat seemed to have less physical problems, than he had in Series Three. We were amazed, because we knew what he'd been told by the doctors, before he did the third one."

This was probably because they'd dosed him up, and he wasn't wearing any kind of drip, (albeit concealed), as he was for Series Three. So ostensibly, he was in better shape.

"Yes, although he did have a bad time while we were in Santo Domingo," explains Kevin. "I remember he was talking to Doctor Amos, a brilliant young doctor, who was assigned to us, full time. I think at one time, he'd wanted to be a Plastic Surgeon. Pat found out from Doctor Amos, that Scans were much cheaper in Santo Domingo, so he went and got one. I can remember Doctor Amos turning up with this big brown envelope. We were using the hotel as a changing unit. I saw him come through the garden and going up to Pat's room, to give him the results of this Scan. About ten or fifteen minutes later, I realised that he hadn't come out, and my heart sank. I went up and knocked on the door, to see if Pat was alright. He said, 'Come in kid – come and have a look!' They were holding these X-rays up to the light. One of the X-rays in particular, showed that the lung cancer tumour had almost completely disappeared and Pat was thrilled to bits! The doctor was just talking him through all the other parts it. So my worst fears weren't well founded at all; they were celebrating the fact that it hadn't got any worse."

Even beyond my wildest dreams, I never thought about 60 million viewers, in 6 episodes – something like 13 million viewers for one particular episode – and neither did anybody else. So here we were – we were on our way – it was all going to happen!

Over the next few months, I started to think: 'What am I going to do – how am I going to do it? What sort of problems would arise for me?' I decided that I didn't want the aggravation of the Yard premises and the Salvage Company, which had nearly driven me barmy. Every day they'd phone up and tell me that we'd been broken into again – or set on fire again; the dog had bitten the cat again – that sort of thing – it was terrible. So I got rid of the yard: I practically gave it away. There were one or two other reasons, but the fact that we were doing 'Auf Wiedersehen' again was enough.

Chapter Sixteen

CHAMPNEY'S GYM

When we used to go back to the hotel, The Meridian, in Piccadilly, we always stayed there because it had a great gym and then we could walk into town. I spent every night with him there. I had to go back and spend time on my own there recently. It was really tough staying there, while we were finishing off the 'Christmas Special', in August 2004. I didn't feel right, for the first time, you know what I mean? It didn't feel the same. 'Cause I just kept expecting to go out and knock on his door, and hear him say: "Alright our kid? Off we go!" Ready – and down to the gym. So I'll probably never stay there again now, because I've got memories of it, where every time I walk down the corridor, he's with me.

Tim Healy

Tim began his career as a Stand-up Comedian. It seems more than likely that this aspect of their personalities is one of the elements that drew them together. During a television interview, with *BBC Midlands*, on Thursday 25 November 2004, I made the point that Pat was actually a comedian in his own right, with a very good line in sardonic humour and mimicry, based on comical situations, drawn from his own experience. It was entirely different from the Situation Comedy of *Auf Wiedersehen Pet*, and a side of Pat that most people would be unaware of. From early childhood, Pat enjoyed entertaining his friends. "Oh he loved a laugh!" agrees Tim.

The interview was in the grounds of St. Paul's Church, in the Jewellery Quarter. Just twenty minutes later, I was one of three speakers, paying tribute to Pat at his memorial service described more fully in Chapter 20.

I'm delighted to say that, right out of the blue, Tim Healy suddenly began training, while we were in London, and he took it up – robustly. He's trained very hard ever since – he really does well; he's keen. We'd be on call just after six o'clock every morning. We stayed at the Meridian Hotel, in Piccadilly. Champney's Gym is immediately underneath. It meant travelling forty-five minutes, and sometimes longer, to the location. But we didn't mind, because we wanted a gym facility.

The cast returned each evening, after eight o'clock. Tim and Pat would dive straight into their rooms – straight into their gym clothes – straight into the gym.

We'd come out of the gym, under the shower, then we'd go out and have a quick couple of drinks. Then Tim Healy would say: "Right, come on – bed!" And we'd go straight to bed. Very often it was just a few minutes after ten o'clock. Then up again the next morning at six. Week in and week out – that's what we did. We trained very hard, and I became so proud of Tim. He used to say all the time: "You know Pat, you've got me training." And I'd say: "No, no, I haven't got you training at all – you got yourself training." He used to try to give me the credit, but the credit was all his.

Pat returned from the Dominican Republic, having taken a collection of unique photographs; some of them are included in Gallery 2 of this book. On Saturday 21 June 2003, he used a few, to illustrate his account of events:

Approaching the start of this fourth series, I had other little problems, which I won't go into at this stage. Very hurriedly, (and I stress this), the BBC switched the whole thing to the Dominican Republic, which I'm sure they don't regret. It probably would have had a little more edge, had we gone to Cuba, but we didn't – 'C'est la vie'. We can't knock what happened – it was absolutely wonderful.

We didn't manage to visit Cuba after all – it was too restricted. Haiti – we were terrified – wouldn't go into it! When we got to the Dominican Republic, we got off the plane and stepped into a cauldron – it was so hot! The rehearsal time in London, beforehand, was about a week: we didn't get much of that. The boys dropped straight into the characters – it was really rather wonderful, the way they did. We stayed at the Ambajjador Hotel – which I suppose, means 'Ambassador': spelt with two J's. It was a business hotel, rather than a tourist hotel, in the capitol, Santo Domingo; but it was very good.

They went out filming every day. According to Pat, the Art Department surpassed themselves, building a *fabulous* ambassador's villa, which the team were supposed to be 'doing up'. They also put tremendous effort into creating the boys' living quarters.

It was the jungle, man – an hour-and-a-half out into the jungle – each way! We actually climbed for forty-five minutes every morning, in a four-wheel drive. Each day – an hour and a half's journey to the set and the same for the return journey, for most of the time.

We'd be called at 5.45 – 6am, to go to the set. When we got there, breakfast would be laid out for us – there's be tents out there – gazebos. They found four very old, (but by no means is this a complaint), Winnebagos, with cooling systems: they were very good. They later found us a great big one, which we used as a Green Room.

Numerous injections were required, before they left England.

You name it – we had it! So we're in the Dominican Republic – and we're travelling an hour and a half. You've seen the photographs of that guy in the hut – well that's how they live. I have to say that they're lovely people – they really are! Very much a melting pot: black, Negroid people, Spanish Hispanic-type people.

Pat explained that, in order to film *Auf Wiedersehen*, they had to *make* a clearing in the jungle. Then they actually built the embassy, in between all the trees. It was supposed to have been there for years, so it had to look well established.

So they built it with a tree to the left of it, and another one in front. They imported a fountain, that they had to pay an enormous amount of money for – (which grieved me). So the building looked absolutely original – it looked good. It was mainly an all-British crew, with the exception of one or two native guys. They painted another building, half the size of Rackhams, in Birmingham, for about three hundred pounds – using local labour.

Maurice Phillips and David Innes Edwards were the directors. Maurice directed episodes 1-3; episodes 4-6 were directed by David.

Our journey to the set was marvellous, because we were travelling through the villages, and then into the countryside, then on to another village. You'd pass a television shop and you'd think, 'Good God! Have they got television out here?' But of course, they had; they'd got electricity throughout the island: overhead lines, I suppose – whatever. You'd see these huts: they were just literally corrugated sheets of metal. As the photographs show, at mealtimes, cast and crew sat out, under the trees.

As we drove through these villages, the music (I suppose we've all come to expect it now) was loud; they were playing music all the time. There were shops, which were little more that tins, thrown together, selling food. God knows what the local guys' stomachs were like – how they could absorb all those germs – but they could. We noticed there were very few cats: we only ever saw about three; but that was because they ate them.

In the programme, the boys go into a shop, to buy Che Guevara T-shirts – they needed to give a good impression, locally. Bomber wasn't with them at the time, because he was doing something else.

We did our day's shooting. I photographed a tarantula, but the bloody photograph didn't turn out. We saw a centipede. One particular day, we were filming, and all of a sudden somebody said: "Look!" And there was a snake in the tree. It had a baby bird in its mouth, and it was hanging down from the tree. It wasn't that big a snake, but it had caught the bird, which was trying to fly. The snake was just about to devour the bird. As the bird tried to fly, it dislodged the snake, so that it was now hanging down from the tree. The bird's parents were flying down, and attacking the snake. Someone actually got the snake down later and shot it – which was a shame; they shouldn't have done that, because it wasn't a poisonous snake. But the snake had half eaten the bird, they threw things at it, and it fell out of the tree. I don't know whether the little bird was dead or not – I didn't ask. It would certainly have been scared out of its wits. But that was an experience – watching the snake in its own environment – taking a bird.

The 'shanty' type villages and primitive living conditions that the *Aufpet* entourage saw on their travels, were in complete contrast to the up-market business hotel they returned to, each evening.

We also saw a land crab there; he was light grey all over. You could hear his pincers snapping. I bet he was six inches across. When I first saw it, Tim 'ealy had got it, on a lead – the funniest thing you ever saw!

Who's Timeeli... one of the natives?

No – Tim Healy! He came walking up with it, as if he was walking a dog. He'd just found it in the bush. They teased the bloody thing for about three hours. I said, "Let it go," because they'd already killed the bloomin' snake – you know what I mean? We learned the next day that one of the locals had caught and eaten it. I thought: 'How do you eat a great big crab?' But apparently, they're much the same to eat as a sea crab.

What's the story behind the muddy faces, in the two photos at the top of page XXVII?

The wagon just slew of the road one day and went into a stream – which is another sad story. We all got behind it to push it, but with the wheel spin, we all got mud in our eyes. In actual fact, we should have got a shot of it, but we missed the opportunity. They might pick that up later, at Pinewood Studios.

I'm looking at a photo of a coffin, in a cemetery, high up in the mountains, with a panoramic view of the rainforests below. Was that the episode you described on our previous *Aufpet 4* tape, where a hearse has fallen into a ditch?

Yes, we help transport the coffin to the cemetery. Then we lose Barry and the bath, and all sorts of things happen. But what you're looking at there, on the photograph, is jungle – absolute jungle; it's unbelievable! I mean, we drove along the road and we could actually pick bananas, if we wanted to, or pick a coconut, or a mango. I saw mangos yesterday in London, for around £1.60 a piece. When we were on location, I could have had forty of these at the roadside, for ten pesetas, which is about thirty pence, as opposed to one for £1.60. There are no poisonous snakes there, apparently. What is sad is that the Canadians are there, taking the gold out of the mountains.

According to Pat, the government had drawn up a contract with the Canadians, without stipulating that they should put the mountains back as they found them.

Can you imagine – all that beautiful greenery – and they're making it barren? So-called 'civilization' is creeping in there, and it's just an awful shame. Because with all that gold coming out, Joe Average 'man-in-the-street' doesn't get anything out of it – the poor devil – he's not getting anything.

Nothing's been said – not a word – about Bomber's circumstances. Oz, Dennis and Bomber come out of the *OED* building, and they each say: "Right, OK, I'm going to get a train now, back up," and "I'm going to do so-and-so," and somebody said: "Well, where does Bomber live?" Because he'd come from Canada to Russia, to do the Russian job.

Then suddenly, there's Bomber, whose clothes have been blown up in the explosion in Russia, and he's wearing a blazer again, so we don't know where he's got that from; we presume he's bought it – I suppose. But we don't even know where he's living in London – whether it's a flat or a hotel. Someone suggested: "Should we say: 'Are you going back to you digs in London, Bomber?' In the end, they didn't mention it, but it is a 'moot' point: when Oz goes back to Newcastle, and Dennis to where he's going to go, where does Bomber go? But we didn't pursue it. Bomber just appears and there's no mention about his illness or anything. At this stage, we haven't yet gone to Cuba.*

So there we are, doing an hour and a half trip into the jungle every day, and back again. People were called at 5.45, 6 and 6.15am, and we were getting back at 8pm. In six weeks abroad, I only missed four nights in the gym. Apart from that, I was in the gym every single night – I just forced myself to go there; got myself into a right good condition – got my weight down.

Noel Clarke trained in the gym alongside Pat too, as he did during *Aufpet 3*.

So the filming was going on. We saw the centipede, the snake and the crab and it was all very interesting; we saw the big hairy spider. There are always very few re-writes, with 'Auf Wiedersehen', because Dick and Ian know the characters better than anybody. Even when they saw the very subtle changes that we made during the making of 'Aufpet 3', it had probably registered with them, before they came to write this new series. Although they may have written something one day, which wasn't quite right, by the merest fraction of a per cent, one of the boys would have put it right. Ian and Dick would have noticed that, and the result was therefore, very few re-writes.

The directors made no major changes without Ian and Dick's approval, but they'd make *small* changes, like dropping a line, or adding a word or two.

Bear in mind, that anything minor would be major to us, if you know what I mean? Because everything is so important: minor things are so important. Ian and Dick just had a short stay in DR for the whole six weeks, as they were very busy, writing a major Broadway musical.

Our conversation, at that point, was interrupted by Pat's mobile phone. As I switched the tape back on, the phone appeared to ring again, on tape re-play – so Pat reached for his mobile again

Shirley one, Pat nil! You could play that ringing over and over, couldn't you? And I could keep saying: "Hello?" Funny that!

Looking at the photo of the boys, lined up behind an abandoned, rusty vehicle, what's actually happening there?

They're all standing up having a 'wee-wee' – relieving themselves. Can't you see the look on their faces? They all got off the van; it's called the 'Pee Break'. Trust you to pick up on anything...

Well, I did ask! Pat one, Shirley one.

So I didn't eat that night – I believe they all ate quite well. Obviously, I don't eat late, and in England, you wouldn't want to anyway. We used to be in bed at ten o'clock every night, because we'd be setting off at six, the following morning, reaching our destination (the set) for half seven. We had breakfast when we arrived on the film set. The only trouble was it upset your whole system; no one was going to the toilet properly.

According to Pat, they all had bad stomachs, and were dashing for the toilets. Pat was vomiting on the set one day – retching! (There's nothing like a bit of detail, is there?!)

Coming out of both ends it was! Well – lack of hygiene, wasn't it? Every lunchtime, one guy used to be there, just wiping thousands of flies off the food; you just couldn't keep them off! I don't think the British Dominicans bothered about flies on food at all – because there's nothing they can do about it; but we did. So they put a wooden floor down, and a big tent up, with just one completely open side. I have to say that the food, under the circumstances, was quite well presented – was quite adequate. They had to make it in the middle of the jungle – and I mean the jungle! Coconuts, mangos and bananas growing everywhere – centipedes here, tarantulas there, albeit a small one. We actually saw a humming bird.

You were frightened to sit down, because of the ants in your pants! All those little things. There are no chicken predators out there, (except the humans), so they're just walking around. There were mosquitoes – ugh! We were in a rainy area of jungle – Tropical Rainforest. Every day around three o'clock, there'd be rain. But we never used to bother. We'd all get wringing wet, then twenty minutes later we'd be dry again.

You'd be on the road and you'd look down – hundreds and hundreds of feet down – and yet there'd be trees, growing above you: because they were reaching for the sunlight. So these trees would grow to enormous sizes: great big tall trees. Everything was just so beautifully exotic: it was a wonderful island, with lovely, grand people.

The archways, on one particular photograph, are part of the embassy complex.

Yes, that's a part of the embassy, which the Art Department built. Credit to them – they did ever so well, they really did. So – the whole trip was great. We returned to the hotel every night – it was smashing! We took over the entire 7th floor. It had an eighth floor, which had a special room, to relax in. The local 'Presidential' beer was free, and so was the local rum – but I'd stopped drinking a month before – would you believe it? They used to put food on – free! There was actually sushi every night – free – upstairs. Jimmy and Chris would have their pots of tea; the other boys would have a beer. I used to drink pure lemon juice. It was there for you – so it was no trouble at all. They just stuck half a dozen lemons in, squeezed them, and brought them out, threw in some ice, and there you were, drinking pure lemon juice – great!

The producer was Chrissy Skinns. As you can see from the photograph, she's a lovely lady. Game as a pebble – and she put up with the boys swearing in front of her!

By 'game as a pebble', Pat meant that he felt completely at ease in Chrissy's company and that they didn't have to modify their behaviour, in her presence. Chrissy recalls the making of one particular episode as follows:

"Episode Three of the series had a particularly clever storyline: the lads had to deliver an antique bath, in their old lorry, to Fidel Castro, across the winding mountain roads of (supposedly) Cuba. Of course, this was not going to be easy for them: in story terms, and, as it turned out, in reality. It was going to mean all the actors filming for days, up in the mountainous forest, in the searing heat and humidity, sitting in the back of a vehicle whose suspension was not exactly 'state of the art'. Knowing that this would be arduous for anyone, let alone someone who'd been seriously ill, I felt it only fair to suggest to Pat that he might want to sit this one out, which would have been perfectly understandable and acceptable. I knew Dick and Ian would be able to find a ploy in the script to ensure that 'Bomber' had to remain behind, so that wasn't a problem. I just felt that Pat should have the choice himself. So I sat opposite him in the Hotel Frances in Santo Domingo (which we used as a green room whilst shooting in the town) and asked him straight. He didn't pause, didn't falter; just said, "No, I came here to work and I'm going to work" and that was that: it just didn't occur to him to let up at all. In fact, I got the distinct impression that it was work, and the need to keep fit for all that entailed, that was keeping him going."

We weren't all called every day, so there are some of us lying in the sun. Meanwhile, actors are taking planes – flying backwards and forwards; one actress did this about five times – helluva trip as well.

One of the main actresses was Sandra James Young, who played Chrissie, Wyman's mother. There was the embassy guy's wife, Erica Trasker, who dances with Wyman, and then there's Pru, who works for the embassy; so they flit in and out a lot. And of course, Julia Tobin's the only one of the original wives. She comes into it when Neville phones home, then he returns home, between the Russian episodes and the Dominican ones.

When Neville goes back home he finds that Brenda's on a course; he goes there – 'puts his foot in it' – says all the wrong things. At that stage, he decides that he won't go abroad again, to work, but he does, when he's persuaded to become a spy.

Barry, on the other hand, is driving the truck when we have an accident; he hits a guy on a bike, and the police take him in. Out there, that's what happens: you can be locked up for nine months, for the slightest misdemeanour. So he's locked up for nine months. While he's in prison, they discover that he was involved with this Mafia man in Russia, whose house got blown up. Also, that he was involved, in England, with the drug people in Arizona, so they decide to check him a little bit further. As Pru says, thinking from their point of view, "We all know that Barry's a 'radish' – but nobody else knows he is." The Cubans don't know – so they kick him in jail, which of course, is while he's doing the film in New Zealand with Tom Cruise - 'The Last Samurai'.

On returning to London, Tim went straight into *Harry Potter*, re-joining the *Aufpet* cast, at the back end of that.

He's in jail again, while he's doing Harry Potter! So our Tim Spall's doing well: he's doing a Tom Cruise and a Harry Potter film – two of the top films in the world. They made lots of allowances for him, because obviously, he's been a tremendous asset to the programme. We were all booked well ahead. But Tim had these two big projects in the offing, and he had to make room for them, when he accepted the 'Auf Wiedersehen' contract.

There were some hilarious moments during filming, when the crab was chasing everyone around, with its jaws snapping open and shut. When they threw the tarantula, everyone jumped and ran!

It was chaotic when they were all under the tree, looking up, and suddenly the snake dropped out. Jimmy saw somebody running naked along the motorway. It was all happening there! You'd be driving along, and you'd see something like a counter top, with a pen (not a biro) underneath, and some sheep in it. On the top of the counter top would be a kind of frame, and a recently gutted sheep would be hanging from it – with the other sheep watching – a terrible shame for them. You had to pay to go on the motorway, but when you did, there were cars going the wrong way – you couldn't believe what you were seeing! You could look at a car, and there would be no grille, no front bumper, no front headlights: not even the buckets that the headlights fit into. All you saw was the radiator – nothing! Not even number plates. And that same car might not even have back lights. I saw many a car like that – not even a bulb!

Despite all the aforementioned, they drove in the dark too. Some had no driving licenses, no insurance. You'd perhaps see a car with no *bulbs* on the back of it; then, in total contrast, the next car might be a £20,000 '44'.

Columbus founded the Dominican Republic – there are statues of him everywhere, and a marvellous museum about him. They're Roman Catholics of course. It's a very interesting island. We were there for six weeks. I think everybody enjoyed it. I should have thought that after two weeks we'd have had enough – but of course, we were there working, and that's what we were prepared to do. From my hotel room I could see the ocean. There was a beach, but not the sort of beach we'd go on. It was a sandy beach, but there was a lot of – what is it?

Sewage?

Yes, I pointed to me bum then – and she said sewage! Because Kevin went for a walk one day, and all of a sudden there was a 'Sh, shhh' noise. He looked, and there was all the sewage – up against the rocks: they hadn't put the pipes far enough out to sea! Funnily enough, I made the point of saying: "Look, when you go to Spain, for example, you can smell the sewage there, can't you?" But you couldn't, on the island; even in the little villages, which were nothing more than a collection of tin huts – just like they are in one of those photographs; now isn't that strange?

Maybe there's something in the surrounding vegetation that masks it. On Madeira, for example, in the woodland areas, up in the hills, the eucalyptus trees have a very pungent smell. I only realised that it was about because Kevin told me. But I would never have identified it. It was a Spanish-speaking island.

On returning to London, about five weeks' filming remained, at Pinewood and various other locations around that area.

I was standing outside Hornsey Town Hall, which is now hardly used at all, and somebody came up to me and said: "Did you wrestle here Pat?" I looked at it and said: "God Blimey yes, I did – funnily enough!" I didn't realise that I had wrestled there – for a guy called Tony Costan. He just put the one show on there. And who should be an 'extra' on 'Aufpet 4', but Prince Kumali, (Gordon Kumali) who comes to the annual wrestlers' meetings. I see him every year. He came as an 'extra' – as a black man. I made a great big fuss of him and introduced him to all the actors. Bill Bridges, Gordon Kumali and myself were in Japan together. I was thrilled to bits!

Meantime, they've laid on a limousine for me again, which is all rather lovely – and a chauffeur. I asked for Steve – the same fella. We're all happy doing what we're doing. Jimmy, as we speak, is having his house pulled down and rebuilt, so he's living in a hotel, in London. For the first two nights he was booked in, he had a ticket on his vehicle, both nights – so he wasn't very pleased about that! And we're all living in the Meridian Hotel, in Piccadilly. Our rooms are three and four hundred pounds a night; we're getting special deals through the BBC; it's got a lovely gym and swimming pool.

Jimmy and Kevin are multi-millionaires – so is Chris. Tim Healy is in so much demand – you can't believe it. Spalley is even bigger than before!

When Jimmy Nail phoned up to say: "Pat, do you want to do another Auf Wiedersehen?" I nearly fell through the floor – or should I say – the caravan in the scrap-yard! But after twenty years, the boys just wanted to be back together again (whispers this). That's really got to mean something. And now here we are, having almost completed the fourth.

One of the funny things was, that when we got back to London, one or two of the boys were as brown as berries – but we had to film the snowy Russian scene (we're filming some of the scenes from back to front). They're very good at creating artificial snow: we were very impressed. They created a massive snow scene outside the building. It took about six hours' preparation, to blow it up, together with the money – all the American dollars. That was funny, because I think one or two must have gone missing!

But of course, shooting is back-to-front, all the boys are brown as bloody berries, and they had to 'damp them down' with flour – or something similar; like they had to do with Gary Holton, during the filming of 'Aufpet 2', when he'd disobeyed instructions and sunbathed in Spain.

We filmed the Russian scene at Luton Ho, which became the house that we 'did up' for the Russian gangster. Twenty years to the day – almost – they've shown the film 'Never Say Never Again'. So by pure coincidence, for 'Aufpet 4', I was in the same room, filming, as the one I'd shot that fight scene in for 'Never Say Never Again' – almost twenty years to the day. And it was on the telly!

When we all got back, people couldn't stop talking about the camaraderie that had come about in DR – about the friendships. That's what happens with the crew, isn't it? They get together and do things. We filmed all around London; some parts were filmed at Pinewood Studios. We shot at Hampstead Town Hall. It was absolutely the wrong time to go, because they were working on the Hampstead Flyover at the time, which made accessing the area quite difficult. But that couldn't have been foreseen, at the planning stage. It was difficult to get there, because all the roads were up. That doubled as the British Embassy in Russia.

According to Pat, they didn't film any night scenes in Britain, because, plot-wise, they were only back in Britain for a very short time, before heading for Cuba – so there's not much of a story-line in Britain at all. At the point where *Aufpet 4* actually finishes, what is the specific situation that the characters find themselves in? For example, is Bomber OK?

Well, we're still in Cuba. And you will have seen by then, the end 'frames'. At this moment, I'm not exactly sure what they'll be. I think they'll be of us all dancing in a Cuban nightclub, and learning the local customs and things like that. So it's left open-ended – as far as the boys' future is concerned.

There is talk of doing a 'Christmas Special' for next year. They're also, allegedly, talking about doing the next series in Baghdad. They won't actually film it there (they'll probably go to Kuwait or Tunisia, or somewhere like that). So when we got back, people were brown. The funny thing was that we had a continued heatwave – so we all felt very much at home.

Pat was still taking malaria tablets on his return to London. Just as well, because he was about to have an unnerving experience:

I went back to the hotel one night, only two weeks ago, and I'm lying on the bed watching telly. I'm going to get an hour in, before I go to the gym. I'd finished early, so I thought I'd have an hour's relaxation. This is back in England now. I've jumped the story, but you've jogged my memory. I'm lying there and all of a sudden I felt freezing. I was so cold that even though I'd got my clothes on, I just dropped straight under the sheets. I was shivering – and continued to shiver. I pulled all the sheets over me (I'm talking June now, aren't I?).

Then all of a sudden, I'm perspiring. I thought: 'Bloody Hell!' Then the next thing I know, the whole bed, right around me, was just as if I'd thrown a bucket of water over it! It became so uncomfortable, that I had to get out of my clothes (which were absolutely 'wringing'), throw them on the floor, and I rolled to the other side of the great big, king-sized bed. I'm staying in the Meridian Hotel, right in the middle of Piccadilly (£330 a night, the rooms are, but the BBC got a special deal); £20 breakfast – my God!

So there he was, stranded, on the dry side of an enormous bed.

And I wake up about three o'clock in the morning; again – absolutely drenched – like a bucket of water – maybe two buckets! So I thought: 'I can't lie in this again!' By now, I wanted to go to the toilet. I couldn't get back into the bed, because it goes cold, as soon as you move; I'm still freezing, and my teeth are chattering. So I pulled the pillows, which I hadn't been using, to the bottom of the bed – across the bed; pulled the top eiderdown, (which wasn't wet) put a dressing gown on, (which I don't normally wear, because they never bloody well fit), but I had no choice. So I put it on, curled up across the bottom of the bed, and went to sleep. Woke up, 'as right as rain'. But very, very weak. I told everybody about it, and they said: "Oh dear – that's strange." It didn't strike me, until about a week later, it might have been a mild attack of malaria.

But was that the end of it? Normally, it stays in your bloodstream, for several years.

Well, maybe I'll get it again – I don't know, but I'm still taking the quinine tablets. I must be on my last one. That reminds me, I should have taken one last night, so I'll take it today.

According to Pat, they were all too 'cream-crackered' to enjoy the sights of London. By the time they returned to their hotel at eight o'clock at night, they were in no state to start looking for restaurants! Tim Healy has fond memories of those evenings spent with Pat.

"We'd finish filming at seven o'clock and get to the gym for about eight. By that time, Pat was putting me through all this boxing training: getting me to punch a bag; then he'd have me doing squats. He was so *proud* of me: he would brag to the other lads, every day. My body shape was changing. He'd come in, in the morning and say: (imitates Pat): 'Have you seen Healy's legs? Look at them!' I became his apprentice. We'd be finished in the gym by nine o'clock, get showered and changed, then walk around the corner to a little bar, just behind the *Meridian*. Every night we'd go to the same bar. We'd buy a jug of beer – four pints – then we'd share it between us: two pints each. Then that was it – off to bed. I was bloomin' thirsty too - trying to keep up with him. Even though he was ill, he was still as strong as a bull!

"He looked a lot better than he did on the third, because he'd gone 'puffy', hadn't he – at *that* time? But when we did the series last year, I thought he was getting through it. He used to say things to me, at the end of the night, like: 'I'll not see you again kid, in a couple of years time.' I used to say, 'Ah, bugger off - what are you talking about? This has got to be you – you're a Superman!' He was a lot stronger and he was back in training. I was slowly getting stronger every week."

Timmy Spall had fish, chips and mushy peas in a restaurant the other day – twenty-five quid! Then Jimmy ordered a sandwich, which came to twenty-four quid. Tim Healy had a bowl of soup – eight quid, a cheese sandwich and a cup of tea, and it came to twenty-four quid! It was five pounds to bring your food to your room: bowl of soup eight quid and a five-pound delivery charge. A pot of tea is £4.50. Afternoon tea, with biscuits – (to be fair, you probably get a couple of cakes), is £12.50 per head. So if you and I decide to have tea there: "A pot of tea for two please" – that's nine quid. But afternoon tea for you and I would be £25.00. So that is why you're not invited!

I must phone Len Edwards up, because there's a meeting Monday night, which I really should go to. He's Secretary of the Birmingham branch of 'Equity'. I'll ring him up, to see what's happening, because I'm trying to put together a Charity Show, in Acocks Green soon, which will raise two or three thousand quid. It's an 'Auf Wiedersehen Pet Night'.

Julia Tobin recalls: "Pat always remained the most tremendous professional and never *ever* let it affect his work, in any way whatsoever. There wasn't a *glimmer* of pain, or any uncomfortable feelings that crossed his face. I particularly noticed that he'd lost weight, and of course, being the big man that he was, it did point itself out as being a worrying aspect, to me.

But when we were filming at the hotel, in Ealing, for the last series, Kevin, Tim Healy, Pat and myself were all sitting outside, because it was nice and sunny, although it was meant to be a rainy day. We were all sitting around chatting – and I was just looking at him. I walked over to him and took his face in my hands. I looked in his eyes and said: 'Now come on Pat. Tell me how you really *really* are.' And he said: 'Jules, let me tell you something. I'm not well, but I'm managing.' But that's the most he would tell me. He had great determination and the most phenomenal strength, in all areas; he was one hundred per cent strength."

Chris Fairbank still feels that first series in Germany was the best of the four. They say that it's 'a small world'. Seamus Dunleavy, featured in our wrestling chapters, recalls: "I gave Chris Fairbank a lift one day, Shirley. I went to my hotel up in Selly Park, the *Copperfield*. We had some of the *Pebble Mill* people staying there. The word came up from *Pebble Mill* to Chris Fairbank – he'd to go to *Pebble Mill Studios*. He was acting the part of a pirate in some play or other and they wanted him down there straight away. As I drove him to the studios I said: "If you ever get on *This Is Your Life* Chris, you can say that you remember me giving you a lift!"

Pat invited Bernard Guest to a preview of the new *Aufpet 4* series. "He phoned me up and said: 'There's a *Water Rats* 'do' down in London, at the *Grosvenor Hotel* in Park Lane. Do you fancy going?' They gave you special concessions. We had separate rooms. I wouldn't have a double room with him! He said that also, on the same day they were doing the previews of *Auf Wiedersehen Pet*, in Kilburn High Street, in a special studio. I picked him up and took him down there. Jimmy Nail was there, Chris Fairbank, Kevin Whately and the Director of BBC Television.

"The people there were really sociable. I've met Kevin Whately and Jimmy Nail before. Timothy Spall wasn't there, but Noel Clarke who plays Wyman was... nice lad he is. Then they showed us the preview of Episodes One and Two, because it would have taken too long to show them all. It was quite funny, the comments that were coming out! Jimmy Nail invited us over to his house for tea. He lives on Clapham Common, but unfortunately we hadn't got time. We'd got to go back to the *Grosvenor* to get changed.

"I got on all right with Jimmy. I said: 'Do you really support *Newcastle United*?' He said: 'Wayaye man!' His wife, Miriam, was with him.

"Anyway, we went to the 'do' at the *Grosvenor*. I came down from the room, in the lift, before Pat did. Joe Pasquale crushed in, right at the side of my face. He was looking at me – all the way down! Fixing me with a gaze – you know what I mean? I got out and walked around the corner, and he bumped into me. He said: 'We'll have to stop meeting like this!' – (in his squeaky voice).

"The table we sat on, was with Derek Fowlds, who plays Bernard in *Yes Minister*, and Jeffrey Holland, out of *Hi-De-Hi*! Also an Irish pop star – Marianne, and Nerys Hughes, out of *The Liver Birds*. Les Dawson's second wife was sitting by me; his daughter was there as well. There were some lovely people there. I was talking to quite a few of them.

"I spoke to Marty Wilde, in the foyer. I said, 'You wouldn't know who I am,' but he remembered me from when he worked at my club. I asked him how Richard was – his son. He said: 'You're one of the few people who call him that. They all call him Dickie.' His daughter's Kim Wilde. I was talking to the little fella who played R2D2." This was Kenny Baker, who is featured in *Pat Roach's Birmingham*, together with a photo of him as the *Star Wars* robot.

And so it was that the Cuban-based fourth series of the much-loved drama returned to BBC1 screens on Sunday 4 January 2004, at 9.00pm. Speaking on BBC WM's *Late Show*, on the Monday evening immediately following this first transmission, a rather hoarse-sounding Pat, (who clearly wasn't well, but had nevertheless made the effort), summed up the camaraderie between the cast, in the following way:

We're in touch all the time. One of the remarkable things about the whole production is that everyone gets on – everyone understands that each character is written to enhance the other characters. That's the structure of the group; you can have no number one, two or three.

Tim Healy, Madelaine Newton (Kevin Whately's wife) and Tony Green, at the Whately's home, during the earlier years of Auf Wiedersehen. *By permission of Tony Green.*

The very first series of Auf Wiedersehen Pet *was set in Germany. "We can always change the script Pat!" Ian La Frenais and Pat have a* minor *altercation, outside a German Guest-house. Photographer unknown.*

Cast and crew Aufpet 2 *around the Spanish villa pool,* Central TV 1985. *From Julia Tobin's private photograph collection.*

Karen Karlsen (Hastings) c. 1985, aged 20. She played a hotel receptionist, in Aufpet 2. *By permission of Val Hastings.*

Gary Holton's mother, Joan, loves children. Here she nurses Gary's baby son, Red, who was her first grandchild. By permission of Joan Pugh (Holton).

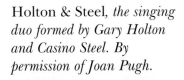

Holton & Steel, *the singing duo formed by Gary Holton and Casino Steel. By permission of Joan Pugh.*

From L-R, on a Marbella beach, during the making of Aufpet 2: *Doreen, Gary Holton, Timmy Clarke and his wife, Diane Clarke. By permission of Doreen Roach.*

Auf Wiedersehen 2 *Marbella Marina Party: L-R: husband-and-wife Jimmy Nail and Miriam Jones, with Chris Fairbank (wearing sunglasses). Madelaine Newton and Kevin Whately have found a shady spot at the back. Gary Holton's dresser is immediately to the left of Pat. Gary Holton and Tim Spall are in the centre foreground. From Doreen's private collection.*

Jimmy Nail, Doreen and Tim Spall on a Marbella beach. By permission of Doreen Roach, Jimmy Nail and Tim Spall.

The cast of Auf Wiedersehen 3, *enjoying the Middlesbrough climate, with the Transporter Bridge in the background. By permission of Doreen Roach.*

A very young Rafe Spall, Tim and Shane's son, going through his paces with Pat, at the Spanish resort where they were staying. By permission of Julia Tobin.

Writing partners Shirley and Pat in Noel's room at Bray Studios. Pat is wearing his 'Bomber' outfit, as filming continued after lunch. Photographer Noel Clarke.

Shirley with Noel Clarke, following an initial lunchtime interview for this book. Photographer Pat Roach. By permission of Noel Clarke.

Pat and Noel prepare to film the Middlesbrough boat ride, described by Noel in Chapter 14. By permission of Doreen Roach.

Pat lined the chairs up for this very special photo, taken in the Arizona desert. At the time he had no way of knowing whether he would be around to make a fourth series. By permission of Doreen Roach.

Tim relaxes at the poolside of their Arizona hotel. Chris Fairbank is in conversation behind him. By permission of Doreen Roach.

Pat, with his driver, Steve Gibson, who was a 'Tower of Strength' to him, throughout the third and fourth series of **Auf Wiedersehen Pet.** *By permission of Doreen Roach.*

Pat, Doreen and Chris enjoy their day trip to Monument Valley. Photographer: Steve Gibson. By permission of Doreen Roach.

Relaxing in front of a Lodge: Kevin, Doreen and Chris. Photographer: Pat Roach. By permission of Doreen Roach.

Steve Gibson and Doreen, photographed by Pat, against a backdrop of deep blue sky and red-rock canyons. By permission of Doreen Roach.

Bomber and Lainie (played by Georgina Lightning) get a second chance at happiness in Auf Wiedersehen 3. *By permission of Doreen Roach.*

Kevin Whately and Julia Tobin look too happy to be 'in role' as Neville and Brenda Hope! By permission of Julia Tobin.

Kevin, Noel, Tim Healy and Pat, on location for Aufpet 3, *outside a London hotel. The observant amongst you will have noticed that's it's the same location as the previous photo - (see the red car with boat). From Julia Tobin's private photograph collection.*

*Pat, with his surgeon, Dr. Ian Geh. Pat writes: "All credit to Doctor Geh, for everything that he and his nurses have done for me." (*Aufpat, *Chapter 18). Photographer: Shirley Thompson, 2002*

Pat's three chemotherapy nursing sisters administered vital treatment to him. From L-R: Jayne Illsley, Christina Hughes and Clare Horrobin. Photograph taken at Heartlands Hospital, by Shirley Thompson, 2002.

Pat and Shirley continued to maintain a positive outlook, as they planned future books. Photographer: Rob Knight.

Rob Knight was Pat's 'Right-hand Man', and a loyal friend throughout. Photograph taken by Shirley Thompson, at Pat's Erdington gymnasium.

Aufpet 4: *The following 15 photographs were taken either by or for Pat, on location in the Dominican Republic, as a private collection to be included in this book. They are now in my own private collection, as he gave them to me, during one of our last meetings - a unique 'thank you' present. (Aufpet 4 collection see chapter 16).*

Aufpet *Producer Chrissy Skinns takes a break with Pat.*

Tim Spall, Patrick Roach Junior and Tim Healy at Pinewood Studios, during the closing stages of Aufpet 4. By permission of Doreen Roach and both Tims.

A further photo of Tim and Pat, taken on DR, when the friends were still together. By permission of Tim Healy.

Book Launch for Pat Roach's Birmingham, *at the* Museum of The Jewellery Quarter *in Birmingham, on Friday 25 June 2004. From L-R: Jack Perkins, Jack Taylor and John Kowalski (all former wrestlers) and friends of Pat's. Jack Taylor's driver is on the right. Behind them are Bernard Newbould and John Bevis. Dr. David Thompson, the writer's husband, is standing just behind them. To the far left is Cynthia Berrington. Photographer: Jean Newbould.*

From L-R: Rob Knight, Shirley Thompson, Denise Welch and Bernard Guest.

Dolly Roach, Pat's mother, with Tim Healy and Denise Welch. Photographer: Shirley Thompson.

Reception at Gems Wine and Dine, after the St. Paul's Memorial Service, in November 2004. From L-R: Brendan Breslin, Johnny Farrington, Dennis Sullivan, Lisa Flynn, 'Con' and Johnny Harris, Freddie Frost and Don Fewtrell. Photographer: Shirley Thompson.

Pat has always had a natural affinity with water. He is pictured here at Gas Street Basin, when George Smith took us on a trip, for If – The Pat Roach Story. *Photographer: Shirley Thompson.*

This was Pat's final view of the world, before leaving with Doreen and Bernard for the Hospice. Photo taken by Shirley, at Pat and Doreen's canalside home.

Floral tributes at Pat's graveside in Bromsgrove, shortly after his 30th July 2004 Memorial Service. Photographer: Shirley Thompson.

Pat's grave, in the spring of 2006. The contrasting flowers seem to symbolise the saying: 'In the midst of life there is death.' Photographer: Shirley Thompson

The bell casting at John Taylor Bellfounders, *Loughborough, on Friday 2nd September 2005. The set of ten bells, cast for the new peal of ten, at St. Paul's Church in the Jewellery Quarter, were subsequently blessed at a special ceremony at St. Paul's on Sunday 3 October 2005. Photographs by Shirley Thompson.*

From L-R: Master of the bell-ringing guild, Richard Grimmett, with the Reverend Tom Pyke, vicar at St. Paul's Church, in the Jewellery Quarter. Tom's help and understanding have been invaluable, *not only for Pat's two memorial services, but throughout the making of this present book, and the previous one,* Pat Roach's Birmingham.

Alan Berry, (in the white shirt), a former Managing Director of John Taylor Bellfounders, provided an excellent guided tour.

Doreen stirs the molten metal for the 8th bell of the Peal, on which Pat's name has been engraved, in company with others, including the parents of Godfrey and Lionel Nall.

Chapter Seventeen

RUSSIAN ROULETTE

When Pat eventually found that conventional treatments weren't producing any long-lasting cure, he began to consider the alternatives. It was rather like Russian Roulette – in that he could never be certain when his time was up. So there was a very strong incentive for him to do whatever he could, to find a remedy.

Shirley Thompson

Having been told I've six to twelve months left, I realised that they said the same thing with Chrissie Fewtrell, but he only lasted through the summer, and was very quickly gone. I'm of the opinion, although I try to keep a very positive head on my shoulders, that I'm probably looking at the end of the summer – I won't see Christmas. But I might – I'll be in there pitching all the time.

Carl Chinn's BBC WM interview with Pat, on 19 August 2002, was four months after *Aufpet 3* was first televised. Carl said: "We've been talking about the book that Pat's written, with Shirley Thompson – *If* – published by Brewin Books. You're involved in a canal production, aren't you, with *British Waterways*?"

Yes, 'Blue Spirit Productions' are involved with 'British Waterways', to put before the Birmingham public a story called 'So Far So Good'. Shirley has a role in it too. It's a modernised version of the Greek story of Orpheus and Eurydice.

Pat was to play Hades, King of the Underworld, or as he put it: "Big ugly Pat again!"

Pat mentioned Jonathan Holmes, the director, and the enthusiasm and professionalism of the cast. One particularly novel aspect of the show was that it had a 'moving venue'. Pat would always make time for anything that enhanced or promoted the Jewellery Quarter. The show was scheduled to run from Tuesday 27 August – Saturday 31 August 2002, beginning at *the Tarnished Halo*. Unfortunately, it had to be cancelled at the very last moment, as the requisite paperwork hadn't been completed. Having been to rehearsals, I can confirm that it would have been spectacular!

Carl concluded his programme with two very apposite comments about Pat: "This is a man who can talk to Harrison Ford, Arnold Schwarzenegger, but he'll talk to us all – at the same level – as he does to all the big stars. I think that's the measure of Pat Roach. He's also a man who has a wide range of involvements in so many different things, and has put himself into raising funds for good causes." Although neither of them could have known at the time, Carl would eventually be one of the Speakers at Pat's Memorial Service, just two years later.

Below is the final extract from, Ed Doolan's broadcast, on 2 March 2003, *The Other Side of Pat Roach*. For ease of reading it remains in 'Question-and Answer' format:

E: Great stories. Everybody says you're a great storyteller, which means there must be a lot of stories you can't tell, in fact, there must be a lot of stories that you *won't* tell?

P: Yes, I always say that you've got to *live* with someone, to *know* them. You can spend your life *liking* someone. But you spend a few days with them, and you soon find that they leave the toothpaste in the bathroom sink, or they don't pull the toilet chain – whatever it is. If you live with someone and you share their secrets, it's very *unfair* to 'kiss-and-tell'. In my books, I haven't done one 'kiss-and-tell'; there's not a mention of sex, not a mention of drugs. Not that I'm suggesting that anyone I work with takes drugs – or even has sex! Not a mention!

E: Are you a sensitive person. You've talked about one or two of the emotional aspects of things that have happened to you, and the way you felt. Are you an emotional person? Can you weep?

P: Oh yes – *Danny Boy*. I didn't have the privilege of hearing it today, but if I had, you'd have seen me shed a tear. But I don't know why. I'm not Irish – I'm English.

E: Oh yes – right!

P: No, really. I was born in the Jewellery Quarter, in Ladywood. Both of my parents are English.

E: Apart from *Danny Boy*, what makes you cry?

P: D'you know, I could almost shed a tear when I hear the French National Anthem!

Ed's programme concluded with ten questions, which originally came from a French series, *Bouillon de Culture*, hosted by Bernard Pivot. They are probably more familiar to many as the questions James Lipton asks at the end of *Inside the Actor's Studio*:

E: Are you ready for your ten questions? Every guest gets these – and it's fascinating to compare what other people say, Pat. What is your favourite word?

P: Awareness – total awareness. There's a book written called *Awareness*. I pride myself in being able to wear the other person's shoes, at all times.

E: Why?

P: Because people rarely do. We're all so self-centred in the things that we think people should do for *us*; you've got to wear the policeman's hat – everyone's hat.

E: What's your *least* favourite word?

P: 'Can't'. I hate it!

E: I'll second you there! What turns you on, creatively, spiritually or emotionally?

P: 'Endeavour' – people that *try*. I'm a member of the *Special Olympics*, which is the Olympic organisation for people with various handicaps. Because it *is* such a wide and varied field, they tend to 'lump' people in together: people who are retarded are in there with Downs Syndrome competitors – and so on.

E: What turns you off?

P: I suppose negativity – this thing about can't do it – it's too much trouble.

E: Right – you can't *say* this next word. What is your favourite curse word?

P: Right, it's the usual profanity, begins with an 'f', is in the past tense, and ends in 'ed'. That's changed over the years, hasn't it? It's become almost acceptable – but not on the BBC.

E: Almost! Well – even on the BBC. What sound do you love?

P: (Pause) Oh yes – I had to think about it for a second, because there are so many lovely things, aren't there? I made a film on a big bird sanctuary – the early morning sound of birds.

E: What sound do you hate?

P: I'm not sure about what sound I *hate* – the sound of screeching brakes – I think.

E: Alright. What profession other than your own, would you like to attempt?

P: I think I'd like to become a musician-cum-singer, because of the opportunity to create.

E: What profession would you *not* like to do?

P: I'd hate to be in the media, where you have to get a story, and you have to *fabricate* it, to make it work.

E: Really?

P: Oh, I'd *hate* it!

E: And if heaven exists, when you arrive at the Pearly Gates, what would you like to hear God say?

P: I'd like him to say: "Pat, I've made my mind up. I'm doing away with all religious sects. You've *all* got to believe in the same one thing. What we've got here is a mountain, with God at the top, and all the religious sects are trying to get to the top – to God; all spread around this mountain. Some are within sight of each other like the Muslims and the Christians. Others are completely out of sight. But they're all trying to get to the top – to God. And I'd like God to say: "No more religions – just one," that would do for me.

E: It's been such a pleasure to talk to you, Pat Roach. We're going out with a touch of Pavarotti – and *Nessun dorma* – because…?

P: Just to impress the public out there, that I'm a little cultured…

Plays *Nessun dorma*.

E: And that was *The Other Side of Pat Roach*. Thanks to all of you sending e-mails in, first of all, those of you enjoying Pat Roach. Thank you for that.

As Pat mentioned earlier, Ed telephoned him afterwards, to say they'd had a tremendously favourable response to the programme. Moving forward another six months, we find that Pat's future continued to be uncertain, as the following diary entries show:

Thursday 3 July 2003:

Pat and I had a business meeting at *Angels Restaurant*, Warstone Lane, appropriately enough in Birmingham's *Jewellery Quarter*, close to where his life first began. The irony of the restaurant's title hadn't escaped me! Almost since our very first meeting, in 1999, Pat and I had been scrupulously careful to keep his cancer a secret. He only told those who had to know, for practical reasons.

Ronnie Callow, featured in Chapter 5, called in to the restaurant, that afternoon. He and Pat had arranged to meet for a chat. Pat also had leaflets with him, about a drug he'd been using to combat cancer, as Ronnie had been fighting the disease too.

Paddy White, the former manager at *The Rendezvous* nightclub, which Pat had owned many years previously, came in for a coffee too, purely by chance. The afternoon was full of irony: the nightclub had been situated just a short distance away, in Hockley Street, and Paddy and his wife Jill had popped into *Angels*, purely by chance, as she had a watch that needed repairing. Jill had been a barmaid at *The Rendezvous*, which is how she and Paddy originally met. The couple subsequently featured in *Pat Roach's Birmingham*.

Until that day, I'd had been extremely reluctant to make a start on this present chapter. When tempted to begin, on previous occasions, I'd held back, for fear that once these facts 'hit' the word processor, the secret would be out; it seemed like a form of betrayal. But if I didn't record events, they would be lost to me forever. So – on 3 July 2003, this chapter was begun.

That same afternoon, Pat's chauffeur employed by the BBC, was collecting him from the restaurant, to whisk him back to London, for further filming of *AWP 4*. The sub-plot of Pat having to contend with his illness, hovered menacingly, like some *Dark Angel*, whom we hoped would never materialise. But he was becoming noticeably thinner, and his 'insurance', or 'yardstick', around his waistline, seemed to be fast disappearing.

The previous day, during time off from filming, Pat had attended his cancer clinic, for a further CT Scan. As he explained, that afternoon, the results of the scan wouldn't be available for a further two weeks – a lot could happen in a fortnight. He had no choice other than to continue with *Aufpet 4*, without knowing whether he needed further life-saving treatment. On several occasions, over a five-year period, he had received life-saving treatment. But would the same thing happen this time? His final scan was scheduled for Friday 19 December 2003, but would he rally sufficiently to receive it? It was a nerve-wracking time for me, as his co-writer, so I can only *imagine* what it must have been like for Pat and his family.

Since writing the above, a lot of water has 'flown under the bridge':

Friday 28 November 2003:
We read through a couple of Jewellery Quarter transcripts and discussed one or two other matters relating to our forthcoming book, *Pat Roach's Birmingham*. But from that point onwards, Pat's health *seemed* to go into free-fall. The following day, I left for a fortnight's holiday in Devon and Cornwall. By sheer coincidence, Pat's condition worsened, although he wasn't sure exactly why, at this point. He spent the next three weeks or so, either in bed, or unable to do much. From this point onwards, I was obliged to work on our book by myself, making all the decisions relating to it. What little conversation I was able to have with Pat, meanwhile, was in short bursts, of a few seconds duration only, and often monosyllabic.

In most cases, his friends were unable to contact him, as his mobile remained switched off for considerable periods of time. He was unable to absorb information that others wanted to give him, and could only have one-way conversations, as nothing else would register. What eventually emerged, when test results came through, was that his brain tumour, previously reduced with lasers, had grown significantly large again to warrant an operation.

Saturday 3 January 2004:

Having made it to yet another family Christmas, Pat telephoned me to confirm that a second brain tumour had developed. He was going to hospital on Monday 5 January, to see whether a second operation was possible. I was researching in the Jewellery Quarter that day; Pat asked me not to phone him, because he would be heavily sedated. He *hoped* to be capable of phoning me some time during that week.

That same evening, Monday 5 January 2004, he took part in a broadcast on BBC WM's *The Late Show*, although, at times, he was clearly struggling with his words. The show, (mentioned briefly at the end of the previous chapter), was presented by husband-and-wife team, Tony and Julie Wadsworth. Pat spoke about the series and about a Fitness Initiative that he was currently supporting. Episode One of *Auf Wiedersehen 4* – the Cuban-based series had been televised the previous evening, so the subject was very topical. He explained that the crew had recently been featured on the front cover of a TV magazine, as a sign of the appreciation that the cast felt, for the tremendous support that the crew always gave them.

He also mentioned that the two of us were co-writing *Pat Roach's Birmingham*. Despite feeling ill, he made a point of 'plugging' the biography *The Original Alton Douglas*, which I'd recently co-written with Alton; and the fact that I was becoming a 'well known author in my own right'. This illustrates well the point made in this and previous biographies, that if Pat is your friend, he will always have your interests at heart. He also mentioned that we'd plans to co-write a wrestling book with a difference; perhaps I'll eventually be able to deliver it for him!

Tony concluded: "It's been a pleasure seeing you. Don't make it *too* long, before you come in and see us again. Let us know when your book's out and come in and chat to us about it, in more detail. I know you're not feeling too well tonight, so there's even more reason for saying thanks for coming in and talking to us. All the best with the new telly show. *Auf Wiedersehen Pet* is on BBC 1, Sunday nights – don't miss it!"

Sunday 11 January 2004:

Meanwhile, unfortunately, The *News of the World* had been probing. Without any warning, on Sunday 11 January 2004, it published an article, announcing that Pat was dying of cancer. Being a national newspaper, everyone heard about it, and we were now presented with a much more difficult situation. Our publisher, Alan Brewin and Pat's close friend and wrestling spokesman, Bill Bridges, were forced to deny the rumours or disclaim knowledge, which in Alan's case, was to some extent true. To make matters worse, the photo accompanying the article, was grotesque: taken when he was just about to sneeze, as he walked past Ken Schofield's Jewellery Quarter warehouse.

We received many calls from his friends and family, which had to be 'side-stepped', to a certain extent, to allay people's anxiety. The article presented a real problem for Pat and his brother Pete Meakin. "When Pat told me and my wife Shirley, back in 1998, that he'd got cancer, he said that he wasn't going to tell mom, because it would upset her too much. He just hoped that, when we eventually did have to tell her, mother would forgive him, for not having told her.

"When we eventually had to tell mom, we sat her down and we made believe that we hadn't known." Pete's wife Shirley explains: "Pat phoned us up just before and asked if we could all come down to mother's: 'I want you to be there for me.' He didn't want her to read about it in the papers, before he'd had a chance to explain." "He wanted us all there together," continues Pete, "probably to make it easier on everybody. It was obviously a big thing for Pat to have to tell mom."

The best case scenario, as Pat said on several occasions, was never having to do it: in the nicest possible way, if he managed to outlive her. "He sat mom down in the Living Room and we sat with him," Pete recalls. "That was a very emotional thing, because we didn't know, with mom's health, how she was going to take it. He said: 'Mother, I've got something I've got to tell you.' I was thinking: 'How's she going to take this?' He was holding her hand when he told her." "But we had to make out that it was as big a shock to us as it was to her," adds Shirley.

On Sunday 18 January 2004, Pat went into the Queen Elizabeth Hospital, Birmingham, and had surgery, to remove a brain tumour, the following day. Over the next three days he was incommunicado, but late on Thursday evening, 23 January, at about 9.20pm. I had a call from Pat, from the hospital. Having had no idea, like the rest of his friends, whether he was alive or dead, I'd left a message on his mobile. When he rang, I knew that things couldn't be too bad, because he joked about having come back from the dead to speak to me!

Tuesday 3 February 2004:
Pat came to my house; in my opinion, quite a feat in itself, as, only days earlier, he'd had difficulty in simply walking, and continues to experience dizzy spells. Although not presently happy with climbing stairs, he has

sufficient determination to have begun exercising. He managed one hundred press-ups yesterday. Some days are better for him than others. Either way, it's a tremendous relief to see him back on his feet again, after such a major operation.

He's trying certain homeopathic remedies at present. Hopefully, when he goes for a CT on the 19 February, his specialist, (who is still Doctor Geh), will be able to confirm that the homeopathy that Pat is using, will be compatible with any radiotherapy or chemotherapy that may prove necessary. Pat's hoping to avoid the aforementioned treatments, if possible, as they damage other body cells in the process.

According to Pat, Dr. Geh has told him that he's one of only six people in the country to have continued to combat the disease, to date. I hope the 'Big'un continues to do so – he's so courageous! Pat also made the point that he'd mistakenly thought that the reason the doctor hadn't wanted to see him before the 19th was because there was no need for radio or chemotherapy. What he now realises is that it's because the doctor knew that his body couldn't *take* it any sooner.

On Wednesday 11 February 2004, I had another editorial meeting with Pat at my home; on 24 February, feeling that time was running out, we had a further meeting at the Gym, during which we reaffirmed a series of past agreements that we'd made, regarding many aspects of this book. This particular chapter is a 'case-in-point'.

* * * * *

We put 'on hold' the two opening chapters of this book, plus many verbatim passages from Pat, and our final chapter *The Joke's On Me*, as we were convinced that he would to die much earlier. Meanwhile, Pat continued to run a showbusiness career, plus his scrap yard, as best he could. However, only months before Pat's passing, someone tried to kill him at his yard. He telephoned me, in a state-of-shock, saying that two men in a car, whilst in the process of stealing parts from him, (one of a number of such incidents), had driven the car straight at him, as they made their getaway. It was only Pat's stuntman skills that saved him, but they knocked him to the ground and bruised him. The police never caught them.

I discovered later that Alfie Evans, (see Chapter 3), actually witnessed this, first-hand: "He told me about selling the yard: 'I've got to get out Alf, otherwise I'll be up on a murder charge! They're driving me mad, they're coming in and stealing.' His yard was broken into and they stole all of his burning gear. He phoned me up and he said: 'They've robbed my yard.' I said: 'Well, you can have all of my burning gear, oxyacetylene equipment. I've got lots of guns – I can bring them up. I'm not using them any more.' So I went to the yard and Pat was outside – messing. All of a sudden, he's opened a car door and they drove past – to hit him. Pat tried to jump out of the way, but the driver knocked him on the floor. It bruised all of his one side. A coloured kid was driving the car. He hit him and tried to run him down." Pat rolled under another car, to get out of the way. He told me later that he was convinced that the driver was 'high' on drugs.

Mentioning the incident to Seamus Dunleavy, the following year, he commented: "We owned a lot of houses in Winson Green, (we've just sold them). That's when I used to go up and see him a lot, when I was popping up there. Pat always said: 'It's a *very* dangerous area.'" On the rare occasions that his co-writer picked him up from the yard, it was always at a pre-arranged time, so that I wasn't parked there for long.

In October 2004, discussing the reasons why Pat managed to survive as long as he did, Doreen commented: "I think it was his determination: he just wouldn't give in. The alternative remedies that he tried gave him hope. He really thought that *some* of them would work." The history of his treatment is rather complicated. "He tried some nuts – I think they were Chinese. You had to eat about seven – three times a day. Oh dear – he tried those! Then some kind of tea that you brewed up: later, he found that they sold it in a bottle. So I was pleased with that – no more brewing up! Then he sent to America – for the Oxygen Machine."

With access to the Internet, I had assisted Pat in obtaining information about this from America, together with various components. "He tried that for quite a while," Doreen continues. "Then there was Noni Juice. I've got a bottle of it. I can show you." The large bottle of juice, according to the label, is Tahitian. It says: 'mixed fruit juice beverage.' "Robert Knight, at the Club, used to order it and then go and pick it up for him. He'd have it morning and night. It was supposed to clean you all through. I suppose the theory was that it cleared all the impurities out of you." Several of the alternative treatments, like the later German one, described in the next chapter, and the Ozone Machine, seem to involve various natural gases. He was using the Ozone Machine both ends, I believe! It must have been really unpleasant for him.

"Yes – but I don't think any of these things really *worked*. It was just his determination to keep going," Doreen explains. "There were some crystals too, that he mixed with water and drank." I think that was a Red

Indian/Canadian remedy. Another cancer patient had already ordered the crystals, but died before being able to use them. So Pat bought them from the supplier. But he *was* concerned that he might be wasting his money! "Of course, it was only towards the end that he was trying all these alternatives," Doreen observes.

Pat remarked on several occasions, that the NHS Staff were wonderful. Did Doreen meet any of them? "Yes – Dr. Geh and his nurses; also, staff at the Queen Elizabeth, when he was having his brain operations. David Talboys used to fetch him out and I'd pick him up, to bring him here, because, in my experience, the parking situation was terrible." We're both in agreement, as was Pat, that the medical staff who treated him, were first-rate.

In an earlier chapter, Kevin Whately refers to the scan that Pat had in DR, during the filming of *Aufpet 4*. "Yes, Pat showed me," Doreen confirms.

"I had cancer myself," Doreen continues. "My treatment was *absolutely* marvellous. I went in and had a biopsy and within a week, I'd had the operation. Absolutely fine."

Pat fought the cancer by every means available, using alternative treatment too, during his final years. It comforted him to know that he was trying everything possible and that he was being proactive. His personality was such that he could never allow the disease to simply take over; He fought it, with all of his resources and inner strength, to the end.

Doreen had a premonition about Pat, which he'd previously described, at one of our meetings: "One day I had a feeling that Pat was ill. I picked up the phone and I said to him: 'Are you alright?' He said: 'No, I've just been ever so bad.'" According to Pat, he normally would have made light of it and said: "Oh – I'm fine!" But because it was uncanny that Doreen phoned so quickly after he'd felt really ill, he simply couldn't hide it from her.

I asked Doreen about the month or so prior to Pat's death, when he decided that he didn't want even some of his *closest* friends to see him. When they phoned me for news, they were naturally upset that they couldn't visit him. "Yes, he didn't want anyone to see him that ill. He wanted them to remember him just the way he had been – big and strong," Doreen confirms. Pat liked to feel in control of situations. So the fact that the disease was now controlling *him* must have been very hard for him to take. "Yes, in the end I used to wash him and help him change," comments Doreen. "He *hated* it – he really did!"

Pat and myself were very keen to provide financial help to at least one major cancer charity, via this final book. We are currently liaising with Cancer

BACUP, a charity which provides information and support to anyone affected by cancer. Pat found their meetings particularly supportive, and described a Support Group, recommended by the Cancer BACUP Centre, based at Walsgrave Hospital, in Coventry. He made friends with one gentleman in particular, who attended the group, but unfortunately, I don't have his name on record, ('Murphy's Law' being what it is!). However, the man in question had survived cancer for several years and continued to lead an active life. Pat drew particular comfort from his example. The Cancer BACUP freephone helpline, (0808 800 1234 – UK only), is staffed by cancer information nurses able to answer any question on any cancer. Donations to the charity can be made by calling 0207 920 7871 (standard rate). For additional details about the organisation, log on to www.cancerbacup.org.uk.

It's a sobering thought that variations on Pat's experience of cancer continue to be repeated countless times, within so many families, in Britain and throughout the world. Partners and spouses have to totally re-examine their priorities, and re-adjust their lives, to cope, once a diagnosis has been made.

Wait a second –

Maybe it's only –

Ssh! Just be quiet for a minute. While we've spent this time together, talking about my life, you've made a great attempt towards an awareness, so that you're able to feel more than ever, for people who are confronted by terminal illness. I know it has touched you deeply that there are situations where people are totally alive and kicking one moment – and struggling and striving towards death the next.

I wanted to ask you, my co-author, who has now become my friend for life – or dare I say it – my lifelong friend – to put something of yourself into the book, as I feel that you have a lot more to offer than merely co-writing it. Because of your tenderness and the way you have received many of the things I have said, I know that you are able to make a major contribution towards this part of the book. As you are a rather poetic type of person, perhaps that's the form it should take?

A wise person once said: "It is only with the heart that one can see clearly: what is essential is invisible to the eye." Accordingly, (and with no wish to be maudlin or to intrude on anyone's private grief), the following poem, which has Pat's blessing, is dedicated to all those couples who have lost, or are *likely* to lose, the person most precious to them, through terminal illness.

When a cancer diagnosis is made, the first things that inevitably disappear, are the freedom and independence of both partners, as the one cares for the other. The essence of this poem is two-fold: that love will endure *beyond* the grave, and that although physical circumstances may suddenly restrict our lives, true freedom lies closer than we may imagine.

Despite the sadness of Pat's death, five months later, it gave him his final *freedom*, releasing him from all the pain and suffering; so the poem's *title* has a dual significance too.

* * * * *

FREEDOM

Had we but time and worlds enough
I'd take you to a place
Where time suspends eternity
Far from life's fraught 'rat-race'.

And if we'd the will... and cared enough
We'd find an inner peace
Where death and wealth don't signify
And worldly cares just cease.

Our health and youth restored again
We'd wander through woods alone,
On riverbanks we'd take our ease
And join – 'til our hearts were one.

But where is the time, and where is this place
Where we could slip away
To find our desires and souls again
Be together, come what may?

Through peaceful ways we'll discover a dawn
Where the path to freedom starts.
Place gentle hands love... feel the beat
For it lies within our hearts.

© Shirley Thompson 2004

This poem is also on page 541 of the *Celebrations Anthology,* Forward Press, 2006.

Chapter Eighteen

MIDNIGHT MERCHANT

Pat phoned me up and said: "I've found this place." He'd been telling me about his treatment – his 'chemo' and so on. Some of it had been doing him good, but some hadn't. This place in Germany had been recommended as a good thing. If he could go, they would help him out. But he couldn't fly, because of his 'chemo' and all the other treatment. I said: "Well, we'll drive there and I'll take you." He said: "What?" I said: "I'll take you." That was on the Friday. On the Monday, I booked a boat straight away; it was in Ludwigshafen. I knew where that was, in Germany. We drove down through England all day. We were booked on the boat, and went on the company called 'Norfolk Line'; the name of the boat was the 'Midnight Merchant'.

Bernard Guest

Bernard had been a military man, for almost twelve years, and a close friend of Pat's since the 1960s. As Wayne Bridges explained in Chapter 10, Pat regarded Bernard, who subsequently became a businessman-entrepreneur, as a man whom he would "trust above all others." A measure of his trust in Bernard is that Pat asked Bernard and myself to coordinate his funeral together, in conjunction with Wayne Bridges and a few other trusted friends.

Bernard and Pat met in the late 1960s, when Bernard was still in the armed forces. "The first time I met Pat was at Roy O'Neill's yard in Church Road, Lozells, in Birmingham. I was with a friend of mine who was ex-Para, named Wallis, when I went to meet Pat, in civilian clothing. I hadn't used to wear my uniform... posing!"

In those days, Bernard was sometimes referred to as a 'Black Country Kid'. "In the 1970s, Pat phoned to say he'd heard that I'd got a 2½ ton crane for sale, and would I be interested in selling it, on a part-exchange basis for a weighing machine? We agreed the price; he came over and looked at it. I expected him to have a 'low-load' or something to take it back – but no. He said: 'I'm going to drive it back to Birmingham!' That was fourteen miles, along the roads. I couldn't *believe* it – but he did it. I lived in Willenhall at that time and had just started out on my own." It was virtually impossible for Pat to steer the machine, but somehow he managed it. Passing his test in a Tipper Truck, at the age of seventeen, probably gave him a head start!

On the subject of unusual vehicles, according to wrestler John Kowalski, around this same period, "Pat had a Second-hand Car Pitch at Washwood Heath. For some time, the main attraction was a 1930s hearse, a really big one, with a shovel leaning against the bonnet. A large sign on the windscreen said *Do-it-yourself Funerals – For Hire*. I don't remember if he *did* have any takers, but it certainly created much interest!" remembers John.

"After that, I did quite a few deals with him," Bernard continues. "We've never been in each other's pockets. I wouldn't see him for years and then he would pop up. But we had an affinity. I haven't got many friends. I mean, my birthday's in two week's time. I'm asking all my friends and we're going to hold the party in a telephone box!

"We were working on one particular job, doing some insulation for an underground building. The first night, we were in Kemptown, which is part of Brighton: they called it 'Camptown' – we found out later! We go in this bar and I'm wearing black trousers and a white polo-neck sweater, which (I didn't realise) is the 'Puffs' uniform. I was standing at the bar, and, looking across, I said: 'The barmaid needs a shave!' Comes close, and it was a fella! So I said: 'Let's go – we'll go somewhere else.' We went to another pub, and I'm approached by this fella who comes up to me and says, 'How would you like me to buy you a drink?' I said: 'How would you like to spend three months in Intensive Care?'"

Bernard has a wealth of hilarious tales about his years in the building industry. Sadly, we don't have space in this chapter, so they'll have to keep for another time! However, Pat was keen to include some of their mutual acquaintances. The first of these was Fidemann. "We just called him 'Fiddy'," recalls Bernard. "He was like a gorilla. But he was a nice fella. He looked like Jean Claud Van Damm actually – his face, but he was much bigger. I met him in the middle-to-late 1970s. He was a Brummie, from around Northfield way.

"Fiddy said: 'Roy O'Neill's here and he pointed you out.' I used to specialise in electrical stuff: buying it and selling it on. He said: 'We'm looking at this stuff in the Refrigeration Room. Could you have a look at it and price it for us?' I said: 'I've got no problem with that.' Then at that, little Harry Dossiter comes. It was just like *Little and Large*." (No wonder Pat wanted them included!) "Fiddy was a very quiet, laid-back 'hard man'. Harry was like a typical little bloke: he was 'flash', jumped about – nice fella, always

'Jack-the-Lad'," continues Bernard. "Always immaculately dressed. But I hadn't realised how frightened Brummies were of rats." Bernard had taken a torch into the back room of an old building. "I'm looking round and Fiddy was saying: 'What do you think of that?' I was just giving him the benefit of my experience, because that was the way you *used* to be – you'd help each other, if you were stuck for something; there were very few arseholes, because they didn't last long. There were very few Black Country Kids who went into Birmingham at all, in the 1970s. 'Oh,' I says, 'there are some rats in here!' As soon as I uttered the words, there was a *mass* exodus: not just those two. I thought there was a fire or something. They were all galloping out and I thought: 'What's going on?' They hadn't just left the room: they were outside in the car park! I said, 'What's up? What's up?' We had a lot of long-tailed rats: these so-called 'hard men' were terrified of them – it was like a 'thing' in the town. I've come across a lot of it in the scrap trade – in 'Brum'. I've never seen any in the Black Country – it doesn't bother us – you know?

"Harry Dossiter was a tough little man, but he's gone – like – about five years ago; Fidemann died quite a while ago. They all went on about him, but Harry and 'Fiddy' were always OK to me – and I treat people as I find them. I can't say how they were to others. Pat's father, Frank Roach and Dennis Sullivan were well matched as dealers and friends. Billy Ward – he was another one: 'Here's me hand, here's me heart.'" In *If – The Pat Roach Story*, Pat refers to 'Wardie' and 'Clarkie'.

On Tuesday 9 March 2004, Pat went to Germany to begin his first course of Alternative Treatment, for cancer. He phoned me from Germany, on 12 March to say that the cancer was spreading, but he thought that the medics might be able to help. The three of us describe that visit:

As I speak, at this second, I'm probably three weeks down the road from my friend Bernard Guest, having taken me to Germany. He literally threw me into a car, gave up all of his work. He said: "Look – nothing else matters – except you." Which is a rather lovely thing to say. Our trip was from 9 – 17 March 2004.

Bernard and myself go back many years. He gave up his business, gave up everything. He said: "Right – I'm taking you!" Threw me into the car, and drove me, literally, into the middle of Germany. And I have to say – if it turns out that way – he will have saved my life!

Pat selected this particular clinic from a videotape, which arrived with his HO3 Machine, from America. The tape, which had been made a few years previously, described progress in the Ozone World: "very convincing stuff," according to Pat. An interview, with Doctor Kief from Ludwigshafen, was included on the tape.

Such was the strength of Pat and Bernard's friendship, that when Pat needed him most, Bernard was there for him, as the opening paragraph of this chapter explains. Bernard simply decided: 'This is it – he's going!'

One of the first things I said to Bernard was – "Well, OK – if you drive me there, but your money's no good." So obviously, I paid all the expenses. The whole trip came to maybe three and a half thousand pounds, including the treatment as well – the very thought of people in Britain being kept alive, for that amount! There are people up the hospital now, and it's costing far more than that, to treat them. And that's only to try to stop the cancers growing – when they could send them abroad to this guy and get them cured, for a fraction of the price.

But they can't accept his work – it's outside the etiquette of the British Medical Council. This may not be true, but one of the wonderful things that I'm looking forward to – (I think about it a hundred times a day) – is that I might have a message for people, that "You don't have to die from cancer – you can be cured!" Can you imagine saying that to people? I'm not being entirely selfish about his – because I've resolved myself to die – you know that. But it would be wonderful if I could say that to people.

"One of the strange things," continues Bernard, "was that when we wanted to go up four flights of stairs, to the seating deck, Pat had to stop at each flight of stairs.

"We got off the boat in France, and drove down through France for two days – right the way down. We stopped just outside Saarbrücken, the first night, at eleven o'clock at night, having just gone through snowstorms and God-knows-what! I thought: 'We're not going to make it through this!'" Pat was wide awake whilst this was happening, and had a similar reaction to Bernard. "When we crossed on the boat, I changed my car for a BMW of the 'Seven' series – in Belgium: it was more comfortable to drive," explains Bernard. "Then we reached Mannheim and I drove from there to Ludwigshafen. There we found a place called Phinklewierde, not far from Frankenthal."

There are certain similarities between Pat and Bernard: "We're not afraid of anybody. I don't need money that much. I've had quite a comfortable life, but I shall never stop working until I'm ninety! The point is, is not *what* you do – it's *why you do it*. I mean, there are many opportunities for you to make lots of money, in many nefarious ways, that I wouldn't touch. But basically, I enjoy doing the *deal*. That's me. Sometimes I lose money, but you've got to *enjoy* it."

Bernard was making friends with everybody at the clinic. He gathered information off various people, as he speaks German fluently.

"We sat in the ante-room. Then Pat went in for his interview with the Consultant. I was talking to two Americans first – Vincent and Evan. Vincent had Aids; Evan is a lawyer in Manhattan and he's got a twin brother. I said: 'Is your twin brother a homosexual?' Because he was quite open – you know? He said: 'No, he's married to an exotic dancer. But I can't see what he sees in her!' Evan's phoned me from America since, because Vincent died."

Vincent told me that he'd got three weeks to live. They'd had friends who, a couple of years ago, had been cured of colon cancer, by this guy: not just stopped – cured – a whole new ball game! Vince told me that he hadn't had a shower for weeks. He couldn't put his clothes on. He used to cry every day, with his itching and irritation, through psoriasis, because his immune system was so low, as a result of HIV. It was terrible: his appearance was like someone a Biafran would take the Mickey out of. He was like a stick man. When he crossed his legs, there was nothing on them. How he held on I don't know. I was really taken aback!

"It was the first time Vincent could have a shower, when he was at the German clinic," explains Bernard.

When I arrived the second day, this bloody guy Vince jumped up out of the chair and shook my hand – with a big smile on his face. I couldn't believe it! We both went in for treatment again and were telling each other how much better we felt.

"Pat was having his treatment, and there was a woman in there, with a little girl, who had eczema. Her mother had a photo of her, with the rash all over her. After treatment at the clinic it was reduced to just a little on her hand. These people had cured her. There were so many positive things that people said there."

There was a guy there, about seventy-odd, who'd been going blind for a while and they'd saved his sight.

"They weren't trying to sell you something: they were actual patients. Quite a few of the things that had happened to them were positive. It was just individual people. It was a big house, rather than a *conventional* clinic. I should have taken a picture of it really."

They were delightful people, almost a family business. Ludwigshafen is quite a big city, in the centre of Germany, on the River Rhine. I'd already inquired, (because it was on the video), about the Blood Washing. I'd spoken beforehand to the staff. They said yes, so I was delighted, because I knew that I wasn't going to last five weeks. I was going downhill so quickly. Of course, there was always the risk that Doctor Kief's treatment might not work for me, but could work for somebody else.

They put Pat on a machine, which extracted 150mm of blood, then pumped HO3 into it, through another machine.

It comes out as ozone at the other end. Then they pump that into your blood. It's a ratio of what density is needed and for how long. There may well be some magic ingredient. They inject some high-powered Vitamin C into it. Basically, they're looking at your own body's antibodies. I'm jumping the gun a bit. So the treatment is, they take out a certain amount of blood, HO3 it – put it back into me – maybe with a secret ingredient added – I don't know.

"The doctor's daughter, Mia came in," recalls Bernard. "I was talking to all these different people. A seventy-six-year-old woman arrived, with her husband, who was two years older. He'd improved no end, since he'd been going there. The doctor came out – the one in charge. He was very explicit and explained exactly what was going on. The first thing he told Pat was: "Your blood reading is very high. But now we know, we can do something about it."

But all credit to Doctor Geh – for operations and everything he and the nurses have done for me. You and I know, and everybody else knows, that you die from cancer. And certainly, when you've got a tumour in each lung and one in your liver, as I have at present, you die from it. I've got three at the moment. My German consultant came up with a blood test. I've got the results in my pocket here – to show you. He said: "Oh, it's bad news Mr. Roach. Your cancer is really galloping – it's really accelerating. But I can still help." So, as of now, two weeks down the road from here, I'm going to need another injection – and – I dunno. Let's see whether that does any good.

Bernard confirms Pat's description of Doctor Kief's approach: "It was like: 'In three months time, I won't need to see you.' Whether that was psychological, I don't know. Pat had his injections, every day, so he had to go there each day, and stay there. But that night, after he'd had his first course of treatment, he walked nearly a mile. Then he had a pint of beer. He got better while he was there."

The day I arrived there, I couldn't walk five paces, without gasping for air... there was no doubt about that. I couldn't walk upstairs – I was in terrible trouble. I'd get to the top of seven single steps – one flight – and I'd have to rest, then repeat the process, with each flight. But that same evening, we went out looking for a Chinese Restaurant, because my walking seemed to improve almost immediately.

"We had to stay there over a week," continues Bernard. "They weren't open on a Saturday or Sunday, because of the laws in Germany. They're fighting for their license, because there's problems with what they're doing anyway. So we stayed there over the weekend. On the Monday morning we went back again. The doctor said to me: 'You're a bit of a realist, aren't you?' I said: 'What do you mean?' He said: 'Well, if you'd got this, what would you do?' I said, 'I'd let it go its own way. You can't fight it, so what's the use?'"

It's now late March and the brain tumour thing is fairly well behind me now. I was warned about various side effects of the operation. As I sit here now, in Shirley's Study, I've got very clouded vision in my left eye. I don't know whether it's a result of that operation. They did say I could lose the sight of my left eye – and I'm just getting a clouded thing in my eye. I intend to see an optician – today if possible, to find out what's wrong with me. My immune system's on the floor: the very least thing that happens to me, cold or rain, for example, I'm in trouble. What really confuses you is that if you've got a bit of brain trouble, although you're conscious, at the same time you're thinking: 'What the bloody hell's going on?' Suddenly I realised that amongst everything else, I couldn't walk from one door to another, without being in terrible trouble – breathing-wise. And that I couldn't walk five paces without staggering.

Meanwhile, I'd got my Ozone-HO3 Machine, from America, which I'd been using for a while. Then again, I don't know that that's been doing me much good. I've been pumping that stuff into almost every orifice that I've got – as advised.

When Pat asked Doctor Kief if he should stop using the American machine, he said: "No, pump it into you – you can't get enough HO3." So Pat continued to use it.

Tony Green remembers: "On the very last occasion I saw Pat, he came into the office and he sat in the same chair that you're sitting in now. He kept clutching his side, and was obviously in tremendous pain. But he put on a brave face and said that he hoped that this new treatment was going to cure him. There was the German treatment, and he'd been in touch with America. When he was using the Ozone Machine, from America, he had to wear a rubber suit, where you pump air into it! It was a bit difficult to say: 'You don't look well,' so I asked him if the pain was bad: he said: 'Oh it's not too bad.' Pat would always pass things off."

Pat tried to see as many of his old friends as possible, during the three years preceding his death, when he thought he hadn't long to go. His excuse for giving them a big hug was that he hadn't seen them for ages, whereas in his *own* mind, he was actually saying goodbye to them. "Pat used to hug me quite frequently – he had done for years," Tony continues. "It was a regular thing: he'd put his arms out and kind of bearhug you. No kisses or anything like that. I don't think he hugged many people."

In British hospitals, once you get there, everybody's wonderful. It's not the staff's fault, that there's sometimes a shortage of equipment. But they can send you abroad on a return flight, to the Dominican Republic, and do the scan for £150. At the moment, I can have a CT Scan in Belgium, for about £170 – I can walk in off the street. I wasn't allowed to fly for eight weeks, which is one of my problems. But when I told the American guys about my symptoms, they said: "Come over here. We'll sort you out," with all that confidence. "Never mind the fact that you're dying of cancer, come over here and we'll sort you out!"

Pat returned from Germany, on Wednesday 17 March, saying that the next four or five weeks were crucial. He drove to my house, on Thursday 25 March 2004. Unbeknown to me, this would be his very last visit. That same day, we made the following reprise of his medical history:

You still look in the mirror every day and wonder if you're going to start dying that day, or if you can hang on a little bit longer. I went to the hospital and a doctor came in – not the usual one – and endorsed the fact that the tumour in my lung is starting to get bigger, and the other one, that has been very quiet, has started to become active. And yes – I've inherited another one as well: I've got one in my liver – which I wasn't very pleased about! I've been taking my bits-and-pieces, my 'Flora' stuff, B17s for about five months, and a couple of other things.

All of the 'tried-and-tested' remedies haven't done the trick, because I've inherited new cancers. They said that they weren't in a great dash to see me, because they were growing very slowly – small compensation, I suppose. Then, in the next few weeks, I started to fall about, all over the place; got some nasty headaches, as I'd done before, with the tumour I had in my brain. Just before Christmas 2003, because my Immune System is always so low, I caught a chest cold. Two courses of antibiotics didn't resolve it. Then there was a mixture of heavy chest colds, head colds and I wasn't quite sure where I was, or what I was doing. All of this went on over Christmas 2003. The reason was, as it turned out, that I'd developed a brain tumour.

I went to the Alexandra Hospital, where they gave me a brain scan, plus a chest-and-abdomen scan, which endorsed the fact that I'd got the brain tumour and that my other tumours were still growing. As we mentioned in the previous chapter, I was then referred to the Queen Elizabeth, in January 2004, where I saw a guy who decided to operate, and take out this brain tumour forthwith.

Pat would have preferred to keep his final stay at the Queen Elizabeth Hospital, Birmingham a secret, but as one might expect, this proved impossible. Although he'd kept his whereabouts secret from me too, ironically, one or two people telephoned, to tell me where he was!

Following your German visit, are you still able to walk a reasonable distance again?

Yes. When I was a week down the road in my treatment there, I'd improved. I'm now a fortnight on from that, and I'm still doing ever so well. But there's no doubt about it – my Immune System is haywire. I've got some trouble with my left eye now. I don't know what it is. I've got to get it sorted.

Pat told me later that, following brain tumour surgery, he'd been warned that he might lose some of the feeling in the left-hand side of his body, together with the eyesight of his left eye. Shortly afterwards, by early April 2004, he'd completely lost the sight in his left eye.

I tried to lance a boil on my foot – and that's gone all stiff on me. It just seems that my Immune System is fairly low.

You're not able to do much at all now, are you?

No, I do very little. All my life you see, if I saw a set of stairs, I'd run up the bloody things – you know what I mean? I've been a 'hustler-and-bustler' all my life. But now, I don't meet challenges. I can't, because I get out of breath – very quickly. I'm trying to hold out for another two weeks, and not go downhill – until I can get the serum injected into my stomach. I keep harping back to looking at Doctor Kief's face – his expression and his attitude towards the cancer. 25,000 a year die of Prostate Cancer – but he shrugs it off – as if he doesn't even need to talk about it! Then he says that the next most successful cancer treatment he's good at treating is lung cancer, which is good news – obviously. Then liver cancer comes in. He doesn't refer to any procedure, once you've had your jabs, which means one of two things: either, that you're going to die, or, that he's going to cure the cancer. I have to believe that he believes, (and I'm swayed in that direction) – that he is going to cure me.

Perhaps it's all part of the treatment: by not acknowledging the possibility of failure, and by maintaining a positive attitude, he hopes to cure you?

Well, yes. But you and I know that you don't get cured of cancer. We know that, don't we? You get cancer and some people are lucky and go on for years, but a lot of people die from it. I mean, I'm at the stage now, where I'm going to die from it. Because I've had seven cancers now, and it's obviously spread, right through my body. It's only a matter of time.

Bernard confirms that he and Pat were in Germany, for only the one week. "I went over on my own, the second time, three weeks later, because his further medication wasn't delivered. They had given him enough medication to last him for two weeks, but originally, Mia was going to deliver it to him in London, but she didn't. Some of the e-mails weren't replied to, so I sent a very nasty e-mail to them. Then they replied. Pat said: 'I need this other stuff, because I've run out of this liquid.' But of course, you can't fly out and bring it in by 'plane, because if you do, they're going to see it. There were two kinds of liquid, which were for injections." Pat, by this time, had no choice other than to inject himself.

"But he wanted the small pins, so I got those for him, as well. When he phoned me and said that he needed this liquid, what could I do? I couldn't fly it in, because of legal restrictions regarding medical supplies. So I said: 'I'll fetch it for you.' I went across again, and drove straight the way through France, then down into Germany. Drove back out of Germany and France, caught the ferry at Dunkerque, then back across England. I brought the needles and liquid to him, that night. It took me two-and-a-half days to do all of that."

On Sunday 4 April 2004 there was an OLRA meeting (*Old Ladywood Reunion Association*), at the *Clarendon Suite,* Hagley Road. Despite being so ill, Pat attended for a couple of hours and was able to say goodbye to all of his friends. Whether or not they realised what he was doing, I'm not sure. Certainly, there was an undercurrent of sadness.

On Friday 9 April, he telephoned to say that he'd lost all sight in his left eye and had been advised that he should no longer drive, so he was now 'grounded'. Pat tried his best to remain cheerful, but I was about to take a fortnight's holiday in Florida from 17 April to 1 May, and was very concerned that something would happen to him in my absence. He said: "Don't worry – I'll be around for a while longer!" It was his 67th birthday on 19 May. I was praying that he lived to see it. The *O.L.R.A.* meeting was the last time I saw him, for some weeks. All communication, for some time thereafter, was by phone.

Returned from Florida on Sunday 2 May, but was perturbed to find that Pat wasn't answering any calls on his mobile, either to myself or other friends. This continued for several days, during which time I kept in touch with Ronnie Callow and Bill Bridges.

Pat eventually telephoned from the Queen Elizabeth Hospital, on Saturday morning, 8 May, whilst I was in Solihull, to say that he would let me know what was happening.

On Monday morning 10 May 2004, He left an Answerphone message, confirming where he was, and that he would phone as soon as he was able. The message sounded as though he was speaking underwater. It was clear that something was radically affecting his brain and therefore his speech:

Hello… a message for Shirley. I'm in the Queen Elizabeth Hospital. I will know more what's happening to me on Monday. I will tell you on Monday what's happening. Maybe they will give me more radiotherapy, or maybe they will operate. Until Monday I can't tell you anything else.

Bill Bridges was in touch with the hospital, using a predetermined password, and kindly kept Bernard and myself informed. I phoned Ronnie Callow, and vice versa. This arrangement continued until Wednesday 19 May. Pat remained out of touch with many of his friends during this period. From time to time, some of them would phone. I promised to let them know if something major happened. Ronnie discovered that this third recurrence of the tumour was large and pressing down heavily on Pat's optical nerve. So, for a week or so, prior to the operation, they applied radiotherapy to reduce its size. By pure coincidence, Harold Evans took his wife, Beverley to the same hospital and met Pat as he was being pushed back to his ward, following an MRI Scan. Harold asked: "Paddy, what's wrong?" Pat replied: "I've had it!" According to Harold, Pat seemed to be in a really poor state.

Monday 17 May 2004:
Pat had this third operation. Bill told me that evening that Pat had come round afterwards and was sitting up in bed.

Wednesday 19 May:
Pat telephoned at 7.24pm., very briefly, to assure me that he was OK.

Thursday 20 May:
8.30am: Pat phoned early this morning, and for the first time in weeks, spoke reasonably clearly. His ability to communicate comes and goes, so we're playing everything 'by ear'. He was due to leave hospital in two days. He had ideas for various books, and was still very keen to be on the *Jewellery Quarter Association Committee*. If possible, would like to be buried in a Jewellery Quarter plot. The loss of sight, in his left eye, appears to be irreversible. He's working on his right eye – hopes to keep sight in that one. He can no longer drive, as it's far too dangerous.

Sunday 23 May 2004:
Pat phoned at 4.50pm. (I'd phoned the day before, i.e. Saturday, to check that he'd been safely discharged from hospital). Got an unusually abrupt response, which was rather worrying. Today's call was to apologise for being so abrupt. He'd discharged himself from hospital, apparently thinking that he could get safely back home, by car, but the battery was completely flat! Luckily, one of his fans just happened to be nearby, came to the rescue and got him moving again!

Wednesday 26 May:
Pat phoned at 4.40pm, to 'touch base'. Despite taking sleeping pills, he is unable to sleep at night. Gave him the excellent news from our publisher, Alan Brewin, that *Pat Roach's Birmingham* was currently being printed. To expedite matters, Alan's asking the same company to do the binding too. I briefly mentioned the proposed Launch, but as this is a month away, quickly dropped

the subject. Impossible for me to phone Pat, as only he knows when his brain is lucid enough for a coherent conversation, (albeit, for a minute or two only). I passed on the love and good wishes of the *many* people who had contacted me. He told me that on one particular day, recently, he had 48 phone calls!

Progress is slow. He's spending a great deal of time in bed, just resting and coming down for the occasional meal. It's only during his 'clear-headed' periods that he's able to do light exercise, although he'd done 500 today. For the past few days he's hardly been able to walk, but has now graduated to 50 yards.

Friday 28 May, 18.06h
I updated him about our arrangements for *Pat Roach's Birmingham*. We agreed that in present circumstances, I should distribute the copies. Told him I'm expecting the books next week. He was driving his car, with just one good eye – don't know how he manages it! Said he'll try to help me with *Redditch Festival* signing if he's well enough. IT IS NOW JUST OVER 8 WEEKS SINCE PAT AND I HAD A MEETING.

The very *last* time that I saw Pat was between 4.30 - 6.30pm on Tuesday 8 June 2004. I had collected 102 copies of *Pat Roach's Birmingham*, newly published that morning, from my publisher's son, Alistair Brewin, in Studley. Pat was supposed to visit me about 2pm that afternoon, but phoned to say that he was too ill to make it that distance. He was *adamant*, however, that I should meet him. Despite the fact that it was a baking-hot day, he insisted on signing forty of the new books, so that I'd have some special copies, and gave me some signed photos of scenes from his various films. When I said that I'd plough the proceeds from the photographs back into this third book, he left me with a parting quip: "No – buy yourself some lipsticks!"

It's a two-hour period that I'll never forget: Pat almost bald, wearing his baseball cap, whilst the two of us signed books, over beer and shandy – his eyesight severely impaired. I was close to tears as we eventually parted; then I watched his red Mondeo disappear up the country lane… and out of sight. On the journey home I was crying… Pat had just asked me to begin his funeral arrangements.

On Friday 25 June, we launched *Pat Roach's Birmingham* at the *Museum of the Jewellery Quarter* in Birmingham, with the kind assistance of Victoria Emmanuelle and her staff. It was just as if the book itself had suddenly come to life, as most of the people featured in it were present, including several people from the Jewellery Quarter itself. The speakers were John Kowalski, Ronnie Callow and myself. The day was a great success, but it was tinged with sadness, because Pat was too ill to attend, and we were all painfully aware of the fact.

What most of the guests *didn't* know, for fear of upsetting them further, was that on the 22 June, just three days before, I'd visited the Reverend Nigel Marns, at St. John's Church of England, Bromsgrove, to plan Pat's Thanksgiving Service. We had also taken a walk through the church grounds, to discuss security logistics. At regular intervals, during the Launch, my mind kept straying back to that meeting, the entire church site itself, and the inevitable implications...

Rob Knight met Pat the following day: "I had a phone call on 26 June, asking me if I would mind helping him to tow a car, which needed a replacement engine." Pat asked Rob to use two ropes to secure the towed vehicle, but because of his tumour, almost immediately forgot his request. "We proceeded, with him driving and me behind, in the car that was being towed. Not a short distance – as I'd imagined – but to Earlswood – a forty-minute drive, with Pat having to judge several different roundabouts, road junctions, traffic lights etc. To his absolute credit, despite the fact that he was very ill, and blind in one eye, he got us there, brilliantly. When we arrived he congratulated me, saying that I'd done really well, I'd 'got the job'. Another example of him praising someone else, whilst working under very difficult circumstances himself."

Rob saw Pat for the very last time, on Saturday 10 July 2004, when he picked him up, to take him to a favourite countryside spot. By this time, filming of the *Christmas Special* was well under way, in Thailand. Somewhere in Pat's life, he had stumbled on a rural haven complete with pond, ducks and other water birds, where he could relax when the mood took him. He had become very fond of the various waterfowl and enjoyed feeding them, from a small jetty; they each had their own names and personalities! "I picked him up from there, as usual, which I had been doing regularly, on a Saturday," explains Rob, "and took him back, at about 4.30pm in the afternoon. As I was dropping him off, he asked me whether I was busy the *following* day – the Sunday. Straight away I said: 'No – just call me and let me know.' He shook my hand before I got out of the car and... that was the *last* time that I ever saw him."

Filming for the *Auf Wiedersehen Christmas Special* had begun at the end of June and took seven weeks. It was more or less completed by Monday 17 August 2004, according to Chris Fairbank, whom I interviewed the following day, as the final touches were being made. Chris explained: "The script was originally written to include Pat. Within the first twenty minutes of the

Christmas Special, Bomber would have quietly made an announcement, at first to Dennis, that he's going back to Arizona. It was all beautifully done, was totally credible and believable, and picked up the relationship that Bomber had with Lainie and Paulie, the boy. But Pat wasn't able to film *anything*. He came down, the day of the Read-through, which was due to start at ten o'clock – they usually do. Pat only managed about two hours and the Read-through was then going to be at two o'clock, because, as we'd been told, Pat had lost his voice and couldn't actually speak. So there was no point in him trying to read, because he couldn't."

Rob recalls that Pat's mind was sufficiently alert at this stage for him to comment: "I'll show my face and say that I've lost my voice through shouting at the football!" He adds that Pat had been doing regular vocal exercises, with a view to getting his voice back to normal. "We were also told that he was ill," Chris continues, "but nobody mentioned his cancer of the brain, because nobody actually knew – this was the thing."

Determined as ever, Pat took the view: "I'm going to do everything I can to take part. Everything's looking OK." So I said: "Oh that's great Pat!" I knew really, that it was highly unlikely, but I didn't want to disillusion him. It was a tragic situation all round, as he'd come so far.

"Joy Spink was very worried beforehand," Chris continues. "She'd left messages with Pat, which *had* been returned, but there was a two-week period where she couldn't even leave a message, because his Voicemail was so loaded. This was causing concern, quite understandably, because whenever Pat received a message, he would usually respond within minutes, unless he was busy doing something. But he would always return his calls." Meanwhile, back in Birmingham, most of his friends were in the same quandary.

"Anyway, Joy told me that it was now OK," Chris remembers. "She'd spoken to Pat, but he was sounding very hoarse: she could hardly make out what he was saying. That's when I think that the 'order of the day' was changed. When Pat turned up on that Monday morning, it was a helluva shock! He looked so ill... he really did. He'd lost the vision in his left eye; the vision in his right eye was severely impaired. He couldn't speak.

"He had a gauze pad, which we thought was to protect us from him, but of course, it was completely the other way around, because he'd just had a burst of radiotherapy, which had burned his voice box, and left him vulnerable to the least bit of infection. So that's what the gauze was for. He tried to motion to us, not to come too close.

"One of the benefits of being a 'short-arse' is that my head was just above his waist, so I was able to just give him a hug around his waist, making sure that my head was away. I'm glad that I did that. That in itself was a shock, because he'd got a fairly bulky jacket on, on top of a denim jacket, but I could certainly feel that he'd lost so much weight. I remember him saying that his main concern was to keep his weight up."

The *Christmas Special* script was re-edited. "I think the alterations had been done in the best way possible, in so far as Bomber's absence isn't alluded to *continually*. Because the more you do that, the more you notice that the character isn't there. On top of which, you've got Real Life, whereby the audience knows that Pat died back in July."

I asked Chris if Pat's absence had altered the dynamics of the group. "Do you know, it altered it a *helluva* lot – a lot more than we thought it might. We all mentioned that, at various points, while we were out there. This was before we got the awful news, the sad news, that Pat had died. He was really *missed*, but that news brought it into even starker relief. When one of us is down, it really is like losing a limb."

After Rob returned Pat to the cottage, for the last time, on the 10 July, he remained with Doreen, for the next five days. Although Rob didn't actually see him, like myself, he kept in touch with Pat's progress, through Bernard Guest, (who was visiting him every day), and a network of other friends. But the 'Gentle Giant' was becoming progressively weaker...

Chapter Nineteen

THERE'S A STATUE IN MY GARDEN
A VERY SPECIAL CHAPTER
BY TIM HEALY

Pat never looked upon himself as an accomplished actor; he didn't realise how good he was. No one could have played the part of Bomber as well as he did. He was very much loved by everyone he worked with. He had a wonderful sense of humour.

I remember the first day on *Auf Wiedersehen Pet*. We all met for the first time in the rehearsal room at Elstree. Jimmy and I had driven down in my Triumph Spitfire, from Newcastle. We all introduced ourselves to each other. I remember shaking this huge mountain of a man's hand. "Hi, I'm Tim," I said. He looked down at me with a smile. "Pat Roach," he said. "Alright Kid?"

The first thing we did was to go to the Wardrobe Department to try on our costumes. We all filed into this room, with rails and rails of costumes. An Irish 'gay' voice was heard, from behind the costumes: "Won't keep you a minute!" We all looked at each other. Then this little guy came out from behind the rails and banged straight into Pat. He looked up. His head had hit Pat – just above the belly button. "Hello!" was the only word he could get out. This was Sean. He became Pat's dresser and mine too. I must admit, he became quite besotted with Pat, and loved looking after him. We all looked up to Pat from the beginning. He was a famous wrestler. The rest of the lads were all newcomers.

I'd been performing a play called *Bring me Sunshine*, by C.P. Taylor; sadly, his last play before he died. I'd had a stiff neck for months. I went to the doctor and he said: "Have you ever had a heavy bang on your head during your life?" I thought back and remembered when I was five years old, my brother bundled me over a wall and I fell five feet, onto the top of my head. This resulted in my having to wear glasses as a child. The doctor told me that I had damaged a disc in my neck, all those years ago, and advised me to go for traction.

I had been doing this for a couple of months, but my neck was still stiff. Pat noticed me having problems with it, during the first week of filming. I explained to him the history. "Come to my dressing room kid," he said. He sat me in a chair, wrapped his arms around me and told me to breathe in. I did, a couple of times, then he squeezed all the air out of me. There was a huge crack! He said: "Is that any better? Try moving your neck." I was amazed. It had become totally free – not stiff any more! I felt a stone lighter, and my stiff neck has never come back to this day. Pat reckoned the problem had been in my lower back.

We all became good friends over the next few months. I remember filming one day and there was a 30mph sign on one of the walls. We were supposed to be in Germany, and the sign was in shot, so it had to be removed. Richard Lyndsay was desperately trying to pull this sign off the wall with a screwdriver. Pat went over and offered to help. The sign was metal and bolted into the brickwork. Pat grabbed hold of it and pulled it straight off the wall. "There you go kid!" The crew all gave him a round of applause. Pat was the strongest guy I've ever met.

He was a great practical joker. He used one of his favourite tricks, if anyone was out of order, or a 'pain-in-the-arse'. He would put a large apple in the palm of his hand and ask the person if they would like to smell it. Just as their nose touched the apple, he used to squeeze the apple and it would literally explode – covering the culprit with apple sauce!

Pat was always buying and selling things in those days. I still have visions of him walking down the corridor at Elstree, with half a dozen fur coats over his arm. "Do ya want a fur coat Kid? Twenty-five quid." Nobody ever asked him where he got them from! Leather jackets, jumpers – all sorts of things.

Pat was wrestling regularly, while we filmed the first two series. When *Auf Wiedersehen Pet* became a big hit, he became Pat 'Bomber' Roach. He'd always been a Baddie, but his character, Bomber, the Gentle Giant, made him decide to become a Goodie. The audiences loved him in the wrestling halls, as I was about to find out. He invited me to go to Fairfield Hall in Croydon, to act as his Second. "What do I have to do?" I asked him. "Just give me some water and dry me down between rounds," he said.

I'll never forget walking into the ring with him. In the audience's eyes, we weren't Tim Healy and Pat Roach, we were Dennis and Bomber. Pat would pretend to listen to my advice, as if I was the boss – and the audience loved it. Pat was fighting Wayne Bridges and he won – two falls to one. I only ever seconded him once, but it was great fun and I felt proud that he had let me do this.

Pat loved cars; he would turn up to work in all sorts of different vehicles. He had a Rolls Royce in those days, with the number PAT III. It was a Corniche. I always remember him taking me for a ride through Nottingham. I'd never been in a Rolls Royce before. "You will have one of these one day," he said to me.

One day, he turned up to work in a Mini Traveller. I'll always remember him climbing out. It looked almost impossible for him to get in it; he was six feet five inches and twenty stone at the time.

Pat turned up one day in a Porsche 911. We were filming the second series at Nottingham. We travelled to Derbyshire, to film Thornley Manor Scenes. I'd asked Pat if I could have a ride in the Porsche with him, so we set off from the George Hotel in Nottingham, in the Porsche. The rest of the lads followed behind in the Minibus.

There was heavy traffic all the way there, so Pat said that he couldn't let me see how quick it was. There was a long drive leading up to Thornley Manor: about a mile long, very straight, but up and down. We got there at about 7am. so we were the first to arrive at the long drive. I said to Pat: "Go on mate – give it a go!" So Pat opened it up. I was looking out of the side window, when I heard Pat say "Shit!" We'd gone over a brow in the road and there, straight in front of us, was the Designer, coming the other way, in a Sierra.

Pat hit the breaks; everything went black for me. I woke up at the side of the road, desperately trying to breathe. I hadn't been wearing a seat belt; neither had Pat. The windscreen had shot out. I had followed it: hit my head on the dashboard and gone through the empty screen. I hit the dashboard so hard, I moved it five inches out of line, according to the Paramedic who arrived.

As he wasn't wearing a seatbelt, Pat had grabbed the steering wheel and held it rigid. He pushed the steering column into the other car's engine and sprained his back a little bit. He then grabbed me, pulled me to safety, and checked on Mike, the Designer, who had whiplash. Then he stayed with me until the ambulance arrived.

I was taken to hospital, where I stayed for four days. Luckily, I was only very badly bruised. If anyone else had been driving, the steering wheel would have taken his head off, according to the Paramedics. Pat felt so guilty that I was hurt and spent hours in the hospital with me. It was my fault – I asked him to open it up. We were all very lucky, and we'd laugh about it many a time, for years afterwards.

Pat was a gentleman and a joy to work with. He had a wonderful sense of humour. He could never tell a joke without falling about laughing, before he got to the punchline. He had a really high-pitched laugh for such a big bloke. I'll never forget his laugh. But he wouldn't suffer fools.

When he became ill with this terrible disease he decided to fight and fight it. He did, for six-and-a-half years, after being given six weeks to live, back in 1998. His surgeon told him that he was one of only six people in the country, to have survived for so long.

I watched him train every day, during the last series. He used to squat a thousand times every day. When he got back from Arizona, I decided to train with him. We spent a lot of time together, as we both stayed at the *Meridian Hotel* in London, where there was a great gym. I remember my first night. He got me to squat with him. I did a hundred – and I was knackered! Then we would go into the Weights Room, where he put me through a series of exercises. The first night I was so knackered, I threw up. The squats started to become easier after a while; it took me three months before I managed a thousand. We used to go for a couple of pints after training.

A lot of famous people don't handle fame very well. Can you imagine being six foot five and walking into a bar? No one could miss Pat! He would walk into the bar, head held high. Anyone who looked at him would get the eyeball – straight back. I would follow him. Nobody would see me until we got to the bar!

I said before that Pat didn't suffer fools. I remember one night, we'd been training together, and went for a pint. I followed Pat to the bar, as usual. We always used to share a four-pint jug between us and were just waiting for it to arrive, when this big fat bloke came over and said to Pat: "How heavy are you?" "I beg your pardon?" Pat replied. "How heavy are you? I'm twenty stone," he bragged. "Yes, but you're a fat git," said Pat. If you got rid of that gut, you'd be lighter than The Healy!"

He would talk to anyone, if they were polite; if not, he wouldn't give them a second of the day. I hope I carry that with me now. I learnt so much from him. I miss him dearly, as a great actor, and moreover, as a wonderful friend.

Pat always had his life organised. He even planned his funeral. Knowing he would die eventually from this terrible illness, he planned the whole thing. He started selling up, as it were. He rang me during this time and said: "Listen Kid, I've got this statue of Hercules; it's been in my gym. You can have the first offer Kid – £700.00. It's modelled on my body." "Oh right," I said. "Yeah – great. I'll have it pal." He said he would organise the delivery of it.

I hadn't mentioned this to my wife, Denise. About a fortnight later, I was in London. My mobile went off: "What on earth is this statue, being loaded off a wagon?" "Oh," I said, "it's been modelled on Pat. He's selling some of his possessions." Over the next few weeks, the statue 'grew on her'. It is now my prize possession. It's a three-quarter size of Pat. You will see from the photograph that he's still head and shoulders above me, even when he's three-quarter size!

When Pat died, I was in Thailand. I rang the missus and asked that she put a black armband on Hercules. I took it off when I got home. He will stand there in perpetuity… whenever I look at him. I have some wonderful memories, often very sad. But I know Pat is there for me.

There's A Statue In My Garden

There's a statue in my garden,
They call him Hercules.
He's modelled on Pat, dear friend of mine,
Who could lift a car with ease.

For years and years I watched him
Squatting up and down.
I'd eat all the sandwiches and biscuits,
Then I'd hit the town.

"Take it easy kid," he'd say to me
At the early morning call.
"Life's about moderation,
If you want to stay on the ball."

He never asked me to join him,
Working in the gym,
But always when he came out
He'd give me a cheeky grin.

"I've done more squats for you kid,
I've done Kev's and Jimmy's too.
I did a thousand tonight –
Do you fancy a pint or two?"

Then one day I followed him,
I thought I'd try my best.
I said: "Will you go easy pal
And let me have a rest?"

"Don't you worry The Healy,
You just take your time.
Try these for starters,
These are squats of mine."

For the next few months we squatted
I tried to keep in time.
I became his apprentice,
He said I was "doing fine".

I'll never forget that time together
Working in the gym
Or the pint or two that we shared
When we felt all in.

There's a statue in my garden,
They call him Hercules.
He stands in Perpetuity,
And I know Pat's always there for me!

Tim Healy, July 2004

Chapter Twenty

UP... OR DOWN?

Pat had the kind of indomitable spirit that never really dies: it lives on, not only in his many performances, but in the hearts and memories of his fans, and, above all, those closest of all to him – his family and friends. (I was about to write 'his many friends', but I know that he'd consider that far too pretentious a way of putting it – even though it's perfectly true)!

Shirley Thompson

In this chapter, we recall the final three days of Pat's life, through the eyes of family and close friends, who spent those last hours with him. The two subsequent church services, held in his memory, are also included. On Thursday 15 July 2004, Bernard Guest sent a message to Rob Knight, saying that Pat had been taken to the Primrose Ward of the *Princess of Wales Hospice*, Bromsgrove. "It was described to me how he'd left the house, and how determined he was to go out in his own way – to walk, almost unaided," Rob recalls.

Bernard Guest continues the story: "We're talking about the 15 July 2004. I'd been to see Pat, three or four days previously, and he was very agitated about some bank account that he wanted me to sort out. On the morning of the 15th when I went to see him, he kept drifting in and out of sleep. His wife, Doreen, said: 'Will you stop with me, because the Macmillan Nurse is coming?' Pat appeared to be a bit hostile to the nurse, for some reason. So I waited at their house and was talking to him about this and that. He was quite compos mentis but he still kept mentioning this account that he wanted to sort out. He said: 'I want to give you this company.' When the Macmillan Nurse arrived, she said, 'Pat, your medication isn't working and your symptoms have become more pronounced. I think it's best to take you to this new place – and have you assessed.'

"Pat looked at me," continues Bernard, "and the nurse said: 'I can get an ambulance here for four o'clock.' The Duchess of Kent was opening the place on that same day. Pat turned round and said: 'No, no, I don't want an ambulance! Bern – you'll take me – won't you?' I said: 'Of course – no problem. I've got something to do first, but I'll be back at half past three.' That was about one o'clock. I hadn't been away twenty minutes when the phone rang. It was Doreen: 'They want you at two o'clock.' I went straight back and walked him out to the car.

"Then I took him directly to the *Princess Diana*, in my car: Doreen sat in the back and Pat in the front," explains Bernard. "When we arrived at the hospice, I went in to check with the people there. The doctor came out with me – a really nice fella. He brought a wheelchair out. I explained to Pat: 'You can't walk, because it's quite a long way.' The doctor pushed Pat in the wheelchair, into the Hospice. I was walking alongside him.

"We went into the actual room. The doctor left us there... alone with him. Pat turned to me and said: 'Is this a Dying Room Bern?' I said: 'Yes mate, it is.' He went: 'Tchh... oh well.' We sat down and the doctor started asking him questions – his name, his date of birth, and so on; which didn't really matter, because they knew that he was going to die, within three days maximum. Don't get me wrong, the people in there were *exceptionally* nice. They were handpicked... really beautiful people; with these nurses – I could see halos! That's how nice they were. The bed was a bit too short for a bloke like him. I took Doreen home, because she didn't stop long. Pat was still sitting in the chair, when we left – one of those special reclining chairs that lift up and down. Then I went back again with Doreen, that same evening, to see him."

The following morning, Friday 16 July, was Doreen's birthday. "Doreen said to me: 'Oh, he didn't die on my birthday then.' I went to the ward that morning, on my own," Bernard continues. "Then Doreen, Mark and Diane came, and stopped about twenty minutes, because he wasn't compos mentis. It was my wife Jan's birthday on the day he actually died – the 17th." Pat had been drugged through a special tube. Whenever possible, he'd resisted taking drugs, certainly during his first two operations, preferring natural remedies to pharmaceutical ones. However, Bernard observes: "He was taking morphine most of the time, to kill the pain, although he may not always have realised." Rob recalls that the dried apricot kernels, which Pat ate, also had a drug-like effect and acted as alternative painkillers.

Pat had requested that I should set the record straight with regard to Diane, Mark' wife, thinking at first that Pat was trying to take over Patrick's upbringing. Doreen confirmed that as long as I put it in a tactful way, she has no objection to my including a posthumous note, to the effect that Pat only ever wanted to help Diane with Patrick, and was in no way trying to take over.

Doreen continues: "Pat said: 'I don't want this box on any more. Take it off!' But I couldn't could I? That was on Friday 16th, the day after he went in. I think he knew that once that box was on, he was really on his way out. Maybe he thought that if he took it off, he'd come round and fight again?"

A close family friend said that when Pat *originally* went into hospital, back in 1998, wearing his long wax jacket, although he was feeling really ill, he strode very purposefully towards the ward, in much the same way as he used to stride into the wrestling ring. In similar fashion, Pat strode out of the back door of his house, for the *last* time, aided by a walking stick, and wearing his black and white tracksuit. Rob recalls: "He would always leave by the back door, when I visited him; he would never answer the front door."

Pat walked down the path – head held high, then stopped and paused at the end of the path, facing the canal. He surveyed the entire scene in front of him: the little humpback bridge, the boats and his picturesque cottage... taking in every detail. Then, with a final shake of his head, he got into the car. "But he was still in control," observes Rob. "That was Pat. He was doing it his way. He was very upright – going out – in style. The only time I ever saw him revert from his full height was when he was at the Fitness Centre, because he used to worry about being intimidating. If he was talking to a female client he would shrink: change his whole persona – even his voice. But with males he was always very upright. I'm sure that would have been very important to him, to leave his home like that – in that manner. It was his final goodbye... in the way that *he* wanted to do it."

Despite being a summer's day, there was hardly anyone about. Pat had a natural affinity with 'water' locations. "That particular location gave him a great deal of pleasure," Rob continues. "Obviously it related to his childhood as well – the canals and everything." Pat attributed his fascination with water to some kind of genetic memory: his grandmother, Amelia, had been a water gypsy. One can only *imagine* the emotions and the thoughts running through his mind, at that point. But at least he was in familiar surroundings, as he said his final farewell, to the countryside that he'd loved since his boyhood. It was around 2.15pm. when he left his canalside cottage, for the very last time. For the final few yards, Pat put his arm around Bernard's shoulder for support, and the stick was dispensed with.

Rob describes Pat as: "... very warm, very open, very approachable. He would always finish any conversation with, 'You be lucky!'" He signed his letters with those identical words too, as I know from the substantial amount of joint correspondence that we sent, over the years. Pat's warm personality undoubtedly came from Dolly.

Rob noticed, on the mobile phone record of Pat's last telephone conversations, there was an entry for the 16 July at 10.29 in the morning. "He'd accessed his Voicemail messages, because it had run for a period of three minutes and thirty-six seconds. There was an entry for the day before, so he'd listened to them prior to that as well. But on this particular occasion, rather than just delete them, he'd taken time to listen to all his messages. To me, it was a mark of the fact that it was 'business as usual'." Or – perhaps it was even *more* significant than that? Given that he knew he didn't have much longer, it may have been his only means of saying silent good-byes to everyone. Rob agrees: "It could well have been a case of hearing people's voices, for the last time."

Pat's widow, Doreen, recalls: "Pat sat in that chair, where you're sitting now, saying that there was something that he wanted to tell David Talboys. He was desperate to tell him, but we couldn't get him on the phone. In the end he just sat here and I kept dialing. David said it was strange, because that was the only time that he and Brenda went out all day.

"It was just before he went in the Hospice, on the Thursday. I managed to get in touch with Dave on Thursday night and took him to see Pat. It was about eight o'clock – a night visit. I said: 'Look who I've brought to see you.' Pat sat straight up and said: 'Oh, David!' But then, what he wanted to tell him just went out of his mind, probably because the drugs were in him. I took Mark and Diane there on one occasion, but Patrick never saw his Granddad in there. David went back to see him again, on the Friday night, but the nurses wouldn't let him in. They said: 'No, it's no good upsetting him.' Once he had that black box on, with the different drugs in it, he seemed to go downhill. He said, 'Don't worry about me, because I'll be out of it. I won't even know if you're there or not.'"

"I went back to the ward again, at about ten o'clock on the Friday night," continues Bernard. "I was talking to Pat about one or two things, but he wasn't really making much sense. I said to the nurse: 'He's not too good, is he?' She said, 'No, he's comfortable but...' They're telling you that he's going to die really – and it's imminent.

"He was still talking – he was saying a couple of things. You can put that in the book about me calling him 'Pat the Puff', from years ago. It was a kind of joking thing that we had – at a nightclub. Dancing like a big fairy he was, after he'd had a drink. So I always used to call him 'Pat the Puff' and he called me 'Bernie the Bastard'! Late on this Friday night – I was joking with him about the fact that they'd booked him in as Francis Roach."

As previously explained, Pat used the name Francis during each hospital stay, hoping to preserve his privacy. It was the name he was christened with, and also his father's name. Bernard continues: I said: 'What kind of a name is that? It's a 'Puff's' name, that is!' He said: 'Bern – f*** off!' Then he went to sleep – and that was the last thing he *ever* said to me.

"At half past one in the morning, of Saturday 17 July 2004, I had a phone call to say that he'd passed away, at 1.20 am. So I got into my car and drove over to Doreen's, to tell her, at about half past two in the morning. She said, 'Oh yes? OK.'" Doreen was wearing pyjamas when Bernard arrived, as she'd been sleeping. "I didn't want to go in. I just stood on the doorstep and told her." Bernard very thoughtfully left a message on my Answer-phone. "You were one of the first to know – so that you knew he'd gone. I left messages for the people who needed to know. Then I came home and went back to bed. I went to see Doreen again the next day, to sort out what I'd got to do. I helped with all the arrangements, such as the Death Certificate, and went to the hospital to collect his personal effects."

Dave Talboys and myself had already begun the funeral arrangements. Luckily, Pat had given us clearance to make these arrangements, and those for his Thanksgiving Service, nine days previously; ironically, on the very same day that *Pat Roach's Birmingham* was published. So that was already in place – thank goodness! As explained in Chapter 18, I'd also had a meeting with the Reverend Nigel Marns, vicar of St. John's and St. Andrew's Churches in Bromsgrove, who handled the whole proceedings with tremendous sensitivity and professionalism. Together, we devised an Order of Service, as close to Pat's *precise* instructions as possible. As it was to be a high-profile funeral, the vicar put me in touch with Nicola Currie, the Communications Officer for the Diocese of Worcester, so that we could quickly put security arrangements and press releases in place, to be ready, the moment they were needed. Pat had never forgotten the 'Field Day' that the Press had, at Gary Holton's funeral; there was no way that anyone wanted a repeat performance of that!

"Then on the Saturday Lunchtime, 17 July, we all went to see him at the Hospice," Bernard recalls. "Doreen, Mark, Diane, Patrick, and you and myself." When family and friends visited him at the Chapel of Rest shortly afterwards, Pat looked really noble – like the Pat we all remember. Bernard comments: "I was pleased he was no longer suffering, because it wasn't Pat anyway; it was just a shell of himself and he wouldn't have wanted people to see him like that. Without the drugs he would have been in terrible screaming pain; he wasn't in any pain at all, towards the end: he was heavily sedated. But I think that *he* knew and *I* knew – and to be quite honest, I was pleased that he'd gone." I felt the same. He'd endured so much, for over six years, but had suffered enough. "All of his suffering and all of his turmoil had gone for good," Bernard concludes. Pat remarked on several occasions that, when he eventually passed away, he'd have a nice long rest... and he'd be at peace.

The funeral at Bromsgrove:
Pat planned his funeral with great care, down to the finest details: "Make sure that my mom's sitting down – and Aunt Freda – if she's there, otherwise they'll collapse." We discussed the arrangements several times, over a period of at least five years, as we had no way of knowing how much time remained. Towards the end he commented: "I don't want people standing around, saying what a great guy I was – or anything like that." But as I pointed out, during my Thanksgiving Service tribute to him, "People will say exactly what they want to say at funerals. It's not a situation you can control!" Our Chapter Title derives from the fact that at one time, Pat planned to have cut-outs of two up-ended feet glued on the end of his coffin, with a label – 'Up or Down?!'

We delayed the funeral for a fortnight, so that the *Auf Wiedersehen* cast could return from Thailand, which was one of his dearest wishes. At the request of Pat and his family, the initial Thanksgiving Service, at St. John's Church of England, Church Lane, Bromsgrove, on Saturday 30 July 2004, was a private ceremony. Almost two hundred guests were invited, comprising family, close friends, wrestlers, actors et cetera. (Pat's mother, Dolly, was in a wheelchair – her son, Pete Meakin had organised this; sadly, Aunt Freda was too indisposed to attend). Pat's wrestling friends and principal members of the cast and crew of *Auf Wiedersehen Pet*, were amongst the mourners.

The congregation filed in to St. John's, to music from *Classic Moods and Serenity* tapes; five minutes before the opening address, Pavarotti's *Nessun dorma* began to play. There were floral displays of wild flowers around the church, as Pat preferred them to the cultivated varieties. The congregation had also included them in their wreaths.

Order of Service:
Welcome and prayers, by The Reverend Nigel Marns.

Reading by Christopher Fairbank, from Ecclesiastes 3, v. 1-12. (a 'time and a purpose for everything, under heaven').

Four additional speakers:
Shirley Thompson, Pat's friend and biographer. *A brief summary of Pat's life, with particular reference to those present and Pat's final wishes. Concluded with Emily Brontë's poem, 'Last Lines', chosen by Pat, plus another short verse.*

Bill (Wayne) Bridges – wrestler and lifelong friend, representing his fellow wrestlers: *Included remark: "If anyone makes a comment about Pat still being as stiff as ever, he's going to come back and haunt the so-and-so!" Most of Bill's tribute can be found in Chapter 10.*

Kevin Whately read *If* – by Rudyard Kipling.

Fellow *Auf Wiedersehen Pet* actor, Tim Healy: *A very humorous tribute, to cheer people up. He also mentioned that Jimmy Nail would be singing 'Danny Boy', at the graveside, at Pat's special request.*

Address, by The Reverend Tom Pyke, vicar of St. Paul's Church in the Jewellery Quarter, (about Pat's connections with the Quarter).

Closing Prayers, led by the Reverend Marns – including the Lord's Prayer; Commendation. The approximate length of the ceremony was forty minutes.

*　*　*　*　*

As the service ended, the six pallbearers, Bill and Sarah Bridges, Pete Roberts, John Kowalski, Dave Bond and Johnny Kincaid lifted Pat's coffin and led the Congregation out, in procession, whilst Pat's recording of *Fighting Man* was played. *Nessun dorma* followed, plus music from the church organist, as the processional exit took some time.

The Reverend Nigel Marns led the able-bodied members of the congregation, through the church grounds, to a separate cemetery, some five-to-ten-minutes walk away. Others travelled there by car. Once all were assembled at the graveside, there was a short burial service, during which

Jimmy Nail sang *O Danny Boy*, at Pat's special request. It was a particularly poignant rendition of the song, made even more so by Jimmy's adaptation of the closing lines – "Oh Paddy Roach, oh Paddy Roach, we love you so."

Once the coffin had been lowered, individual wild flowers were thrown into the grave by many of the mourners. On a humorous note, and by prior arrangement with Doreen, Tony Green poured in a bottle of *Bollinger* champagne, to give Pat a last drink! "We'd shared that many bottles of *Bollinger* together, it was my way of paying a special tribute to him."

The Graveside Ceremony was conducted jointly by The Reverend Nigel Marns and the Reverend Tom Pyke, Vicar of St. Paul's Church. This included a Sixteenth-century prayer, read by the Reverend Marns:

> *God be in my head*
> *And in my understanding;*
> *God be in mine eyes,*
> *And in my looking;*
> *God be in my mouth,*
> *And in my speaking*
> *God be in my heart,*
> *And in my thinking;*
> *God be in my end and at my departing.*

*   *   *   *   *

The congregation walked or drove back to the Reception, at a *Ramada Hotel*, the *Perry Hall*, just a short distance from the church. The hotel's *Clent Room* had also been hired, to provide additional privacy for the *Auf Wiedersehen* cast and production team.

Rob Knight observes: "The funeral was exactly as Pat would have wanted it to be. It was private, dignified and respectful. Pat wouldn't have wanted a media circus. There could have been thousands of people there, I'm sure, but he was selective about the people he invited, purposely, to keep it 'low-key'; typical of Pat – not wanting to draw a lot of attention to himself, or his family. It was a gathering of lovely people who had many wonderful things to say, about Pat; a very special celebration of his life."

I found the burial part of the ceremony, in Bromsgrove Cemetery, particularly moving. His ninety-year-old mother, Dolly, was talking to Pat at the graveside: "If there's anything that you need Paddy, let me know."

"When I spoke to her afterwards", Rob recalls, "she said that she couldn't understand where he got the strength from, to carry him through all the suffering. I said, 'Well, I can see straight away, that he obviously got it from you'... a lovely lady. The wild flowers were especially dear to his heart, very symbolical and typical of the sharing approach that he wanted to create."

Patrick waited until the rest of the congregation had moved away from his Granddad's graveside. Then he went over by himself, picked up a handful of clay soil and threw it in. Standing alongside the grave, he seemed to be having a private conversation with Pat – a rather mature reaction, for an eleven-year-old boy.

Kevin Whately commented afterwards that we'd achieved the right balance, and that the atmosphere was just right. Subsequent 'feed-back', received by Bernie Guest and myself, was that people came away, feeling content to have paid their respects in a more celebratory way. Jack Taylor, who has attended several wrestlers' funerals over the past few years, commented that Pat's had the best atmosphere of them all.

Pete Meakin remembers: "The main wreath on the coffin was beautiful. It was the biggest one I've ever seen. And the amount of people there, paying their last respects... I thought how nice it was of them all to be there – and that the *Auf Wiedersehen* cast and crew had all been able to get back in time. Mom said what a long coffin it was! Obviously it was an emotional day and you're just trying to get through it. Tim Healy really made light and comical work of it – that kept it going for the rest of the day. He really was *just* what we needed at that point. He got a lot of people through the day, actually, on that one.

"Mom loved the lads, especially when they were paying their last respects. She was so pleased that they'd actually come. To get mom from the road to the graveside, we had to pick her up! She couldn't make it. We carried her over and she was able to say goodbye to Pat and have a talk with him."

With the Jewellery Quarter cemeteries being unavailable, Bromsgrove was chosen, as the most convenient location for Pat's family. Doreen commented later: "When I'm shopping, I can just pop into the cemetery. I've ordered the Memorial, to go on his grave – it's an open book." The rectangular grave, as our photograph shows, is completely enclosed in black granite, filled with green chippings. The book is open at the two centre pages, with a gold chord and tassel down the centre. The inscriptions are all in gold lettering. The left-hand page reads as follows:

On the top line – "IF" – (in 1½ inch letters).

PAT ROACH
1937 – 2004
LOVING HUSBAND,
FATHER,
GRANDFATHER
AND SON
IN OUR HEARTS
FOREVER

The words: 'AUF WIEDERSEHEN, PAT' are emblazoned across the front, below the book headstone.

Pat thought that Doreen might prefer to be cremated, "...but with cremation, you're just finished – you've gone," she decided. "The right-hand page of the book has been left blank for me, when the time comes! When Pat and I talked about dying, before any cancers came – (mine or his) – I used to say: 'You've got to die first, so that you can go down first and see what it's like. Then I can come down on top, later!' That was always my wish – although I never really *wished* for it – I didn't want it to come true. It's funny isn't it – how things just happen?

"Pat seemed to have an opinion about everything and to know a bit about most things. He tried to make sense of everything," Doreen observes. "He usually thought about things carefully, but he could also come back with an answer as quick as anything! I have to sit and think about things. I think our grandson's following in Pat's footsteps, and he's a romancer – he's got a good imagination."

Talking to Tim Healy about the *Christmas Special*, which was later televised in two halves, on 28 and 29 December 2004, he described the three contingency plans, drawn up to allow for changes in Pat's illness. In the end they reverted to Plan C, whereby Tim reads the letter from Bomber to the rest of the boys.

Kevin described what followed after Joy Spink had phoned me from Thailand. "We'd done almost all the day's filming. We'd just moved location, really out into the Wild. It was actually a building site but in our film, it was a clearing in the jungle. We were about to do a scene around the campfire, when Joy called us away. It didn't cross my mind. She'd only heard a rumour – she hadn't heard for sure," recalls Kevin. "I thought she was just going to say: 'Look, we're going to run over tonight. Do you mind going on for a bit longer?'

"When she told us – not to make too fine a point of it – there were a *lot* of tears. She said, 'We can pack up now and go home. If you don't feel like doing this, we can continue another day.' Chris said: 'I think Pat would be *irate* if we did that – if we didn't carry on.' And actually we used it: it was a scene where we were all quite frightened, out in the jungle and just about to get kidnapped – and being a long way from home anyway."

Tim Healy recalls: "It came as a big shock to all of us, when Pat came to the first day of rehearsals. What I'll always remember is the *determination* of this man. He came to show us what he was – do you know what I mean? It was the first day of the *Christmas Special* and he desperately wanted to be in it. But the illness had taken over. It must have been such hard work for him, just to get from Birmingham to London and to come in this Rehearsal Room, so again, that shows you just what sort of guts he had.

"I must admit, he was always invincible, in my eyes. For five or six months, before that first rehearsal day of the *Christmas Special*, I didn't see him at all. So it came as a big shock to me, to see that this illness had really grabbed him. We all went off to Thailand, worried, and just hoping that he'd be there when we got back. Joy broke the news to us. The Press had been ringing my wife, Denise Welch, all day and she'd been trying to ring me, but of course, I was on set, otherwise I would have heard from her."

I'd tried to ring the *Auf Wiedersehen* Production office, (Kevin had given me the number, in case of an emergency), but as Pat died on a Saturday, there was no one available. Madelaine Newton, Kevin's wife, managed to get a message through to Thailand for me. Joy Spink subsequently telephoned from, Thailand, on the 17th, asking me to confirm the details. I reassured her that we would put the funeral 'on hold', so that cast and crew could be home in time.

"When Joy relayed your message, it was then about seven o'clock in the evening," remembers Tim Healy. "We all agreed: If he'd been here he would have said, 'Get on with it kid, don't you bloody dare stop work for me kid – just 'cause I've died like.' It was such a fitting scene to do… if there was one scene that came at the right time – after this terrible news. We were all just lying around the campfire – ready to fall asleep. It was a very peaceful and laid-back scene: the only moment like that in the whole show. It was quite extraordinary that this news happened, at that point, and of course, now, I'll never forget that scene, because that's when we found out the news."

Tim elaborates: "Plan B was if he was very ill, but we could get him to record – we could get him on the set, and he couldn't speak. Chris Fairbank was going to dub Pat's voice, because Chris is very good with voices. The third plan was if he died, so in this *Christmas Special*, I read a letter out to the lads. Bomber wants to build a shed in his back garden. He's had enough of travelling round the world, his son's thirteen now. He's got two reasons to stay at home: one's his son and one's his new wife. Thanks for the good times – that's it.

"It actually finishes where we started. The first series started with us going out to Germany. This one finishes with just the three of us together, going out to Germany and they play the old theme music again – you know (sings it): "Breakin' away, got to find…" – says bye-bye, you know? I say to Neville: 'Oh, what did your Brenda say when you told her you were going back to Germany?' Neville says, 'She said "Auf Wiedersehen Pet,"' – bash – that's it! The first time it's ever been mentioned. A great way of finishing – but quite sad as well." Does Tim think that it *will* be the last? "It is. It wouldn't be the same without Pat." At the end of the *Auf Wiedersehen Christmas Special*, they dedicated the programme to Pat and gave his dates – 1937 –2004: a very poignant moment.

An official BBC press statement was released, on the day of Pat's death, from the cast and crew – filming in Thailand. It read: "We are completely heartbroken and our hearts and condolences go out to Pat's family." Laura Mackie, BBC Head of Drama Serials, said: "Pat made a fantastic contribution to *Auf Wiedersehen Pet*, over the years and he created a much loved character in the gentle giant, Bomber. Our thoughts are with his family at this sad time." Franc Roddam commented: "This really is auf wiedersehen, Pat. Pat was a wonderful, wise and gentle man, much loved by all the series' other actors and we're all devastated by his death."

Kevin continues: "That news set the mood of the scene. We all stood up and had a two-minute silence around the campfire, which was *very* emotional. Not for the Thai Crew, because they weren't aware of what had happened – or who Pat was. But it was very emotional for us. The crew were probably told at the same time as us; they just left us all alone. We were mostly in silence. Then after about half an hour we just started telling each other stories about Pat and trying to cheer ourselves up. Talking about things that he'd said, laughing, and trying to get into perspective the fact that he'd had three years more than the doctors had expected. It was a pretty *miserable* time."

The eventual timing was a tremendous relief, because there were only two days in it. Not to put too fine a point on it, we had to keep him embalmed for two weeks, so we only had a two-day leeway. If he'd died two days earlier, we'd have been in trouble!

"Well it wouldn't surprise me if Pat had that in mind!" observes Kevin. "Jim had the idea of putting something of Pat's into that scene, but there wasn't anything, they hadn't brought any of his costume out. Then the next morning, Jim went down to a beautiful monastery, the local 'wat', near the hotel, and asked them to say a prayer. He took the priest three items of food, as an offering, and they say a prayer for you. They brought them all in and did a chant for Pat. They got Jim to pour the water from one vessel into another, then pour it onto a tree, out in the grounds; that was the spirit of the Departed. Jim came back and told us about it. The rest of us, subsequently, were due back in Bangkok after that, so we all went to various wats and places at that point."

The task of trying to make all of the arrangements for Pat's Thanksgiving Service, whilst at the same time keeping over two hundred people informed and happy with what was 'going down', is a story in itself. One person was suggesting this – another wanted that. At times it was a logistics nightmare. That's apart from the security arrangements and a constant stream of calls from the Press, for days on end! To their credit, the Press, for the most part, handled the situation with great sensitivity. Throughout all of this, Bernard Guest and I hardly had time to draw breath! Luckily there were other friends on hand too, to help. Bill Bridges was kept very busy, in Kent, making all the arrangements for his fellow wrestlers.

A last minute 'glitch' produced a rather comic scenario, which would definitely have appealed to Pat! It concerned his request, that friends and family should throw individual wild flowers onto his coffin. The flowers were still tightly bound together, in two huge bundles. So whilst walking to the graveside, Kevin Whately came to the rescue, helping me to tear individual flowers from the bundles, so they were *just* ready as we approached the cemetery gateway. I didn't have a strong enough grip to pull enough of them out, in the time available. Despite the occasion, we couldn't resist a grin or two!

Wrestling entrepreneur and former champion Jack Taylor, who made an invaluable contribution to Chapter 8 of *Pat Roach's Birmingham*, experienced some rather unsettling events, shortly after Pat's death in July. He has kindly allowed me to include them in this chapter. It was rather brave of him, as the more sceptical amongst us may be inclined to simply dismiss what follows. The passage is in letter format, as that's the way it was received. I'll leave you to make up your own mind, about the phenomena that Jack describes. For my part, I'm sure that he has related this to me in good faith.

*   *   *   *   *

Shirley

Further to our recent conversation, regarding 'messages' from my good friend Pat, (I feel a little embarrassed by this, as it is *not* imagination on my part). But here is a breakdown of events until now:

The aborted trip to the church for the funeral on 28 July:

After getting home, called Ray Crawley to make sure that he got home safely, as he had gone by train. He was tired but OK, having to walk the ten miles from Burton-on-Trent, to his home in Netherseal... he had missed the last bus by fifteen minutes.

That night, I went to bed at midnight, after compiling articles for *Fanzine*. Awoke with a start at precisely 2am. It was as if someone was banging on the bedroom door. Nothing there, got up, made a Horlicks, went back to bed. Nothing further next night, but I was keyed up, as the funeral proper was the following day, 30 July, and I was a little apprehensive.

Wednesday 4 August: Sound asleep in bed, felt the bed shake and covers seemed to be pulling away. Voice just whispered: "It's me – Paddy, everything is OK." Sat bolt upright: another cup of Horlicks. The time then was 2am – as before.

Friday 6 August: I always sleep with the window slightly open. A noise woke me up, as if the catch had been lifted off. It had – window was virtually shut. Re-opened it and put the latch back on, got into bed. Then the bed shook – another whisper... "Look in the box, under vehicle,"... nothing more.

Saturday 7 August: After late night, got into bed, again awoken with shivers, and again the whispered voice, saying: "Tell them to look in the box. Under vehicle..." Then it trailed off. Saturday afternoon I went into town. Saw someone at the Spiritualist Church, off Charles Street, who said it was unusual to get messages so soon after a person had passed away. Suggested I should go along to one of their séances...

Monday 9 August: About 4am in the morning, the wind seemed to howl around my bungalow, then went quiet, and the voice repeated again: "Get them to look in the box, under vehicle..." and it trailed off.

Thursday 12 August: Just could not sleep. Had got up several times to get a drink, and finally went off. Again, the bed shook, and I had the impression that the top cover was being pulled away. Sat up, clutched the cover, then the voice again said: "It's Paddy... look in the box, it's under the motor..." By this time, I was getting used to this happening, and I just said: "Okay Pat, I'll certainly pass the message on."

Since then – nothing; but I do seem to be sleeping much better and feeling in better form in the mornings, when I get up. But I have not, as yet, been to a séance.

Jack Taylor

*   *   *   *   *

Tony Green recalls a six-mile boat trip with Pat down to the riverside location of Cookham, just above Maidenhead. "We'd had quite a lot to drink and of course, we came back in the dark. Unfortunately, let's say, with the moonlight and the drink, I ran the boat aground. Pat looked at me, all glassy-eyed and said: 'The driver's pissed!' We both sat there, killing ourselves laughing. Our passengers had to jump into the water, to free the boat. Pat said he often used to sit – and that memory would come back. He'd laugh his socks off! He'd got a very good sense of humour, Pat had.

"I always thought that if Pat had got out of the scrap business and got himself on a level plain; if he'd stopped mucking about, trying to do this and do that, he'd have been a lot better off. Sometimes, he penny-pinched. He could have portrayed his image better and done a lot better in life. Pat didn't like people to be false. He wasn't perfect. I'm not perfect and neither are you. But Pat would never bullshit you. He would tell you straight – this is how it is. He would never pretend to be what he wasn't.

"Seeing him on a regular basis, initially, when he told me, it was a big shock. I found that the best way of talking to him about it, was to be head-on direct. He wouldn't have appreciated me waffling about it. He never complained really. I think his approach to it was incredible, because he accepted it, but made a façade, even when he was in pain, that he was doing well and that things were going to be OK. When he sat in that chair, he was really in pain."

Tony's boathouse was a special haunt of theirs. Since Pat's demise, Tony has felt his presence really strongly there. "Pat and I spent a lot of time there - he 'switched off', relaxed and was at ease. We used to do a run through the woods, which was quite demanding, on a regular basis. We'd probably run four or five miles through Quarry Woods, between 1984 to 1989."

Pete Meakin recalls happier times too: "Pat invited Shirley and me over to the house by the river, in Upton-upon-Severn, for a Barbecue. He had a forty-five gallon drum, which he'd cut in half, to use as a barbecue. Doreen said: 'Would you believe it – he's got a 'state-of-the-art', gas-fired barbecue – and look what he's cooking on!' He'd got old logs in this half of a forty-five gallon oil drum and he's cooking great big 'wadges' of liver on it! Pat said, 'Keep an eye on that liver Pete,' then disappeared. I thought, 'Keep an eye on it? There's nothing to turn it with!' I could see it frizzling up. There was steak as well, but what had been a ten-pound lump of liver, ended up as two ounces!"

Shirley remembers: "Pat was wearing an old tracksuit, (inside-out), an old pair of carpet slippers and there he was, sat on the front of his boat, messing around with an old fishing rod. It was just so comical to see him – nothing *ever* bothered him in that way. He never dressed up for anybody, unless it was a celebration! Then later we all 'tootled' off on the boat. There was a captain's peaked cap and we all took it in turns to wear it and have a go at steering the boat; there was me, Pete, Doreen and Dolly. It was a really wonderful day." Pete adds: "If Pat loved you, he loved you – he couldn't do enough for you. But if you were on his Bad List, there's no way he'd tolerate you."

*   *   *   *   *

Although we could have filled an extra chapter with concluding comments, here are just a few more observations, from some of the people who knew him well:

Brendan Breslin
"Pat was a 'Gentle Giant'. He'd never pass you by, he always had time to come over and speak to you and shake hands. Even though he was a celebrity, Pat made you feel good – a bit special."

Ray Robinson
"This guy said: 'What did you think of the match Ray?' I said: 'Yes, it was fine.' Pat just looked up and said: 'Ray – tell him the truth!' That was Pat. He stopped me straight away and said: 'It's no good being nice to him Ray. Tell him the truth.' I admired him for that. That was years ago – probably in the first year or two that I met him."

Peter Charlesworth (Pat's Agent) and Sharry Clark, Peter's Associate
"We looked after Pat for over twenty years. He was never less than absorbing, as a man and a client. Full of ideas and schemes, some of which worked out and some that we restrained him from, for his own good. But at all times a delight to work with, great fun, and a complete gentleman."

Wayne Bridges
"When Pat was wrestling, there were the likes of Mick McManus, Jackie Pallo, Les Kellett, Nagasaki – (I can go on and on with names). But they didn't come to any of those – they came to Pat. He was added to the *Hall of Fame* quite recently, an honour usually given to people when they've passed on, such as André the Giant, who is mentioned in Arnie's *Foreword* to *If.* André wasn't put in the *Hall of Fame* when he was alive, but Pat was."

Dave Talboys
"Pat was very proud of what he did – and he should be. Because he did it from nothing – and that makes it *doubly* good. He wasn't going without a fight, because he'd fought all his life: that's why he achieved so much. Forget the fallacy that big fellas are 'dumbo'. You didn't invade his privacy, else he would completely ignore you – and that's fair enough. This fella was very intelligent… very up-front."

Jim Collins
Pat's chauffeur friend, like Pat, has long been interested in Parapsychology. He also proposed the theory that if the pineal gland, which lies dormant in most human beings, is ever reactivated, it can make an individual more insightful: "I thought that Pat had got the gift." The gland in question is a small outgrowth, behind and above the third ventricle of the brain.

Harold Evans
"Pat was one of these people who was a gentleman, well mannered, respectable and would respect people. If he took a dislike to you, he'd find it hard to talk to you and he'd just practically ignore you. You couldn't borrow much off him, because he had to work for every penny that he had, so he'd think that he wasn't going to give it away and he wasn't going to let anyone take it off him."

Pete Roberts
"He was such a character. Pat just had a certain charisma. There are certain people that you can *always* listen to – and some that you can't. Like most of us, I like certain people, but not others. But Pat found something nice in everybody. That was basically the difference between the two of us."

* * * * *

Doreen Roach

"Whenever we were out in the car and we were coming back in the early or late evening, sometimes part of the sky would be red. He used to love the sky. It really used to give him a lift – and the trees. We both liked them: a lovely big tree. We'd stop and look at them."

In *If – The Pat Roach Story*, Pat recalled how, if he was driving through the countryside, and suddenly saw a field of golden flowers, he'd stop the car and just sit there, enjoying the view. The sight of them filled him with at least as much joy and elation as if he'd suddenly been given a part in a top Hollywood film! That's why the plot where he's buried is so ideal: surrounded by Nature, in a country churchyard.

Doreen continues: "Pat didn't care what people *thought* of him, he was just himself. Nearly every weekend I have Patrick. Of a Sunday, we go to the grave... and Patrick talks to his Granddad, just as if he's alive. 'Granddad, I've had trouble at school. But Nanny will help me. It will be alright. And we're going on holiday Granddad.' He tells him absolutely everything. 'Well we're going now Granddad – see you next Sunday!' Pat thought the world of Patrick."

A public memorial service was held at St. Paul's Church, in Birmingham's Jewellery Quarter, on Thursday 25 November 2004, a few streets from where Pat grew up. It had originally been Pat's wish to be buried in the Jewellery Quarter, but we discovered that the cemeteries had been closed. The speakers were Tim Healy, Wayne Bridges, Shirley Thompson and Professor Carl Chinn, who spoke about Pat's particular association with Birmingham. Doreen and the family were again present and the ceremony was well attended. (Wayne and Sarah, unfortunately, got trapped in the Blackwall Tunnel, en route, – but that's another story)!

The Reverend Tom Pyke, Vicar of St. Paul's, who had also participated in the Bromsgrove ceremony, led the service. He described this November service as, "... a celebration of Pat's fascinating life and the fact that he was a native son of the Jewellery Quarter," according to Poppy Brady, of the *Birmingham Mail*. The ceremony began with an evocative, half-muffled 'passing bell', in memory of Pat.

Afterwards, a Reception was held at *Gems Wine and Dine*, in Branston Street, thanks to the generosity of the owner, Lisa Flynn. Photographs of the event can be found in this book. Video clips from some of Pat's films were screened, during the afternoon. Pat's good friend, Kenny Schofield, was the main organiser of the event, ably assisted by Jewellery Quarter writer, Marie Haddleton. Doreen is particularly grateful that Kenny arranged for a 'signer' to be present at the service, to assist Mark and Diane. A substantial number of the contributors to our three books were present at one or both of the July and November ceremonies. According to the Reverend Pyke, Pat's name will be included on a bell, as part of the brand new ring of ten bells, at St. Paul's. This has now taken place, and his name will remain there, for posterity.

*   *   *   *   *

I have no regrets about my life, but my regret is leaving behind grief and aggravation for other people. For instance, it might even be for you to mention in the book, the worry of you having to finish this third book on your own. It might not be relevant if I'm here when you finish it – but then again – I might not be.

*   *   *   *   *

Pat had a determination and strength of character, which more than equalled his physical stature. It's a quality that helped him conquer the earlier disadvantages of his childhood, and later, to overcome all manner of difficulties. Despite sometimes being on a short fuse, generally speaking, he had a tremendous regard for the needs of others, coupled with a desire to lend a hand, provided those involved show sufficient drive and determination themselves. No one got a free ride with Pat – as several contributors have observed. He was a 'driven man' – and a fighter: both in the ring and throughout his life. This, combined with the fact that he was multi-talented, goes a long way to explaining why he managed to achieve so much. Pat and I became close friends during the six years that we knew each other: a friendship that I shall cherish until the end of my days. The mighty presence that one felt, whilst in his company, was only part of the picture. The true situation was far more complex and intriguing, for there was another, highly imaginative side to him, which emerged even more, when we worked on projects other than his biographies.

Over the course of co-writing this Trilogy of books, I have been privileged to meet and interview almost two hundred people – not to mention their families and colleagues! My heartfelt thanks go to you all, for your hospitality, your generosity, and your invaluable insights. Without your help, it would have been impossible to relate Pat's life story in such intimate detail.

We shouldn't finish, however, without mentioning the sad irony of the death of two of Pat's closest friends, (who also featured in his books), shortly after Pat's funeral, before even a year was out. Jim White, Pat's fellow judo expert, sadly died in the latter part of 2004, leaving a widow, Sylvia, and family. Pete Berrington's funeral followed, on Wednesday, 6 April 2005; his widow, Cynthia, kindly allowed me to attend, to pay my respects. Jim and Pete were both kind and thoughtful men. Our condolences go to both families. On an even sadder note, Cynthia Berrington has now died too – exactly a year and a day after Pete. More recently, Pete Evans telephoned to say that he was en route to Ronnie Taylor's funeral service. It was being held that day, Tuesday 1st August, at Gloucester Cathedral.

A final message from Pat awaits you, in Chapter 21 – as always, he gets the last word! Meanwhile, his close friend, Tim Healy, provides our concluding tribute:

"Bomber's character was similar to Pat in a lot of ways. He was the Headman of the team, really. I was the boss, but he was like the Voice of Wisdom. I just didn't pay tribute to that aspect of him at the funeral and I wished I'd said that now. He'll be missed so much, as an actor too. I mean, he got a wonderful tribute from Wayne Bridges on behalf of the wrestling side, but nobody said how brilliant an actor he was. It was a fantastic performance as Bomber and the great thing is that it's there forever... it will last, forever."

Today's date, as I make some of the final editorial changes to our book, is ironically, 31 July 2006, just two weeks after the second anniversary of Pat's death. Whilst working with his last thoughts, and the memories of our contributors, I have been constantly aware of Pat's presence, and all the happy moments come flooding back. But as we draw to a close, let me just say, on behalf of his family, and countless friends and fans across the globe: "This is not a *final* goodbye, Big Fella, but simply... Auf Wiedersehen, Pat."

Chapter Twenty-One

THE JOKE'S ON ME

Here we are – the three of us – my friend Dave Talboys, Shirley, and myself, discussing backwards and forwards what we're going to do about my funeral arrangements. Dave's saying: "We've all got to go sometime," followed by my reply: "Wouldn't it be funny if after asking you to arrange my funeral, I ended up at yours!" And having a laugh that he might pop off any day, with his dodgy heart! So we all finish up having a real laugh, rolling about on the floor, talking about the fact that I might be doing Dave's funeral, instead of him doing mine!

And Dave and I are explaining that I will actually go home tonight, as I have done every night since my sentence, and before I go to bed, I will take three melatone tablets, which are well known cancer preventatives. And the greatest irony of all – I'm still taking a three-milligram aspirin, to prevent prostate cancer!

After all the health tips I've given you people out there, whether you've been my friends, or students in the judo and health clubs, here I am, dying of lung cancer. You're all smoking your cigarettes, drinking your pints, eating your fish-and-chips, not taking your vitamins in the morning – and I'm dead; all of you people, who're now reading this additional chapter, who I preached to over the years about taking your vitamins. Everybody in the world is laughing at me: you're all out there, laughing your balls off, and I'm 'brown bread' – I'm 'Hovis'! I've got more cancer in me than you can shake a stick at. Surely... the joke is on me.

SELECTED BIBLIOGRAPHY

A Northern Soul, The Autobiography - Jimmy Nail, Michael Joseph (an imprint of Penguin Books) 2004.

The Auf Wiedersehen, Pet Story – That's Living Alright – Franc Roddam and Dan Waddell, BBC Books 2003.

You Grunt and I'll Groan – Jackie 'Mr. TV' Pallo, Macdonald Queen Anne Press, 1985.

If – The Pat Roach Story – Pat Roach with Shirley Thompson, Brewin Books 2002.

Pat Roach's Birmingham – Pat Roach and Shirley Thompson, Brewin Books 2004.

The Cancer Guide for Men – by Helen Beare and Neil Priddy, Sheldon Press, 1999.

Understanding cancer of the oesophagus – BACUP Cancer Charity Information and Support for people affected by cancer – BACUP Cancer Charity (website: www.cancerbacup.org.uk).

Newspaper articles and magazines

(Many and varied relating to Pat and/or *Auf Wiedersehen Pet*) in the following publications:

The Birmingham Post; The Birmingham Post and Mail: The Brew 'Us Bugle – (the magazine of the Ladywood History Group).

Carl Chinn's Brummagem; The Evening Mail .

Cheshire Life, November 2002 'It's Alderley, Pet', article about Tim Healy and his family.

The Daily Mail; The Independent; The Mirror; The News of the World and The Sunday Mercury.

Radio Times, 27 April – 3rd May 2002 – 'Have a nice day, Pet', Special Feature Edition about *Aufpet 3*.

Yours Magazine, August 2003 – 'Don't call me a Celeb', article about Kevin Whately.

July 2004, following Pat's death: *numerous* articles about him, in the majority of national and local newspapers.

INDEX